BUILDING AND ECONOMIC GROWTH
IN SOUTHERN EUROPE (1050–1300)

THE MEDIEVAL COUNTRYSIDE

VOLUME 26

PETRIFYING
WEALTH

The four-volume sub-series 'Petrifying Wealth' explores the sudden ubiquity of masonry construction between 1050 and 1300 in Southern Europe and its profound effect on the European landscape. New questions about wealth, society, and medieval building are explored, which highlight the link between construction in durable materials and the shaping of individual, collective, and territorial identities: the birth of a new, long-lasting panorama, epitomising the way we see the space and territory of Europe nowadays.

VOLUME 2

Building and Economic Growth in Southern Europe (1050–1300)

Edited by

SANDRO CAROCCI *and* ALESSIO FIORE

BREPOLS

***Petrifying Wealth. The Southern European Shift to Masonry as Collective Investment in Identity, c. 1050–1300* is funded by an ERC/European Research Council Advanced Grant (grant number 695515).**

Cover image: 'Stonemasons at work', Girona Cathedral, Romanesque cloister, west gallery. Twelfth century. Photo: Federico Del Tredici.

British Library Cataloguing in Publication Data
A catalogue record for this book is available from the British Library.

ISBN: 978-2-503-60541-8
e-ISBN: 978-2-503-60543-2
DOI: 10.1484/M.TMC-EB.5.132952

ISSN: 1784-8814
e-ISSN: 2294-8430

Printed in the EU on acid-free paper.

D/2024/0095/138

Table of Contents

Part II
Manufacturing

Part III
Connecting

List of Illustrations

Petrified Nodes: Bridges and Economic Growth (Tuscany, 1050–1200) — *Paolo Tomei*

ALESSIO FIORE

Introduction

Building Economic Growth in Southern Europe

As recent studies have acknowledged, economic growth in Europe between the eleventh and thirteenth centuries is still an unresolved historiographical problem;[1] scholars have yet to shed light on many aspects of the subject, some of which are of key importance.[2] One of the most hotly debated topics is undoubtedly the issue of the chronology of growth itself. While economic expansion in the period between the latter part of the twelfth and (especially) the thirteenth century is well established, and is clearly supported by the numerous written and material sources increasingly at our disposal, the dynamics of the preceding historical period are much less clear and require more specific research; the geographic distribution of the sources for the earlier period is more problematic and elusive than is the case for the subsequent phase. This book is aimed partly at identifying possible avenues for research to help enhance the written and material sources at our disposal, with a view to better understanding the chronologies of growth, with a particular focus on southern Europe.

In order to better define our objectives, I should briefly explain the specific research context out of which this book developed. It has its origins in a conference (organized in late 2021 by Sandro Carocci and myself) which formed part of the ERC project *Petrifying Wealth. The Southern European Shift to Masonry as Collective Investment in Identity, c. 1050–1300*, directed by Ana Rodríguez and Sandro Carocci. This ERC project investigates the use of masonry (in stone, bricks and other durable materials) which from the mid-eleventh century onwards became increasingly evident as one of the privileged means of representing and affirming identity on the part of individuals, families, secular communities, religious institutions, and nuclei

1 The publication of this research was financed by the European Research Council (ERC) under the European Union's Horizon 2020 research and innovation programme (grant agreement 695515), project *Petrifying Wealth: The Southern European Shift to Masonry as Collective Investment in Identity, c. 1050–1300*.

2 Franceschi, ed., *La crescita economica*.

Alessio Fiore (alessio.fiore@unito.it) obtained his PhD from the University of Pisa, and is at present professor of Medieval History at the University of Turin.

Building and Economic Growth in Southern Europe (1050–1300), ed. by Sandro Carocci and Alessio Fiore, (Turnhout: Brepols, 2024), pp. 9–15 BREPOLS PUBLISHERS 10.1484/M.TMC-EB.5.137971

of political power. In this wider context, the specific aim of the conference and the subsequent book was to focus on the relationship between functional buildings and economic development in this period. From this perspective, *Petrifying Wealth* (henceforth *PW*) can be framed within a broader series of research projects that seek to better understand the specific trajectory and strength of economic dynamics in this crucial phase; in this case using the development of building in durable materials in southern Europe as a qualifying indicator. While economic growth is not the main focus of the research conducted in *PW*, it is a prerequisite for this area of study: it was growth that lay behind the building boom (in stone and brick), and it is therefore both a manifestation and a valuable quantitative and qualitative indicator of this growth.

Within the various lines of research pursued by the project, this volume attempts to shift the perspective, and to focus on the obvious premise of *PW*, namely economic development in and of itself, seeking to conduct a more specific and in-depth examination of the relationship between building investments on the one hand, and the dynamics of production and trade on the other. More specifically, the aim of this book is to focus in the broadest possible sense on buildings and functional structures whose main purpose was to serve the economy, from the production of artefacts to agricultural activity, from trade to the material infrastructure that made this possible. Any phase of intense growth of course triggers an increase in the number of constructions associated with economic activity; this is often accompanied by a marked material transformation of their structures (internal and external) and/or their location.[3] A study of the dynamics more specifically related to these buildings can provide a new and promising perspective from which to examine the forms and dynamics of growth itself. The proliferation of buildings linked to production and trading activities, as well as changes in their structure, presents a privileged vantage point from which to observe this crucial phase of economic expansion, particularly when dealing with the rather obscure phase prior to 1200, for which there are decidedly fewer examples of illuminating source material available than for the later period. Information about these buildings can indeed provide us with valuable clues as to the identity of and choices made by the key figures involved in the economic expansion of the period, as well as the chronology of growth itself, which is still debated by scholars today.[4] If the selection of written and material sources is not sufficient to allow us to make solidly grounded quantitative discourses, perhaps focusing on buildings, and in particular on productive buildings, might open up new perspectives for analysis. However, it should be emphasized that the decision to focus on their functional and economic value does not mean that these buildings (such as a bridge or a

3 Kriedte and others, *Industrialisierung*.
4 Wickham, *The Donkey*.

craftsman's house-cum-workshop) are not also a means of expressing and conveying identity or ideological content; but there can be no doubt of the relevance, and often preponderance, of their economic value particularly in the case of flour mills, oil mills, fulling mills, and ironworks. We have therefore decided to venture beyond the traditional thematic boundary of *PW* and to also examine those functional structures where stone and brick were only occasionally or never used, such as canalization works, or where wood was a common component, as was often the case with mills, bridges, and forges.

Relatively few comprehensive studies of structures connected with economic activity have been undertaken, at least as far as our period is concerned.[5] Research in the field has tended to focus on the latter part of the Middle Ages, which offers the advantage of more abundant sources.[6] Our aim is to try to fill a significant historiographical gap by focusing on southern and Mediterranean Europe, specifically Spain, southern France, and Italy in accordance with *PW*'s general guidelines. Authors were specifically requested to focus their studies on the period beginning no later than the twelfth century, and preferably as early as the end of the eleventh, notwithstanding the greater difficulties presented by more archaic sources. The aim of this is to better grasp the chronologies connected with the transformations in buildings specifically related to production, particularly with regard to the problematic period prior to 1200.

With these objectives in mind, contributions to the volume have been organized into three different thematic sections: the agricultural sector; the production of artefacts; and communications infrastructure. Needless to say, while some essays deal exclusively with the subject matter of the section in which they appear, others cover a broader area. Due to the nature of the specific subject of this research, some structures are characterized by their wide range of uses: mills, for example, were associated with both the production of manufactured goods (energy for processing in the textile and metal sectors) and with the agricultural sector (milling of cereals); while canalization works were involved not only in the irrigation and drainage of agricultural land, but also in the supply of hydraulic energy to mills, as well as serving as a communication route for transporting goods or people by ship.

It is no coincidence that the book begins by focusing on the agricultural sector, as this comprised not only the bulk of the economy in terms of overall volume during the period under review, but was also key to the developments behind the growth in the complexity of the economic system as a whole. This was not a simple case of an increase in production driven by population growth, but rather a progressive transformation aimed at increasing agricultural

5 An important exception is Arnoux, 'Les moulins'.

6 Some good examples of research focused on the late Middle Ages are: Verna, *Les temps des moulines*; Mugueta Moreno, 'Les territoires de la sidérurgie'; Cosi, 'L'attività laniera'; Deyá, *La manufactura de la lana*.

output (probably associated with a rise of productivity). A crucial element of research into these changes is the study of the investment in rural production structures that made this shift possible: this is key to our understanding of the extent to which these structures were transformed. It was precisely the progressive increase in production in the sector that facilitated the release of human resources and energy which could then be assigned to other sectors, and thus constitutes the indispensable premise for generalized economic expansion. Our objective is to fully understand how investment in structures linked to agricultural activity led to a transformation in production methods and profitability, and to identify the key figures behind this transformation process.

The first section opens with an essay by Lorenzo Tabarrini, which offers a broad overview of the situation in central-northern Italy, and focuses attention on the buildings associated with an intensification of production in the countryside, such as *cassine*, *casali*, and *grange*. The construction of these buildings was a direct result of the investment of large amounts of capital in the countryside, mostly made by citizens. It was a process characterized by regional differences, which also corresponded to different building realities, but which shared significant common features associated with the increasing commercialization of agricultural surplus in city markets from the late twelfth century onwards.

Víctor Farías Zurita's study concentrates on a smaller geographical area, namely the lands belonging to the monastery of Sant Cugat, in Old Catalonia, whose rich documentation provides a privileged view of the dynamics that lead to the emergence of the Catalan *mas*, regarded as a key moment in the process of the restructuring of aristocratic, or seigneurial power in the region. The article focuses on the material structures of the *mas* and stresses seigneurial creativity in the process of the reorganization of agrarian production.

Giovanna Bianchi's article is devoted to cereal storage systems, drawing primarily on material evidence, and with a special focus on archaeological data. While it concentrates chiefly on Tuscany, the study also looks at the rest of central-northern Italy, as well as the Norman kingdom in the south, and compares systems in the different regions. We are presented with a clear overall picture of the three-way game being played between royal power, lordships, and local communities, and this is crucial for bettering our understanding of the materiality of storage places and their relationship with urban markets.

Josep Torró's essay explores canalization works in eastern Spain, focusing on the transition from Islamic to Christian domination. His objective is to explore the dynamics of transformation that characterize this type of infrastructure, which played a key role in the changes in agricultural activity in the area. The development of the canals is linked not only to a redefinition of the agrarian landscape, but also to profound shifts in the social order, it thus helps to understand the overall changes that were underway in Valencia's social hierarchy as a whole.

Fabrizio Pagnoni focuses on the relationship between economic development and the hydraulic investments which characterized the Po Valley. He emphasizes that the network of canals not only had an agricultural purpose but also crucially provided the energy needed to power manufacturing activity, and at the same time facilitated the transport of commercial goods by water. The construction of canals is seen here as an operation that underlies a wide range of functions and involved many different participants. This multifaceted function of canals is a good illustration of how the various sections of the book should not be seen as hermetically-sealed compartments, but rather as interconnected domains with potentially overlapping subject matter. Pagnoni's essay represents a perfect *trait d'union* with the second section of the book, which focuses on buildings and other structures connected with the production of artefacts (including residential buildings as 'products' for the housing market) and the transformation of raw materials, such as metals. The growth of artisan production is one of the key phenomena of economic expansion: an analysis of the structures connected with this type of production provides important information about the changes in the organizational logistics of the spatial location of manufacturing, but also about the size of these manufacturing enterprises as compared with previous and subsequent periods in history.

Jordi Morello's essay opens this second section with an analysis of the role of mills in Catalonia between the late eleventh and thirteenth centuries. The author highlights the existence of two main types of mills: flour mills and fulling mills. The twelfth century witnessed not only an explosion in the number of mills: it was also a period of change as regards the materials used for building these structures, with a progressive increase in the use of stone. The buildings themselves were larger, more expensive, and equipped with decidedly more sophisticated machinery.

Maria Elena Cortese's article, by contrast, concentrates on structures related to iron-working, which was one of the main sectors of craft production in the high Middle Ages. Her analysis highlights an increase in the production of metal artefacts from as early as the first half of the twelfth century. By the second half of the century, and particularly during the early decades of the thirteenth century, the continuous expansion of production was associated with significant innovations in production processes, which allowed for an increase in volume and quality, while at the same time they brought down production costs. There was a direct link between these improvements and major investments in production buildings: these were technically much more complex than their predecessors and involved a more complex use of resources from the surrounding area, from timber to water power.

The final article in this section is my own, and it explores the production and economic management of a very particular class of artefacts, namely urban dwellings. The period between the end of the eleventh and the beginning of the thirteenth century saw not only a profound transformation in the materials used to build housing in central and northern Italian cities, but also witnessed a new kind of economic exploitation of dwellings, which can be seen as an indicator of the more general transformation of the economy of southern Europe.

The third section of the book looks at transport-related infrastructure. In order for the economy to grow, it was essential for locally-produced commodities, both manufactured goods and foodstuffs, to be transported what might be some distance to reach centres of consumption. The economic integration of ever larger spaces and the creation of locally- or regionally-based production specializations constitute one of the defining features of the process of economic growth. It was the communications infrastructure that made this integration possible, by facilitating a progressively more intense and widespread circulation of goods. Research into the development of this infrastructure is therefore crucial for understanding the transformation which occurred in the various systems that interconnected different economic spaces, at local, supra-local, and macro-regional levels. The final section of the book is therefore devoted to infrastructure connected with the exchange of goods and the movement of people and commodities, such as ports, arsenals, and bridges. Ports, and their related infrastructure, have long been a prime object of research because of their association with long-distance trade.[7] However when it comes to local economic integration — which many scholars hold to be more crucial than the more prestigious long-distance connections — the role played by bridges is fundamental. This type of infrastructure, generally somewhat overlooked by researchers, is examined in two of the studies in this section. Paolo Tomei's essay focuses on bridges in northern Tuscany between the late eleventh and early thirteenth century, and offers a new interpretation that marks a departure from the existing research. Stone bridges — petrified nodes in the trading network — are regarded as the product of the actions (and interactions) of a range of actors, with a marked change occurring between the late eleventh and late twelfth century, in a framework characterized by strong experimentalism. Bridges and the institutions connected to them emerge as a fundamental indicator not only of regional economic dynamism but also of the plurality and polyphony of the actions of the actors involved.

By contrast, Pinuccia Simbula's article examines the difficulties associated with maritime and long-distance travel, which became increasingly important in the European economy between the twelfth and thirteenth centuries. She focuses on the role of seaports and related infrastructure, in particular shipyards and naval arsenals. As early as the twelfth century, the first significant masonry constructions were documented in Genoa and Pisa, and also to a lesser extent, in centres such as Otranto. It was only in the thirteenth century however that the harbour network truly began to develop and that harbour construction became more widespread; it was around the same time that the first proper arsenals for the construction of warships were built. Decentralized commercial

7 Augenti, *Città e porti*.

shipbuilding is an equally problematic field of research, characterized by a large number of small, scattered production sites, whose material structures are not easy to interpret.

The book closes with the conclusions of Sandro Carocci, who analyses the results of the researches presented here, insisting on the plurality of the protagonists of the investment in structures for production and trade, their chronologies and their economic consequences.

Works Cited

Arnoux, Mathieu, 'Les moulins à eau en Europe occidentale (IXe–XIIe siècle). Aux origines d'une économie institutionnelle de l'énergie hydraulique', in *L'acqua nei secoli altomedievali. Atti della LV Settimana di studio (Spoleto, 12–17 aprile 2007)*, (Spoleto: CISAM, 2008), pp. 693–746

Augenti, Andrea, *Città e porti dall'Antichità al Medioevo* (Rome: Carocci, 2018)

Cosi, Cinzia, 'L'attività laniera nel contado fiorentino. Le strutture materiali', *Rivista di storia dell'agricoltura*, 39 (1999), 57–86

Deyá, Miguel J., *La manufactura de la lana en la Mallorca del siglo XV* (Palma de Majorque: El Tall, 1997)

Franceschi, Franco, ed., *La crescita economica dell'Occidente medievale. Un tema storico non ancora esaurito* (Pistoia: Centro Italiano di Studi di Storia e d'Arte, 2017)

Kriedte, Peter, Hans Medick, and Jürgen Schlumbohm, *Industrialisierung vor der Industrialisierung. Gewerbliche Warenproduktion auf dem Land in der Formationsperiode des Kapitalismus* (Göttingen: Vandenhoeck und Ruprecht, 1977)

Mugueta Moreno, Íñigo, 'Les territoires de la sidérurgie médiévale au Pays basque et en Navarre', in *Les industries rurales dans l'Europe médiévale et modern*, ed. by Jean-Michel Minovez, Catherine Verna, and Liliane Hilaire-Pérez (Toulouse: Presses universitaires du Midi, 2013), pp. 63–76

Verna, Catherine, *Le temp des moulines. Fer, technique et société dans les Pyrénées centrales (XIIIe-XVIe siècles)* (Paris: Éditions de la Sorbonne, 2001)

Wickham, Chris, *The Donkey and the Boat: Reinterpreting the Mediterranean Economy, 950–1180* (Oxford: Oxford University Press, 2023)

Part I

Farming

LORENZO TABARRINI

Storing for the Economy?

Landed Estates and their Buildings in Northern and Central Italy, Twelfth and Thirteenth Centuries

This essay is a discussion of landed estates and rural buildings in northern and central Italy during the twelfth and thirteenth centuries; its aim is to link estates and buildings with wider socio-economic transformations. Before I begin, I would like to make some preliminary remarks. The geographical scope of my analysis covers the *Regnum Italiae* and the papal territories, in other words what was originally the Carolingian political sphere. I decided against including southern Italy in the study as this would have required me to consider a partially different set of historical questions, and to harness all the relevant bibliography. The period I chose to analyse is instead easier to justify. I shall focus on the century between *c.* 1150 and *c.* 1250, which is generally recognized as having been marked by a process of substantial economic expansion throughout Western Europe. This consisted — in very broad terms — of demographic growth, increased agricultural production, urban development, and the expansion of commercial and financial activities; what amounts, in short, to an increase in aggregate demand (which, moreover, took place under generally favourable climatic conditions).[1]

This essay is based on a survey of the extant research, both historical and archaeological, although some local studies could be added. Many of the issues that I will discuss are familiar to Italian medievalists, but probably less so to an English-speaking public. In view of this, I shall attempt to provide a synthesis of the secondary literature by shaping my argument around four main themes, which may help to shed light on the relationship between landed estates and rural buildings on the one hand, and patterns of economic development on

* I would like to thank Margaret Goring and Gregory Woods for revising the English, Federico Del Tredici and Tiziana Lazzari for critiquing the content, and Taylor Zaneri for doing both.

1 An overview in Masschaele, 'Economic Takeoff'. Economic transformations and climatic shifts during the Middle Ages are discussed by Campbell, *The Great Transition*. Syntheses written in Italian are Palermo, *Sviluppo* and Cammarosano, *Economia*; cf. also the essays collected in Franceschi, ed., *La crescita*.

Lorenzo Tabarrini (lorenzo.tabarrini3@unibo.it) studied at the University of Pisa and at the Scuola Normale Superiore. He obtained his PhD from the University of Oxford, and he is currently *assegnista di ricerca* at the University of Bologna.

Building and Economic Growth in Southern Europe (1050–1300), ed. by Sandro Carocci and Alessio Fiore, (Turnhout: Brepols, 2024), pp. 19–37 BREPOLS PUBLISHERS 10.1484/M.TMC-EB.5.137972

the other. First of all, I will give a brief description of the four types of estates which, for reasons that will be clarified as we proceed, appear to deserve the most careful scrutiny. I shall then discuss the infrastructure and buildings which characterized these estates, paying particular attention to the materials with which they were built. Thirdly, I will identify the sections of society who paid for the creation of these estates. Lastly, I shall make a number of observations on the reasons behind their creation. At least two caveats have to be borne in mind, however. First, the written and archaeological evidence is not equally distributed across northern and central Italy. It follows that not all the geographical areas that I wish to investigate have received the same amount of attention in the existing scholarship, which cannot be regarded as a coherent body of research, and consists chiefly of regional studies. Second, with regard to this particular field of inquiry, the late Middle Ages have been more closely studied than the twelfth and thirteenth centuries. This fact can be explained by the remarkable wealth of information and internal coherence characterizing fourteenth- and fifteenth-century sources when compared to central medieval documents, which are plentiful but also somewhat erratic. I shall return to some of these points in due course; for now, it is sufficient for them to serve as part of the general background to the analysis that follows.

* * *

Let us begin with a brief description of the four types of landed estates I intend to focus on: *casali*, *cassine*, *grange*, and *poderi*. Other types of estate did exist, and I shall mention these later on; but *casali*, *cassine*, and *grange* are regarded as the most structured landed properties of northern and central Italy during the twelfth and thirteenth centuries, along with *poderi* (whose early history, as I shall explain in the ensuing paragraphs, is however rather obscure). Their construction required substantial investments, which is a key element for the understanding of the overall economic change. Not only were they complex structures. Another characteristic they shared was relative isolation from other rural settlements; they did not form part of castles or villages, despite the fact that, owing to their size and the presence of fortifications, they did in some instances resemble castles or villages. They were also often built from scratch, although in some cases pre-existing settlements and their infrastructures were used as a basis for the creation of *casali*, *cassine*, *grange*, and *poderi*.[2] I have refrained from including those settlements variously labelled as *ville*, *villenove*, *terre nuove*, *borghi franchi*, or *borghi nuovi* in my analysis; these too became more widespread during the course of the thirteenth century and can certainly be regarded as part of a process of small-scale urbanization — and thus of economic expansion. I have not omitted these settlements for reasons of space alone: because of their

2 Accurate and complete accounts of this are to be found in Comba, 'La dispersione'; Comba, 'Le origini'; and, with a focus on south-western Piedmont, Comba, 'Rappresentazioni'. Cf. also Varanini, 'Insediamenti'. A more recent overview is Rapetti, 'Paesaggi'.

size, their appearance was more that of small towns than large farms, which would take us too far from the analysis of landed estates and their buildings. The same is true of *incastellamento*, and particularly of the so-called *secondo incastellamento*, the second wave of castle building, which can be identified in some Italian regions over the twelfth and thirteenth centuries, but whose links with estate-creation would require a separate study.[3]

I shall begin with *casali*. The term *casale* is already attested across northern and central Italy in the early Middle Ages, when it defined an open settlement comprising, or coinciding with, a relatively small estate-centre.[4] The *casali* I wish to focus on here are those that proliferated from the central decades of the twelfth century onwards around Rome, in the *Campagna Romana*, the area extending around the city for between 15 and 20 kilometres; this expansion is referred to as *incasalamento*. One can in fact distinguish two different phases of *incasalamento*, but here we are concerned with the first, which began in the 1150s, intensified in the 1190s, and continued for much of the thirteenth century.[5] Over the course of that century the first *incasalamento* became a phenomenon of substantial agricultural reorganization, with landowners creating large numbers of new isolated rural estates. The size of *casali* is also believed to have been considerable from the start; actual data can be drawn only from fourteenth-century and early modern sources, but already in the thirteenth century they might well have occupied between fifty-five and 555 hectares.[6] The second *incasalamento*, occurring between the fourteenth and the fifteenth centuries, was by contrast a step backwards, the result of the typical late medieval abandonment of open villages and fortified settlements, not only around Rome but also in Italy and indeed in Europe as a whole.[7] It should be noted, as a final point, that the workforce of *casali* seems to have been constituted by salaried workers — even though, again, substantial information on this is available only from the fourteenth century.[8]

---

3 Cf. Settia, *Castelli*, pp. 319–25; Comba, '"Ville" e borghi nuovi'; the collection of essays in Comba, Panero, and Pinto, eds, *Borghi*; and those in Friedman and Pirillo, eds, *Le terre nuove*. On the *secondo incastellamento* in Tuscany cf. Farinelli and Giorgi, 'Fenomeni'; on the construction of *castra* in the *Campagna Romana* from *c*. 1180 cf. Carocci and Vendittelli, *L'origine*, pp. 23–68; on the creation of new castles (and the abandonment of older ones) in western Liguria between the twelfth and the thirteenth centuries cf. Murialdo, 'La riorganizzazione'; on the archaeology of *villenove* in Piedmont cf. Micheletto, 'L'insediamento'.

4 For the Pianura Padana see Fumagalli, *Terra*, pp. 25–60. Cf. Bacchi, 'Conquista', on the Ferrarese. Examples can be found in the documentation from the monastery of S. Salvatore al Monte Amiata, too: cf. Wickham, 'Paesaggi sepolti', esp. p. 113. On the *casali* in the *Campagna Romana* during the early Middle Ages, cf. Lenzi, 'Per una storia'.

5 The landmark monograph on the origins of Roman *casali* is Carocci and Vendittelli, *L'origine*. See also Maire Vigueur, *L'autre Rome*, pp. 86–93; and, with different nuances, Wickham, *Medieval Rome*, pp. 40, 59, 70, 80, 86, and 108.

6 Carocci and Vendittelli, *L'origine*, pp. 12–13.

7 Cf. Brezzi, 'Il sistema'; cf. the following footnotes for further references.

8 See note 5.

Let us now move on to the *cassine*, or (in Italian) *cascine*. As was the case with *casale*, the word *cassina* was employed in the early Middle Ages with its literal meaning of small house, *casa*. In this study, however, the term has a different meaning. These *cassine* extended over much of Lombardy between the twelfth and fourteenth centuries, although the earliest evidence of them dates back to the tenth century; at that time, the term might signify a village or an isolated rural estate, but could also denote a simple storage facility. Around 1350 there were at least thirty-seven *cassine* on the outskirts of Milan, varying in size from three to thirteen hectares; they appear to have been smaller than *casali*, possibly because the immediate environs of Milan were heavily populated and the patterns of landowning and landholding were highly fragmented, with many potentially competing owners.[9] It is important to stress that it was only in the twelfth and thirteenth centuries that *cassine* came to be identified as the permanent place of residence of various groups of rural workers and their families — and this was a new development. Some *cassine*, moreover, were grouped together (in the Italian historiography they are called *cascine a grappolo*) and had a clearly defined collective identity; indeed, they were a kind of local institution, not unlike rural communes. This is the case with the Milanese *Cassine de' Biffi* in the late *Duecento*, which have been studied by Enrica Salvatori.[10] Around Cremona *cascine* appear to have been even larger, to the point that they resembled small towns.[11]

Of the different types of estate examined in this article, it is *grange* that have attracted the greatest amount of interest from researchers. The word *grangia* derives from the late Latin *granea*, *granica*, *grancia*, which means barn or storage facility for cereals.[12] During the twelfth century, the term began to be used to denote the estate-centres belonging to the monasteries of the Cistercian order, and as a result can be found wherever Cistercians became established.[13] In Piedmont, *grangia* had a broader meaning: it could simply define an isolated rural estate, together with the word *tectum*.[14] *Grange* could either be built on the sites of pre-existing settlements or on previously undeveloped land, and could reach a considerable size: in 1275 Villamaggiore, one of the *grange* of the monastery of S. Maria di Chiaravalle Milanese,

9 And this separates the Milanese hinterland from the *Campagna Romana*: cf. Wickham, *Medieval Rome*, p. 39. The standard account on the surroundings of Milan is De Angelis Cappabianca, 'Le "cassine" tra il XII e il XIV secolo'. On eastern Lombardy cf. Menant, *Campagnes*, pp. 124–27. In the fifteenth century, the term *cascina* in the outskirts of Milan denoted all rural settlements that did not develop into a commune: cf. Del Tredici, *Comunità*, p. 59.

10 Salvatori, 'Una comunità'.

11 Grillo, 'Grange e cascine', p. 114.

12 Chiappa Mauri, 'Le scelte', p. 37. Please note that in Italian, *grangia* is singular and *grange* is plural.

13 Comba, 'Aspects'.

14 Cf. as an overview Comba, *Metamorfosi*.

comprised 420 hectares of arable fields and grassland.[15] The workforce on this type of estate was initially composed for the most part of lay brothers, who were responsible for the cultivation of monastic demesnes. Lay brothers were aided by salaried workers and later on by *massarii*; these were tenants whose role became crucial towards the middle of the thirteenth century. At that time many Cistercian abbeys were burdened with debts and were therefore forced to lease out their demesnes, thus abandoning direct exploitation and replacing it with indirect management.[16]

Finally, I shall briefly outline the principal characteristics of the *poderi*. It is well known that the term *podere* refers to a very large, isolated and polyculture-oriented rural estate, usually with a tenant house at its centre, which was sometimes attached to the landowner's house. This type of estate has been the object of numerous studies, as the *poderi* constituted the farming unit to which the *mezzadria* contract was applied. The *mezzadria poderale* can be defined as a particular form of sharecropping tenure. It was characterized, among other things, by the equal division of the harvest between proprietor and tenant, by the joint provision of livestock and seed-corn, and by the short duration of contracts (which, however, were generally renewed). The *poderi mezzadrili* shaped the countryside in much of central Italy throughout the late Middle Ages and the early modern era, and their importance has long been acknowledged.[17] Paradoxically, we have relatively little information about the creation of *poderi*, a process generally referred to as *appoderamento*. Oretta Muzzi and Maria Daniela Nenci have argued that in late twelfth-century Tuscany the word *podere* began to replace the term *mansus*, which denoted the farming unit dating from Carolingian times; they have also maintained, however, that at that stage the *podere* was not the *podere mezzadrile* of the fourteenth, fifteenth, and sixteenth centuries. In the central medieval period, using the term *podere* to describe a tenure was simply a way to emphasize proprietorial rights: the power (*potere* in Italian) that the landowner wielded over that land.[18] Moreover, it should be stressed that in past historiography the

---

15 Comba, 'I Cistercensi', p. 249.

16 Cf. again Comba, 'Le origini', p. 373. On northern Europe see the classic essay by Higounet, 'Effets'. On Lombardy cf. Chiappa Mauri, *Terra*, esp. p. 30 on the leasing out of *grange* (see also Chiappa Mauri, 'Le scelte', p. 43 and following). Some local studies: Saracco Previdi, 'Habitat' (on the Marche region); Cortese, 'Gli opifici' (on S. Galgano in Val di Merse, in the Sienese); Grillo, 'Dal bosco' and Comba, '"In silva Stapharda"' (on S. Maria di Staffarda, close to Cuneo, and the *grangia* of Aimondino). More local studies will be cited in subsequent footnotes.

17 The bibliography on *mezzadria poderale* is vast. With regard to Tuscany, I have recently summarized it in Tabarrini, *Estate*, Introduction, note 11, but I will cite some of it in subsequent footnotes.

18 Muzzi and Nenci, eds, *Il contratto*, p. 55. There are various — and sometimes divergent — views on the development of *poderi* in medieval Tuscany. According to Enrico Fiumi, *poderi* can be identified around S. Gimignano in the fourteenth century: Fiumi, *Storia*, pp. 129–40. Elio Conti sees the creation of *poderi* as the late medieval re-composition of the fragmented

concept of *appoderamento* has not always been used to indicate the spread of the *mezzadria* contract. *Appoderamento* might simply designate the process by which landed estates were made larger and more uniform, mostly through the purchase of bordering land plots — a practice known as *ingrossatio* in Latin sources.[19] This distinction is relevant to this study: *ingrossatio* did take place over the twelfth and thirteenth centuries, and we shall see this again when discussing the landed patrimony of Cistercian *grange*. By contrast, the creation of *poderi mezzadrili*, as a late medieval and early modern phenomenon, falls outside the chronological scope of this essay.

There are some further structures that need at least to be mentioned, namely *bastite, casamenta, caseforti, motte, torri,* and *tumbe*. These were all fortified buildings (and were all to be found in a rural setting, except for the *casamenta,* which were located within the city of Vercelli)[20] usually situated at the centre of landed estates or areas in which land-clearing was required. In some instances, they fulfilled a mainly military function; in others, they developed into actual villages. For reasons of space, I cannot devote much time to them here; but it should be emphasized that these structures began to appear across many regions of northern and central Italy during the late twelfth and, above all, thirteenth centuries.[21] This is significant: they testify to a generalized endeavour aimed at investment in rural buildings, broadly speaking over the same period in which *casali, cassine, grange,* and (bearing in mind the caveats mentioned above) *poderi* started to take shape in the countryside. In this sense, they can be seen as further manifestations of the process of economic development outlined above.

---

patterns of landowning and landholding that had characterized the countryside of Florence during the central Middle Ages: Conti, *La formazione*. Philip Jones acknowledges that the construction of isolated rural houses on the *poderi* was a remarkably obscure process: cf. Jones, 'From manor to mezzadria'. According to Giovanni Cherubini, the process of *appoderamento,* along with the dispersion of settlements, can be identified in some parts of Tuscany in the fourteenth century: Cherubini, 'Forme'. Giuliano Pinto has stressed that the contract of *mezzadria* began to be inextricably linked to *poderi* only during the sixteenth century: Pinto, 'Per una storia'. Franca Leverotti has hypothesized that the term *podere* may have been applied in the twelfth century to lands which formerly belonged to the fiscal domain: Leverotti, 'Scomposizione'.

19 This point was made by Klapisch-Zuber, 'Mezzadria' and reiterated by Comba, 'La dispersione'. Cf. also the contribution by Giuliano Pinto cited at note 18.

20 Cf. Gullino, *Forme*.

21 See as an overview Settia, *L'illusione*; Comba, *Metamorfosi*, pp. 77–78 on the *bastita* of Pogliola, close to Cuneo; Comba, 'Le origini', esp. pp. 377–81; Settia, 'Tra azienda agricola e fortezza'. Cf. also the essays in Comba, Panero, and Pinto, eds, *Motte*: namely, Grillo, 'Fra poteri pubblici e iniziative private', on the outskirts of Milan and Como; Mannoni and Sicios, 'Le torri', which argues that *torri* in Liguria emerge in our records between the twelfth and the fourteenth centuries; Tiberini, 'Colombaie', esp. pp. 287–90 on the slow expansion of *torri* in Umbria from the first decade of the thirteenth century on. It should be noted that in some areas *motte, torri* and *caseforti* did not appear until the late Middle Ages: this is the case with Friuli (cf. Degrassi, 'Motte').

My second point concerns the infrastructure and materials that characterized these estates, once again looking first at the Roman *casali* during the first *incasalamento*. The *casali* were often grouped around a tower made of bricks (*turris*), which was sometimes more than twenty metres high — indeed, many of these towers have survived and are still visible in the *Campagna Romana*; they were enclosed by a *castellarium*, a word used to describe diverse types and sizes of walls. Since the *castellarium* encompassed the whole *casale*, the two terms sometimes became synonymous. Within the *castellarium*/*casale*, were various residential buildings: single- and two-storey houses (*solarate*), which were sometimes fitted with chimneys (and were therefore called *caminata*), as well as arguably imposing constructions named *palatia*. Importantly, the *casale* also comprised a substantial set of outbuildings, such as storage facilities for cereals, cisterns, and artificial caves, called *arnaria*, complete with niches and air-holes.[22]

The Milanese *cassine* appear to have been less complex, which can be explained, to an extent at least, by their smaller size in comparison to Roman *casali* (which, as we recall, measured a maximum of thirteen hectares as opposed to 555). The most significant source of information regarding these small estates are the *cascine a grappolo*, which were structured around common spaces: these areas usually contained a well, an oven, and a press. An important role was played by mills and, at a later date, around the middle of the fourteenth century, by fulling machines used for paper production.[23]

Significantly more information is available regarding Cistercian *grange*. As I mentioned earlier, *grangia* originally denoted a storage place for cereals — a form of infrastructure which indeed appears to have been central to Cistercian communities, to the extent that it came to define the entirety of their landed estates. Rinaldo Comba suggested in 1985 that the aisled warehouse may have been the sole unifying architectural element of Italian *grange*; however, this can only be proved by a comprehensive archaeological survey of all the surviving *grange* — and such a survey has yet to be carried out.[24] Let us now look more closely at two examples. The *grangia* of Valera must have been a particularly impressive structure: it was located near Lodi, which belonged to the abbey of Chiaravalle Milanese, and was the centre of a substantial land-purchasing operation, which led to the creation of a compact body of landed properties by the middle of the thirteenth century. By 1236 it was encircled by a ditch, and by 1255 an enclosure wall had been added, probably built of stone. It contained a brick kiln and it had a *lobia* (literally, an arcade) which might have been

22 Carocci and Vendittelli, *L'origine*, pp. 69–78, 85–89; Carocci and Vendittelli, 'Casali', pp. 299–300.

23 This is the case with the *cassine* outside Porta Ticinese, in Milan: cf. De Angelis Cappabianca, 'Le "cassine" tra il XII e il XIV secolo', esp. pp. 379–84.

24 Comba, 'I Cistercensi', pp. 241–42. A recent overview of the Cistercian *grange* located, for the most part, in modern France (some of them, like Vaulerent and Foncalvy, are monumental buildings, which have survived up to the present day) is Blary, 'La question'.

a dormitory or, again, a storage facility.[25] The second example concerns the monastery of S. Croce al Chienti, which was a dependency of the Cistercian abbey of S. Maria di Chiaravalle di Fiastra, in the Marche region. It deserves some scrutiny, as an inventory drawn up in the thirteenth century provides many details of the infrastructure and outbuildings included in S. Croce and its neighbouring *grangia*. *Infra claustrum* (that is to say, within the monastery) S. Croce had one storage facility, one infirmary, two cellars, kitchens, two larders, and a number of rooms for working with fabrics. *Extra claustrum* (outside the monastery) one could find various rural buildings as well as the *grangia*, which was surrounded by two ditches and provided shelter for a large number of farm animals.[26]

We shall focus only briefly on *poderi* — since, as I remarked earlier, there is little information available about them during the twelfth and thirteenth centuries. What we can however say is that, firstly, late medieval Tuscan *poderi* were often created by reusing pre-existing structures, thus pointing to a certain degree of continuity in the patterns of at least some rural settlements — even though it is difficult to gauge exactly how far back this practice goes. It was not infrequent for groups of five to ten peasant houses to be combined to create a single *podere*, possibly also as a result of the demographic crisis marking the fourteenth and fifteenth centuries.[27] This same kind of development can at least be hypothesized with regard to Umbria and Marche, for which however written evidence is less plentiful than is the case for Tuscany.[28] As to their infrastructure, it should be emphasized that the largest *poderi* were cultivated by more than one peasant family, and usually included underground arcades, *colombaie* (that is, towers for the breeding of doves), gardens enclosed by masonry walls, and buildings for the maintenance of canals. Finally, it is worth noting that the landowner's house was frequently used as a storage facility.[29]

The next point I wish to analyse is critical to the understanding of the relationship between landed estates and their buildings on the one hand, and overall economic change on the other. Who paid for these estates and buildings, and how? Here the emphasis is on the social position of the key figures involved, rather than on the types of estates. First and foremost, it was

25 Chiappa Mauri, 'La costruzione'.

26 Saracco Previdi, 'Grange'. An overview of the documentation of S. Croce al Chienti up to 1291 is Borri, 'Documenti'.

27 Mazzi and Raveggi, *Gli uomini*, pp. 130–31.

28 The classic reference work on the development of *mezzadria poderale* in Umbria is Desplanques, *Campagnes*, pp. 176–81. He argued that the *mezzadria* contract started to take its definitive form during the thirteenth century, whereas one needs to wait for the decades straddling the sixteenth and seventeenth centuries in order to observe the process of *appoderamento*. For a different view, stressing the earlier spread, in the countryside of Perugia, of isolated rural houses (which would be typical of the *mezzadria poderale*) cf. Grohmann, *Città*, II, pp. 893–913. On the Marche region, and the countryside of Ancona in particular, cf. Villani, *I centri*, pp. 63–66.

29 Cf. again Mazzi and Raveggi, *Gli uomini*, esp. pp. 132–34.

the mercantile classes of urban society who were the principal force behind the development of *casali*, *cassine*, and *poderi*. From the 1190s onwards, Roman merchants were fully engaged in European-wide trade networks; the profits derived from this activity were then reinvested in the purchase of land, thus paving the way for the first *incasalamento* and its distinctively expansionist character.[30] Milanese *cassine*, too, particularly in the thirteenth and fourteenth centuries, were built on the initiative of the merchants and bankers who gradually began to replace the old consular aristocracy of the commune.[31] The same pattern applies to Tuscan *poderi*, although the relocation of city-based owners to the countryside becomes clearly visible only in the fourteenth and fifteenth centuries.[32]

The Cistercians are the second group to be considered, in particular the ways they financed *grange*. Firstly, the monks could benefit from donations of landed goods from bishops and major lay aristocrats; moreover, the exemptions from many tributes conceded by popes and emperors further contributed to their wealth. Two examples will suffice. In an attempt to establish good relations with the abbey of S. Maria di Morimondo, which stood on the boundary between their two dioceses, the prelates of Pavia and Milan conceded numerous estates to the resident Cistercian community, thereby playing a pivotal role in the creation of the abbey's substantial landed patrimony over the course of the twelfth century.[33] My second example regards S. Maria di Lucedio in Piedmont, which in the late 1180s was granted by the papacy a series of exemptions from the payment of tithes and tolls (namely those regarding cattle transhumance) which would later be confirmed by Emperor Frederick II; furthermore, over the same period S. Maria received donations from the bishop of Vercelli and the marquis of Monferrato.[34] Nevertheless, the support from aristocrats and sovereigns can hardly account alone for the monumental land-purchasing operations undertaken by Cistercian communities; and it is worth emphasizing that, in some instances, we have no idea where the money came from. This is notably the case with the *grangia* of Valera, which, as I mentioned earlier, was quite possibly one of the grandest Italian *grange* in terms of fortifications and rural buildings, judging from written evidence. It is therefore striking that, as Luisa Chiappa Mauri has argued, it is not at all clear how the landed patrimony

30 Cf. the list of families involved in the creation of *casali* provided by Maire Vigueur, *L'autre Rome*, p. 88.

31 Cf. De Angelis Cappabianca, 'Le "cassine" tra il XII e il XIV secolo', pp. 398–99; lists of families who took part in the creation of *cassine* can be found in De Angelis Cappabianca, 'Le cascine', p. 10, and in Salvatori, 'Una comunità', p. 204.

32 Classic references are Herlihy and Klapisch-Zuber, *Les Toscans* on the Florentine *catasto* drawn up in 1427; Cherubini, 'La "Tavola delle possessioni"' and Cherubini, 'Proprietari', on the Sienese countryside in the fourteenth century.

33 Occhipinti, 'Il monastero' and Occhipinti, 'Fortuna'.

34 Cf. Panero, 'Forme'. An overview of the privileges granted by popes to Cistercian communities in northern Italy is Cariboni, 'Esenzione'.

of Valera was financed.[35] I would hypothesize that the Cistercians took out loans in order to purchase new lands, probably with the aim of making a profit by selling the agricultural surplus subsequently obtained. This is difficult to prove: credit transactions were seldom written down, and, when they were, in most cases interest rates were not stated explicitly.[36] What we do know, however, is that many Cistercian abbeys were burdened with debts around the middle of the thirteenth century. The accumulation of these debts can be explained by local dynamics, as was the case at Morimondo, which was destroyed by Pavese soldiers in 1237 and plunged into poverty as a result;[37] but I would not exclude the possibility that other religious foundations fell into debt as a consequence of spiralling interest rates.[38]

With the exception of the Cistercians, religious institutions appear to have played a less prominent role than the urban bourgeoisie in the creation of isolated rural estates. There were, it is true, partial exceptions. Some of the thirteenth-century Milanese *cassine* were built by the chapter house of S. Giovanni di Monza and the hospital of S. Simpliciano in Milan. The landed properties of the Church dominated the *Campagna Romana* at least up until 1150, and continued to play an important role after that date; and in the second *incasalamento* it was the clerics who were the protagonists. J.-C. Maire Vigueur has calculated that over half of the Roman *casali* attested between 1348 and 1428 were owned by clerics. But churches and monasteries ceased to be promoters of *cassine* after 1300, and the second *incasalamento* was a retrograde step, resulting from the abandonment of castles and open settlements (named *ville*), which were turned into *casali*; this would appear to confirm the relatively marginal role played by clerics other than Cistercians.[39] The same can be said for rural lay aristocracies, who acted as patrons or benefactors of new Cistercian foundations by granting them lands, but who were in general less proactive than urban owners.[40] Finally, a brief mention should be made of the peasant class, as they too were behind a number of initiatives. The following are a handful of examples. From 1192 onwards notarial documents in Umbria begin to record the existence of *castellaria*, that is, small fortified

35 Cf. again Chiappa Mauri, 'La costruzione', p. 287.

36 An overview, focused on credit granted to agriculturists in Italy from the twelfth to the fourteenth centuries, is Gaulin and Menant, 'Endettement'. A point of comparison is provided by the brilliant analysis conducted by Chris Briggs on fourteenth-century England: Briggs, *Credit*, esp. p. 30 on the problems posed by the sources on credit transactions.

37 Cf. the articles cited at note 33.

38 I myself have struggled to explain the widespread indebtedness of Florentine ecclesiastical institutions at the beginning of the thirteenth century, and have had to resort to hypotheses: Tabarrini, *Estate*, ch. 2.

39 De Angelis Cappabianca, 'Le "cassine" tra il XII e il XIV secolo'; Maire Vigueur, 'Les *casali*', pp. 66–67; Wickham, *Medieval Rome*, p. 59. On the second *incasalamento* cf. also Carocci and Vendittelli, 'Casali', pp. 297–98.

40 Examples are Chiaravalle Milanese (Radaelli, 'Archeologia', pp. 297–98), Lucedio (Panero, 'Forme'), Morimondo (Occhipinti, 'Fortuna', p. 316), and Staffarda (Panero, 'Formazione').

rural estates which were apparently constructed by local landowners.[41] Some of the *tecta* in Piedmont were named after the people who built them; these did not belong to any recognizable aristocratic family and are therefore likely to have been small-scale landowners.[42] The creation of rural estates known as *casarene*, in the Marche region, can also be ascribed to the peasant initiative, although these are attested only in the fourteenth century.[43] On a general level, these structures do not appear to have been particularly grand: the written evidence points in that direction, while archaeological remains are virtually non-existent. This is not difficult to comprehend, as small to medium owners were unlikely to have had the wherewithal to make substantial investments in rural buildings and fortifications.

We shall now move on to the final point of my essay — that is, the purposes for which these estates were created. Again, this is to an extent implicit in previous comments, but some aspects require further development. First of all, one characteristic common to all the types of estates discussed so far was the proximity between cultivators and the land they worked. *Casali*, *cassine*, *grange*, and *poderi* were intended to be places of residence for agricultural labourers; it can be inferred that such a proximity derived from an attempt at enhancing productivity on the part of landowners. In relation to this, landowners were evidently endeavouring to improve agricultural production. This is best demonstrated by the Roman *casali*, where wheat-farming and animal husbandry were closely interconnected; large grain fields such as those found in *casali* required the use of draught animals, which could clear far larger areas of land than a human workforce.[44] For the same reason, the aforementioned *grangia* of S. Croce del Chienti employed a number of farmhands exclusively tasked with tending cattle.[45] Another example is the *grangia* of S. Maria di Campo Imperatore, in Abruzzo. The excavations carried out there from 1997 revealed the presence of small stone buildings called *condole*, and of arcades called *locce* which served as shelters for the monks when they moved the cattle from the mountains down to the plain — also known as vertical transhumance.[46] The exploitation of watercourses and the creation of canals was similarly geared towards the increase in overall agricultural output: this emerges clearly from the documentation concerning the Milanese *cassine*, namely those located right outside Porta Vercellina, and also from the excavation (started in 2013) of the *grangia* of Nosedo, which belonged to the abbey of Chiaravalle Milanese.[47] As a final point, it is worth noting that cereals appear to have been stored

41 Tiberini, *Le signorie*, p. 191 and following.

42 Comba, *Metamorfosi*, pp. 78–79.

43 Cf. again Saracco Previdi, 'Habitat'; an overview of Marche, Umbria and Lazio in Ait and Lanconelli, 'Successi'.

44 Cf. again, for an overview, Carocci and Vendittelli, 'Casali'.

45 See again Saracco Previdi, 'Grange'.

46 Gabay, 'Grangia'.

47 Cf. note 9 on Milanese *cassine*; on Nosedo, see Radaelli, 'Archeologia'.

in one of the outbuildings which were a constant feature of *casali, cassine, grange,* and *poderi*. We may assume that a proportion of the stored cereals was not destined for home consumption, but was set aside in order to be sold at market — there was also possible speculation on the price of grain over bad years or bad seasons. This is consistent with evidence from England pointing to an increase in the number of barns and granaries after 1200.[48]

* * *

We can conclude that the creation of *casali, cassine, grange,* and *poderi* reflects the increase in aggregate demand that characterized the period between *c.* 1150 and *c.* 1250. I would like to briefly outline three possible research avenues which, I hope, may be opened up by this review of the literature on isolated rural estates. First, this literature ought to be re-read in the light of what is known about credit to agriculturists: it cannot be a coincidence that the proliferation of storage facilities coincides, by and large, with the earliest evidence of increasingly consistent loans to peasants, both in cash and kind (which could be added to their sometimes meagre income, and possibly used to pay rent). Second, it should be emphasized that, with the important exception of Cistercian monks (who however would find themselves beset by debts by the middle of the thirteenth century), the social class that on the whole was best placed to finance structured estates and costly rural buildings was that which derived its income from commerce and finance. One might infer that these were the main drivers of economic change over the central Middle Ages, since they delivered the highest profits and therefore facilitated substantial investments; and if the role played by the merchant class in determining and furthering medieval economic growth is beyond dispute, the debate regarding the fundamental causes of that growth, and the relationship between the two, is still an open one.[49] Finally, it should be stressed that only considerable investment could provide tenants and rural workers with costly infrastructures. As Maria Serena Mazzi and Susanna Raveggi have suggested, this helps explain why harsh agrarian regimes, such as the *mezzadria poderale,* might have appeared more convenient and attractive than independent ownership. Whatever their difficulties, *mezzadri* were better equipped and could therefore in some respects enjoy less severe conditions than free peasants.[50] The study of landed estates, their buildings and the way these were financed may therefore shed light on the long-term success of the *mezzadria poderale*.

48 This topic has been studied with particular regard to the modern age: cf. the collection of essays in Ronsjin, Mignemi, and Herment, eds, *Stocks*. On England cf. Gardiner, 'Stacks', p. 34. The potentially speculative nature of stockpiling grain was already well known by the Carolingians: cf. Devroey, *La Nature*, esp. pp. 141–42.

49 See once again the essays in Franceschi, ed., *La crescita*.

50 Mazzi and Raveggi, *Gli uomini*, esp. pp. 132–34.

Works Cited

Secondary Works

Ait, Ivana, and Angela Lanconelli, 'Successi e crisi delle nuove fondazioni. Modelli insediativi a confronto nell'Italia centrale: Marche, Umbria, Lazio', in *Fondare abitati in età medievale: Successi e fallimenti. Omaggio a Rinaldo Comba. Atti delle giornate internazionali di studio (S. Giovanni Valdarno, 15–16 gennaio 2016)*, ed. by Francesco Panero, Giuliano Pinto, and Paolo Pirillo (Florence: EDIFIR, 2017), pp. 195–219

Bacchi, Teresa, 'Conquista del territorio e modificazione dei modelli insediativi: Le aziende fondiarie nel Ferrarese (secoli XI–XII)', in *Le campagne italiane prima e dopo il Mille: Una società in trasformazione*, ed. by Bruno Andreolli, Vito Fumagalli, and Massimo Montanari (Bologna: CLUEB, 1985), pp. 135–61

Blary, François, 'La question des clos symboliques et fortifiés des établissements cisterciens (XIIIe-XVe s.)', *Bulletin du centre d'études médiévales d'Auxerre*, hors-série 12 (2020), 197–241

Borri, Giammario, 'Documenti per la storia del monastero di Santa Croce al Chienti (1085–1291)', *Studia Picena*, 69 (2004), 7–87

Brezzi, Paolo, 'Il sistema agrario nel territorio romano alla fine del Medio Evo', *Studi romani*, 25.2 (1977), 153–68

Briggs, Chris, *Credit and Village: Society in Fourteenth-Century England* (Oxford: British Academy, 2009)

Campbell, Bruce M. S., *The Great Transition: Climate, Disease and Society in the Late-Medieval World* (Cambridge: Cambridge University Press, 2016)

Cammarosano, Paolo, *Economia politica classica e storia economica dell'Europa medievale* (Udine: CERM, 2020)

Cariboni, Guido, 'Esenzione e formazione del *Privilegium commune*: Osservazioni a partire dai cenobi dell'Italia settentrionale', in *Papato e monachesimo 'esente' nei secoli centrali del Medioevo*, ed. by Nicolangelo D'Acunto (Florence: Firenze University Press, 2003), pp. 65–107

Carocci, Sandro, and Marco Vendittelli, *L'origine della Campagna Romana: Casali, castelli e villaggi nel XII e XIII secolo. Con saggi di Daniela Esposito, Mauro Lenzi, Susanna Passigli* (Rome: Società Romana di Storia Patria, 2004)

Carocci, Sandro, and Marco Vendittelli, 'Casali e castelli nella Campagna Romana (XII secolo – metà XIV secolo)', in *Motte, torri e caseforti nelle campagne medievali (secoli XII–XV). Omaggio ad Aldo A. Settia. Atti del Convegno (Cherasco, 23–25 settembre 2005)*, ed. by Rinaldo Comba, Francesco Panero, and Giuliano Pinto (Cherasco: CISIM, 2007), pp. 295–302

Cherubini, Giovanni, 'Forme e vicende degli insediamenti nella campagna toscana dei secoli XIII-XV', *Quaderni storici*, 24 (1973), 879–904 [also in Cherubini, Giovanni, *Signori, contadini, borghesi: Ricerche sulla società italiana del basso medioevo* (Florence: La Nuova Italia, 1974), pp. 145–74]

——, 'Proprietari, contadini e campagne senesi all'inizio del Trecento', in Cherubini, Giovanni, *Signori, contadini, borghesi: Ricerche sulla società italiana del basso medioevo* (Florence: La Nuova Italia, 1974), pp. 231–311
——, 'La "Tavola delle possessioni" del comune di Siena', *Rivista di storia dell'agricoltura*, 14.2 (1974), 5–14
Chiappa Mauri, Luisa, 'La costruzione del paesaggio agrario padano: i Cistercensi e la grangia di Valera', *Studi storici*, 26.2 (1985), 263–313
——, 'Le scelte economiche del monastero di Chiaravalle milanese nel XII e XIII secolo', in *Chiaravalle: Arte e storia di un'abbazia cistercense*, ed. by Paolo Tomea (Milan: Edizioni Electa, 1992), pp. 31–49
——, *Terra e uomini nella Lombardia medievale* (Rome: Laterza, 1997)
Comba, Rinaldo, 'Aspects économiques de la vie des abbayes cisterciennes de l'Italie du Nord-Ouest (XIIe-XIVe siècle)', in *L'économie cistercienne: Géographie — Mutations du Moyen Âge aux temps modernes (Flaran, Troisièmes journées internationales d'histoire, 16–18 septembre 1981)*, ed. by Charles Higounet (Auch: Presses Universitaires du Midi, 1983), pp. 119–33
——, 'I Cistercensi fra città e campagne nei secoli XII e XIII: Una sintesi mutevole di orientamenti economici e culturali nell'Italia nord-occidentale', *Studi storici*, 26.2 (1985), 237–61
——, 'La dispersione dell'habitat nell'Italia centro-settentrionale tra XII e XV secolo: Vent'anni di ricerche', *Studi storici*, 3 (1984), 765–83
——, *Metamorfosi di un paesaggio rurale: Uomini e luoghi del Piemonte sud-occidentale fra X e XVI secolo* (Turin: CELID, 1983)
——, 'Le origini medievali dell'assetto insediativo moderno nelle campagne italiane', in *Storia d'Italia. Annali, VIII: Insediamenti e territorio*, ed. by Cesare De Seta (Turin: Einaudi, 1985), pp. 367–404
——, 'Rappresentazioni mentali, realtà e aspetti di cultura materiale nella storia delle dimore rurali: le campagne del Piemonte sud-occidentale tra XII e XVI secolo', *Archeologia medievale*, 5 (1978), 375–414
——, '"In silva Stapharda": dissodamenti, grange e villenove in un grande complesso forestale (XI–XIV secolo)', *Archivio Storico Italiano*, 167:4 (2009), 607–24
——, '"Ville" e borghi nuovi nell'Italia del Nord (XII–XIV secolo)', *Studi storici*, 32.1 (1991), 5–23
Comba, Rinaldo, and Grado Giovanni Merlo, eds, *L'abbazia di Staffarda e l'irradiazione cistercense nel Piemonte meridionale. Atti del Convegno (Abbazia di Staffarda — Revello, 17–18 ottobre 1998)* (Cuneo: Società per gli Studi Storici, Archeologici ed Artistici per la Provincia di Cuneo, 1999)
Comba, Rinaldo, Francesco Panero, and Giuliano Pinto, eds, *Borghi nuovi e borghi franchi nel processo di costruzione dei distretti comunali nell'Italia centro-settentrionale (secoli XII–XIV)* (Cherasco: Società per gli Studi Storici, Archeologici ed Artistici per la Provincia di Cuneo, 2002)
Comba, Rinaldo, Francesco Panero, and Giuliano Pinto, eds, *Motte, torri e caseforti nelle campagne medievali (secoli XII–XV). Omaggio ad Aldo A. Settia. Atti del Convegno (Cherasco, 23–25 settembre 2005)* (Cherasco: CISIM, 2007)

Conti, Elio, *La formazione della struttura agraria moderna nel contado fiorentino* (Rome: Istituto Storico Italiano per il Medioevo, 1965)

Cortese, Maria Elena, 'Gli opifici idraulici dell'Abbazia cistercense di San Galgano in Val di Merse (Siena)', in *Dalle abbazie, l'Europa: I nuovi germogli del seme benedettino tra primo e secondo millennio (secc. X–XII). Atti del Convegno di Studi (Badia a Settimo, 22–24 aprile 1999)*, ed. by Alessandro Guidotti and Gabriella Cirri (Florence: Maschietto, 2006), pp. 303–11

De Angelis Cappabianca, Laura, 'Le cascine del suburbio di Milano tra il XII e il XIII secolo', *Bollettino della società pavese di Storia Patria*, 88.40 (1988), 5–12

——, 'Le "cassine" tra il XII e il XIV secolo: l'esempio di Milano', in *Paesaggi urbani dell'Italia padana nei secoli VIII–XIV* (Bologna: GEM, 1988), pp. 373–415

Degrassi, Donata, 'Motte, torri e caseforti nelle campagne friulane: Prime indagini e orientamenti di ricerca', in *Motte, torri e caseforti nelle campagne medievali (secoli XII–XV). Omaggio ad Aldo A. Settia. Atti del Convegno (Cherasco, 23–25 settembre 2005)*, ed. by Rinaldo Comba, Francesco Panero, and Giuliano Pinto (Cherasco: CISIM, 2007), pp. 195–208

Del Tredici, Federico, *Comunità, nobili e gentiluomini nel contado di Milano del Quattrocento* (Milan: UNICOPLI, 2013)

Desplanques, Henri, *Campagnes Ombriennes: Contribution à l'étude des paysages ruraux en Italie centrale* (Paris: Colin, 1969)

Devroey, Jean-Pierre, *La Nature et le roi: Environnement, pouvoir et société à l'âge de Charlemagne (740–820)* (Paris: Albin Michel, 2019)

Farinelli, Roberto, and Andrea Giorgi, 'Fenomeni di sinecismo e accentramento demico-insediativo pianificato: Il "secondo incastellamento" nella Toscana dei secoli XII e XIII', in *V congresso nazionale di archeologia medievale [Palazzo della Dogana, Salone del Tribunale (Foggia), Palazzo dei Celestini, Auditorium (Manfredonia) (30 settembre – 3 ottobre 2009)]*, ed. by Giuliano Volpe and Pasquale Favia (Borgo San Lorenzo: All'Insegna del Giglio, 2009), pp. 406–11

Fiumi, Enrico, *Storia economica e sociale di San Gimignano* (Florence: Olschki, 1961)

Franceschi, Franco, ed., *La crescita economica dell'Occidente medievale: Un tema storico non ancora esaurito. Venticinquesimo convegno internazionale di studi (Pistoia, 14–17 maggio 2015)* (Rome: Viella, 2017)

Friedman, David, and Paolo Pirillo, eds, *Le terre nuove. Atti del Seminario internazionale organizzato dai Comuni di Firenze e San Giovanni Valdarno (Firenze, San Giovanni Valdarno, 28–30 gennaio 1999)* (Florence: Olschki, 2004)

Fumagalli, Vito, *Terra e società nell'Italia padana* (Turin: Einaudi, 1976)

Gabay, Noémie, 'Grangia cistercense Santa Maria del Monte a Campo Imperatore: Rilievo e studi di un insediamento medievale della transumanza in Italia centrale', *Chronique des activités archéologiques de l'École française de Rome* [https://doi.org/10.4000/cefr.2058], *Italie centrale*, online since 17 October 2018, site visited 24 August 2021

Gardiner, Mark F., 'Stacks, Barns and Granaries in Early and High Medieval England: Crop Storage and its Implications', in *Horrea, Barns and Silos: Storage and Incomes in Early Medieval Europe*, ed. by Giovanna Bianchi, Juan Antonio Quirós Castillo, and Alfonso Vigil-Escalera Guirado (Bilbao: Universidad del País Vasco, 2013), pp. 23–38

Gaulin, Jean-Louis, and François Menant, 'Crédit rural et endettement paysan dans l'Italie communale', in *Endettement paysan et crédit rural dans l'Europe médiévale et moderne. Actes des XVIIes journées internationales d'histoire de l'abbaye de Flaran (Septembre 1995)*, ed. by Maurice Berthe (Toulouse: Presses Universitaires du Midi, 1998), pp. 35–67

Grillo, Paolo, 'Dal bosco agli arativi: La creazione della grangia di Aimondino in una raccolta di testimonianze degli inizi del Duecento', in *L'abbazia di Staffarda e l'irradiazione cistercense nel Piemonte meridionale. Atti del Convegno (Abbazia di Staffarda — Revello, 17–18 ottobre 1998)*, ed. by Rinaldo Comba and Grado Giovanni Merlo (Cuneo: Società per gli Studi Storici, Archeologici ed Artistici per la Provincia di Cuneo, 1999), pp. 269–86

——, 'Grange e cascine in area lombarda (secoli XII–XIII)', in *Attività economiche e sviluppi insediativi nell'Italia dei secoli XI–XV. Omaggio a Giuliano Pinto. Atti del Convegno (Cherasco, 25–27 ottobre 2013)*, ed. by Enrico Lusso (Cherasco: CISIM, 2014), pp. 107–18

——, 'Fra poteri pubblici e iniziative private: Torri e aziende rurali fortificate nell'area milanese e comasca (secoli XII–XIII)', in *Motte, torri e caseforti nelle campagne medievali (secoli XII–XV). Omaggio ad Aldo A. Settia. Atti del Convegno (Cherasco, 23–25 settembre 2005)*, ed. by Rinaldo Comba, Francesco Panero, and Giuliano Pinto (Cherasco: CISIM, 2007), pp. 167–83

Grohmann, Alberto, *Città e territorio tra Medioevo ed età moderna (Perugia, secc. XIII–XVI)*, 2 vols (Perugia: Volumnia, 1981)

Gullino, Giuseppe, *Forme abitative a Vercelli: Questioni e problemi per una ricostruzione del processo terminologico dei manufatti edilizi dal secolo X al secolo XIII* (Vercelli: Società Storica Vercellese, 1980)

Herlihy, David, and Christiane Klapisch-Zuber, *Les Toscans et leurs familles: Une étude du Catasto florentin de 1427* (Paris: Presses de Sciences Po, 1978)

Higounet, Charles, 'Effets des mutations de l'économie rurale cistercienne (XIIIe-XIVe siècles)', in *Agricoltura e trasformazione dell'ambiente: Secoli XIII–XIV. Atti della XI settimana di studio (25–30 aprile 1970)*, ed. by Alessandra Guarducci (Florence: Le Monnier, 1984), pp. 119–30

Jones, Philip J., 'From manor to mezzadria: A Tuscan Case-Study in the Medieval Origins of Modern Agrarian Society', in *Florentine Studies: Politics and Society in Renaissance Florence*, ed. by Nicolai Rubinstein (London: Faber & Faber, 1968), pp. 193–241

Klapisch-Zuber, Christiane, 'Mezzadria e insediamenti rurali alla fine del Medio Evo', in *Civiltà ed economia agricola in Toscana nei secc. XIII–XV: Problemi della vita delle campagne nel tardo Medioevo (VIII convegno internazionale, Pistoia, 21–24 aprile 1977)* (Pistoia: Centro Italiano di Studi di Storia e d'Arte, 1981), pp. 149–68

Lenzi, Mauro, 'Per una storia dei *casalia* del territorio romano nell'alto medioevo', in Sandro Carocci and Marco Vendittelli, *L'origine della Campagna Romana: Casali, castelli e villaggi nel XII e XIII secolo. Con saggi di Daniela Esposito, Mauro Lenzi, Susanna Passigli* (Rome: Società Romana di Storia Patria, 2004), pp. 307–24

Leverotti, Franca, 'Scomposizione e ricomposizione di un "podere": il caso di Colognole in Colline', in *Un 'filo rosso': Studi antichi e nuove ricerche sulle orme di Gabriella Rossetti in occasione dei suoi settanta anni*, ed. by Gabriella Garzella and Enrica Salvatori (Pisa: ETS, 2017), pp. 209–30

Maire Vigueur, Jean-Claude, *L'autre Rome: Une histoire des Romains à l'époque des communes (XIIe-XIVe siècle)* (Paris: Tallandier, 2010)

——, 'Les *casali* des églises romaines à la fin du Moyen Âge (1348–1428)', *Mélanges de l'École française de Rome. Moyen Âge, Temps Modernes*, 86.1 (1974), 63–136

Mannoni, Tiziano, and Matteo Sicios, 'Le torri della Liguria extraurbana tardo-medievale e l'evoluzione dei metodi di studio archeologici', in *Motte, torri e caseforti nelle campagne medievali (secoli XII–XV). Omaggio ad Aldo A. Settia. Atti del Convegno (Cherasco, 23–25 settembre 2005)*, ed. by Rinaldo Comba, Francesco Panero, and Giuliano Pinto (Cherasco: CISIM, 2007), pp. 125–34

Masschaele, James, 'Economic Takeoff and the Rise of Markets', in *A Companion to the Medieval World*, ed. by Carol L. Lansing and Edward D. English (Oxford: Wiley-Blackwell, 2009), pp. 89–110

Mazzi, Maria Serena, and Sergio Raveggi, *Gli uomini e le cose nelle campagne fiorentine del Quattrocento* (Florence: Olschki, 1983)

Menant, François, *Campagnes lombardes au Moyen Âge: L'économie et la société dans la région de Bergame, de Crémone et de Brescia du Xe au XIIe siècle* (Rome: École Française de Rome, 1993)

Micheletto, Egle, 'L'insediamento rurale in Piemonte tra X e XIII secolo: I contesti archeologici', *Archeologia medievale*, 37 (2010), 15–28

Murialdo, Giovanni, 'La riorganizzazione signorile del territorio tra XII e XIII secolo: Incastellamento e decastellamento nel Finale', in *L'incastellamento in Liguria, X–XII secolo: Bilanci e destini di un tema storiografico. Atti della Giornata di Studio (Rapallo, 26 aprile 1997)*, ed. by Fabrizio Benente (Bordighera: Istituto Internazionale di Studi Liguri, 2000), pp. 101–29

Muzzi, Oretta, and Maria Daniela Nenci, eds, *Il contratto di mezzadria nella Toscana medievale*. II *(Contado di Firenze, sec. XIII)* (Florence: Olschki, 1988)

Occhipinti, Elisa, 'Fortuna e crisi di un patrimonio monastico: Morimondo e le sue grange fra XII e XIV secolo', *Studi Storici*, 26.2 (1985), 315–36

——, 'Il monastero di Morimondo in Lombardia tra tensioni locali e antagonismi di potere (secoli XII – inizi XIII)', *Nuova rivista storica*, 68.5/6 (1983), 527–84

Palermo, Luciano, *Sviluppo economico e società preindustriali: Cicli, strutture e congiunture in Europa dal medioevo alla prima età moderna* (Rome: Viella, 1997)

Panero, Francesco, 'Formazione, struttura e gestione del patrimonio fondiario dell'abbazia di Staffarda (secoli XII–XIV)', in *L'abbazia di Staffarda e l'irradiazione cistercense nel Piemonte meridionale. Atti del Convegno (Abbazia di Staffarda — Revello, 17–18 ottobre 1998)*, ed. by Rinaldo Comba and Grado Giovanni Merlo (Cuneo: Società per gli Studi Storici, Archeologici ed Artistici per la Provincia di Cuneo, 1999), pp. 239–58

——, 'Forme monastiche di conduzione diretta della proprietà fondiaria: I Cistercensi di Lucedio', in *Grandi proprietà ecclesiastiche nell'Italia nord-occidentale: Tra sviluppo e crisi (secoli X–XIV)*, ed. by Francesco Panero (Bologna: CLUEB, 2009), pp. 171–93

Pinto, Giuliano, 'Per una storia delle dimore mezzadrili nella Toscana medievale', *Archeologia medievale*, 7 (1980), 153–71

Radaelli, Ricky, 'Archeologia di una grangia: Il caso di *Nocetum* presso Chiaravalle Milanese', in *Costruzione identitaria e spazi sociali: Nuovi studi sul monachesimo cistercense nel Medioevo. Atti dell'incontro di studio (Milano, 1–2 dicembre 2015)*, ed. by Guido Cariboni and Nicolangelo D'Acunto (Spoleto: CISAM, 2017), pp. 291–315

Rapetti, Anna Maria, 'Paesaggi rurali e insediamenti nell'Italia del Basso Medioevo', in *L'Italia alla fine del Medioevo: I caratteri originali nel quadro europeo*, ed. by Francesco Salvestrini (Florence: Firenze University Press, 2006), pp. 25–56

Ronsijn, Wouter, Niccolò Mignemi, and Laurent Herment, eds, *Stocks, Seasons and Sales: Food Supply, Storage and Markets in Europe and the New World* (Turnhout: Brepols, 2019)

Salvatori, Enrica, 'Una comunità familiare nel suburbio milanese: Le Cascine Biffi-Bulgaroni', in *L'età dei Visconti: Il dominio di Milano tra XIII e XV secolo*, ed. by Luisa Chiappa Mauri, Laura De Angelis Cappabianca, and Patrizia Mainoni (Milan: La Storia, 1993), pp. 199–216

Saracco Previdi, Emilia, 'Grange cistercensi nel territorio maceratese: Insediamenti rurali monastici dei secoli XII-XIII', *Proposte e ricerche*, 7.1 (1981), 15–23

——, 'Habitat sparso ed accentrato nell'entroterra della 'Marchia' nei secoli XI–XIV', *Archeologia medievale*, 7 (1980), 367–73

Settia, Aldo A., *Castelli e villaggi nell'Italia padana: Popolamento, potere e sicurezza fra IX e XIII secolo* (Naples: Liguori, 1984)

——, *L'illusione della sicurezza: Fortificazioni di rifugio nell'Italia medievale, 'ricetti', 'bastite', 'cortine'* (Vercelli – Cuneo: Società per gli Studi Storici, Archeologici ed Artistici della Provincia di Cuneo, 2001)

——, 'Tra azienda agricola e fortezza: Case forti, "motte" e "tombe" nell'Italia settentrionale. Dati e problemi', *Archeologia Medievale*, 7 (1980), 31–54

Tabarrini, Lorenzo, *Estate Management around Florence and Lucca, 1000–1250* (Oxford: Oxford University Press, 2023)

Tiberini, Sandro, 'Colombaie e torri nelle campagne umbre: Dagli studi di Desplanques alle ricerche più recenti', in *Motte, torri e caseforti nelle campagne medievali (secoli XII–XV). Omaggio ad Aldo A. Settia. Atti del Convegno (Cherasco, 23–25 settembre 2005)*, ed. by Rinaldo Comba, Francesco Panero, and Giuliano Pinto (Cherasco: CISIM, 2007), pp. 279–94

——, *Le signorie rurali nell'Umbria settentrionale: Perugia e Gubbio, secc. XI–XIII* (Rome: Ministero per i beni e le attività culturali, Ufficio centrale per i beni archivistici, 1999)

Varanini, Gian Maria, 'Insediamenti e territorio nella storia d'Italia', *Quaderni storici*, 21.63/3 (1986), 981–94

Villani, Virginio, *I centri murati in età medievale* (Ancona: Sistema Informativo Territoriale della Provincia di Ancona, 2004)

Wickham, Chris, *Medieval Rome: Stability and Crisis of a City, 900–1150* (Oxford: Oxford University Press, 2015)

——, 'Paesaggi sepolti: Insediamento e incastellamento sull'Amiata, 750–1250', in *L'Amiata nel Medioevo. Atti del convegno internazionale di studi storici (Abbadia San Salvatore, 29 maggio – 1 giugno 1986)*, ed. by Mario Ascheri and Wilhelm Kurze (Rome: Viella, 1989), pp. 101–37

VÍCTOR FARÍAS ZURITA

El *mansus* de la Cataluña Vieja medieval

La implantación de un señorío constructivo

El año 1286 el abad Guerau y los monjes del monasterio de Sant Cugat del Vallès *establecían* (*stabilimus*) a Pere de Quadre y su esposa, Bonanata, *et vestris omnique proieniei*, el *mansus* Vives, alodio del monasterio y emplazado en la parroquia de Sant Cebrià d'Aiguallonga. El *mansus* se establecía *cum introitibus, exitibus, terminis et affrontacionibus suis et cum domibus ibi constructis et construendis et cum olivariis et aliis arboribus diversorum generum que ibi sunt et erunt et cum universis pertinenciis et tenedonibus suis et cum omnibus ad dictum mansum pertinentibus et pertinere debentibus, in monte et plano, et cum orto sive ortis, cum aqua ad rigandum*. A cambio, el matrimonio daría, además de un par de gallinas, una parte proporcional de las cosechas de las tierras de cereal y de viña y un censo en granos por el *mansus* y sus pertenencias. Los monjes prometieron no exigir otros *censos* ni *agrarios*. Los esposos, por su parte, se obligaron no reconocer *alium dominum* y ser *in dicto manso solidi habitantes et affocati dicti monasterii et sue sacristie mayori*.[1] Las fuentes nos permiten afirmar que hacia 1300 el *mansus* (catalán *mas*), tal como se presenta en esta *stabilitio et in emphiteosim donatio et concessio*, se había difundido y consolidado como una *estructura* que sostenía los señoríos de la Cataluña Vieja, señoríos como podía ser el de Sant Cugat del Vallès, un monasterio emplazado a unos quince kilómetros al norte de la *civitas* capital del condado de Barcelona. La abadía era uno de aquellas a las que los conquistadores francos impusieron la regla benedictina y que luego los condes de Barcelona sometieron a su especial *tuitio*. En los siglos venideros sería una de las comunidades monásticas más ricas de la región.

En las páginas que siguen estudiaremos, sobre todo, la *constitución* del *mansus* en el sentido más material del término, esto es, el proceso que, a partir de una serie de decisiones bien calculadas, llevó a reunir aquellos elementos que consolidarían el *mansus* como explotación que debía ser viable en términos económicos y que pretendía asegurar los *redditus* al *dominus*

1 Barcelona, ACA, Notariales St Cugat del Vallès, Reg. 1, fol. 70v.

Víctor Farías Zurita (victor.farias@upf.edu) teaches in the Facultat de Humanitats of the Universitat Pompeu Fabra, in Barcelona.

Building and Economic Growth in Southern Europe (1050–1300), ed. by Sandro Carocci and Alessio Fiore, (Turnhout: Brepols, 2024), pp. 39–56 BREPOLS PUBLISHERS 10.1484/M.TMC-EB.5.137973

mansi, por una parte, y asegurar la diversidad de *expleta* que el titular y su familia requerían para subsistir, por otra. Nuestro cometido será mostrar los diferentes aspectos de dicho proceso con la ayuda de un importante conjunto de fuentes que proceden de lo que fueron en su día los archivos del monasterio de Sant Cugat y de sus notarios. Una parte los pergaminos de los archivos monásticos se conservan en el Archivo de la Corona de Aragón, en la sección Órdenes Religiosas. El mismo archivo conserva un cartulario del siglo XIII que ha sido editado.[2] Otra parte de los pergaminos se conserva en el Archivo del Monasterio de Montserrat. Los registros de la notaría pública de Sant Cugat, cuya serie se inicia el año 1283, se conservan en la sección Notariales del Archivo de la Corona de Aragón.

Acumulación y reorganización

El señorío de Sant Cugat tiene una larga historia. A mediados del siglo XI el monasterio había realizado una primera fase de extraordinaria acumulación de bienes. La procedencia de éstos era diversa: en buena parte se trataba de *alodia* donados por agricultores del entorno; el mayor número de estas *donationes* se registran para la segunda mitad del siglo X. Pero también hay que destacar las importantes donaciones realizadas por la aristocracia curial y los condes de Barcelona: el año 988 Borrell, *duci atque marchio*, donó al monasterio un extenso *alodem* emplazado *in suburbio Barcilonense, in commisso Octaviano*; este alodio, *nomine et vocabulo Rixago*, incluía *terras et vineas, pratis, pascuis, aquis aqualibus, scopolis ac calculis, arduum et declivum, cultum et incultum*.[3] La acumulación realizada por los monjes fue un proceso sistemático y llevó a una redistribución de la propiedad a gran escala. Los dominios del monasterio no eran en su origen sino unos conglomerados heterogéneos de *alodia* que podían estar más concentrados en unas áreas que en otras; las fuentes los describen como una mezcla de parcelas cultivadas (*terras, vineas*), espacios sin cultivar (*silvas, pascuas*), instalaciones (*molendinos*) y edificaciones (*casas*). La explotación de este dominio se realizó hasta mediados del XI mediante contratos *per precariam*. A menudo podemos constatar que los beneficiarios de estos contratos habían sido los propietarios de los predios antes de donarlos a la *domum Sancti Cucuphatis*.[4]

Una profunda reorganización de estos conglomerados puede datarse hacia mediados del siglo XII y la misma se presentó sobre todo como la creación calculada por parte del señor de unidades de explotación estables a partir de los antiguos componentes de los dominios. En el caso de Sant Cugat, las primeras referencias a *mansi* propiedad de la abadía y localizados

2 Rius Serra, *Cartulario*.
3 Para lo que sigue cf. Farías Zurita, *El mas i la vila*, pp. 103–54.
4 Rius Serra, *Cartulario*, doc. 160 (984).

en su entorno más cercano datan de la segunda mitad del siglo XI, aunque estas referencias no se multiplican hasta el siglo siguiente. Los primeros contratos otorgados por los monjes (*stabilimenta*) datan de los años 1045 y 1077, respectivamente; los mismos se hacen cada vez más frecuentes a partir de 1150.[5] Así, en un dominio como el de Sant Cugat, las *precarias* y las *donationes* se vieron reemplazadas por los *stabilimenta* y *stabilitiones*, como el citado en un comienzo, instrumentos perfeccionados y estandarizados gracias a la práctica notarial y la aplicación del derecho enfitéutico. Se puede afirmar, por lo tanto, que la difusión del *mansus* en los dominios monásticos se inició a mediados del siglo XI para acelerarse a mediados del siglo siguiente. El agregado de *mansi* que se constituyó así en torno a la abadía se amplió con las donaciones de *mansi* por parte de fieles de toda condición y por las compras de *mansi* realizadas por los propios monjes.[6]

Seguidamente, los dominios de Sant Cugat, como los de otras abadías catalanas, pasaron a presentarse como grandes agregados de *mansi*, sobre todo allí donde la acumulación previa había sido más intensa. Podemos estimar en un centenar los *mansi* dominio de los monjes hacia 1200 en la quincena de parroquias de Sant Cugat y su entorno.[7] Para nuestro monasterio se constata la existencia de otros dos grandes agregados, alejados de la abadía: un primero en la comarca del Penedès y un segundo en los márgenes noreste de la comarca del Vallès. Hacia 1200 los tres agregados pasaron a ser administrados, respectivamente, por cada uno de los tres pavordes del monasterio: el *prepositus Maioris*, el *prepositus Penitensis* y el *prepositus Palacii*. En los dominios asignados a la *prepositura maioris* se incluía la *villa Sancti Cucuphatis*, el modesto centro urbano que en el siglo XIII se consolidó junto al monasterio. La gestión óptima de unos dominios como los de Sant Cugat impusieron el reclutamiento de cuadros cualificados que asumieron dicha gestión específicamente y en representación personal de su señor. Para designar estos cuadros se impuso el término *baiulus* (*batlle*). Los primeros *baiuli* del monasterio constan para la segunda mitad del XII, aunque las noticias sólo se multiplican a partir de la segunda mitad del siglo, lo que permite datar entre 1150 y 1200 la difusión general del *baiulus* como oficial señorial, responsable, en virtud de su cargo (*baiulia*), sobre todo, de *fideliter congregare* los *fructos et expletos et redditus et proventus*.[8] Esta difusión resulta, pues, paralela a la reorganización de los dominios y la difusión del *mansus*.

5 Barcelona, ACA, Órdenes religiosas, Perg. St Cugat del Valles, 177 A.2 (d) (1045) y 333 (1077).
6 Rius Serra, *Cartulario*, doc. 1173 (1187) y doc. 1026 (1159).
7 Barcelona, ACA, Órdenes religiosas, Perg. sin catalogar, numeración provisional, C-559.
8 Farías Zurita, 'Sobre la reorganización del señorío rural', pp. 887–916.

Constitución

El *mansus*, en tanto que unidad de explotación, se presenta como un conjunto que incluía, por una parte, una diversidad de elementos materiales y, por otra, una serie de derechos y servicios que se consideraban indispensables para garantizar la buena marcha de la explotación. El *mansus* era, por lo tanto, una *estructura* compleja. Se distinguen los elementos materiales de los elementos no-materiales; y se distinguen, entre los primeros, los bienes muebles (*mobilia*), por una parte, y los bienes inmuebles (*immobilia*), por otra.

1) *Mobilia*

Los *mobilia* que nos interesan son los que, en su conjunto, han de considerarse como el equipamiento tecnológico del *mansus*.

a) *Animalia*

La composición de la cabaña y el número de *bestias* que mantenía un *mansus* resulta imposible de precisar para cada caso. Un inventario *post mortem* redactado el año 1305 y relativo al *mansus* Otger, de la parroquia de Sant Martí de Cerdanyola, permite constatar una cabaña que se componía de un buey de piel negra, una burra también de piel negra, cinco lechones, seis carneros de dos años, tres carneros de un año, veintisiete ovejas, cuatro corderos, cinco gallinas y un gallo.[9] Según las fuentes, un *mansus* mantenía una cabaña diversificada: un conjunto de *bestias grossas et minutas*, aunque modesto en términos cuantitativos, aportaba una importante diversidad de recursos a la economía del *mansus*. Las *bestias* proporcionaban materias primas como fibras (*lana*), pieles (*pelles*) y cueros (*quir*). El ganado también suministraba los *fimos* para regenerar las tierras; el estiércol procedía tanto de los cuadrúpedos como de las palomas criadas en los palomares.[10] La cabaña abastecía la familia del *mansus* con la mayor parte de los alimentos de origen animal. Estos alimentos eran diversos y entre ellos destacan la leche y sus derivados (*caseos*), por una parte, y la carne y la grasa, por otra. Cada una de las especies animales respondía a necesidades diferentes y ofrecía recursos diversos. El cerdo se criaba sobre todo por su carne, la oveja por su lana, la cabra por su leche… Pero, entre las funciones del ganado, la de proporcionar alimentos y materias primas podía ser secundaria. Así, el ganado mayor se mantenía porque aportaba su energía para los diversos trabajos que requería la explotación. Los bueyes se empleaban para *triturare* las mieses en la era y los asnos se hacían servir para las *traginas*; las *bestias honeratas* designaban aquellas que se utilizaban para cargar con el estiércol, la paja y la leña. Como *bestias aregas* se consideraban casi siempre los bueyes: los *boves aratores* tiraban del arado y proporcionaban la fuerza para llevar adelante la *laboratio*

9 Barcelona, ACA, Notariales St Cugat del Vallès, Reg. 11, fols 104^{v}–105.
10 Barcelona, ACA, Notariales St Cugat del Vallès, Reg. 7, fol. 91^{v} (1300).

requerida por la cultura de los cereales. La cabaña de las *bestias maiores* se componía básicamente de especies que podían dedicarse a trabajos diversos y que eran resistentes, dóciles y relativamente económicas.

A cambio de ofrecer estas diversas posibilidades al titular del *mansus*, los *animalia tam grossa quam minuta* requerían para ser mantenidas un esfuerzo diferenciado en función de las diferentes especies. Este esfuerzo integraba la cría de las diversas especies animales en un sistema agrícola complejo que, a escala de cada explotación, vinculaba diferentes sectores ecológicos (monte y llano) y sus respectivos sistemas de explotación (pastoreo y agricultura). Las deficiencias de estos vínculos se han de recalcar. La cría de *porcos, oves* y *capras* se relegaba a los espacios del *incultum*, imponiéndose una trashumancia a pequeña escala como sistema generalizado: se llevaban las *bestias* a pasturar en los bosques y las garrigas de las montañas más cercanas, así como en los prados de las riberas. Sólo los bueyes y los asnos se beneficiaban sistemáticamente de la estabulación y de la producción de gramíneas forrajeras (*ordeum*). Nuestra región compartía, así, los rasgos más propios del *modo de producción mediterráneo*, esto es, la disociación más o menos marcada entre agricultura y ganadería.[11] Una consecuencia económica de este hecho fue la imposibilidad de aprovechar para las *tenedones mansi* una buena parte de los abonos de origen animal.

b) *Vascula*

Para almacenar y conservar las diversas cosechas (*expleta*) un *mansus* necesitaba una serie de recipientes que se consideraron siempre como parte básica de su equipamiento. La variedad de estos recipientes viene testimoniada por los inventarios *post mortem*. El *mansus* Otger, de Cerdanyola, disponía en 1305 de dos *botas*, dos *botas parvas*, dos *portadores* y dos *cubos parvos*.[12] Entre la variedad de recipientes, las fuentes destacan por su importancia la *vascula vinaria*, recipientes de morfología diversa y destinados, sobre todo, al almacenamiento de los *racemos* y del *vinum*. En cuanto a sus materiales se observa un predominio de la madera (*vasos ligneos*). De estos recipientes se distinguen otros, hechos de materiales diversos, que servían para almacenar el grano (trillado) y la harina. El inventario del *mansus* Otger menciona *unam gerram in qua tenetur oleum*. Pero, muy poco sabemos de las técnicas de almacenamiento de los productos de la horticultura y la arboricultura.

c) *Ferramenta*

El mencionado inventario del *mansus* Otger permite constatar que estaba equipado con dos arados (*vomeres*), dos ligones (*ligones sive exades*), una podadora (*podadoram*), un hacha (*securim*), dos azuelas (*exols*), dos barrenas

11 Toubert, 'Les féodalités méditerrannéenes', pp. 1–13.

12 Barcelona, ACA, Notariales St Cugat del Vallès, Reg. 11, fols 104v–105.

(*triba, tribanellam*) y un cincel (*escarpre ferri*).[13] Entre estos instrumentos de trabajo del *mansus* ocupaban un lugar destacado las herramientas de la labor (*vomeres et alia aratoria instrumenta*), esto es, aquellas necesarias para las *terras laborare* y *arare* y las *vineas cavare* y *fodere*. Entre las mismas se contaban el arado (con reja de hierro) y los diversos tipos de azadas y azadones. Las herramientas de la cosecha (*podadoras, falces, coltellos*) eran necesarias en los trabajos de todas las culturas. Entre las demás herramientas pueden mencionarse las palas, los rastrillos, los mayales, las hachas, las azuelas y las sierras. El conjunto de estas *ferramenta* constituía una variedad de medios de trabajo, bien adaptados a las determinantes ecológicas y las exigencias que imponían las culturas del *mansus*. Una buena parte de las herramientas estaban compuestas de partes (cortantes) hechas de hierro.

2) *Immobilia*

El *mansus*, en tanto que explotación, reunía un conjunto de diversos elementos inmuebles; de manera formularia lo ponen de manifiesto los *stabilimenta* cuando nos dicen que la *donatio* del *mansus* se realizaba *cum introitibus, exitibus, terminis et affrontacionibus suis, et cum domibus ibi constructis, et cum terris, vineis cultis et heremis, in monte et plano et per omnia loca, et cum olivariis et omnibus aliis arboribus diversorum generum que ibi sunt et erunt, et cum omnibus ad ipsum mansum pertinentibus et pertinere debentibus*. La composición precisa de esta *estructura* resulta compleja y variable en función del marco ecológico en el cual se insertaba. Entre los elementos siempre asociados al *mansus*, variaciones locales al margen, se distinguen las edificaciones y construcciones, por una parte, y las tierras cultivadas, por otra.

a) *Domos*

El centro topográfico del *mansus* estaba constituido por la parcela en la que se emplazaban las *domos* (*casas, mansiones*), un conjunto de edificaciones donde residía la familia, donde ésta almacenaba las cosechas, guardaba las herramientas y estabulaba una parte del ganado (*animalia conservare et reservare*). Sobre las características materiales de estas edificaciones no sabemos mucho y la arqueología poco ha aportado hasta el momento. Las fuentes escritas sólo permiten una descripción aproximada. Las *domos* de un *mansus* constituían un conjunto de una sola planta y articulado por *parietes* de piedra. El techo (*tegumentum*) era sostenido por vigas (*bigas, cabirons, monals, trabis*) y estaba cubierto de *cannas et tegulas*. Las *domos* (lo habitual es el uso del plural) se presentan como un agregado de edificaciones: el año 1304 la heredera del *mansus* Corts, de la parroquia de Aiguallonga, acordó reservar a su madre, entre otras, *quandam domum que est de domibus dicti mansi*, situada

13 Barcelona, ACA, Notariales St Cugat del Vallès, Reg. 11, fols 104^{v}–105. Cf. también Reg. 1, fol. 6 (1284).

junto al *cellario dicti mansi*; además le reservó *ficulneam albochor* y *unum trocium orti ... in quo possit sibi facere spinargia et erbas sibi necessarias*.[14] El conjunto de *domos* podía rodearse de un *clausum*. El interior de las *domos* se articulaba en ámbitos diferenciados. En uno de estos se cocinaba y se convivía; en el mismo se emplazaba el hogar (*focum*) y se instalaba la mesa con sus sillas y bancos (*tabulam comedendi, cadiras, banchos*). Había también uno o más espacios reservados al dormitorio: aquí se hallaban las camas (*lectos*) y las arcas (*archa, scrinia*). Debió haber, por otra parte, un ámbito donde guardar las herramientas y una parte del ganado, concretamente las *bestias minutas*. Junto a las *domos* se emplazaban patios (*curtis, curtalis*) y edificaciones anexas, cuya función era estrictamente económica: el *cellarium* y la *sala*, para almacenar las cosechas. Las fuentes también mencionan construcciones secundarias como partes del *mansus*: los silos para almacenar los granos (*cigias, foveas*); el estercolero (*femerio*) para depositar los *fimos*; el palomar (*columbarium*); el pozo (*puteum*) para la extracción de agua potable; la balsa (*bassa*) para recoger las aguas de lluvia; y la era (*area*), el recinto de suelo aplanado y endurecido artificialmente, donde se trillaban los cereales y las legumbres.

b) *Tenedones*

Las *possessiones* y *tenedones*, siempre destacadas por los *stabilimenta*, representaban específicamente la diversidad de parcelas que se vinculaban a un *mansus* y que se trabajaban con la ayuda del equipo de herramientas anteriormente descrito. En su conjunto, se trata de predios dispersos sobre un parcelario discontinuo, pero sabemos muy poco acerca del número de *tenedones* para una explotación concreta. Las fuentes casi nunca ofrecen un recuento de las mismas. Pero hay excepciones: el 1160 los monjes de Sant Cugat establecieron el *mansum qui vocatur de Sala, iuxta ecclesiam Sancti Laurencii de Fonte Calciata*. Este *mansus* se componía, en primer lugar, de una *manedia*, a la que se añadían, en el lugar de Fontcalçada, tres *pariliatas*, siete *campos*, una *insulam et isletam* y *fexes dues de terra*.[15] En total, el *mansus* disponía de trece *tenedones* más la *manedia*. Ahora bien, a la hora de calcular las dimensiones del *mansus* hay que tener en cuenta que, en función de opciones que aún conocemos mal, se le podían agregar otros predios a los que ya tenía afectados. Esta práctica de agregar predios a un *mansus* (que podían ser dominio de otro señor) se constata en el citado inventario del *mansus* Otger: entre los *immobilia* enumera, en primer lugar, el *mansus* con sus *tenedones*, a lo que se añade una serie de predios que los titulares habían ido agregando al *mansus*, todos emplazados en la misma parroquia; en total cinco *pecias terre* y dos *honores*.[16]

Las *tenedones* eran dedicadas al cultivo de una variedad de especies vegetales que, a su vez, proporcionaban una diversidad de recursos (no sólo

14 Barcelona, ACA, Notariales St Cugat del Vallès, Reg. 10, fols 52^v–53.
15 Rius Serra, *Cartulario*, doc. 1034 (1160).
16 Barcelona, ACA, Notariales St Cugat del Vallès, Reg. 11, fols 104^v–105.

alimenticios) a la familia instalada en el *mansus* y a su ganado (forrajes). La variedad de estas parcelas es notable y es diverso el vocabulario para designarlas. Se las suele distinguir de diversas maneras: por ejemplo, en cuanto a su tamaño y su morfología (las más largas que anchas, como las *fexias*, y las de forma cuadrada, como los *quadros*). En ocasiones se resalta la existencia de cercados (*clausas, macenarias*) y la particularidad de su emplazamiento (las *insulas*, junto a una corriente de agua). Las *pariliatas* eran las parcelas que se podían labrar *cum parilio bono bovis*. Las fuentes, finalmente, distinguían las *tenedones* en cuanto a las culturas a las que estaban dedicadas; en este sentido, destacan las reservadas a los cereales y la vid: las *terras* (*campos*) y las *vineas*. El equipo de herramientas del *mansus* respondía a las necesidades de estas culturas y sobre todo a las mismas se aplicaban los esfuerzos de la familia. El mayor número de *tenedones* estaban reservadas a las cosechas *fructibus panis et vini*. Eran estas culturas, y sobre todo las reservadas a los cereales (de primavera), las que exigían una adaptación a la fragilidad del ecosistema y, con ello, una inversión de energías y recursos para mantener e incrementar la productividad, aplicando prácticas como la irrigación, el aterrazamiento y la regeneración (fertilización) de los predios.[17] A estas culturas principales hay que añadir otras que también tenían su lugar en la economía del *mansus*. Los *pratos* eran las *tenedones* que proporcionaban la *herba*; los mismos dependían de un suministro constante de agua, al igual que los *linares* y los *cannemares*, que se cultivaban por las materias primas que proporcionaban (*linum, canabum*). Los *ortos*, por su parte, eran las *tenedones* en las que se cultivaban verduras y leguminosas (*porris, caulibus et leguminibus*).[18] La horticultura acostumbraba a asociarse con otras (*orto cum vitis*). Una policultura como ésta proporcionaba una variedad de alimentos a lo largo del año y permitía disponer de unos productos fáciles de conservar. Los rendimientos de estos *ortos* dependían pero de ciertos requisitos: los suelos debían ser de buena calidad; había que procurar una buena insolación y evitar que estuviesen expuestos a los vientos fuertes, secos y fríos; requerían frecuentes trabajos de limpieza; había que reservarles buena parte de los fertilizantes y mantenerlos bien irrigados. Las frecuentes labores y la dependencia de los adobes llevó a emplazar los *ortos* lo más cerca posible de las *domos mansi*.

Las culturas de *terras, vineas* y *ortos* se combinaban a menudo con la arboricultura. Los *stabilimenta* nos describen las *tenedones* como plantadas *cum olivariis et omnibus aliis arboribus diversorum generum*. A los olivos, que las formulas destacan, se añadían siempre otras especies, también mencionadas en otro tipo de *instrumenta*. Así, una *contentio* del 1300 nos informa que el monasterio reclamaba al titular del *mansus* Mora, de Sant Medir, la *tascha* y el *decimum de arboribus et de glandibus, ficubus, cereris, pertegis, malepunicis,*

17 La relevancia otorgada a la práctica de la fertilización se constata a partir de los contratos *ad laborandum*; cf. Barcelona, ACA, Notariales St Cugat del Vallès, Reg. 10, fols 46v–47 (1304).

18 Barcelona, ACA, Notariales St Cugat del Vallès, Reg. 12, fol. 42 (1306).

avellanis et de omnibus aliis fructibus arborum que sunt et erunt in honoribus et possessionibus mansi.[19] La asociación de la arboricultura con otras culturas definía las *trileas*, parcelas cercadas, en ocasiones irrigadas, en las que se cultivaban *vineas* (*maliolos*) sostenidas mediante *arbores trilietani* (*trilea cum vitis et arbores*); en ocasiones parecen confundirse con los *ortos* (*ortum vel trilea*).[20] Los *viridiarios* y *verdegarios* eran parcelas irrigadas (*verdegarios reganeis*), situadas a menudo junto a *aquas* y *casas*. Las mismas se asimilaban a los *ortos* y aparecen plantadas *cum vitis* y *cum arboribus pomiferis et aliis arboribus*. La asociación de los *arbores* a las otras culturas ofrecía una serie de ventajas: fijaba los suelos y evitaba la erosión; también permitía explotar diversos niveles vegetales sobre una misma parcela y obtener al menos dos cosechas anuales de cultivos diferentes.

La importancia otorgada en la economía del *mansus* a la horticultura y la arboricultura la define como un policultivo que siempre se desequilibraba a favor de la cerealicultura y la viticultura, sin embargo bien adaptado a la fragilidad propia de un ecosistema mediterráneo. En éste, la agricultura se practicaba sobre suelos muchas veces mediocres y se enfrentaba a notables retos climáticos, la aridez estival sobre todo. Por esta razón se acompañaba el cultivo del cereal con el cultivo de las *vineas, ortos* y *arbores omnium fructuum*, seleccionando siempre especies vegetales resistentes y evitando la dependencia de especies demasiado susceptibles a los accidentes climáticos. Se lograba así diversificar las cosechas y distribuirlas sobre momentos diferentes del ciclo agrícola anual. Sin embargo, tanto la particularidad del parcelario como la fragilidad del ecosistema y la opción por el policultivo implicaron un sobreconsumo de energías. Las culturas intensivas requerían notables inversiones en trabajo manual (azada). Pero también las otras culturas exigían una adaptación a la fragilidad del ecosistema y, con ello, una inversión de energías y recursos para asegurar la productividad aplicando prácticas como la irrigación. El parcelario fragmentado y discontinuo obligaba a los *cultores agri* a trabajar parcela por parcela; la dispersión de los predios implicaba gastar mucho tiempo en los desplazamientos de hombres y bestias.

3) *Iura*

A la diversidad de elementos materiales presentados se añaden los elementos no materiales del *mansus*, un conjunto de derechos siempre presentes en las clausulas de la *donatio in emphiteosim*. Se incluían entre estos *iura* los que garantizaban la circulación por los caminos y el acceso a las *casas* y a las *tenedones* de hombres y ganado (*viam eundi et redeundi cum bobus areguis et cum aliis bestiis, ad portandum fimos et ad extrahendum inde bladum et omnes alios fructus*).[21] Además del *viam sive transitum* se incluían los derechos de

19 Barcelona, ACA, Notariales St Cugat del Vallès, Reg. 7, fol. 100.
20 Barcelona, ACA, Notariales St Cugat del Vallès, Reg. 8, fols 79–79v (1302).
21 Barcelona, ACA, Notarials, St Cugat, Reg. 1, fol. 63 (1285).

explotar las *aquas* para la irrigación de las *tenedones mansi*.[22] Estos derechos particulares se asimilaban al derecho general de *adimperamentum* (*ademprivium*), un derecho que definía los *spacia heremarum terrarum* como bienes públicos, otorgando a cualquiera su libre explotación. Un derecho que el 1025 el conde Berenguer Ramon I había confirmado a los habitantes del condado de Barcelona como parte de sus *franchitates*.[23] El *adimperamentum* otorgaba a los *laboratores* la facultad de acceder al *incultum* y explotar sus recursos. De hecho, los *stabilimenta* y otros *instrumenta* nos presentan el *mansus* como dotado *cum ademprivis, in prono sive in plano*, enumerando, junto a las *terras cultas et incultas*, los elementos del *incultum* al cual tenía acceso.[24] Estos elementos ofrecían múltiples recursos importantes para la economía del *mansus*. La variedad y el volumen de éstos dependía del marco ecológico concreto en el que la explotación se insertaba. Las *aquas* alimentaban los *regos* y se explotaban para la pesca. Los pedregales proporcionaban *petras* y *lapides* para construir diques y canales, entre otras. Las riberas eran aprovechadas para *mittere animalia ad pascendum*. Los bosques, las garrigas, los pastizales y los prados naturales eran los sectores más valiosos del *incultum* en términos económicos. De éstos se extraían vegetales que, mezclados con abonos, ayudaban a fertilizar los campos; las hojas y las hierbas podían servir como litera. La *silva*, la *garrica* y el *pascuum* proporcionaban una serie de materias primas vegetales (esparto, grana, roldón…) y ofrecían asimismo lugares para la *paschura animalium*, especialmente de los ovinos, caprinos y porcinos (*collectione glandium*). En los mismos se recogían miel, setas y frutos silvestres para el consumo humano. En las *nemora* se explotaban, según sistemas diversos, árboles de especies, tamaños y edades diferentes; las leñas y maderas diversas servían para la industria, los hornos y la construcción de diques, molinos y casas (*ligna ad domos construendas*); para la fabricación de artefactos domésticos, herramientas y recipientes (*scindendo arbores glandiferos quando volebant et faciendo inde tines et vexella*); y para la calefacción (*ligna ad comburendum*) y la elaboración de combustibles (carbón vegetal). Las cortezas de los árboles servían para la construcción de panales y la resina de las coníferas proporcionaba la pez y la brea. La caza, por último, acostumbraba a ser un derecho reservado al *dominus* y sólo muy raramente se otorgaba al titular de un *mansus*.

4) *Servicia*

El *mansus* que hemos descrito hasta aquí requería para su funcionamiento de la aportación de la fuerza de trabajo que proporcionaba año tras año la familia instalada en la explotación (el matrimonio más *omnes progenies atque posteritas*). A la difusión del *mansus* correspondió una consolidación de la

22 Barcelona, ACA, Notarials, St Cugat, Reg. 6, fols 118–118^{v} (1300); Reg. 9, fol. 89 (1304).
23 Font Rius, *Cartas*, doc. 15. Para lo que sigue cf. Farías Zurita, 'El medio natural', pp. 277–99.
24 Barcelona, ACA, Perg. St Cugat del Vallès, 335 (1077); Perg. St Cugat del Vallès, 1042 (1239).

familia nuclear en tanto que unidad doméstica.[25] El cabeza de familia y titular del *mansus* respondía de la calidad del trabajo (*security melioratio*) y lo recibía de su señor *ad bonam agriculturam ducendum*.[26] El trabajo aportado por parte de la familia no era, evidentemente, el mismo para cada uno de sus miembros, sino que variaba siguiendo una división del trabajo en función del sexo y la edad. La presencia de una mano de obra que no fueran los padres y los hijos del matrimonio es algo que sólo muy raramente se puede constatar a partir de las fuentes. Las evidencias se limitan a la ocasional contratación de mano de obra (*nuncios*), incluso esclava, por parte del titular de un *mansus* concreto.[27]

A la hora de estimar el volumen de esfuerzos que la familia invertía en la explotación de cada *mansus* hay que advertir que una parte de los trabajos necesarios para asegurar la viabilidad de la explotación quedaron *externalizados*, esto es, fueron garantizados como *servicia*. Entre estos *servicia* hay que destacar la molinería y la herrería, los que más testimonios han dejado en las fuentes.[28] Tanto una como otra eran instituciones que permitían descargar la familia de ciertos trabajos necesarios pero pesados y complejos: reparar (*locedare, calceare, perbocare*) las herramientas y moler el grano destinado a la panificación. Ambas instituciones compartían dos rasgos que las definían: en primer lugar, su promoción por parte del señor. El esfuerzo de Sant Cugat por equipar sus dominios con molinos, por ejemplo, se constata desde el siglo X; este esfuerzo fue sistemático y no cesaría: aún a finales del XIII los monjes otorgaban *licenciam construendi molendinum novum*.[29] Esto quiere decir que el señorío fue también una red cada vez más densa de instalaciones con funciones de centralidad a nivel local. En segundo lugar, el mantenimiento de estas instalaciones fue encargado siempre a un especialista. Los servicios requerían un personal con ciertas habilidades y dedicado a realizar con pericia sus trabajos: un herrero (*ferrarius*), en el caso de la herrería, un molinero (*molnerius*), en el caso de la molinería. Este personal, frecuentemente titular de un *mansus*,[30] era responsable de mantener la buena marcha de las instalaciones y realizar de manera adecuada su trabajo. El herrero trabajaba en unas *domos fabrice*, dotadas de las herramientas necesarias.[31] La herrería y la molinería requerían del *dominus* unas importantes inversiones para ponerlas y mantenerlas en marcha. La institución de dicho personal y dichas inversiones corrían a cargo del señor. El esfuerzo de éste por hacer del *servicium fabrice* un servicio accesible a las poblaciones locales, y con ello reducir los tiempos de desplazamiento de éstas, explica la multiplicación de las *fabricas* a lo largo

25 To Figueras, *Família i hereu*, pp. 279–347.
26 Barcelona, ACA, Órdenes religiosas, Perg. St Cugat del Vallès, 1192 (1250); Perg. St Cugat del Vallès, 679 ([1195]).
27 Barcelona, ACA, Notariales, St Cugat del Valles, Reg. 7, fol. 12^{v} (1295).
28 Farías Zurita, *El mas i la vila*, pp. 35–62, y 'Les ferreries'.
29 Barcelona, ACA, Notariales, St Cugat del Valles, Reg. 5, fol. 38. Bonnassie, *Catalogne*, pp. 459–64.
30 Barcelona, ACA, Notariales, St Cugat del Valles, Reg. 5, fol. 38 (1295).
31 Barcelona, ACA, Notariales, St Cugat del Valles, Reg. 12, fols 27–27^{v} (1306).

de las comarcas de la Cataluña Vieja y a partir del XII. El *locidum* y la *multura* eran las tasas con los que los *habitatores mansi* remuneraban los servicios que recibían de la herrería y la molinería, respectivamente. Una y otra se hacían efectivas en especie o moneda. Las tasas podían venir fijadas en el propio *stabilimentum*.[32] En el caso del *locidum*, éstas acabaron siendo fijas y anuales. Los servicios, por otra parte, se asociaban (casi) siempre al *districtum*, al poder de mando del *dominus*. En virtud de éste, el señor obligaba a todos los habitantes de un lugar a acudir a sus instalaciones, además de exigir ciertas *missiones* (*iornales*) a la hora de mantener sus infraestructuras, sobre todo en el caso de los molinos (*regos mundare et escurare*).[33] Este *districtum* aseguraba una contrapartida a las inversiones del señor; éste obligaba a acudir a su herrería, pero también garantizaba la disponibilidad de su herrero a la hora de reparar las *ferramenta quae ad usum laboracionis et agriculture pertinent*.

La herrería y la molinería ofrecían unos servicios que eran esenciales para una economía del *mansus* basada en una particular combinación de culturas que, a su vez, requerían la aplicación de una tecnología específica. El *mansus* estaba equipado con un notable y diversificado *stock* de herramientas cuyas partes metálicas se desgastaban con su uso, lo que requería varias reparaciones al año. Las tareas de *calcare* debían realizarse lo más rápidamente posible en momentos críticos como, por ejemplo, cuando había que *expleta segare et triturare*; debía evitarse que alguna incidencia climática pudiera malograr los *expleta*. Esto era algo urgente sobre todo para las culturas del cereal, por la vulnerabilidad propia de las gramíneas y por el lugar destacado que éstas ocupaban en el conjunto de las culturas del *mansus*. La disponibilidad de un especialista que reparase con rapidez las partes cortantes de las herramientas desgastadas por un uso intensivo evitaba perder el tiempo calzando las rejas del arado y las hojas de las hoces. El margen de tiempo del que disponía el titular del *mansus* se veía reducido además por los *iornales, batudas, iovas, podadas* y *traginas* que estaba obligado a prestar para su señor justo en los momentos (*tempore arandi, seminandi, segandi*) en que las *tenedones* requerían el máximo de sus esfuerzos.[34]

Selección, combinación y promoción

La explotación que hemos presentado en tanto que *estructura* suponía una *selección* de elementos productivos: un conjunto de elementos tanto muebles como inmuebles que ofrecían unos recursos y que se complementaba siempre con el acceso garantizado a los recursos del *incultum*. Así mismo, una serie de servicios permitían descargar el *mansus* de ciertos trabajos que quedaban a cargo de especialistas. Esta *selección* era también una *combinación*, en el

---

32 Barcelona, ACA, Notariales, St Cugat del Valles, Reg. 12, fols 88ᵛ–89; Reg. 9, fol. 89.

33 Barcelona, ACA, Notariales, St Cugat del Valles, Reg. 10, fols 71ᵛ–72 (1304); Reg. 11, fol. 69ᵛ (1305).

34 Barcelona, ACA, Notariales, St Cugat del Valles, Reg. 6, fols 156–156ᵛ.

sentido que hubo siempre un *desequilibrio* en cuanto a las culturas propias de la economía del *mansus*. La misma siempre optó de manera deliberada por favorecer los *expleta panis et vini*. A partir de esta particular selección y combinación de sus elementos productivos, quedó definido el *mansus* individual como una explotación notablemente estable. El *stabilimentum* fijaba esta estabilidad y el señor (mediante su oficial local) la garantizaba, al tiempo que vigilaba la integridad y viabilidad de la explotación. La cláusula de la *melioratio* aseguraba, por su parte, el trabajo óptimo de las *tenedones*. De un *mansus* a otro la unidad se presenta como estandarizadada en cuanto a sus elementos: los *mansi* se constituyeron como *estructuras* equiparables en un mismo señorío y de un señorío a otro. Como regla, el régimen de apropiación fue relativamente uniforme, al menos en el marco de un mismo dominio; lo demuestran los *caput brevia* a partir del XIII.[35] Así, podemos deducir que el volumen de trabajo invertido por los *cultores* no debió variar decisivamente de un año a otro, ni de una unidad a otra. Lo mismo puede afirmarse para las cosechas que se esperaban de las *tenedones*. El hecho que fuera la familia nuclear la que proporcionara lo esencial de la fuerza de trabajo puso límites a un incremento de la capacidad productiva del *mansus*, mediante la agregación de predios, por ejemplo. Lo dicho quiere decir también que las posibilidades de una estratificación fueron limitadas. Las diferencias de tamaño de un *mansus* a otro se podían dar, entre otras, porque el propio contrato enfitéutico otorgaba un margen a la gestión especulativa de las *tenedones* por parte de su titular; y también porque no había un impedimento legal para la agregación de parcelas a una explotación ya constituida. Pero dicho esto, cabe resaltar que hacia 1300 no hay evidencias que nos permitan afirmar contrastes relevantes en términos de recursos económicos para nuestra población de *rustici qui teneant mansum et laborent cum pare bovum*.[36]

La constitución del *mansus*, la selección y combinación de los elementos productivos que hemos presentado, no fueron procesos espontáneos: el resultado presenta demasiadas regularidades de un caso a otro y la uniformidad resulta demasiado evidente de un señorío a otro. Esto no niega unas posibles particularidades. Estas se explican, no obstante, por una adaptación a la diversidad de condiciones ecológicas locales y a su aprovechamiento con fines especulativos. Por otra parte, entre las *tenedones* del *mansus* había una parcela que las fuentes destacan y que sirve para ilustrar hasta qué punto la constitución de nuestra *estructura* fue el resultado de un cálculo y de aplicar unos criterios bien definidos a la hora de constituirla. Dicha parcela recibe nombres diversos: *manedia*, pero también *barchera*, *casalaticum* y *quintana*. Además se la denomina genéricamente con el plural *ferragenales*, lo cual indica que era una parcela reservada a la cultura de las *ferragine*, los forrajes (*ordeum*) destinados de manera específica a las *bestias grossas*, los bueyes necesarios para

35 Benito, 'Hoc est breve', pp. 3–27.

36 Bastardas, *Usatges*, pp. 49–50.

la tracción del arado; un arado que, a su vez, era indispensable para la cultura de los cereales, una de las culturas dominantes en la economía del *mansus*.[37] Su función, en este sentido, explica que la *manedia* se considerara un elemento indispensable de las *tenedones mansi*; los *stabilimenta* la individualizan entre las *possessiones* y la graban con un censo particular y modesto.[38] La *manedia* estaba bien delimitada (*signata et fexuriata*) y podía estar plantada con *arbores*;[39] y la hallamos emplazada *ante ianuam sive introitum* de las *domos mansi*.[40]

La constitución del *mansus*, la selección y combinación de elementos de la que hemos tratado, se realizó siguiendo unos criterios que dirigieron las decisiones de los señores; estas decisiones implicaban, de entrada, una *opción*. El momento decisivo se produjo cuando en el curso de aquel proceso de reorganización de los señoríos que hemos descrito se adoptó un modelo de explotación ya establecido, el *mansus*, la *terra unius familie*, componente del *sistema curtense* (la *Villikationsordnung* de los historiadores alemanes), tal como éste se había impuesto sobre todo en las regiones centrales del imperio carolingio en los siglos VIII y IX.[41] Este *sistema curtense* nunca se implantó en las regiones periféricas del imperio. Para la Cataluña carolingia, en los siglos IX y X, el término *masus* (menos frecuente *mansus*) puede documentarse de una manera puntual sobre todo en los condados más septentrionales y frecuentemente asociado a los fiscos condales. Pero en ningún caso podemos afirmar la existencia de un *sistema curtense* que como escribe Toubert se constituyó a partir de *la simbiosis que, en el curso del siglo VIII, se estableció en el seno de la curtis entre el sector de explotación señorial directa y una fuerza de trabajo que, en beneficio de la reserva, entregaba un campesinado que, por otra parte, disponía, con el manso, de una pequeña explotación destinada a la subsistencia familiar y susceptible de dejar un modesta excedente campesino para el intercambio*.[42] El *masus* de las fuentes catalanas lo describe Pierre Bonnassie como una explotación trabajada por una familia y una unidad de apropiación cuya integridad el señor procura mantener.[43] Por lo demás el término *masus* apenas puede documentarse antes del siglo XI en un condado como el de Barcelona; las pocas ocasiones que aparece en las fuentes no es sino como sinónimo de los términos *casas*, *domos* o *mansiones*.[44]

---

37 Montserrat, AMM, Perg. St Cugat del Vallès, 164 (1158); Barcelona, ACA, Notariales, St Cugat del Valles, Reg. 12, fols 55ᵛ–56 (1306).

38 Barcelona, ACA, Notariales, St Cugat del Valles, Reg. 3, fols 96–96ᵛ (1293).

39 Montserrat, AMM, Perg. St Cugat del Vallès, 72 (1171).

40 Barcelona, ACA, Notariales, St Cugat del Valles, Reg. 12, 45ᵛ–46 (1306).

41 Toubert, *Castillos*, pp. 17–149. Para el *masus* en los condados catalanes cf. Bonnassie, *La Catalogne*, pp. 242–47. Para el *mansus* carolingio cf. Verhulst, 'La diversité du regime domanial', pp. 133–48; Schlesinger, 'Die Hufe im Frankenreich', pp. 41–70.

42 Toubert, *Castillos*, p. 39.

43 Bonnassie, *La Catalogne*, 246.

44 Barcelona, Archivo Capitular de Barcelona, Diversorum 1.4, 151 (1047).

En nuestra región, por lo tanto, se constata una general reorganización de los señoríos que se data hacia mediados del siglo XII, una reorganización que se presenta sobre todo como la creación calculada por parte de los señores de unidades de explotación estables a partir de la diversidad de elementos que componían los dominios. Es a partir de entonces que se multiplican las referencias a *mansi* y se multiplican sobre todo los *instrumenta* por las cuales un señor *establecía* un *mansus* a un futuro titular. El primero de estos *instrumenta* otorgados por nuestro monasterio data de 1045.[45] Retengamos, pues, que en una región periférica como la Cataluña carolingia lo que se constata es una difusión tardía del *mansus* a gran escala como resultado de la adopción de un modelo de explotación que llevó, a su vez, a la instalación de una *Mansusordnung*. Para explicar la instalación de este orden a nivel regional hemos propuesto trabajar con dos conceptos.[46] Uno de éstos, el de *feudalización*, se refiere a unos procesos que Bonnassie estudia para el caso de los condados catalanes y que, entre otras, le llevan a postular la existencia de una *revolución feudal*.[47] Dicha *feudalización* llevó a lo que Perry Anderson llama una *parcelación de la soberanía*, un proceso de usurpación a gran escala de las parcelas de soberanía y de los recursos a ellas asociadas por parte de un número creciente de titulares que no eran la *potestas publica*.[48] A mediados del XI una nueva clase de señores, más numerosa y más poderosa, impuso lo que Bonnassie califica como *piratería señorial* y permitió la instalación de un *señorío explotativo*, un señorío que se pretendía ejercer sin límites externos y de manera arbitraria. Ello permitió apropiarse una parte notable de los recursos que producía una población de agricultores más numerosa y con mayores capacidades económicas. La generalización de una *lógica de la rapiña*, que las *querimonie* evidencian con detalle,[49] instaló una competencia permanente que, a menudo, se sostuvo de manera violenta, aunque conviene distinguir los diversos tipos de señoríos en función de sus respectivos titulares.[50]

La *feudalización* creó las condiciones para lo que Chris Wickham ha descrito como *estructuras políticas a pequeña escala* y para aquel proceso que llamaremos *señorialización*: el segundo de nuestros conceptos. El mismo se refiere a la *construcción* de un nuevo tipo de señorío y responde a la constatación empírica de *fases* bien diferenciadas en la historia del señorío.[51] El examen de las fuentes de los siglos XII y XIII, tanto de aquellas que presentan un inventario

45 Barcelona, ACA, Perg. St Cugat del Vallès, 177 A.2 (d) (1045) (Rius Serra, *Cartulario*, doc. 579).

46 Farías Zurita, 'El mas y la vila', pp. 119–52.

47 Bonnassie, *La Catalogne*, pp. 539–680. Para una discusión del concepto cf. Bisson, 'The "Feudal Revolution"', pp. 6–42; Bisson, 'Medieval Lordship', pp. 743–59. Para importantes consideraciones y matizaciones cf. Kuchenbuch, '*Potestas* und *Utilitas*', pp. 141–46.

48 Anderson, *Passages*, pp. 147–53.

49 Bisson, *Tormented Voices*; Farías Zurita, 'Una querimonia', pp. 99–104; Salrach, 'Multa placita et contenciones', pp. 197–228.

50 Kuchenbuch, 'Die Klostergrundherrschaft', pp. 297–343.

51 Wickham, *Medieval Europe*, pp. 104–10; Kuchenbuch, '*Potestas* und *Utilitas*', pp. 117–46.

de las prácticas explotativas como de aquellas (cada vez más numerosas) que nos ayudan a reconstruir la rutina administrativa en el marco de los diversos dominios, obligan a constatar una transformación de dicho *señorío explotativo* y su sustitución por un *señorío constructivo*, en el sentido que evidencia por parte de sus promotores la asimilación de ciertos hábitos y habilidades (contabilizar, inventariar, planificar, negociar…), más allá del ejercicio de la *piratería* como medio para multiplicar y acumular *iura* y maximizar *redditus*. La *señorialización* suponía una racionalización en la medida que requería un cálculo cuyo objetivo, entre otros, era crear una *estructura* que sostuviera la apropiación, garantizara la continuidad de la misma y asegurara a los *cultores et laboratores* su subsistencia. Esta racionalización se define en términos de *agencia* en el sentido que estamos ante una *acción* que pretendió tanto una renovación de las estrategias señoriales como una movilización de los recursos diversos a disposición de los señores. La *promoción* de un *señorío transformado*, asumida por éstos, nos permite entender el proceso de reorganización que hemos constatado para unos dominios monásticos concretos. Los diversos aspectos de este proceso se prueban de manera empírica: la constitución del *mansus*, de una unidad estable de explotación, apropiación y residencia, que, como tal, desarrolló una *estructura* modelo que ya en sus orígenes carolingios había funcionado como una unidad de cálculo; la instalación de estructuras administrativas (*baiulia*) a cargo de oficiales responsables de gestionar la buena marcha de los dominios; finalmente, la creación de *servicios auxiliares* y de *instituciones centrales* que permitieron garantizar la buena marcha del *mansus*, entre otras. Este proceso de reorganización respondió a criterios que orientaron las estrategias generales y las decisiones respecto a la gestión rutinaria de los señoríos. La *promoción* de la que hemos hablado, la renovación de las estrategias señoriales y la movilización de los diversos recursos a disposición del señor, son un testimonio de la transformación que definió el nuevo señorío como un señorío también *creativo*.

ABSTRACT Based on extensive and detailed research in Catalan monastic archives, this article examines the process of reorganization of lordship in the Catalan region between the middle of the eleventh and the middle of the twelfth centuries, a process we define as seigneurialization. As a result of that process, the *mansus* became the basic component of what has to be considered a genuine medieval lordship. As a structure, defined by its remarkable stability, the *mansus* had to ensure subsistence of the peasant family, on the one hand, and seigneurial appropriation on the other. This article describes the material and other elements of the *mansus* and stresses seigneurial agency and creativity in that process of reorganizing their domains.

Works Cited

Manuscripts and Archival Sources

Barcelona, Archivo de la Corona de Aragón [ACA], Notariales, Sant Cugat del Vallès

——, Órdenes religiosas, Pergaminos, Sant Cugat del Vallès

——, Órdenes religiosas, Pergaminos sin catalogar

Barcelona, Archivo Capitular de Barcelona, Diversorum

Montserrat, Archivo del Monasterio de Montserrat [AMM], Pergaminos Sant Cugat del Vallès

Primary Sources

Bastardas, Joan, Teresa Gràcia Sahuquillo Gràcia, Lluïsa de Nadal, and Pere Puig i Ustrell, *Usatges de Barcelona. El codi a mitjan segle XII. Establiment del text llatí i edició de la versió catalana del manuscrit del segle XIII de l'Arxiu de la Corona de Aragó de Barcelona* (Barcelona: Fundació Noguera, 1984)

Font Rius, Josep Maria, *Cartas de población y franquicia de Cataluña*, I (Madrid: Consejo Superior de Investigaciones Científicas. Instituto Jerónimo Zurita. Escuela de Estudios Medievales, 1969)

Rius Serra, José, *Cartulario de 'Sant Cugat del Vallés'*, I (Barcelona: Consejo Superior de Investigaciones Científicas. Escuela de Estudios Medievales, 1946–47, Madrid 1981)

Secondary Works

Anderson, Perry, *Passages from Antiquity to Feudalism* (London: NLB, 1975)

Benito Monclús, Pere, 'Hoc est breve… L'emergència del costum i els orígens de la pràctica de capbrevació, segles XI-XIII', in *Estudios sobre rentas, fiscalidad y finanzas en la Cataluña bajomedieval*, ed. by Manuel Sánchez Martínez (Barcelona: Consejo Superior de Investigaciones Científicas. Institución Milà i Fontanals, 1993), pp. 3–27

Bisson, Thomas N., 'The "Feudal Revolution"', *Past & Present*, 142 (1994), 6–42

——, 'Medieval Lordship', *Speculum*, 70.4 (1995), 743–59

——, *Tormented Voices: Power, Crisis, and Humanity in Rural Catalonia. 1140–1200* (Cambridge, MA: Harvard University Press, 1998)

Bonnassie, Pierre, *La Catalogne du milieu du Xe a la fin du XIe siècle. Croissance et mutations d'une société*, 1 (Toulouse: Association des Publications de l'Université de Toulouse-Le Mirail, 1975)

Farías Zurita, Víctor, 'Les ferreries al nordest de la Catalunya Vella (segles XI–XIV). Una contribució a l'estudi d'una institució senyorial', in *L'obtenció del ferro pel procediment directe entre els segles IV i XIX. Actes del 6è curs d'Arqueologia d'Andorra* (Andorra: Govern d'Andorra. Ministeri de Cultura, 2002), pp. 35–62

——, *El mas i la vila a la Catalunya medieval. Els fonaments d'una societat senyorialitzada (segles XI–XIV)* (Valencia: Universitat de València, 2011)

——, 'El mas y la vila. Reflexiones acerca de la señorialización y la urbanización a pequeña escala en la Cataluña Vieja, siglos XII–XIV', *La ciudad de los campesinos. Villas nuevas, pequeñas villas, villas mercado. XLVI Semana Internacional de Estudios Medievales, Estella* (Pamplona: Gobierno de Navarra, Departamento de Cultura y Deporte, 2020), pp. 119–52

——, 'El medio natural en una sociedad señorializada. Composición, explotación y apropiación del incultum en la Catalunya del noreste (siglos X–XIII)', in *El medio natural en la España medieval. Actas del I Congreso sobre ecohistoria e historia medieval*, ed. by Julián Clemente Ramos (Cáceres: Universidad de Extremadura, 2001), pp. 277–99

——, 'Una *querimonia* desconeguda procedente de la antic arxiu de Sant Cugat del Valles (ca. 1160–1162)', *Gausac*, 5 (1994), 99–104

——, 'Sobre la reorganización del señorío rural y la figura del *baiulus* en la Catalunya del noreste de los siglos XII y XIII', *Anuario de Estudios Medievales*, 30.2 (2000), 887–916

Kuchenbuch, Ludolf, 'Die Klostergrundherrschaft im Frühmittelalter. Eine Zwischenbilanz', in *Herrschaft und Kirche. Beiträge zur Entstehung und Wirkungsweise episkopaler und monastischer Organisationsformen*, ed. by Friedrich Prinz (Stuttgart: Hiersemann, 1988), pp. 297–343

——, '*Potestas* und *Utilitas*. Ein Versuch über Stand und Perspektiven der Forschung zur Grundherrschaft im 9.-13. Jahrhundert', *Historische Zeitschrift*, 265 (1997), 117–46

Salrach, Josep Maria, 'Multa placita et contenciones. Conflictos de los siglos XI–XII en el Cartulario de Sant Cugat del Valles', in *Les origines de la féodalité. Hommage á Claudio Sánchez Albornoz*, ed. by Joseph Pérez and Santiago Aguadé Nieto (Madrid: Casa Velázquez y Universidad de Alcalá, 2000), pp. 197–228

Schlesinger, Walter, 'Die Hufe im Frankenreich', in *Untersuchungen zur eisenzeitlichen und frühmittelalterlichen Flur in Mitteleuropa und ihre Nutzung*, 1, ed. by Heinrich Beck (Göttingen: Akademie der Wissenschaften zu Göttingen, Kommission für die Altertumskunde Mittel- und Nordeuropas, 1979), pp. 41–70

To Figueras, Lluís, *Família i hereu a la Catalunya nord-oriental (segles X–XII)* (Barcelona: Publicacions de l'Abadia de Montserrat, 1997)

Toubert, Pierre, *Castillos, señores y campesinos en la Italia medieval* (Barcelona: Crítica, 1990)

——, 'Les féodalités méditerrannéenes: un probleme d'histoire comparée', *Structures féodales et féodalisme dans l'Occident méditerranéen (Xe-XIIIe siècle). Bilan et perspectives de recherches* (Paris: Éditions du Centre National de la Recherche Scientifique, 1980), pp. 1–13

Verhulst, Adriaan, 'La diversité du regime domanial entre Loire et Rhin a l'époque carolingienne. Bilan de quinze années de recherches', in *Villa — curtis — grangia. Landwirtschaft zwischen Loire und Rhein von der Römerzeit zum Hochmittelalter*, ed. by Walter Janssen and Dietrich Lohrmann (Munich: Artemis, 1983), pp. 133–48

Wickham, Chris, *Medieval Europe* (New Haven: Yale University Press, 2016)

GIOVANNA BIANCHI

Reflections on the Archaeology of Cereal Storage in Medieval Italy

Granaries and Silos

The analysis of cereal storage systems, based primarily on material evidence, is a topic that until recently has attracted relatively little attention from archaeologists. This trend has changed over the last decade, and there is now also increasing interest in the subject from scholars of written sources. Significant contributions were gathered both during a conference organized in Vitoria, Spain, in 2011, and in 2018 during the XL Journées internationales d'histoire de Flaran held at the abbey of Arthous.[1]

As regards Italy, the geographical area which I will focus on in this study (fig. 4.1), an article has recently been published that provides an overview of the subject and further enriches the data presented during the Spanish conference of 2011, thanks to an updated survey of the storage systems documented throughout the Italian peninsula, accompanied by a first typological subdivision.[2] The details provided on specific southern contexts, such as the case of north-western Sicily or Ordona, that implement the existing in-depth studies in the area of Apulia known as Capitanata, are also significant.[3] The recent conference at Flaran, which provided a more up-to-date European overview than the earlier one in Spain, gives us a clearer and more multi-layered perspective (starting from the geographical one) of the possible differences and analogies between Italy and the rest of Europe. In the following pages I shall attempt to compare the different settings, with the aim of focusing attention not so much on specific case studies as on the systems of clientelism and on the importance of storage in the wider political-economic context.

1 Vigil-Escalera and others, eds, *Horrea, Barns and Silos*; Lauwers and Schneider, eds, *Mises en réserve*.
2 Ebanista, 'La conservazione del grano'.
3 Alfano and D'Amico, 'La conservazione dei cereali'; Favia, *Ordona XII*.

Giovanna Bianchi (giovanna.bianchi@unisi.it) is currently Professor of Christian and Medieval Archaeology at the University of Siena. She was co-beneficiary of the ERC Advanced Grant *nEU-Med-Origins of a New Economic Union (seventh–twelfth centuries)*.

Building and Economic Growth in Southern Europe (1050–1300), ed. by Sandro Carocci and Alessio Fiore, (Turnhout: Brepols, 2024), pp. 57–78 BREPOLS PUBLISHERS 10.1484/M.TMC-EB.5.137974

Figure 4.1. Location of sites mentioned in this chapter.

The starting point of my line of thought derives from what a review of the published material indicates were the main systems of storing cereals for Italy between the early and late Middle Ages, namely silos and granaries. As Ebanista has shown, within these two broad categories some differences can be observed: silos are classified according to whether they were fully or partially buried, and whether or not they had an internal lining. Likewise, granaries can be grouped into two macro-categories, depending on the different building materials used (perishable and non-perishable).

In Italy, a series of problems still remain for archaeologists who set out to study this kind of evidence: sketchy descriptions; vague assessments of the state of conservation (which, for example, in the case of silos, makes it impossible to verify whether they were found completely preserved);

a frequent absence of observations on the link between storage evidence and the coeval stratigraphic context (with the risk of missing the association with elements such as kilns for preliminary drying of cereals); a chronology often set in too broad timespans; scarce archaeobotanical analyses; and very weak connections between storage systems and possible patrons commissioning such work. This explains the difficulty in defining more detailed typologies as well as the presence in the list of 154 sites surveyed by Ebanista of as many as fifty storage elements in which the evidence does not correspond to the typologies identified by the author.[4]

Beginning with this list and counting the material remains surveyed, out of 104 traces of storage systems, only twelve belong to granaries while ninety-three can be traced back to silos, either individual or often in more or less numerous groups. This is part of a general trend that is typical of the entire Mediterranean area and beyond, as silos are frequently documented in both northern Spain and France. It is likely that this type of storage system would once also have been dominant in a place like the British Isles; however for reasons probably related to technical knowledge or local customs, after the Iron Age the conservation of foodstuffs in granaries was favoured over below-ground storage systems.[5]

Regardless of these numbers, early medieval Italian granaries have always attracted a certain amount of interest in archaeological literature, especially in Tuscany, as they helped highlight the narrative of the well-known model elaborated by Riccardo Francovich.[6] At Montarrenti, the site where Francovich conducted much of his research, the wooden granary found in the topmost area of the site is possible material evidence that the site was a *caput curtis*, reflecting a new policy of the control of agricultural resources by landowners that emerged at the height of the Carolingian period. Later, the discovery of other granaries, again constructed with perishable materials, confirmed Francovich's hypothesis, which was later taken up and expanded upon by Marco Valenti.[7] These granaries were located inside the early medieval Tuscan settlements of Miranduolo and Rocca degli Alberti which, like Montarrenti, dated from the ninth century or the early decades of the following century. The granary, more suitable than the silos for short- to medium-term storage, would have been the best means of collecting and distributing the surplus produce which had increased significantly since the first centuries of the early Middle Ages, the result of an agrarian policy that sought to exploit cereal resources more fully. More recently, Simone Collavini has tackled the subject of granaries in documentary sources, with a focus on Tuscany. The data thus acquired, relating to granaries attested between the ninth and tenth

4 Ebanista, 'La conservazione del grano', p. 477.

5 Ebanista, 'La conservazione del grano', p. 476.

6 Francovich, 'The Beginning of Hilltop Villages'.

7 Valenti, *L'insediamento altomedievale*.

Figure 4.2. Rocca degli Alberti (Monterotondo M.mo, GR). In the centre of the photo are the remains of the silos. Photo courtesy of Paolo Nannini, SABAP-SI.

centuries, allowed him to draw some significant conclusions: this kind of storage system, which was increasingly present in the countryside and outside urban contexts, would initially have belonged to important members of the lay and ecclesiastical aristocracy (for example counts and bishops), and later appeared on the estates of less politically significant landowners; the granary, part of the manorial management system of rural properties, would have been a relevant symbol of the landed seigneuries' more pervasive ability to control cereal output.[8]

Many of the granaries for which material evidence exists are located in the uppermost areas of the settlements in question, within the *dominicum* space of the *curtes*: in Tuscany this is true of Montarrenti, Miranduolo and Rocca degli Alberti at Monterotondo Marittimo (fig. 4.2). This evidence disappeared when areas of high ground at all three locations were redeveloped during the twelfth century, with the construction not only of new wall circuits, but also and more importantly of seigneurial residences featuring stone towers or keeps.[9]

It seems therefore that, in the twelfth century, Tuscan granaries lost their significance as a symbol of power for the ruling classes or at least, as

8 Collavini, 'Luoghi e contenitori di stoccaggio'.

9 Bianchi and Grassi, 'Sistemi di stoccaggio'.

demonstrated by the archaeology, it was no longer necessary for them to be located in the upper part of a settlement. This is borne out by the fact that, apart from the aforementioned examples, no storage place of this kind was detected at the majority of the twelfth-century castles investigated by archaeologists, either in Tuscany or in the rest of the north central part of the peninsula.

As far as silos are concerned, evidence of these can be found in all parts of the country, with a greater concentration in the southern central part; as previous studies have suggested, this is possibly due to climatic issues and the nature of the soil.[10] According to the literature on the subject, the silo is the storage system most closely associated with local and community knowledge, and its presence, often in the form of single features inside domestic environments, is widespread proof of this. As shown by experimental archaeology and also by contemporary evidence in North Africa,[11] if hermetically sealed, silos allow grain to be stored for many years, therefore providing a valuable reserve at times of famine.[12] When considering medieval silos and their material characteristics it is possible to observe, on the one hand, the widespread presence of types designed for medium- and large-scale storage (with relatively distinct forms), and on the other, a common variable linked to the chronologies of the activities taking place on the site. In the case of France and Spain, for example, the tenth century clearly marks the beginning of an increase, at times truly exponential, in the number of silos; a similar, albeit less marked, trend can also be observed in Italy. The other feature shared by silos in all three countries is their absence from the written sources, a fact already noted in the past by various authors, and this also emerges quite clearly in Nicola Perreaux's recent article based on a systematic investigation of the sources referring to medieval storage in the documentary corpus of the *Cartae Europae Medii Aevi* (CEMA) which holds a collection of digitalized editions of more than 225,000 documents.[13] This data has led Perreaux to speculate that perhaps the sources only mention above-ground storage sites, and that in all likelihood the landowners were not particularly interested in monitoring these resources, at least until the beginning of the twelfth century when granaries are mentioned with considerably more frequency.

This observation is complementary to to the excavation results from a wide range of territorial contexts, such as the Spanish Basque Country, and Roussillon and Languedoc in southern France.[14] In both cases, the creation

10 Gelichi, 'Conclusioni'.

11 Peña-Chocarro and others, 'Técnicas de almacenamiento'.

12 Alongside the actual silos, in domestic households, small grain pits are often found, connected to a much more restricted consumption over time; these were dug in holes not much larger and deeper than those used as postholes, or in cavities within the rock, as were discovered, for example, in the excavation of the mining castle of Cugnano. For more details, see Bianchi and Grassi, 'Sistemi di stoccaggio'.

13 Perreaux, 'Prélèvements, organization spatio-temporelle'

14 Quirós Castillo, 'Silos y sistemas de almacenaje'; Maufras and Puig, 'L'apport de l'archéologie'.

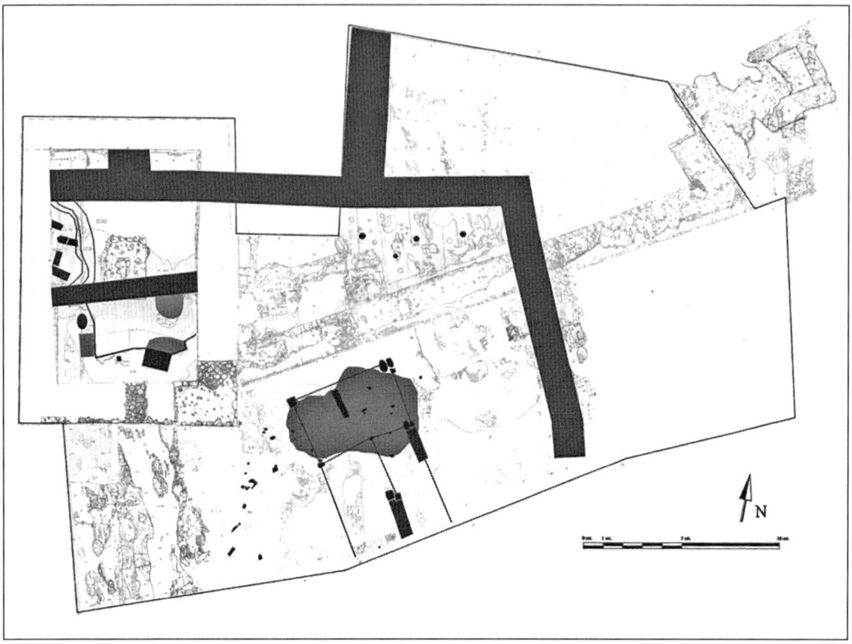

Figure 4.3. Rocca degli Alberti (Monterotondo M.mo, GR). The excavation area with the tenth-century walls and the remains of the granary marked with dark shading.

of a strikingly large number of silos in the early medieval period has been attributed, more decisively in the Spanish case and less so in France, to strategies associated with rural communities. A similar interpretative trajectory was followed in the case of Rocca degli Alberti at Monterotondo Marittimo in Tuscany.[15] Here, the building of a granary on the site where a group of eight silos had previously stood was read as proof of a renewed interest in these structures on the part of landowners: the new building was superimposed, both physically and figuratively, on the existing storage strategies of the community living there (figs 4.2–4.3).

This interpretation might lead us to believe that the transition from community administration to an increasingly pervasive seigneurial management between the tenth and twelfth centuries was straightforward and direct. However, certain anomalies must be taken into account: silos, at least in Italy, are also found in distinctly seigneurial locations, such as the castle site of Brina[16] in Liguria, or Tusculum, in the hills near Rome, with connections to the counts of the same name and where, from the end of the tenth century, a

15 Bianchi and Grassi, 'Sistemi di stoccaggio'.

16 The silos were found inside the upper area corresponding to the seigneurial area of ownership, also marked by the presence of a tower; see Baldassari and others, 'Indagini archeologiche'.

large number of silo groups were established in a specially designated location.[17] In the case of the silos in central and southern France, archaeologists who have studied their settings have repeatedly questioned whether the presence of these features in large numbers can be entirely attributed to community strategies, given the discovery of artefacts that indicate that these sites were at the centre of extra-regional trade in a territory that, from the tenth century onwards, was controlled by the powerful counts of Toulouse.[18] In southern Italy, as we shall see, the presence of silos went hand in hand with the rule of the Normans and subsequent overlords, perpetuating the powerful ruler/silo combination for much of the late Middle Ages.

These observations raise fresh questions: can we speak of a distinction at the level of patronage between silos and granaries? Are there significant chronological and geographical variations that discriminate between the two types of storage? What are the most marked peculiarities for the Italian peninsula?

Between Signs of Change and Silent Witnesses

Using the data currently available to compare Italy with other western European settings, we can observe how the Italian peninsula, unlike for example France or Spain, is clearly divided into two parts in terms of storage types.

The area of the northern centre, which broadly coincided with the Kingdom of Italy until halfway through the Middle Ages, has yielded a smaller amount of material evidence than the southern centre. Silos outnumber granaries, although they are always present in numbers that almost never exceed ten units, if we exclude the smaller family silos, which were connected to individual dwellings and usually consisting of cavities that are neither particularly deep or wide (on average between 0.60 and 1.20 metres in diameter and 0.60 and 2 metres deep), and were quite different in size from those in the Norman south (diameters between 2 and 6 metres with a depth sometimes over 8 metres). Even the granaries do not appear to be especially large. An idea of the scale is provided by those in Tuscany which measure 5 by 4–6 metres, with the exception of the granary at Montarrenti, whose dimensions are 13 metres long and 4 metres wide.[19] With regard to the chronology of the granaries, in the course of the European project nEU-Med,[20] on the basis of historical research topics included in the project, the need arose to verify certain chronologies, in

17 Beolchini and Delogu, 'La nobiltà romana'.

18 Maufras and Puig, 'L'apport de l'archéologie', pp. 65–66.

19 Cantini, *Il castello*, p. 31.

20 This is an ERC Advanced Grant 2014 project entitled *Origins of a new economic union (7th-twelfth centuries): resources, landscapes and political strategies in a Mediterranean region (nEU-Med)*, which was a collaboration between the Principal Investigator Richard Hodges, and myself. The host institution was the University of Siena, www.neu-med.unisi.it.

particular for the case studies of Rocca Alberti and Montarrenti. The structure on this last site was dated to the ninth century according to elements that could be inferred from the relative chronology. In the absence of indicators capable of precisely defining the time of its construction, the granary had previously been included in the earlier sequences, and was dated between the second half of the eighth and the ninth century, and was thought to have been abandoned following a great fire traced to the end of the ninth century. Grain would therefore have been stored and dried in the kiln located near the granary at the height of the Carolingian period, and its sequences would later have been sealed by the fire and reconstruction activities that took place in the summit area between the tenth and eleventh centuries.[21]

However, new radiocarbon analysis of the burnt seeds recovered both inside the granary, in the layers that relate to the fire and the subsequent abandonment of the structure, as well as inside the kiln, lead to fresh conclusions. A more in-depth discussion of this site must be left to future publications specifically devoted to the case. We can however state that the dating of the seeds from inside the kiln (thus contextual to its use) to a period between 952–1024 (cal. AD, sigma1) and that of the seeds charred as a result of the burning of the granary to the years between 969–1040 (cal. AD, sigma1) has led to a cautious hypothesis, if not a different chronology, that there was a more prolonged use of the granary itself and the related structures until the end of the tenth century.[22] Similar assertions can be made for the granary found at Rocca degli Alberti, Monterotondo Marittimo, previously dated to between the ninth and tenth century and now placed in a chronological timespan stretching from 983 to 1051 (cal. AD, sigma1).

It had also been assumed that the granaries hypothesized at Miranduolo had been in prolonged use up until this period.[23] Moving the use of the Tuscan granaries forward to the tenth century is more consistent with the chronologies of other storage sites in northern Italy, such as those at Montecastellaro di Groppallo in Emilia Romagna or Broili in Illegio, in Friuli.[24] In the last two instances, moreover, the granaries were located inside the ground floors of walled structures, interpretable as a tower in the case of Broili and of more uncertain use at Montecastellaro. The increase in the number of granaries in the course of the tenth century is consistent with the more frequent mentions of these structures in documentary sources, coinciding, in the Tuscan case,

21 Cantini, *Il castello*, pp. 30–34.

22 Radiocarbon dating of the samples from Montarrenti and Rocca degli Alberti was carried out at the Università della Campania Luigi Vanvitelli, Dipartimento di Scienze e Tecnologie ambientali, biologiche e farmaceutiche with the collaboration of the Istituto Nazionale di Fisica Nucleare of Florence, Laboratorio di Tecniche Nucleari applicate ai Beni Culturali.

23 Ebanista, 'La conservazione del grano', pp. 510–11.

24 In the case of the site at Brina these were silos; see Baldassari and others, 'Indagini archeologiche'; for Groppallo, see Bazzini and others, 'Un'officina per la lavorazione'; for Broili, see Cagnana and others, 'Accumulare e difendere'.

with the widespread transformation of the landscape: these changes affected large swathes of territory in the southern centre of the region and were characterized by greater deforestation and controlled burning to clear of areas destined for agricultural use or grazing.[25]

In a recent publication, I hypothesized that the phase of transformation that characterized the countryside of central-northern Italy between the second half of the tenth century and the first decades of the following century was closely connected to a broad political and economic strategy pursued by the Ottonian dynasty.[26] The establishment of the first fortified centres, already referred to in many sources as castles, along with the transformation of the natural landscape, went hand in hand with significant investments in the various royal courts of the Italic Kingdom, linked to the exploitation of specific resources (such as iron and salt). This royal programme, implemented with the consent of the leading aristocratic families, but also with the agreement of the rural communities themselves, was one of the first steps towards the great economic development that characterized Tuscany and the northern centre of the peninsula from the twelfth century onwards.

The increase in the number of granaries (with the new chronologies of use for Montarrenti and Rocca Alberti) would therefore be set in this context. During the phase in which the foundations were being laid for a more structured formation of territorial nobility, thanks also to the donations of public land, the granary was undoubtedly an important symbol for these growing powers, emphasizing not only their own social prestige, as Collavini suggests, but probably also their adherence to the royal project. This point is particularly interesting when we look at the history of built structures more generally, given the parallels that this volume seeks to identify. In both Tuscany and elsewhere (similar observations also apply for vast portions of the Po Valley), it was precisely during this phase, coinciding with Ottonian domination, that important transformations were recorded at many sites belonging to those aristocratic families closely connected to royal strategies: the construction of new stone enclosures; the planning of settlement areas; and the building of the first stone towers.[27] It is precisely at this stage that stone begins to be used more widely as a building material in secular architecture, coinciding with the first episodes of *incastellamento*.

Stone however was not yet in general use. In Tuscany, for example, we find it only at sites linked to the exploitation of specific resources or belonging to important lineages; in the Po Valley, wood continued to be used, although construction techniques were being adopted that reflected the presence of specialized craftsmen.[28] In any case, in Tuscany at least, the stone tower seems

25 Buonincontri and others, 'Shaping Mediterranean Landscapes'.
26 Bianchi, *Archeologia dei beni pubblici*.
27 Bianchi, *Archeologia dei beni pubblici*, pp. 233–42.
28 Bianchi, 'Dalla pietrificazione dei poteri'.

to have become one of the most characteristic symbols of participation in the royal political programme. In this regard, I have written that the tower represented a sort of symbol of the *qualità pubblica* (i.e. public quality) of the settlement, its patronage, and its political orientation. This was a symbol that, indisputably in the case of Broili di Illegio and perhaps also in that of Montecastellaro di Groppallo, performed a dual function, with a grain store located on the ground floor.

It is therefore possible that granaries and towers constituted two key elements in the seigneurial (and/or royal?) architecture of the time, even though archaeological records shows that this was not an univocal unambiguous situation condition. In addition to the aforementioned cases of the castles at Brina and Tusculum, a number of silos were excavated, for instance, at the prominent bishop's court at Chieri and at sites of certain strategic importance during the Ottonian phase such as Bovolone, Piadena, and Nogara, although these were limited to a rather small number of units.[29]

To return to the initial reflections of this section, although we are aware of a symbolic valorization of granaries and of their relative increase in number in literary and material sources during the tenth century, they do not appear to have increased in number throughout the northern centre, on a par with the silos themselves. This is certainly not due to a lack of archaeological investigations; while only a limited number of these have been carried out in the region, they have certainly been more numerous than those conducted in southern Italy, where the remains of storage structures are more abundant. In Tuscany, extensive excavation activities at the centre of the royal court of Valli,[30] as well as at the marquis's court of San Genesio,[31] have not unearthed any particular or extensive storage structures. It is of course possible that these field excavations did not examine the areas where such storage facilities were located; however, taking this evidence into account, we are faced with a 'significant absence' as far as public goods of considerable importance are concerned. Is it therefore possible that many sites in the centre-north used different storage methods than silos or granaries? To try to find an answer to this challenging question, or at least put forward some hypotheses on the subject, we must return to Tuscany, where the greater number of excavations may provide us with data upon which to formulate some theories.

Collavini has repeatedly drawn attention to the fact that, in documents from the central centuries of the Middle Ages, we find references to arks: these were portable containers where grain surpluses were stored, and which were placed inside churches, cloisters, or in the homes of secular owners.[32] Is it conceivable, therefore, that at the same time as the existence of silos and

29 Ebanista, 'La conservazione del grano'.

30 Bianchi and Hodges, *The nEU-Med Project*.

31 Cantini, 'Per un'archeologia dei *vici*'.

32 Bianchi and Collavini, 'Lieux de stockage'.

granaries, the landowning nobility were also in possession of these storage features which, being portable, have left no archaeological trace? As far as Tuscany is concerned, we could also consider this supposition to be valid if we took into consideration the data after the end of the tenth–first half of the eleventh century, when the general political-economic situation underwent a decisive change.

I have stated in previous articles, as well as in the present one, that the material remains of both silos and granaries disappear in the twelfth century. Of the two distinguishing symbols of the early fortified centres in the Ottonian period, it is the tower that seems to survive the test of time while the granary does not. The reason behind this was the change in the political-economic situation alluded to above. The public programme of redefining the man-made and natural landscape, along with the more intensive exploitation of specific resources, came to an end with this new, more violent phase.[33] It was during this period that, in Tuscany at least, the high-ranking protagonists — the marquises and the kings — who had once been responsible for maintaining the political balance, acting on behalf of not only the various aristocratic groups but also the local communities, found themselves deprived of this fundamental role.[34] During the second half of the eleventh century, the political fragmentation of the rural territories, triggered by the more incisive emergence of the territorial lordships exercising rights that had previously pertained to the public sphere, took place within a new context that bore little resemblance to what had gone before: this had been a 'traditional' world represented by the rural royal courts, and by settlements that had acted as intersections in this public network. These, in most cases, found themselves materially obliterated either through abandonment or destruction. These include the court at Valli and the granaries at Montarrenti and Rocca degli Alberti, as well as other important sites in Tuscany and beyond.[35]

Past studies, and especially the more recent ones, offer descriptions of this new world characterized by fierce rivalries that also included frequent episodes of conflict and violence, with a systematic use of military force.[36] Against this backdrop, the castle with its fortifications became the clearest material manifestation of the new local powers; the tower, once a public symbol, now became the castle's principal emblem, reinforced by its role during the Ottonian period when it became associated with the wielding of power. These fierce conflicts and ongoing hostilities were undoubtedly a major obstacle to the process of economic growth initiated by the Ottonians, but the basic conditions for this kind of growth that had been established under their rule meant that the economies were able to recover, albeit slowly, once

33 Fiore, *The Seigneurial Transformation.*

34 Cortese, *L'aristocrazia toscana.*

35 Bianchi, *Archeologia dei beni pubblici*, pp. 189–98.

36 Fiore, 'I rituali delle violenza'.

the local seigneurial powers were in place. This coincided with a new period of castle building between the eleventh and twelfth centuries, in which stone featured prominently: the visible surfaces of castle walls were almost always constructed with well-crafted stone.[37] In both Tuscany and the northern centre of the peninsula, granaries and groups of silos were located in the central areas of agricultural estates, making them part of a specific setting inextricably linked to the manorial system. Until the end of the eleventh century, it was common for landlords to be absent from their rural estates, preferring instead to reside in large towns and cities in order to maintain a close proximity with the dominant political scene.[38]

When this system broke down, large numbers of nobles relocated to the countryside, and as a result suitable space had to be found for their new stone-built seigneurial residences: as a result material evidence of granaries and silos became more scarce. Since written sources still attest to the existence of granaries, in line with the increase in cereal production, it is possible that these structures, having lost their symbolic value, were located in parts of the settlement that have not as yet been investigated by archaeologists.

Where Tuscany is concerned, given the exponential increase in references to arks, it is possible to hypothesize that, as a continuation of the more sporadic early medieval tradition, during the twelfth century the use of portable containers became the most widespread and appropriate solution to a series of new conditions: the need to quickly dispose of more abundant cereal resources as a result of their increasing commercialization; the fact that ever more fragmented and therefore smaller individual landed estates, ruled by a larger number of nobles (with the corresponding reduction in the amount of harvested crops and their storage) meant that fixed, and above all, larger storage places were no longer necessary; the progressive reduction in the size of manors and a certain lack of interest on the part of landowners in accumulating these resources on the manorial farmstead; and the increased prevalence of indirect tenure, as can be inferred from the conditions appearing in agrarian contracts, especially from the mid-twelfth century.[39]

This did not affect the pervasiveness of the rural overlords, who were still capable of drawing surplus with collection strategies that gave rise to a different organization of labour and crop distribution. Of the various storage methods in use in the early Middle Ages, arks or portable containers in general were best suited to the needs of landowners in the contemporary political-economic context. Within these new production systems, communal areas may have existed for the threshing and possibly drying of grains close to the fields, where they were then directly stored in portable containers (arks or other storage systems such as receptacles made of pottery or other materials). It is

---

37 Bianchi, 'Dalla pietrificazione dei poteri'.

38 For Tuscany see Cortese, *L'aristocrazia toscana*; and Tomei, *Milites elegantes*.

39 Bianchi and Collavini, 'Lieux de stockage', pp. 140–42.

virtually impossible to identify material traces of these methods of production as they were most likely to have been located at some distance from the principal site, and would be difficult to recognize even using archaeological diagnostics. The discovery of an interpretable context of this kind in the very last habitation layers of the power centre (or *dominicum*) of the royal court of Valli was therefore a real stroke of luck (fig. 4.4).

In a series of close sequences dated to between the twelfth and early thirteenth century, by which time all the functions that had characterized the royal court during the Carolingian and especially Ottonian periods had been abandoned, extensive scatterings of burnt seeds (mainly barley, wheat and legumes) were recorded in some parts of the site not associated with storage features.[40] The presence of small kilns suggests that, after harvesting, the seeds would be dried before being transferred into portable containers. By that date the entire area, once the property of the royal court, had been divided up and appropriated by a number of castles in the surrounding territory, including the one at Valle, which had taken its name from the court. It is therefore possible that cereal products from the domain of one or more castles were collected in this lowland area, which had good connections to land and sea routes (given its proximity to a port that was operational at the time). The lack of similar material evidence at other sites leaves us wondering whether this was common practice at the time or whether it represented an exception.

As for other parts of the northern centre of the Italian peninsula, a lack of specific studies of these areas makes it difficult to speculate. What has been written so far may however encourage a more thorough investigation of a wide geographical area where, as far as the twelfth and thirteenth centuries are concerned, no obvious traces of granaries and silos remain, with the exception of possible storage sites of an uncertain date at a number of castles in the Euganean Hills, and references to 'storage' castles found in documentary sources but as yet not investigated by archaeologists.[41]

One thing is certain: at the same time as evidence of storage sites was gradually disappearing in this part of the peninsula, in the south of Italy, from the eleventh century onwards and under Norman domination, these sites began to proliferate. This is clearly visible in Apulia where, thanks to the work of Pasquale Favia, a greater amount of detailed research on storage areas is available than for other regions.[42] Although the most recent research records increasing structured traces of storage sites as early as the period of Byzantine rule, it was with the arrival of the Normans that large silos begin to appear (in the case of Fiorentino or Ordona between 260 and 270 kilos of produce could be stored). The pits were constructed with a certain degree of skill, and

40 Marasco and Briano, 'The Stratigraphic Sequence'.

41 For the castles in the Euganean Hills, see Calaon, 'I castelli dei Colli Euganei'; for a discussion on the so-called castle deposits, see Settia, *Castelli medievali*, pp. 115–26.

42 Favia, 'Fovea pro frumento mittere'; Favia, *Ordona XII*.

Figure 4.4. Vetricella. Aerial view (drone) of the excavation of the centre of the court of Valli. Circles indicate places where the remains of seeds (carporests) accumulate. Photo by nEU-Med project.

it is possible that specialized personnel were assigned to this task. Alongside the silos we also find, albeit in smaller numbers, granaries built of masonry: the one at Castelpagano consists of small rooms with a height of around 3 metres. Silos at a number of sites, especially in central-southern Apulia, were located in specific open spaces. This was the case at Ordona, between the mid-eleventh and twelfth centuries, or at San Lorenzo in Carminiano, where a certain degree of planning of the areas destined to house these features is evident, often in the vicinity of new settlements; hence the hypothesis that the presence of these large storage areas was aligned with or promoted new forms of aggregation characterized by centralized settlement solutions. These complex storage systems were set up in both inland and coastal areas, the latter in anticipation of their contents being exported to market by sea. Excavations have also revealed twelfth- and thirteenth-century grain pits inside dwellings that appear to be contemporary with those in open areas (Ordona, Fiorentino). The size of these pits (in the case of Ordona they are even larger than those outside) suggests a possible commercialization of cereals or the need to prepare for tax levies.[43] Generally speaking, these large storage sites were abandoned at some point during the fourteenth century.

Pasquale Favia links the presence of silos to the strategies of central powers connected with both the monarchy and the nobility's need for large storage facilities: this was driven by their policy of profit and intensive territorial exploitation, and was buttressed by solid policies supporting a well-conceived operational chain of storage, transport, and trade. A similar interpretation has also been proposed for the areas of Jato and Belice in Sicily, where recent research has highlighted the presence of twenty-four silos connected to Norman agricultural policies in territories with a strong Islamic presence. The pits, like those in Apulia, were of considerable size, measuring on average between 4 and 8 metres in diameter, with a depth between 3 and 8 metres. Unlike those in Apulia, however, these silos were located at some distance from the settlements, always along the main roadways, and it is assumed that ad hoc craftsmen were employed in their construction.[44]

The juxtaposition between royal power and local nobility, within a shared strategy of agricultural exploitation, was also the interpretation of the situation in the Norman south, as developed in the article I published jointly with Francesca Grassi in 2013, where this policy was contrasted with the fragmentation of the seigneurial domains in the northern centre of the peninsula and the distinct systems of storage chosen as a consequence. This was followed by the publication of Sandro Carocci's important book which studied the nobility of the so-called Mezzogiorno (i.e. southern Italy).[45]

43 Favia, 'Fovea pro frumento mittere', p. 270.

44 Alfano and D'Amico, 'La conservazione dei cereali', p. 74.

45 Carocci, *Signorie di Mezzogiorno*.

Inspired by the fresh insight provided by this work, it is perhaps now possible to move a little further in the search for a correlation between the picture outlined by the written sources and that provided by the material ones. Carocci focuses in particular on two historical peculiarities of Apulia, a region rich in archaeological data: the nobility, whose offices were assigned by those who reigned and who did not have much control over their possessions, levvied taxes that were lower than those imposed by the lords in the northern centre of the peninsula; and village communities, which played a more active role, were characterized by the presence of representatives who the crown usually protected by granting them, with the partial exception of Sicily, room for political action.[46]

These hypotheses might lead to a reassessment of the role of village communities in a joint strategy of cereal exploitation with the monarchy and the nobility, connected to the local leading figures and carried out with a certain degree of autonomy. The large family silos inside dwellings, present above all in the Capitanata, might be material proof of less oppressive seigneurial levies, and the capacity of members of local communities to accumulate grain with a view to potential commercialization. This provides a marked contrast with the condition and organization of the small family silos in the northern centre, which existed against a backdrop of much greater seigneurial control. The abandonment of the Apulian silos and their entire management system in the fourteenth century would appear to be a continuation of the changes, which, as Carocci's book explains, were already occurring at the end of the thirteenth century during the reign of Frederick II. These resulted in the establishment of what the author defines as 'normal' aristocratic rule, that is, with characteristics that were much more in line with that of the northern centre of the peninsula.

In Conclusion

The editors of this volume requested that the contributing authors focus on functional buildings or structures connected to specific production or exchange processes, in order to be able to suggest a narrative connected to economic expansion prior to the thirteenth century. The aim was to relate this type of data to the great building boom which was largely characterized by the use of durable materials (stone and brick) that marked the period between the mid-eleventh and early thirteenth century. As I have sought to demonstrate in this study, tackling these issues from the point of view of storage structures is not particularly straightforward, since their history is marked, in alternating phases, by their presence and absence, with a strong

46 Carocci, *Signorie di Mezzogiorno*, pp. 519–21.

imbalance — more marked than in other European countries — between the north and south of the peninsula.

In the northern centre the relatively scarce material evidence for silos and granaries (accompanied by a small number of references in documentary sources) is the dominant feature for much of the early Middle Ages. This leads us to hypothesize other possible means of storage, potentially portable containers made of pottery or perishable materials; or possibly arks, perhaps made of wood or stone, which are invisible archaeologically but have nevertheless been present in Tuscan written sources since the ninth century. Although not existing in large numbers, it is nevertheless evident that, until the late eleventh century, the granary was an important symbol of prestige for its owners, who generally belonged to the middle and upper aristocracy. There was an apparent increase in the number of storage structures during the second half of the tenth century when, thanks to a series of important investments by the Ottonian dynasty, at least in Tuscany, the stage was set for greater economic growth. The nobility, especially those of higher political rank, actively participated in this scheme, and gained significant benefits in terms of the expansion of their landed estates. Over this period, which lasted at least until the mid-eleventh century, the granary continued to have a strong symbolic value, and it also became a symbol of participation in a political-economic programme that in many areas saw the conquest of new areas destined for cultivation with the clearance of woodland and controlled fires

With the gradual, but inexorable, disengagement of the central power and the strengthening of the territorial aristocracy, within the framework of the struggle for investiture, political fragmentation also gave rise to new strategies for cereal exploitation and storage. The granary lost its symbolic value and its dominant position in the manorial farmsteads, with seigneurial residences and particularly towers and keeps becoming the necessary symbols representing the military powers in a climate of fierce competition that involved all levels of aristocracy. For the many reasons outlined in the previous paragraph — at least in the case of Tuscany which has been the object of more numerous studies — portable containers seem perhaps to have been the solution that best suited the policies of the new seigneurial powers. The stark absence of material evidence, although partly compensated by more abundant documentary sources, is in any case proof of a new world order that, after a slowing down of the initial boom that began in the Ottonian Age, was revived with the arrival of the territorial nobility, moving towards increasing growth as testified by the substantial investments in new castles, now built entirely of stone. The mounds of cereal in the now-abandoned manorial centre of the royal court of Valli in southern Tuscany are, in my opinion, the most striking material evidence of this change, seen from the perspective of cereal exploitation systems.

In contrast, in the south, where the government of the Normans was particularly efficient and closely linked to the local aristocracies, the large number of silos is palpable proof of economic growth, which similarly began at the end of the eleventh century. This lead to the formation of new settlement nuclei, and also resulted in the active involvement of the local leading figures and the communities themselves, to a much greater extent than in the north. This pattern endured for many years until the 'genetic' profile of the southern lordships came to resemble those of North; it is no accident that this shift coincided, at least in Apulia, with the disappearance of the system of large silos.

Works Cited

Secondary Works

Alfano, Antonio, and Gabriele D'Amico, 'La conservazione dei cereali a lungo termine nella Sicilia medievale. L'importanza del dato archeologico per una nuova prospettiva di ricerca', *Archeologia Medievale*, 44 (2017), 73–94

Baldassarri, Monica, Alessandra Frondoni, and Marco Milanese, 'Indagini archeologiche al castello della Brina (SP): i risultati delle campagne 2005–2007', *Archeologia Medievale*, 35 (2008), 101–20

Bazzini, Marco, Gian Piero Devoti, Angelo Ghiretti, Enrico Giannichedda, Renata Perego, and Stefano Provini, 'Un'officina per la lavorazione della steatite (X–XII secolo) ed un granaio carbonizzato (inizi XI) al Monte Castellano di Groppallo (comune di Farini, media valle del Nure, Piacenza). Prima campagna di scavo 2006–2007', *Archeologia Medievale*, 35 (2008), 453–89

Beolchini, Valeria, and Paolo Delogu, 'La nobiltà romana altomedievale in città e fuori. Il caso di Tusculum', in *La nobiltà romana nel Medioevo*, ed. by Sandro Carocci (Rome: École Française de Rome, 2006), pp. 137–69

Bianchi, Giovanna, *Archeologia dei beni pubblici. Alle origini della crescita economica in una regione mediterranea (secc. IX–XI)* (Florence: All'Insegna del Giglio, 2022)

——, 'Dalla pietrificazione dei poteri alla pietrificazione della ricchezza. Uso funzionale e simbolico della pietra tra Toscana e Centro-Nord della penisola (X–XII secolo)', in *Il paesaggio pietrificato. La storia sociale dell'Europa tra X e XII secolo attraverso l'archeologia del costruito*, ed. by Fabio Giovannini and Alessandra Molinari, *Archeologia dell'Architettura*, Special Issue, 26 (2021), 97–118

Bianchi, Giovanna, and Francesca Grassi, 'Sistemi di stoccaggio nelle campagne italiane (secc. VII–XIII): l'evidenza archeologica dal caso di Rocca degli Alberti in Toscana', in *Horrea, Barns and Silos: Storage and Incomes in Early Medieval Europe*, ed. by Alfonso Vigil-Escalera, Giovanna Bianchi, and Juan Antonio Quirós Castillo (Bilbao: Servicio editorial Universidad del Pais Vasco, Documentos de Arqueologia Medieval, 2013), pp. 77–102

Bianchi, Giovanna, and Richard Hodges, eds, *The nEU-Med Project: Vetricella, An Early Medieval Royal Property on Tuscany's Mediterranean* (Florence: All'Insegna del Giglio, 2020)

Bianchi, Giovanna, and Simone M. Collavini, 'Lieux de stockage des céréales et formes d'extraction du surplus paysan, entre sources matérielles et sources écrites (Italie du Centre et Septentrionale, IXe-XIIe siècle)', in *Mises en réserve: production, accumulation et redistribution des céréales dans L'Occident médiévale et moderne*, ed. by Michel Lauwers and Laurent Schneider (Toulouse: Presses Universitaries du Midi, 2022), pp. 129–42

Buonincontri, Mauro Paolo, Pierluigi Pieruccini, Davide Susini, Carmine Lubritto, Paola Ricci, Fabian Rey, Willi Tinner, Daniele Colombaroli, Ruth

Drescher-Schneider, Luisa Dallai, Lorenzo Marasco, Giulio Poggi, Giovanna Bianchi, Richard Hodges, and Gaetano Di Pasquale, 'Shaping Mediterranean Landscapes: The Cultural Impact of Anthropogenic Fires in Tyrrhenian Southern Tuscany during the Iron and Middle Ages (800–450 BC/ AD 650–1300)', *The Holocene*, 30.10 (2020), 1420–37

Cagnana, Aurora, Eliana Bertamoni, Elisabetta Castiglioni, Roberto Degano, Piermassimo Ghidotti, Paola Greppi, Enrico Roncallo, Filippo Rosset, Mauro Rottoli, and Marco Vignola, 'Accumulare e difendere nelle Alpi carniche dell'XI secolo: gli scavi nel sito fortificato di Broili di Illegio', *Archeologia Medievale*, 46 (2019), 97–120

Calaon, Diego, 'I castelli dei Colli Euganei tra fonti scritte e archeologia', in *Castelli del Veneto tra archeologia e fonti scritte*, ed. by Gian Pietro Brogiolo and Elisa Possenti (Mantova: SAP, 2005), pp. 93–116

Cantini, Federico, *Il castello di Montarrenti. Lo scavo archeologico (1982–1987) per la storia della formazione del villaggio medievale in Toscana (secc. VII–XV)* (Florence: All'Insegna del Giglio, 2003)

——, 'Per un'archeologia dei *vici* tra tarda antichità e medioevo. Il caso di vicus Wallari-Burgus Sancti Genesi', in *Paesaggi, comunità, villaggi medievali*, ed. by Paola Galetti (Spoleto: Fondazione Centro Italiano di Studi sull'alto medioevo), pp. 511–24

Carocci, Sandro, *Signoria di Mezzogiorno. Società rurali, poteri aristocratici e monarchia (XII–XIII secolo)* (Rome: Viella, 2014)

Collavini, Simone M., 'Luoghi e contenitori di stoccaggio dei cereali in Toscana (VIII–XII s.): le evidenze delle fonti scritte', in *Horrea, Barns and Silos: Storage and Incomes in Early Medieval Europe*, ed. by Alfonso Vigil-Escalera, Giovanna Bianchi, and Juan Antonio Quirós Castillo (Bilbao: Servicio editorial Universidad del Pais Vasco, Documentos de Arqueologia Medieval, 2013), pp. 57–76

Cortese, Maria E., *L'aristocrazia toscana. Sette secoli (VI–XII)* (Spoleto: Fondazione Centro Italiano di Studi sull'alto medioevo, 2017)

Ebanista, Carlo, 'La conservazione del grano nel medioevo: testimonianze archeologiche', in *La civiltà del pane. Storia, tecniche e simboli dal Mediterraneo all'Atlantico*, ed. by Gabriele Archetti (Spoleto: Fondazione Centro Italiano di Studi sull'alto medioevo, 2015), pp. 469–521

Favia, Pasquale, 'Fovea pro frumento mittere. Archeologia della conservazione dei cereali nella Capitanata medievale', in *Puer Apuliae. Mélanges offerts à Jean-Marie Martin*, ed. by Errico Cuozzo, Vincent Déroche, Annik Peters-Custot, and Vivient Prigent (Paris: Collège de France-CNRS Centre de recherche d'Histoire et civilisation de Byzance, Monographies 30, 2008), pp. 239–75

——, *Ordona XII. Un casale nel Tavoliere medievale* (Bari: Edipuglia, 2018)

Fiore, Alessio, 'I rituali della violenza. Forza e prevaricazione nell'esperienza del potere signorile nelle campagne (Italia centro-settentrionale, secoli XI–XII)', *Società e Storia*, 149 (2015), 435–67

——, *The Seigneurial Transformation: Power Structures and Political Communication in the Countryside of Central and Northern Italy* (Oxford: Oxford University Press, 2020)

Francovich, Riccardo, 'The Beginning of Hilltop Villages in Early Medieval Tuscany', in *The Long Morning of Medieval Europe*, ed. by Jennifer R. Davis and Michael McCormick (Aldershot: Routledge, 2008), pp. 55–82

Gelichi, Sauro, 'Conclusioni', in *Horrea, Barns and Silos: Storage and Incomes in Early Medieval Europe*, ed. by Alfonso Vigil-Escalera, Giovanna Bianchi, and Juan Antonio Quirós Castillo (Bilbao: Servicio editorial Universidad del Pais Vasco, Documentos de Arqueologia Medieval, 2013), pp. 217–23

Lauwers, Michel, and Laurent Schneider, eds, *Mises en réserve: production, accumulation et redistribution des céréales dans L'Occident médiévale et moderne* (Toulouse: Presses Universitaries du Midi, 2022)

Marasco, Lorenzo, and Arianna Briano, 'The Stratigraphic Sequence at the Site of Vetricella (Scarlino, Grosseto): A Revised Interpretation (Eighth–Thirteenth Century)', in *The nEU-Med Project: Vetricella, An Early Medieval Royal Property on Tuscany's Mediterranean*, ed. by Giovanna Bianchi and Richard Hodges (Florence: All'Insegna del Giglio, 2020), pp. 9–22

Maufras, Odile, and Carole Puig, 'L'apport de l'archéologie des quartiers d'ensilage du haut Moyen Âge à la connaisance du stockage céréalier. À propos de l'organisation des sites de Missignac (Gard) et de Taxo-d'Avall (Pyrénées-Orientales)', in *Mises en réserve: production, accumulation et redistribution des céréales dans L'Occident médiévale et moderne*, ed. by Michel Lauwers and Laurent Schneider (Toulouse: Presses Universitaries du Midi, 2022), pp. 49–66

Pegña-Cocharro, Leonor, Jesus Emilio González Urquijo, Juan José Ibañez, and Lydia Zapata 'Técnicas de almaceniamento de alimentos en el mundo rural traditional: experiencias desde la etnografia', in *Horrea, Barns and Silos: Storage and Incomes in Early Medieval Europe*, ed. by Alfonso Vigil-Escalera, Giovanna Bianchi, and Juan Antonio Quirós Castillo (Bilbao: Servicio editorial Universidad del Pais Vasco, Documentos de Arqueologia Medieval, 2013), pp. 209–16

Perreaux, Nicolas, 'Prélèvements, organization spatio-temporelle et domination sociale. Les mentions de lieux de stockage dans le chartes médiévales (VIIe-XIIIe siècle)', in *Mises en réserve: production, accumulation et redistribution des céréales dans L'Occident médiévale et moderne*, ed. by Michel Lauwers and Laurent Schneider (Toulouse: Presses Universitaries du Midi, 2022), pp. 179–92

Quirós Castillo, Juan Antonio, 'Silos y sistema de almacenaje en el Pais Vasco en la Alta Edad Media', in *Horrea, Barns and Silos: Storage and Incomes in Early Medieval Europe*, ed. by Alfonso Vigil-Escalera, Giovanna Bianchi, and Juan Antonio Quirós Castillo (Bilbao: Servicio editorial Universidad del Pais Vasco, Documentos de Arqueologia Medieval, 2013), pp. 171–92

Settia, Aldo, *Castelli medievali* (Bologna: Il Mulino, 2007)

Tomei, Paolo, *Milites elegantes: le strutture aristocratiche nel territorio lucchese (800–1100 c.)* (Firenze: Reti Medievali e-book 34, 2019)

Valenti, Marco, *L'insediamento altomedievale nelle campagne toscane. Paesaggi, popolamento e villaggi tra VI e X secolo* (Florence: All'Insegna del Giglio, 2004)

Vigil-Escalera, Alfonso, Giovanna Bianchi, and Juan Antonio Quirós Castillo, eds, *Horrea, Barns and Silos: Storage and Incomes in Early Medieval Europe* (Bilbao: Servicio editorial Universidad del Pais Vasco, Documentos de Arqueologia Medieval, 2013)

JOSEP TORRÓ

Extrahere cequiam

Irrigation Canal Building and Agricultural Hydraulics in the Crown of Aragon (1170–1300)

Introduction

In the eleventh century, the frontier that divided al-Andalus and the Christian kingdoms within the Iberian Peninsula constituted a boundary not only between two different political and religious dimensions: it was also a dividing line between markedly different forms of social organization, each of which had produced and perfected their own ecological systems.[1] As Thomas F. Glick observed, broadly speaking, the agrarian order being developed in the Christian north focused chiefly on cereal growing and livestock farming, while in the Muslim south the cultivated landscape offered greater diversity, in which cereals played a comparatively less significant role, with the produce from olive groves, vineyards, and *huertas* featuring more prominently. Here artificially irrigated areas, denser and more localized than the extensive dryland crop fields, guaranteed a large part of the agricultural output, to the extent that Arab authors generally considered al-Andalus to be a country where irrigated agriculture was predominant.[2]

It should be mentioned that two basic forms of irrigation existed in al-Andalus. The first type was dependent on bringing water up from below ground using animal-driven water wheels, or harnessing rivers to power *norias* — water wheels moved by the force of the current. In this way limited or intermittent flows were obtained for unconnected irrigated areas. This type of irrigation was characteristic of the south-west of the peninsula and the Guadalquivir valley. The other solution was that of irrigation based on the diversion and transportation of water along canals using the force of gravity. These were sometimes simple systems, originating from springs, with the water

1 This work was carried out within the framework of the project ERC-SYG-101071726: MEDGREENREV ("Re-thinking the 'Green Revolution' in the Medieval Western Mediterranean, 6th–16th centuries").

2 Glick, *Cristianos y musulmanes en la España medieval*, p. 110.

Josep Torró (josep.torro@uv.es) is Associate Professor of Medieval History at the Universitat de València – Estudi General, Spain.

Building and Economic Growth in Southern Europe (1050–1300), ed. by Sandro Carocci and Alessio Fiore, (Turnhout: Brepols, 2024), pp. 79–100 BREPOLS PUBLISHERS 10.1484/M.TMC-EB.5.137975

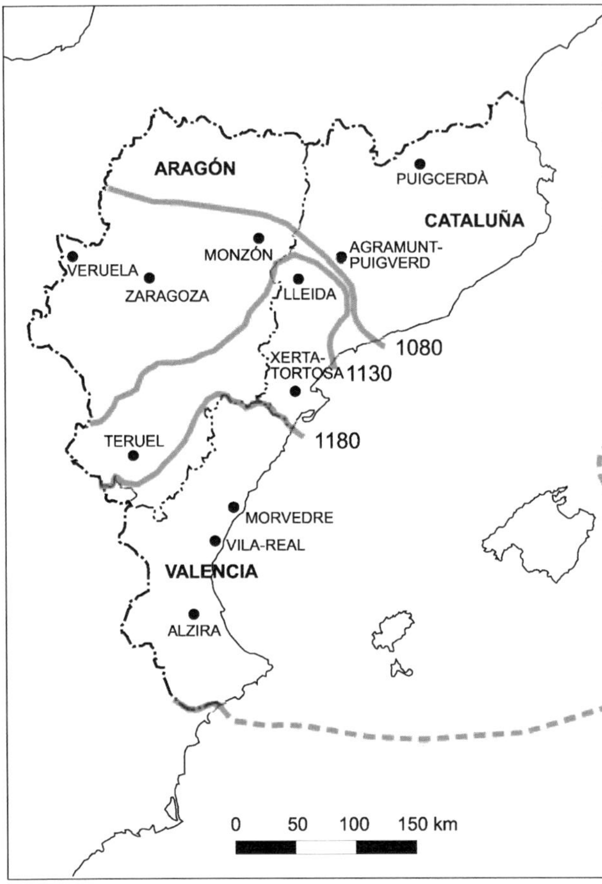

Figure 5.1. The Crown of Aragon: frontier advances (1080–1245) and the location of major Christian hydraulic works (not all mentioned in the text).

usually collected in ponds prior to its distribution; but irrigation with water diverted by gravity also gave rise to the complex systems of the *huertas* in the east and south-east of the peninsula, located principally in Granada, Murcia, the floodplains of Valencia, and the Ebro basin. These systems depended on long canals that originated in dams placed obliquely across riverbeds and which transported the water for several kilometres.

Of course, irrigated agriculture was not entirely unknown in the Christian kingdoms of the north. Their laws allowed water to be appropriated by private individuals or ecclesiastical institutions, but the prime objective of hydraulic devices was usually to power mills, only indirectly supplying water to irrigate meadows and vegetable patches.

Nevertheless, when as a result of major Christian advances in the twelfth and thirteenth centuries the frontier moved southwards (Figure 5.1), the complex hydraulic systems of the south fell into the hands of the conquerors, and this produced a completely new scenario. These systems were based on the large-scale distribution of water through dams diverting rivers and long canals with a multitude of small branches; their management clearly had a very particular impact on the Crown of Aragon, into whose territory the important *huertas* of the Ebro basin were incorporated in the twelfth century, followed by those in Valencia, after their conquest in the thirteenth century.

The Christian conquerors' contact and familiarization with Andalusi irrigation systems was to have an interesting effect on the hydraulic vocabulary of the Iberian Romance languages, the most significant examples of which were the adoption of the Arabic terms *sāqiya* (canal) and *sudd* (dam), giving rise to their respective derivations: *acequia* and *azud* in Castilian, *séquia* and *assut* in Catalan (not to mention the Arabic terminology relative to lesser hydraulic devices, with its huge geographical variability).[3] These words were not only incorporated into Romance spoken languages, but also into Latin charters, despite these already having their own hydraulic terminology, which survived mainly in the Pyrenees and in some diplomatic formulae. This terminological replacement suggests that the Arabic vocabulary prevailed due to the more widespread presence in the Muslim south of hydraulic devices and their close identification with the practice of irrigation.

It should however be emphasized that the endurance of Arabic hydraulic terminology, together with allusions in documents to the 'time of the Saracens' as a reference to a status quo that apparently ought to be preserved, has long been an obstacle to a proper understanding of the situation regarding irrigation systems in the years following the Christian conquests.[4] For a long time, it was supposed that Andalusi irrigation systems remained unchanged in Christian hands. However, research carried out over the last twenty years in both the Ebro valley and in Valencia has shown beyond dispute that not only did the new seigneurial authorities and Christian settlers introduce changes to the legal organization of irrigation, but that they also altered the physical structure of the systems, extending the networks of *acequias* and making them denser in order to expand the irrigated surfaces as far as possible.[5]

These initiatives were not an isolated phenomenon: they were part of a more diverse process of land reclamation, one that included sowing crops on barren dry land and previously drained marshland. It is however equally true that, in this context of general expansion, the prime objective seems to have been to encourage irrigated farming.[6]

The agricultural hydraulics initiatives carried out after the conquests were not restricted to the modification or enlargement of the pre-existing irrigation systems; new irrigated areas were created where previously — in the Muslim period — none had existed, with important financial investment in the

---

3 Neuvonen, *Los arabismos del español en el siglo XIII*, pp. 84–85, 132–33.

4 Guinot, '"Com en temps de sarraïns"', pp. 192–93.

5 Ortega, 'La agricultura de los vencedores', pp. 137–41; Guinot and Esquilache, 'La reorganización del paisaje agrario'; Esquilache, *Els constructors de l'Horta de València*, pp. 221–29.

6 Torró, 'Field and Canal-Building', pp. 85–96; Torró, 'Paisajes de frontera', pp. 31–32.

digging of large-flow canals over long courses. It is on these new enterprises that I will focus my attention in this article. They have the advantage of being physically more easily identifiable than the changes to the 'inherited' hydraulic systems, detection of which requires detailed archaeological and morphological studies. Moreover, unlike these earlier modifications, which were usually intermittent, the new irrigation works were often large-scale undertakings that required political decisions and an important mobilization of wealth, and were consequently more visible in documentary references.

In the Settlers' Home Regions

Although less common and clearly not as sophisticated as contemporary Andalusi agricultural hydraulics, canal-digging was not unknown in the Christian societies of the north. We therefore need to determine whether the work carried out in the conquered lands was merely a reproduction of local technological traditions — those typical of Muslim society — or whether they depended to some extent on expertise introduced by the new settlers.

When seeking to determine the nature of the conquerors' expertise with regard to hydraulics, the case of northern Catalonia may serve as a reference. Helena Kirchner has established three stages in the development of hydraulics in this region. To begin with, during the ninth and tenth centuries, there is evidence only of what she terms 'small peasant hydraulics', consisting of a short diversion towards a mill (often with a number of different owners), from which water was taken to irrigate a small garden situated between the irrigation canal, the watercourse, and the mill. From the mid-tenth century and during the eleventh, we witness a process of the gradual appropriation by the lords (through donations, purchases and exchanges) that barely affected the physical structure of the canals. Even the long millstreams owned by the Count of Barcelona and Girona, recorded from the eleventh century, were not new projects: all evidence would appear to suggest that they were old Roman conduits which had been repaired and modified. It was not until the end of the twelfth century that some larger-scale canal-digging work began, promoted above all by the king and the urban communities. These initiatives, recorded in Catalonia until the middle of the fourteenth century, have been linked to the increase in cereal production and the growing commercialization of grain, although in principle they were not intended for the irrigation of fields.[7]

These systems were in effect designed to provide mill complexes with energy: in the majority of cases, irrigation was of little importance and played a secondary role. This can be seen, for example, in a number of the canals in Roussillon studied by Sylvie Caucanas, such as the Rec de Millars (1163) or,

7 Kirchner, 'Hidráulica campesina', pp. 43–45.

further south, the Séquia del Molinot in Agramunt (after 1150).[8] But the most significant example is perhaps the Puigcerdà canal in La Cerdanya. Completed shortly after 1180 and based on a diversion of the river Aravó, its opening was linked to the foundation of the town of the same name by King Alfonso II, although it was not built from scratch: many small rudimentary diversions already existed on the banks of the river, supplying water to power mills and irrigate a number of meadows, to the extent that a saturation point had been reached and that technically 'there was no room for any more mills or canals'. In order to obtain the gradients necessary to generate hydraulic energy at new mill sites, the water had to be diverted upstream away from the valley bottom for a distance of more than nine kilometres to its principal objective: the urban mills (for flour and cloth) in the new town of Puigcerdà. This was the sole purpose of the canal; irrigation was therefore prohibited along the entirety of its course, although it *was* permitted after the water had passed through the town's mill complex, with water concessions being granted to irrigate some gardens and meadows in the immediate vicinity of the town.[9]

In Conquered Lands

Mills ceased to receive preferential treatment when irrigation canals began to be dug in the conquered lands from the late eleventh century onwards, following the victors' first encounters with irrigated Andalusi agriculture. The Christian lords regarded this hydraulic technology more as war booty than an 'inheritance' (in some cases pockets of the Muslim population remained and continued with farming work), as did the new Christian settlers who received irrigable plots. This inherited technology did not however prove sufficient. Despite the massive scale of the appropriation of functional hydraulic systems, not only did numerous initiatives spring up to create new irrigated areas, but they also came soon after the end of the conquests, that is, from the middle of the twelfth century in the Ebro basin and southern Aragon, and from the mid-thirteenth century in the case of Valencia (Figure 5.1). We shall now consider a number of examples of this type of initiative.

Following the conquest of Lleida (1149), there was a considerable increase in irrigation dependant on the volume of the flow of the river Segre and its tributaries. Jordi Bolòs has succeeded in identifying at least three major operations: the new *acequia* whose construction between Castellpagès and Torres de Segre was initiated by the nobleman Ramon de Cervera in 1184, with the king's authorization; the extension of the Andalusi Fontanet canal, which involved moving the diversion dam further up the Segre; and most

8 Caucanas, *Moulins et irrigation en Roussillon*, pp. 260–62; Eritja, 'Assentaments i sistemes hidràulics', p. 184.

9 Kirchner and others, *Aigua prohibida*, pp. 21–23, 31–40.

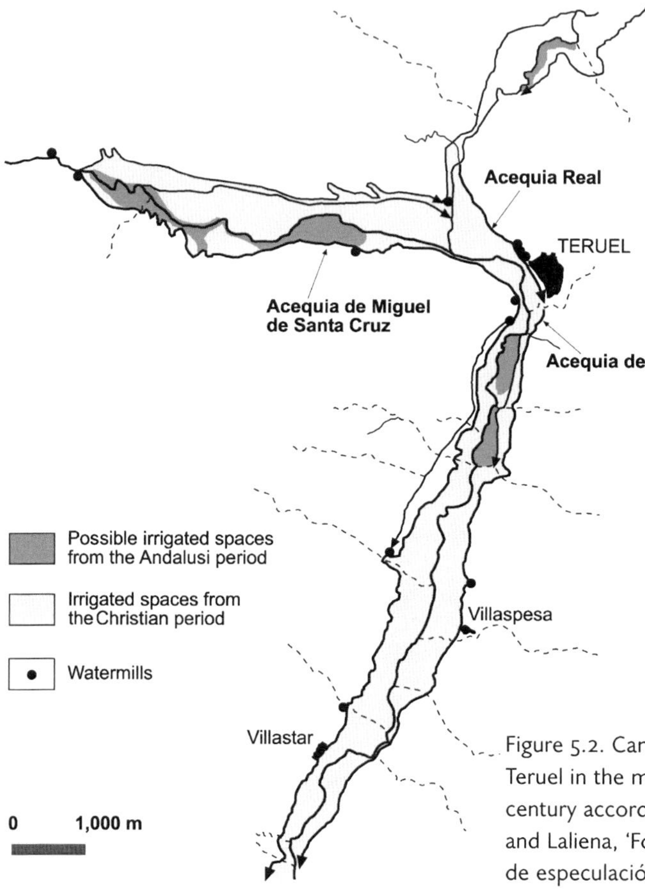

Figure 5.2. Canal network in Teruel in the mid-thirteenth century according to Ortega and Laliena, 'Formas feudales de especulación agraria', p. 83.

importantly, the long Segrià or Pinyana *acequia* whose construction appears to have commenced at the end of the twelfth century. This project may well have taken advantage of a shorter pre-existing canal and other smaller local *acequias*, but the end result was a vast new system that was dug across the domains of several lords on its long route from the dam on the river Noguera Ribagorçana. In Bolòs's view, the choice of locations for these operations suggests that the lords only appreciated the importance of irrigation in places where it might be conducive to cereal production.[10]

In southern Aragon, the Teruel area, dominated by the depression formed by the rivers Alfambra and Guadalaviar-Turia, was settled quite rapidly by Christians following its conquest (*c.* 1170), resulting in the large-scale

10 Bolòs, *Els orígens medievals del paisatge català*, pp. 370–71. The Torres de Segre *acequia* has been studied by Marfull, 'Un sistema hidráulico feudal en el valle del Segre'.

transformation of irrigated areas. According to the study by Julián Ortega and Carlos Laliena, an indeterminate number of canals appear to date from the period prior to the conquest, but there can be no doubt that most of the hydraulic network that was functioning around 1240 was the product of later initiatives. Of particular note was the building of the Miguel de Santa Cruz *acequia*, which was named after the *senior* who was in charge of the *honor* (royal land grant) of Teruel between about 1172 and 1182: this was an extremely long canal, spanning a distance of at least fifteen kilometres, which supplied water to several *aldeas* (villages). Other irrigation projects inaugurated around this time include the *acequia Real*, whose main function was to power the king's mills and irrigate the adjacent lands; and the Uclés canal, mentioned in 1196, which seems to have taken advantage of part of the Andalusi infrastructure (Figure 5.2). The irrigated lands were basically used for growing cereals and vines, although the frequency of the references to irrigated vines in documents and the local jurisdiction (*Fuero de Teruel*) seems to indicate a certain preference for winegrowing by the landowners who ruled the town.[11]

In the kingdom of Valencia, where the principal military operations were concluded in 1245, documentary references to new hydraulic works are more numerous and precise. They also begin to appear not long after the conquest. Two major initiatives stand out: the *acequias* of Alzira and Vila-real. The former, begun in 1258, was the result of a particularly ambitious agricultural transformation plan. The lower course of the Júcar, unlike the medium-sized and small rivers, had not been diverted for irrigation purposes in the Muslim period, given the danger posed by the violent rises in the water level of this mighty river. Its floodplain was irrigated by diversions of its tributaries, catchments of springs, and water wheels. In order to divert the flow of the Júcar, a very large solid dam was required, quite different from the precarious diversion devices constructed by the Muslims before the conquest. The initial objective was to carry the waters of the Júcar to the southern edges of the *huerta* of Valencia, which was irrigated by another river, the Turia. Thus, in contrast to the previously mentioned examples at Lleida and Teruel, the course of this canal remained at a high level that gradually moved it away from the course of the river and the newly irrigated areas surrounded the pre-existing ones, situated lower down. Although the ultimate goal was not achieved in that period, by about 1273 when the essential part of the work was completed, the canal was twenty-two kilometres long (Figure 5.3).

The other major canalization project was the Vila-real *acequia*, on the river Millars, whose volume flow rate was five or six times smaller than that of the Júcar. The canal that irrigated the lands adjacent to the small *madīna* of Borriana had already been diverted from its course in the Muslim period, and for this reason the new canal was built upstream: the area it was destined to irrigate was juxtaposed, on higher levels, to that of the old Andalusi *huerta*

11 Ortega and Laliena, 'Formas feudales de especulación agraria', pp. 82–88, 93–95.

Figure 5.3. The new canal of Alzira built by royal initiative in 1258–1272. The possible Andalusi *acequias* are based on an unpublished work by Lydia Castan.

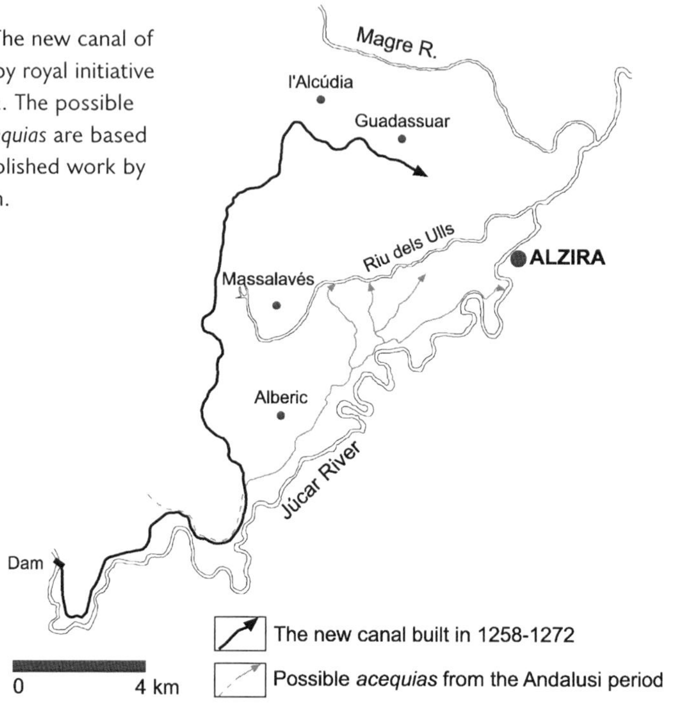

of Borriana, whose large *acequia* would now form the lower edge of the new irrigated area. It should be pointed out that the excavation of the new canal was an undertaking closely linked to the founding of the new town of Vila-real, its objective being the distribution of irrigation water on land that had previously been dry or left uncultivated. It is useful to observe that the twelve-kilometre long canal was split into two main branches, with the mills located on the lower one; this explains why it loses height, while the upper one remains at the highest possible level in order to maximize the irrigable surface area (Figure 5.4). The information relative to this work dates from between 1272 and 1281.[12]

Technological Aspects

The irrigation schemes described above share undeniable similarities with the hydraulic systems of the Muslim period. It is equally true, however, that these similarities derive fundamentally from the technological requirements necessarily involved in digging irrigation canals in the geo-climatic environments

12 Guinot and Selma, 'La construcción del paisaje en una huerta feudal', pp. 115–17.

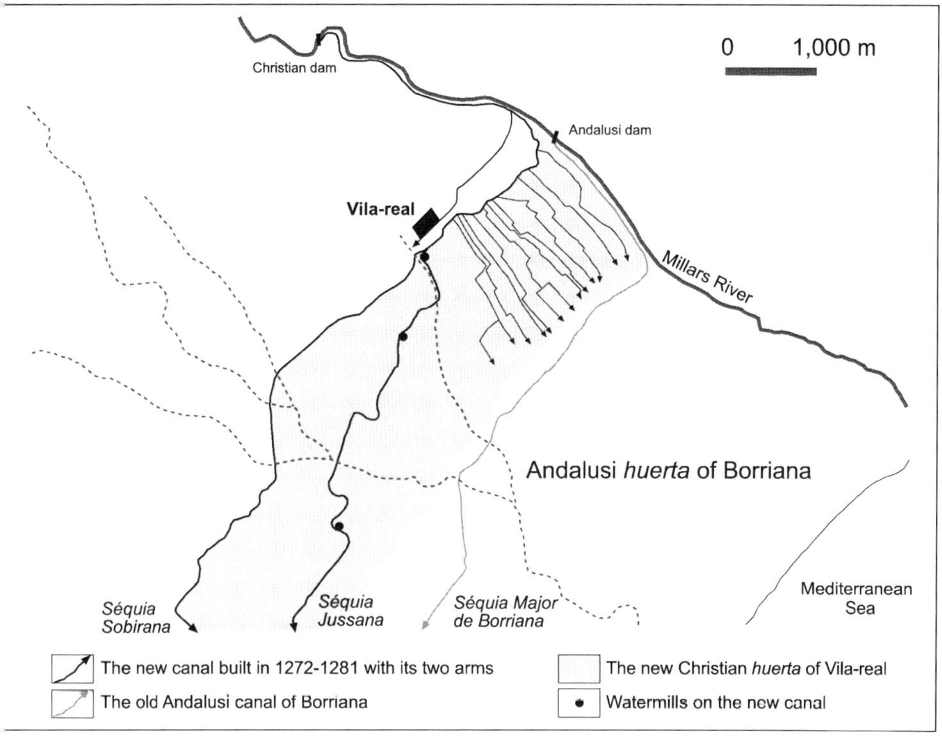

Figure 5.4. The new canal of Vila-real built by royal initiative in 1272–1281. Based on Guinot and Selma, 'La construcción del paisaje en una huerta feudal', p. 144, and González Villaescusa *Las formas de los paisajes mediterráneos*, p. 278.

typical of Mediterranean rivers. Beyond the series of architectural accessories or minor elements, in fluvial irrigation systems we find three basic components: diversion dams, canals dug out of the ground, and divisors (*partidores*) by means of which canals were split into two in order to distribute the water.

In the Andalusi period, the divisors of the floodplain irrigation systems branched the continuous flow of the water diverted from the river, dividing the water in circulation into proportional parts. In order to maintain the stability of these parts, structures were adopted in the form of starlings built of hewn stone. These were a key component of the architecture of hydraulic systems, ensuring the supply of water to the irrigated areas of each settlement (*qarya/s*) that had taken part in the construction project.[13] In the systems created by the Christians these mechanisms were replicated, although less frequently. This type of divisor, called a 'tongue' (*llengua*), splits the Vila-real canal into its two main branches (Figure 5.4). Like the system itself, it was clearly built

13 Guinot, 'El paisaje de la Huerta de Valencia', pp. 103–05; Esquilache, *Els constructors de l'Horta de València*, pp. 238–43.

by Christian settlers to perform a function similar to dividing the current; however, unlike the Andalusi divisors it does not guarantee a continuous flow of water to different local communities, but is instead subordinated to a general distribution by turns.[14]

Diversion dams (*azudes*) were obliquely-positioned rectilinear structures that did not traverse the entire width of the river; constructed from stakes or canes and filled with loose stones or balls of earth, these dams had to be rebuilt periodically due to the habitual floods of the Mediterranean rivers. Although this kind of device was in widespread use amongst Christian settlers, the newcomers also introduced fixed masonry *azudes*, built of stone and mortar, of whose existence there is no record in al-Andalus.[15] The aforementioned *azud* in the Alzira canal might be assumed to be unique, given the magnitude of the diverted flow and the force of the current. This is not however the case: in the kingdom of Valencia, we know of an *azud* built around 1293 at the initiative of the town of Pego, which had to be 'good, firm and sufficient', given that its task was to raise the water to a considerable height so that it could be carried to the land in the valley. A large sum (3000 s.) was spent on the scheme, but it was never completed, nor did it fulfil its functions of irrigation; eventually however the king authorized the construction of a mill which would make use of the water brought to the area.[16] Particularly significant in this respect was the initiative to alter the course of the canal of the town of Morvedre, begun in 1298, which required the rebuilding of the *azud*. An inspection carried out two years later noted that, when the work was begun, 'it was not their wish to make in the said place an *azud* of mortar, but of (loose) stones and wood', but it was eventually agreed to build it using mortar, spanning the entire river.[17] This type of improvement was not widely carried out, but the decision to 'petrify' some *azudes*, replacing them with permanent dams built of masonry, was the result of assessing, on a case by case basis, whether the flexibility of the precarious old devices (if they did not withstand the floods, they could be relocated or changed easily if necessary) made up for the maintenance problems and, above all, the functional limitations they imposed on the needs of the newly irrigated areas (greater flow, more difficult diversions).

Although in the aforementioned inspection of the Morvedre canal it is stated that the new stretch was built 'of both earth and mortar', the fact is that *acequias* continued to be, fundamentally, made of earth, with some masonry reinforcements in the sections most exposed to erosion. The differences between the work carried out in the Christian period and that of the Andalusi-

14 Guinot and Selma, 'La construcción del paisaje en una huerta feudal', p. 117.

15 Cressier, 'À propos des apports orientaux dans l'hydraulique agraire d'al-Andalus'; Bazzana and De Meulemeester, *La noria, l'aubergine et le fellah*, pp. 184–91, 344.

16 Torró, 'Canteros y niveladores', p. 212.

17 *Pergamins, processos i cartes reials*, ed. by Guinot, pp. 279–82.

era can be seen, above all, in the general morphology of the irrigation systems. It should be borne in mind that the network of irrigation canals and ditches had to be adapted to irrigable plots of land that were created with geometric criteria to be distributed among the settlers. That is why branches at right angles were quite usual, arranged also at regular intervals, as can be seen clearly in the hydraulic systems created in the Ebro valley after the conquest or, on a rather smaller scale, in the case of Vila-real (Figure 5.4).[18]

The crucial aspect of the excavation of canals was their suitability for controlling the speed of the flow. It was necessary to plan the course to ensure free-flowing circulation, with no changes in speed that might lead to the deterioration of the sides, uniformly maintaining a very slight gradient (below the threshold of 1 ‰) along the entire course and adapting the canal's section to the gradual reduction of the channelled flow. This was the objective of the master builders who 'extracted' or dug *acequias*. What may perhaps be surprising, given what historically we have been led to understand, is the complete absence of the mention of Muslims as being in charge of this type of building work. We undoubtedly have to take into consideration the paucity of information offered by written sources prior to the fourteenth century, where those who performed this kind of operation are rarely mentioned. But there are no references to 'Saracen' technicians or masters either in the later sources referring to hydraulic works in Aragon and Valencia, although it is highly likely that a great deal of Muslim manual labour was involved. There are, moreover, a number of quite explicit references to the roles played by technicians of Catalan or Occitan origin in charge of building the canals in the kingdom of Valencia during the thirteenth century. One example was the *magistro operis cequie* of Alzira in 1272, Arnau Vidal, who was also the master builder at Valencia Cathedral; or the fact that the inspection made of the building work at the Morvedre canal in 1300 was carried out by four Christian 'masters and stonemasons' from Valencia.[19]

It seems that the knowledge of geometry conferred by the mastery of the profession of stonemason was sufficient to deal with the problems of levelling and hydraulics presented by these long canals. Documentary references also make clear the growing importance of the *azudes* built as fixed masonry structures. However, it is important to point out that, although they built the dams, determined the course of the canal, and established the forks in the main branches, stonemasons and levellers do not seem to have been responsible for the dendritic distribution of the water, i.e. its conduction to the irrigable

18 Ortega, 'La agricultura de los vencedores y la agricultura de los vencidos', pp. 137–39; Bolòs, *Els orígens medievals del paisatge català*, pp. 316–18; González Villaescusa, *Las formas de los paisajes mediterráneos*, pp. 271–78.

19 Torró, 'Canteros y niveladores', pp. 212–14. The same is true of the men who specialized in digging drainage canals, and who worked draining the coastal wetlands in Valencia from the end of the thirteenth century. A significant number of them even came from parts of Europe north of the Alps: Torró, 'Agricultural Drainage Technology', p. 320.

surfaces. Thirteenth-century documents refer to the latter generically as *subtus cequiam*, 'that which is below the (main) canal': the area where the settlers were given plots of land marked out at right angles; a space unified only by its right to receive water, although the interested parties were responsible for making effective use of this resource. At this point it is necessary to consider who was behind these initiatives, and how they were financed.

Promotion and Financing

Naturally, it was the lords who were recorded in the documents as the formal promoters, in particular the great lords who ruled expanses of land where a canal several kilometres long could be dug without provoking jurisdictional conflicts, with no need for agreements with other lords. There is documentary evidence of schemes instigated by the king and also by religious and military orders. In all of these, however, the active participation of the local community — the *universitat* or *concejo* — was essential. Alan J. Forey puts forward the theory that it might even have been the community who proposed the digging of the canals, as opposed to the overlords who were perhaps reluctant to spend large sums on projects whose initial investment would only slowly be recouped.[20]

As mentioned before, the texts enable us to see that the builders of the principal canals did not concern themselves with the dendritic distribution; they did not dig the network of secondary *acequias* and ditches that carried water to the plots. This *modus operandi* derived directly from the mechanisms of seigniorial promotion and their relationship with the community. A good example of this is the *acequia* of Paúles and Sosiles, diverted from the river Cinca, in the Aragonese town of Monzón, which was ruled by the Order of the Temple. In 1250 the Templars reached an agreement with the *universitat* which specified that the Order would take charge of the construction of the canal with its dam and would be responsible for its maintenance, reserving for itself the right to build mills; but it would be the local people who would be in charge of digging secondary *acequias* or ditches and taking the irrigation water to their fields using whatever auxiliary devices were necessary.[21] This agreement is similar to the one formalized by James I in 1273 with the *universitat* of Alzira which gave the king responsibility for the maintenance of the dam, canal, and the dividers of the canal, but allowed the local population 'to dig channels' and take water from the main *acequia*.[22]

Although the construction of the Paúles and Sosiles canal seems either to have been instigated by the Templars or to have constituted a joint initiative

20 Forey, 'Notes on Irrigation in North-Eastern Spain', p. 130.

21 Madrid, AHN, Códices, L. 653, pp. 340–45. Published with many errors by Castillón, 'Política hidráulica de templarios', pp. 393–95, 409–12.

22 Published by Gual, *Estudio histórico-geográfico*, pp. 104–07.

between the Order and the local inhabitants, it was in fact the latter who paid for the work, possibly in full. In Forey's view, the fact that the Order could demand large payments from the inhabitants to pay for the project suggests that the initiative originated with the community rather than with the Templars. Indeed, the text of the agreement does not expressly envisage any payment from the Order, but it does clearly establish the way in which the local people had to contribute: on the one hand, the *universitat* as a whole would provide 1000 *aureos*; on the other, the individuals benefiting from the irrigation water would have to pay an entry fee of 1 *aureo* for each *soga* of land. We do not know how many irrigable *sogas* were paid for, nor is it easy to determine to what exact surface area the said measure corresponded, but we do know that an annual payment (*cequiaje*) was also established of 2½ d. per *soga*. Given the nature of the *cequiaje*, to which I shall refer below, an annual payment of somewhere in the region of 200 s. seems at least plausible, which suggests — and this is pure speculation — that at least 1000 *sogas* were entered in the accounts, that is, a further 1000 *aureos* paid as entry fees. Since in the 1250s *aureos* or *morabetins* were the equivalent of between 6 and 7 s. in *iaccensis* deniers (the currency of Aragon which would be the one used solely or predominantly in the payments), the hypothesis of an approximate cost of 2000 *aureos* would correspond to between 12,000 and 14,000 s: in other words, about 40–45 kg of coined silver for a canal of more than five kilometres in length.[23]

The Templars were very possibly restricting themselves to overseeing and regulating a project undertaken by the local community. Nevertheless, documents tend to show that the Order had technological and organizational means apparently beyond the reach of the *universitat*. It is significant that, a mere two years later, the townspeople of Monzón presented the existing Salobrás *acequia* to the Templars, 'so that they might make and build it' along with its *azud* and take responsibility for keeping both devices in working order. Substantial repair work was undertaken, possibly including a new masonry dam, for which the irrigators paid an unspecified entry fee.[24] The Order's experience in managing this kind of undertaking also seems to have been taken into account by the king. Thus, James I entrusted a Templar, Pere Peironet, knight commander in the town of Borriana in Valencia and royal almoner, with the administration of the works of the Vila-real canal in the 1270s.[25]

---

23 With the amount of the *cequiaje* referred to, 960 *sogas* were needed to collect 200 s. The *soga* of Monzón was a measurement of length that in the sixteenth century was equivalent to 32 *alnes* of Lleida, that is, 28.704 metres (Alsina and others, *Pesos, mides i mesures*, p. 116). If the *soga*, understood as surface area, consists of the square of the length, we would be talking about 823.9 m^2 (a measure very similar to the *fanecada* of Valencia), so 1000 *sogas* would be 82.39 ha. It was probably larger. The *solidus iaccensis* (12 deniers) contained 3.24 g of 0.958 silver.

24 Madrid, AHN, Códices, L. 653, pp. 348–50 (1252).

25 *Documentos de Jaime I de Aragón*, VII, ed. by Huici and Cabanes, pp. 102–03: James I acknowledges that the knight commander Peironet has accounted for the money used in the works

The information relating to the canals promoted by the king during this period is less fragmentary. It at least presents us with two major forms of finance that we shall term 'internal' and 'external'. The former would consist of revenue issuing directly from the acquisition of rights over the irrigation water by members of the local community, as occurred in the case of the Templars' canal of Paúles and Sosiles. The latter, obviously, would be unconnected to these links between the community and the overlords, and is only recorded in the references to the king's canals. We find an example of external finance in 1257, when James I ordered the *baile* (the king's representative in charge of administration and finance) of Lleida to collect a tax to pay for work on the canal of Llitera (*ad opus cequie de Litera*). The majority of the towns on which this *peita* was levied (Tamarit, Almenar, Almacelles, etc.) seem to have been potential beneficiaries of the water, but the lion's share of the tax fell to Montblanc, a town of some importance which was too far away to be reached by the canal. Although it seems that in the end the money collected was not allocated in its totality to the work on the canal, it is worth pointing out that the sum required, a total of 13,350 s. (43.2 kg of silver) was quite close to that of the estimated cost of the *acequia* of Paúles and Sosiles.[26] Digging large irrigation canals was expensive due mainly to the sheer number of manual labourers required for this kind of task. When the work on the *acequia* of Morvedre was inspected in 1300, the notary who drafted the report noticed 'the great company of men' who were preparing to lay the foundations of the dam.

Recourse to external funding by way of generic incomes of the royal *bailía* is more evident in the case of the Vila-real canal. We are not aware of any references to financial contributions made by the potential beneficiaries of the canal, but we do know that funds from the royal *bailía* were used for the *opus cequie* in 1273 (also in Alzira); more specifically, the following year, the sale of two years' worth of the income from the neighbouring town of Borriana were sold for 7000 s. which the purchasers then had to hand over immediately to the Templar Pere Peironet so that he could allocate them to the work on the canal (*ad opus operis cequie nostre Ville Regalis*).[27] Although we do not know the exact cost of the work, contemporary reports suggest that it was considered at the time to be an expensive undertaking: Bertran Albert, from Marseille, who had been contracted to build the canal, died in 1281, shortly after receiving what was described as 'a large sum of money'

---

of the canal (1276). A Templar called Peironet first appears in 1230 associated with the works on the main *acequia* of the *huerta* of Monzón (Madrid, AHN, Códices, L. 653, pp. 338–40). Despite the length of time that elapsed, we cannot rule out that this is the same person.

26 Barcelona, ACA, Cancillería, reg. 8, fol. 31^r (1257); reg. 10, fols 30r, 96r, 106^v (1258–1259).

27 Barcelona, ACA, Cancillería, reg. 19, fols 31^r (1273), 128^v (1274). Vila-real's town charter was granted on 20 February 1274: *Cartes de poblament medievals valencianes*, ed. by Guinot, pp. 342–44.

which now had to be recovered.[28] It is interesting, moreover, to note that, at least in these royal enterprises associated with the settlement of the recently conquered territories, it was possible to pay the master builders without transferring the financial burden to the settlers-irrigators. We know for example that in 1260 Bonfill, the first master of the Alzira *acequia*, had been given land — undoubtedly associated with the canal — as 'a salary for your mastery and work', which he was authorized to sell. The master Arnau Vidal may also have been paid in part with immovable goods.[29]

It may well be that the standard means of financing the king's canals was via a combination of internal and external resources, as was in fact the case with Alzira. While in 1258 James I ordered all the settlers whose lands lay along the course of the new canal 'to pay their part of the expenses that are incurred to extract the said canal from the river Júcar', it is equally true that some years later he did not hesitate to allocate funds from the royal *bailía*, as well as resources unconnected with the canal — such as the revenue collected from tolls and from the Jews of Teruel — for work on the canal.[30]

We obtain a clearer insight into the king's financial involvement in the hydraulic works carried out in his personal domains in the kingdom of Valencia if we observe that James I refers to the canals that he has built as his patrimony (*cequia nostra Algezire, cequia nostra Ville Regalis*). It is therefore logical that the king's officials should have administered the new irrigation systems initially, but that by the end of the thirteenth and the beginning of the fourteenth century these duties had begun to be transferred to the corresponding *universitats*.[31] In fact, in the final years of the thirteenth century, it is possible to document initiatives associated with irrigation in the hands of the local communities in the king's domains, such as the aforementioned failed project at Pego in 1293, or the alteration of the course of the Morvedre canal in 1298. For the latter the king was even asked for help, eventually granting an exemption from taxation for two years, on the condition that the work be completed within that period.[32]

28 Barcelona, ACA, Cancillería, reg. 50, fols 211^{v}–212^{r}: *magna peccunie quantitatem*.

29 *Diplomatarium of the Crusader Kingdom of Valencia*, II, ed. by Burns, doc. 281, pp. 238–39: *salarii quod vobis pertinet pro vestro magistratu et labore çequie Aliezire*. In 1274 four *jovades* (12 ha) and houses in Alzira were granted to a son of Arnau Vidal, *magistro operis cequie Algesire*: Barcelona, ACA, Cancillería, reg. 19, fol. 105^{v}.

30 *Diplomatarium of the Crusader Kingdom of Valencia*, II, ed. by Burns, doc. 162, p. 139: *in extrahendo iamdictam cequiam de flumine Xuchari* (1258); doc. 451 (1263); IV, doc. 1136, pp. 162–64: payment of 2000 s. 'for the work on the irrigation canal of Alzira' (1271).

31 Guinot and Selma, 'La construcción del paisaje en una huerta feudal', pp. 124–26.

32 Barcelona, ACA, Cancillería, reg. 196, fol. 248^{rv}. The royal document refers significantly to 'the work that they [the *universitat*] are attempting to do'.

Objectives and Maintenance

The significance of the external resources contributed by the monarch to these irrigation projects can undoubtedly be explained by their colonizing potential and their contribution to the consolidation of the kingdom of Valencia created by James I. After the old Andalusi *huertas* had been shared out, the construction of the Alzira and Vila-real canals facilitated the continued gifts of land that were attractive for the beneficiaries, in particular those close to the king — servants, relatives, and friends, and others loyal to him — who it was hoped would settle in the recently conquered territory. The location of the plots in the *subtus cequiam* area, systematically specified in the charters, in principle constituted a guarantee of access to the irrigation water that gave the land crucial added value. The continuity between these initiatives is also significant : Vila-real began just when Alzira ended, and two of the first gifts made in the former had originally been promised in the latter.[33] Moreover, both enterprises were closely associated with the creation of new urban centres. There is no doubt that this is the case with the founding of Vila-real, but James I also decreed that the beneficiaries of lands below the *acequia* of Alzira should receive plots to build houses in an area outside the town.[34] At the same time, the creation of this canal made possible the founding of a settlement along the final section of its course: Guadassuar, where forty-two settlers from Navarre set up home in 1270 (Figure 5.4).[35]

The overlords could demand considerably higher rents from the irrigated plots than those paid in areas of dryland cultivation. In Forey's opinion, this fact would explain the increase in irrigated areas in the Ebro basin during the twelfth and thirteenth centuries.[36] However, this explanation could be called into question if we consider the substantial participation of the local communities in the hydraulic initiatives, which Forey has also pointed out. In the territory of Valencia the lands around the new irrigation canals were usually distributed rent-free, so it is obvious that in these cases an immediate return was not expected (although, as we have seen with the Templars in Aragon, the king took care to reserve the building and exploitation of the mills exclusively for himself). What the overlords *did* seek to encourage was a certain type of farming. The donations of irrigable land were so extensive that their beneficiaries would not farm them directly: many are recorded that measured between four and ten *jovades* (16–30 hectares) or more. It was therefore not a case of creating small horticultural areas, but rather of encouraging a yield

33 Torró, 'Field and Canal-Building after the Conquest', p. 98.

34 *Diplomatarium of the Crusader Kingdom of Valencia*, IV, ed. by Burns, doc. 1023, pp. 40–41 (1270).

35 *Cartes de poblament medievals valencianes*, ed. by Guinot, pp. 321–22.

36 Forey, 'Notes on Irrigation in North-Eastern Spain during the XIIth and XIIIth Centuries', pp. 128–29.

of crops that could also be produced on dry land, essentially cereals, and occasionally vineyards.

With regard to the kingdom of Aragon, Carlos Laliena has shown how 'cereals took possession of the *huertas*' between the twelfth and thirteenth centuries, a process intensified from the last quarter of the thirteenth century by the stimulus represented by the growing exportation to urban centres on the Crown of Aragon's Mediterranean coast and the resulting rise in cereal prices.[37] In fact, in the case of the kingdom of Valencia, the production of cereals in the newly irrigated areas was quickly absorbed by domestic demand, most particularly that of the capital itself.

However, creating irrigation systems and putting them into operation was not enough to guarantee their productivity. Maintenance was just as important as construction. While the building work depended on heavy initial investment, the maintenance work required significant periodic expenditure, which included paying the teams of labourers employed to clean the canals, the cost of repair work, and the salary of the *sequier* or *çavacequia*, the officer responsible for the surveillance, conservation, and proper functioning of the system. Maintenance obligations were envisaged in a very similar way in the agreements established between lords and local communities, as we observe if we compare those drawn up between the Order of the Temple and the town of Monzón in 1250 with those between James I and Alzira in 1273. Essentially, these agreements reproduced the division of labour that prevailed in the building of the systems: the cleaning and repair of the main canals, dams, divisors, and sluices were the lords' responsibility, but it would be up to the landowners to maintain the small channels and ditches.

The important thing, in any case, is that although the lords were responsible for maintaining the 'hard' part of the irrigation system, it was the owners of the irrigated land who had to foot the bill. For this purpose, an annual levy for all the canals (whether or not they were newly built) was collected; this was called *cequiaje* or *sequiatge* (also *alfarda* in many parts of Aragon) and was always fixed in proportion to the surface area that each landowner could irrigate. In the case of the agreement reached in Alzira in 1273, the *cequiaje* consisted of 2½ s. per *jovada*, that is, 10 d. or 2.7 grams of silver per hectare.[38]

Thus, receipt of the *cequiaje* was, initially at least, a right accorded to the lord and formal promoter of the canal, who in return took responsibility for its maintenance. But above all it constituted a seigniorial income that could be used for other purposes.[39] In 1271, for example, James I did not hesitate to grant an annual rent of 2000 s. to the nobleman Hug dels Baus (Baux), paid

37 Laliena, 'Agua y progreso social en Aragón', p. 60.

38 On Alzira, see note 22. I have not calculated the equivalence of the *cequiajes* of the canals of Monzón (2 ½ d. or 1 ½ d./*cuerda*) because the surface area suggested in note 23 is speculative.

39 Forey, 'Notes on Irrigation in North-Eastern Spain during the XIIth and XIIIth Centuries', p. 123.

from the *cequiaje* 'and our rights in the *acequia* that we are having built in Alzira'.[40] This situation changed when the local councils began to take over the administration of the hydraulic systems and proceeded to regulate both the rate of the *cequiaje* and the post of *sequier*. This enables us to understand the comparatively modest *cequiaje* established by the council of Vila-real in 1307, consisting of 11d. per *jovada*, that is, 1 gram of silver per hectare — a third of what the king had ordered to be paid in Alzira in 1273.[41]

Conclusions

Despite being built essentially of earth, irrigation canals were singularly persistent and functional features of the rural landscape, outlasting even the majority of stone buildings: all those mentioned in this chapter are still working today. In his now classic characterization of the irrigated areas of al-Andalus, Miquel Barceló defined the main *acequias* with an apt expression: 'lines of rigidity'. And of course, the technological foundations of the hydraulic works are the same in the Andalusi and the Christian worlds: 'the exigency of gravity as the founding fact', structuring the point of water catchment, the course and inclination of the canals, and the location of regulatory devices.[42] However, the boost given to irrigated agriculture in the conquered lands from the second half of the twelfth century onwards arose in a completely different human and social medium, in areas where the Muslim population had been mostly or completely replaced by urban communities of Christian settlers framed in seigniorial contexts. The new hydraulic initiatives and their functional continuity were possible due to the interaction of both seigniorial and communal agencies. This context did determine some technological solutions, such as the more widespread construction of masonry dams, and it gave rise, above all, to irrigated areas of more geometric morphologies.[43]

The new agricultural hydraulics — a singular form of the 'petrification' of wealth — did not result in diversified horticultural landscapes, but they did produce fields of cereals and, to a lesser extent, vineyards, the main crops that could be converted into merchandise and money.[44] Their principal aim was not a direct increase in seigneurial rent, but rather a general increase in population and wealth, which it was hoped would (indirectly) benefit

40 *Diplomatarium of the Crusader Kingdom of Valencia*, IV, ed. by Burns, doc. 1121, pp. 148–49: *in cequiatico et iuribus nostris cequie quam fieri facimus in Algezira*.

41 Guinot and Selma, 'La construcción del paisaje en una huerta feudal', p. 126.

42 Barceló, 'El diseño de espacios irrigados en al-Andalus', pp. 58–60.

43 A magnificent example is the network of hydraulic works and plots of land created in Puçol (in the north of the *huerta* of Valencia) in 1242, studied in detail by Guinot, 'La construcción de nuevos espacios agrarios en el siglo XIII', pp. 128–39.

44 At the beginning of the thirteenth century, in Aragon, the market already makes it possible to absorb each year a volume of cereals large enough so that Peter II can monetize the *pechas* (taxes) on cereal: Ortega and Laliena, 'Formas feudales de especulación agraria', pp. 97–98.

seigneurial incomes. This logic is expressed very transparently in the language of justification that we find in the documents resulting from the implementation of hydraulic projects. The terms used reproduce three clearly defined principles: usefulness, improvement, and increase. The notion of usefulness (*utilitas*) or convenience (*commodum*) highlights the connection between the lords and the communities of inhabitants through shared interests.[45] The second principle, improvement (*melioramentum*), alludes to the territory.[46] It is undoubtedly a part of the discourse of *melioratio terrae,* emanating in the twelfth century from monastic environments, in which the agrarian transformation and the expansion of cereal crops at the expense of other options in the production of foodstuffs is justified and encouraged.[47] Finally, the idea of increase (*augmentum, incrementum*) does not seem to have been made very explicit until the end of the thirteenth century. It refers to both the population and to the seigniorial rents, it being implicit that the growth of the former implies that of the latter. It seems to be associated with the notion of usefulness.[48] It was in the early decades of the fourteenth century that the three principles appeared combined in structured formulae applicable to the goal of legitimizing the king's hydraulic works and, in general, the great schemes associated with settlements of population and agricultural transformation.

45 For example: *Inquisita comuni utilitate et maxima tam Templi quam universsitatis ville Monssonis* (Monzón, 1250); *intelligentes magnum comodum atque utilitatem nostram omnium predictorum et omnium aliorum vicinorum* (Monzón, 1252). See notes 21 and 24.

46 For example: *ad totum melioramentum termini Algezire ... meliorare terminos vestros, scilicet habitatores uniuscuiusque cequie* (Alzira, 1255). Published by Gual, *Estudio histórico-geográfico,* p. 99.

47 Hoffmann, *An Environmental History of Medieval Europe*, pp. 140, 152.

48 For example: *quodam opere quod ipsi intendunt facere seu construere tam ad augmentacionem reddituum nostrorum quam ad comunem utilitatem ipsius loci* (Morvedre, 1298). See note 17.

Works Cited

Manuscripts and Archival Sources

Barcelona, Archivo de la Corona de Aragón (ACA), Cancillería, regs. 8, 10, 19, 50, 196
Madrid, Archivo Histórico Nacional (AHN), Códices, L. 653

Primary Sources

Cartes de poblament medievals valencianes, ed. by Enric Guinot (València: Generalitat, 1991)

Diplomatarium of the Crusader Kingdom of Valencia: The Registered Charters of its Conqueror, Jaume I, 1257–1276, ed. by Robert I. Burns, II–IV (Princeton: Princeton University Press, 1991–2007)

Documentos de Jaime I de Aragón, VII: *1275–1276*, ed. by Ambrosio Huici and Maria Desamparados Cabanes, Textos Medievales, 100 (Zaragoza: Anubar, 2017)

Pergamins, processos i cartes reials. Documentació dispersa valenciana del segle XIII, ed. by Enric Guinot, Fonts Històriques Valencianes, 46 (València: Publicacions de la Universitat de València, 2010)

Secondary Works

Alsina, Claudi, Gaspar Feliu, and Lluís Marquet, *Pesos, mides i mesures dels Països Catalans* (Barcelona: Curial, 1990)

Barceló, Miquel, 'El diseño de espacios irrigados en al-Andalus: un enunciado de principios generales', in *El agua que no duerme. Fundamentos de la arqueología hidráulica andalusí*, ed. by Miquel Barceló, Helena Kirchner, and Carmen Navarro (Granada: El legado andalusí, 1996), pp. 51–71

Bazzana, André, and Johnny De Meulemeester, *La noria, l'aubergine et le fellah. Archéologie des espaces irrigués dans l'occident musulman médiéval (9e–15e siècles)* (Ghent: Academia Press, 2009)

Bolòs, Jordi, *Els orígens medievals del paisatge català. L'arqueologia com a font per a conèixer la història de Catalunya* (Barcelona: Institut d'Estudis Catalans, 2004)

Castillón Cortada, Francisco, 'Política hidráulica de templarios y sanjuanistas en el valle del Cinca (Huesca)', *Cuadernos de Historia Jerónimo Zurita*, 35–36 (1979), 381–445

Caucanas, Sylvie, *Moulins et irrigation en Roussillon du IXe au XVe siècle* (Paris: CNRS Éditions, 1995)

Cressier, Patrice, 'À propos des apports orientaux dans l'hydraulique agraire d'al-Andalus: observations sur le barrage', in *Spanien und der Orient im frühen und hohen Mittelalter*, ed. by Sabine Noack-Haley, Madrider Beiträge, 24 (Mainz: P. von Zabern, 1996), pp. 142–56

Eritja, Xavier, 'Assentaments i sistemas hidràulics a la vall del Sió', in *Paisatge i història en època medieval a la Catalunya Nova. Organització del territorio i societat a la vila d'Agramunt (Urgell) i a la vall del Sió (segles V–XIX)*, ed. by Jordi Bolòs (Lleida: Universitat de Lleida, 2002), pp. 181–88

Esquilache, Ferran, *Els constructors de l'Horta de València. Origen, evolució i estructura social d'una gran horta andalusina entre els segles VIII i XIII* (València: Publicacions de la Universitat de València, 2018)

Forey, Alan J., 'Notes on Irrigation in North-Eastern Spain during the XIIth and XIIIth Centuries', *Anuario de Estudios Medievales*, 17 (1987), 119–32

Glick, Thomas F., *Cristianos y musulmanes en la España medieval (711–1250)* (Madrid: Alianza Editorial, 1991)

González Villaescusa, Ricardo, *Las formas de los paisajes mediterráneos* (Jaén: Universidad de Jaén, 2002)

Gual Camarena, Miguel, *Estudio histórico-geográfico sobre la Acequia Real del Júcar* (València: Institución Alfonso el Magnánimo, 1979)

Guinot, Enric, '"Com en temps de sarraïns". La herencia andalusí en la huerta medieval de Valencia', in *Musulmanes y cristianos frente al agua en las ciudades medievales*, ed. by María I. del Val and Olatz Villanueva (Santander: Universidad de Cantabria, 2008), pp. 173–93

——, 'La construcción de nuevos espacios agrarios en el siglo XIII. Repartimientos y parcelarios de fundación en el reino de Valencia: Puçol y Vilafamés' in *Trigo y ovejas. El impacto de las conquistas en los paisajes andalusíes (siglos XI–XVI)*, ed. by Josep Torró and Enric Guinot (València: Publicacions de la Universitat de València, 2018), pp. 119–60

——, 'El paisaje de la Huerta de Valencia. Elementos de interpretación de su morfología espacial de origen medieval', in *Historia de la ciudad, V. Tradición y progreso* (València: Icaro, 2008), pp. 115–29

Guinot, Enric, and Ferran Esquilache, 'La reorganización del paisaje agrario en la huerta de Valencia después de la conquista cristiana. El sistema hidráulico de Montcada y Benifaraig en el siglo XIII', *Debates de Arqueología Medieval*, 2 (2010), 229–76

Guinot, Enric, and Sergi Selma, 'La construcción del paisaje en una huerta feudal: la Séquia Major de Vila-real (siglos XIII–XV)', in *Hidráulica agraria y sociedad feudal. Prácticas, técnicas, espacios*, ed. by Josep Torró and Enric Guinot (València: Publicacions de la Universitat de València, 2012), pp. 102–45

Hoffmann, Richard C., *An Environmental History of Medieval Europe* (Cambridge: Cambridge University Press, 2014)

Kirchner, Helena, 'Hidráulica campesina anterior a la generalización del dominio feudal. Casos en Cataluña', in *Hidráulica agraria y sociedad feudal. Prácticas, técnicas, espacios*, ed. by Josep Torró and Enric Guinot (València: Publicacions de la Universitat de València, 2012), pp. 21–50

Kirchner, Helena, Jaume Oliver, and Susanna Vela, *Aigua prohibida. Arqueología hidráulica del feudalisme a la Cerdanya. El Canal Reial de Puigcerdà* (Barcelona: Universitat Autònoma de Barcelona, 2002)

Laliena, Carlos, 'Agua y progreso social en Aragón, siglos XII-XVIII', in *¿Agua pasada? Regadíos en el Archivo Histórico Provincial de Zaragoza* (Zaragoza: Gobierno de Aragón: 2008), pp. 53–84

Marfull, Josep, 'Un sistema hidráulico feudal en el valle del Segre: la acequia de Torres', in *Irrigation, Society and Landscape: Tribute to Thomas F. Glick*, ed. by Carles Sanchis, Guillermo Palau, Ignasi Mangue, and Luís P. Martínez (València: Universitat Politècnica de València, 2014), pp. 155–71

Neuvonen, Eero K., *Los arabismos del español en el siglo XIII* (Helsinki: Societas Orientalis Fennica: 1941)

Ortega, Julián M., 'La agricultura de los vencedores y la agricultura de los vencidos: la investigación de las transformaciones feudales de los paisajes agrarios en el valle del Ebro (siglos XII–XIII)', in *Por una arqueología agraria. Perspectivas de investigación sobre espacios de cultivo en las sociedades medievales hispánicas*, ed. by Helena Kirchner, BAR International Series 2062 (Oxford: Archaeopress, 2010), pp. 123–45

Ortega, Julián M., and Laliena, Carlos, 'Formas feudales de especulación agraria: villas, viñas y acequias en el sur de Aragón (ca. 1170–1240)', in *Hidráulica agraria y sociedad feudal. Prácticas, técnicas, espacios*, ed. by Josep Torró and Enric Guinot (València: Publicacions de la Universitat de València, 2012), pp. 79–102

Torró, Josep, 'Agricultural Drainage Technology in Medieval Mediterranean Iberia (13th–16th Centuries)', in *Agrarian Technology in the Medieval Landscape*, ed. by Jan Klápště, Ruralia, 10 (Turnhout: Brepols, 2016), pp. 309–23

——, 'Canteros y niveladores. El problema de la transmisión de las técnicas hidráulicas andalusíes a las sociedades conquistadoras', *Miscelánea medieval murciana*, 37 (2013), 209–31

——, 'Field and Canal-Building after the Conquest: Modifications to the Cultivated Ecosystem in the Kingdom of Valencia, ca. 1250–ca. 1350', in *Worlds of History and Economics: Essays in Honour of Andrew M. Watson*, ed. by Brian A. Catlos (València: Publicacions de la Universitat de València, 2009), pp. 77–108

——, 'Paisajes de frontera: conquistas cristianas y transformaciones agrarias (siglos XII al XIV)', *Edad Media. Revista de Historia*, 20 (2019), 13–46

FABRIZIO PAGNONI

Canal-Digging in the Age of Economic Expansion

Northern Italy, Eleventh–Thirteenth Centuries

Premise

The abundance of research devoted to water management in the Po Valley has clearly demonstrated the importance of the relationship between people and water in the economic, social, and environmental history of this region, both in Antiquity and from the Middle Ages onwards. In the last two decades, however, this rich tradition of studies has undergone an important renewal, due in particular to the stimulus provided by the latest international research trends: it is worth mentioning here the important question of the management and transformation of the commons during the Middle Ages;[1] the prolific field of so-called 'disaster studies';[2] and environmental history.[3] Nevertheless, Italian studies lag behind other European regions, especially when it comes to the interaction between history and archaeology. Compared to Spain, for example, where hydraulic archaeology has enabled scholars to cast light on important medieval phenomena (for example, the development and transformation of *huertas* in urban and suburban areas), an archaeological approach to the analysis of canals and ditches is relatively undeveloped in Italy, although important advances have been made in recent years.[4]

The aim of this study is to reconsider this rich historiographical tradition by focusing on the relationship between economic development and investment in the hydraulic projects that characterized the Po Valley (and, broadly speaking, northern Italy), beginning in the central centuries of the Middle Ages. For this purpose, I will concentrate my analysis on the development of the network of canals, rather than focusing exclusively on the problem of irrigation: this

1 Alfani and Rao, eds, *La gestione delle risorse collettive* (with special reference to the essays devoted in this volume to collective resources in wetlands).

2 See at least Matheus, Piccinni, Pinto, and Varanini, eds, *Le calamità ambientali*; Bianca and Salvestrini, eds, *L'acqua nemica*.

3 Rao, *I paesaggi dell'Italia medievale*.

4 See Ardizio, 'La rete irrigua medievale', pp. 125–28; Labate, 'Archeologia delle acque'.

Fabrizio Pagnoni is professor in the department of Historical Studies at the University of Milan, where he obtained his PhD.

Building and Economic Growth in Southern Europe (1050–1300), ed. by Sandro Carocci and Alessio Fiore, (Turnhout: Brepols, 2024), pp. 101–119 BREPOLS PUBLISHERS 10.1484/M.TMC-EB.5.137976

may be self-evident, but I feel the point should be clarified since agricultural needs were only one (although certainly the most important) of the factors favouring the development of the network of hydraulic infrastructure in the period under review. While agricultural expansion was one incentive for canalization work, for the purposes of drainage (expulsion of the water) or irrigation (and therefore its conduction and division between those who made use of the resource), other factors were equally relevant. These included the need to use water in the production of energy to power the main urban and rural economic infrastructure; and the use of canals for transportation purposes, especially in the direction of the river Po, the area's major commercial route throughout the Middle Ages.[5]

Phases

It has been clearly demonstrated that the network of hydraulic infrastructure first appeared in this region in the early Middle Ages and reached its peak between the fifteenth and sixteenth centuries. Several studies have however helped to identify the twelfth century as a pivotal moment between two quite different stages of development, which François Menant termed respectively the 'age of premises' and the 'age of generalization' of canal excavations in the Po Valley.[6] In other words, the twelfth century has been established as a watershed between two stages of hydraulic initiatives and investments that can be differentiated on at least three levels:

- **Type of initiative:** before the twelfth century the main incentive was principally the need to expel water (not only by canalization but also through specific agricultural practices);[7] while from the twelfth century onwards, water management schemes (not only for irrigation purposes) became more systematic both around urban centres and in the countryside.

- **Scale of initiative:** the first phase was mainly characterized by numerous small-scale operations, sometimes built on what remained of the ancient network of channels from the Roman period. Thereafter, canalizations were pivoted or reshaped based on a network that was gradually provided with large 'axes', in the context of a broader planning and territorial projection.

- **Key figures involved:** despite there being a wide range of potential stakeholders interested in investing in the water regime (ecclesiastical institutions, lay owners, political powers), in the twelfth century we have

5 In the following pages, I shall mention only a small number of other important factors analysed by scholars, such as urban canalization works designed for water supply and wastewater discharge, or canals and ditches built for military purposes.

6 Menant, *Campagnes lombardes*, pp. 182–93.

7 Squatriti, *Water and Society*, p. 78.

documentary evidence of the emerging role played in this field by the rural aristocracy but also and most importantly (from the second half of the century) by the commune. This last factor transformed the status quo, due to the ambition and the quality of the power exercised by urban governments in the reorganization of the hydraulic system within their district.

This periodization, widely agreed upon by historians (although with inevitable local variations), is based chiefly on the intensive use of written records. At present, there are no grounds to fully reject this interpretation; nevertheless, I think it is important to emphasize that, in recent years, archaeology has provided important evidence which justifies a re-evaluation of this chronology of developments. Recent excavations have uncovered indications of relevant canalization work undertaken prior to the twelfth century: these appear to be particularly concentrated in areas where those involved in this type of initiative tended to belong to the highest political and social spheres of the time. This is for example the case with Vetricella, the administrative heart of the *curtis regia* of Valli, which flourished between the ninth and the first decades of the eleventh century as a centre for the storage of goods and the processing of metals extracted from Elba and from the Colline Metallifere. At the same time, the *curtis* was undergoing a process of environmental transformation, which also included an intense hydraulic reorganization of the area. As has been noted by scholars, royal, comital, or marchional powers must have been behind an initiative of this scale.[8]

This relationship between the persistence of the *publicum* and the possibility of pursuing significant hydraulic transformation schemes (in the context of political and economic projection on, at least, a regional scale) is indeed a promising line of investigation, with a number of relevant cases in the Po Valley.[9] It is no coincidence, for example, that one of the oldest pieces of evidence of major canalization in this region is that of the *Fossa Bonifacia*, a navigable canal that was commissioned by the marquis Boniface of Canossa in the first half of the eleventh century. This canal connected the Po to the Tartaro River at Ostiglia, and its construction should be viewed as part of a strategy to reinforce political, territorial, and economic control over the region.[10]

8 Bianchi and Tomei, 'Risorse e contesti insediativi', pp. 160–62.

9 In this perspective, a comparison with the undertakings conceived in the previous centuries is interesting. See for example the *fossatum magnum* between the Rhine and the Danube planned in the late eighth century: Werther and others, '792 or 793? Charlemagne's Canal Project'.

10 Fumagalli, *Storie di Val Padana*, p. 53; Castagnetti, *L'organizzazione del territorio*, pp. 201–02.

Key Players

When focusing on the period examined in this article, it is useful to begin by seeking to determine the kind of people who were involved in this type of transformation and structural investment. The almost limitless amount of documentary evidence concerning hydraulic interventions in the Po Valley between the eleventh and twelfth centuries shows quite clearly that such enterprises, far from being monopolized by one particular social group, were in fact promoted by a range of figures from different backgrounds, albeit with some diversification of type and scale.[11] However, it is possible to identify at least four distinctive features that combined to intensify the impact and ambition of these initiatives; although they did not always necessarily exist concurrently, these factors contributed to the increased significance of the scale of hydraulic investments:

- The possession of privileged water rights.
- The quality and extent of the political power exercised by those involved in these initiatives.
- The amount of resources (not merely financial, but also material: capacity to mobilize men and goods) available to underpin these projects.
- The interest in and ability to address the growing needs of rapidly expanding markets (and especially the urban ones).

Between the eleventh and twelfth centuries, the most relevant canalization enterprises seem to have been concentrated in peri-urban areas, as well as in those parts of the countryside where the presence of the rural lordship was strongest. Just outside the city walls, the digging of canals was stimulated by urban property owners (who did not necessarily belong to the highest ranks of the local aristocracy), often in co-partnership, or at least co-existing with the hydraulic schemes promoted by urban ecclesiastical institutions. In Milan, for example, hydraulic investments were directed — at least until the middle of the twelfth century — towards those areas of the suburbs where water was abundant and immediately available (i.e. the south and west of the city), and where there was a larger number of urban properties.[12] In Bergamo, by the tenth century, a number of hydraulic systems were already in operation to irrigate vegetable gardens and orchards on the outskirts of the city, probably making use of surviving Roman-era canals. However, an important transformation occurred in the second half of the eleventh century: the western and south-western environs of the city were fully irrigated and cultivated thanks to investments made by the local aristocracy and the urban

11 Cortonesi, 'Introduzione'; Panero, 'Canali, fossi, rittani'.

12 Chiappa Mauri, *I mulini ad acqua*; Grillo, *Milano in età comunale*.

ecclesiastical institutions.[13] In Verona (where the hydrography was less favourable to the development of canals along the Adige river) the growth of urban demand encouraged the early establishment of a manufacturing centre close to the city, along the banks of the Fibbio river. As early as the beginning of the twelfth century, this area was crisscrossed by canals that powered water mills controlled by families belonging to the upper ranks of the city's social and political hierarchy.[14]

Outside the cities, the secular and ecclesiastical lordships were often keen to capitalize on the business opportunities resulting from the hydraulic development of the countryside. As recent research has emphasized, these initiatives must be examined in a broader perspective, given the profound redefinition of local powers and forms of domination and dependence which characterized those centuries, the scale of their ambition and territorial projection; nevertheless, the *domini loci* do not appear to have been ignorant of the opportunities provided by this growth in demand.[15]

This was true of Argenta, for example, where the investments carried out at the end of the eleventh century by the local lord (the bishop of Ravenna) must be viewed in the light of his desire to transform the village into the centre of episcopal control over the surrounding territory. At the same time they testify to the aim of making Argenta the central point for the exploitation of the local marshes, thanks to the network of canals that branched off from there.[16] A clear link between economic enhancement through hydraulic investments and the redefinition of the seigneurial power over peasants can also be seen in the agreement reached between the abbey of Nonantola and the rural community of Crevalcore. In the late twelfth century, the generous franchises granted by the abbot to his *homines* residing in Crevalcore came with the condition that they develop the already existing network of canals, which was augmented by the digging of other canals and the construction of mills. The peasants were also required to pay the abbot one-third of the annual income generated by the exploitation of these new infrastructures.[17]

Agreements of this kind might encourage the rural communities themselves to take a leading role in the process, even if not always successfully, as illustrated by what occurred between the canonry of S. Vincenzo, in Bergamo, and the *homines* of Calcinate. Under an initial agreement in 1148, the canons (who were the lords of the village) pledged to invest in the digging of an irrigation ditch, which the community would benefit from in exchange for a commitment to maintain it. Later, the peasants autonomously extended the waterway in the direction of Cavernago, but the high cost of upkeep forced

13 Menant, *Campagnes lombardes*.

14 Varanini, 'Energia idraulica'.

15 Cortese, *L'aristocrazia Toscana*, p. 279 draws attention to the relationship between the extent of the powers exercised by the lords and the quality of the economic investments carried out by them.

16 Fiore, *Il mutamento signorile*, pp. 77–78.

17 Rinaldi, 'La disciplina', p. 26.

them to quickly sell their part of the new canal, which was duly bought by the canons of S. Vincenzo.[18]

Besides these individual cases, the documentation of the period contains useful information for an overall assessment of the phenomenon. Firstly, a correlation can be identified between resources and type of initiatives: the greater the scale of the excavation scheme, the fewer the entrepreneurs with the necessary means (economic or otherwise) to carry them out. Secondly, these initiatives, together with the changes in land properties and management, contributed to the transformation of the hierarchies of the rural environment. Studies of this development have been undertaken for example for the countryside around Milan, where between the twelfth and thirteenth centuries small rural properties disappeared, to be replaced by extensively irrigated estates in the hands of lay owners and ecclesiastical bodies with considerable financial means.[19] The Cistercian granges provide a privileged viewpoint from which to analyse this phenomenon: in the countryside south of Milan, the hydraulic initiatives at Morimondo and Chiaravalle radically restructured the pre-existing habitats (which had hitherto been organized around modest, scattered settlements, that were easier to re-shape than in other parts of the region).[20] This new situation sometimes led to intense disputes with local communities: we have evidence of this occurring at the abbey of Lucedio (south of Vercelli) where the Cistercians' investment in the hydraulic infrastructure on their large estates faced opposition from other prominent local figures (lords, rural communities, other ecclesiastic institutions) whose canals, grasslands, and properties were negatively impacted by the transformations to the hydraulic system instigated by the monks.[21]

Lastly, the disputes over the use of canalized water reported in twelfth-century documents provide a picture of a network that was becoming increasingly dense, and in which the problem of the different uses of water and the hierarchization of activities supported by the infrastructure was particularly evident. We need only think of the well-known disagreements arising from the coexistence of milling activities and expanding irrigation systems, which led to friction between the owners or usufructuaries of the canals over the practices and methods of water exploitation.[22] Written records, especially in the communal period (late twelfth century onwards), also often bear witness to the need to limit or regulate diversions and dams on natural and artificial watercourses whose navigability had to be preserved.[23]

---

18 Menant, *Campagnes lombardes*, p. 295.

19 Grillo, *Milano in età comunale*.

20 Grillo, *Milano in età comunale*, pp. 94–96; Rapetti, *Campagne milanesi*, pp. 99–103; Chiappa Mauri, 'I cisterciensi e le acque'.

21 Bellero, 'I cistercensi e il paesaggio rurale'.

22 For the Milanese countryside, see Chiodi, 'Conflitti per l'uso delle acque'; Rapetti, *Campagne milanesi*.

23 See for example Rinaldi, 'La normativa', pp. 157–58.

Communal Intervention

It was against the background of this growing tension that, at least in some contexts, the urban powers began to have an impact. In Milan and Bergamo, for example, in the central decades of the twelfth century, leading urban groups took on a significant, albeit discreet role as arbitrators between private parties in disputes concerning the use of water and canals in various areas of the countryside. In Milan, Lombardy's largest city, the surviving consular documentation suggests that water management was one of the main issues brought before urban courts (at least forty-six interventions by consuls over issues about water rights survive for the years 1117–1216).[24] Undoubtedly, arbitrating between particular groups or individuals had a role in shaping the prominence and ambition of the communes as the regulator of the urban and rural economic environment. As scholars have emphasized, this role became more extensive in the second half of the century, especially following the granting of concessions to the communes at the Peace of Constance (1183), which further galvanized the role of urban governments in this field.[25] The following list, containing a small number of the most prominent cases, might help to give an idea of the acceleration in hydraulic initiatives generated by the 'communal factor' from the second half of the twelfth century until the end of the following century. From the 1170s onwards, significant additions were made to Milan's network of ditches in the direction of the Ticino, built at the time of the wars against Barbarossa; this canal network underwent further expansion in the middle of the thirteenth century, when the *Naviglio grande* was made fully navigable.[26] In eastern Lombardy, the city of Cremona made vast investments to provide itself with a navigable canal (1231), while Brescia renovated an existing *navigium* extracted from the Chiese River and directed towards the city (1253).[27] In these same decades, the connection between the Serio and Brembo was completed in the countryside around Bergamo, and new canals were dug (the Morla, the Morlana), at the same time as new rural settlements were being founded;[28] in Lodi, the municipality invested in extending the course of the Muzza southwards to Castiglione d'Adda.[29] Challenging work was also carried out in Mantua in 1191 (with the modification of the course of the Mincio and the creation of lakes);[30] Verona in 1196 (when the course of the Bussè River was diverted to allow the drainage

24 Chiodi, 'Conflitti per l'uso delle acque'. On the role played by Milanese aristocracies in legal disputes at that time see Wickham, *Sleepwalking into a New World*.

25 Balestracci, 'La politica delle acque', pp. 437–38; Rao, *I beni del comune*, pp. 45–46; Menant and Campopiano, 'Agricolture irrigue', pp. 301–03.

26 Biscaro, 'Gli antichi "navigli"', pp. 300–09.

27 Greci, 'Le città navigabili', p. 192; Balestrieri, 'Le acque e la loro utilizzazione'.

28 Menant, *Campagnes lombardes*.

29 An overview is to be found in Albini, 'L'ospedale del Brolo', pp. 10–16.

30 Vaini, 'Il controllo delle terre e delle acque'.

of the *Palus communis*);[31] Padua (with the creation of the canal between the city and Monselice in 1189 and the Piovego canal in 1209);[32] Bologna (whose government from the beginning of the thirteenth century extended its control over the Reno sluice and the waterways leading to the city)[33] as well as in Modena and Parma.

As mentioned above, these hydraulic undertakings testify to the ability of urban governments to plan initiatives on a wide scale: most of these were ambitious projects, covering large areas (up to several dozen kilometres) and involving a thorough redesign of the hydraulic system. The projects carried out by municipalities encompassed a wide spectrum of possibilities, ranging from cooperation with private water rights holders to schemes directly promoted by the urban government. These initiatives not only had a material impact: they also had institutional and legal implications that contributed to the reinforcement and definition of the eminent role of the municipalities in the management of canalized waters. Scholars have looked in detail at the process of the statutory definition of water control regulations at both city and district level, which urban governments sought to pursue through the direct involvement of rural communities in the construction, maintenance, and safeguarding of the water supply network, as well as setting up special offices entrusted with territorial and water monitoring tasks.[34] In addition to this, however, a more discreet, but no less important policy was being pursued: during the thirteenth century, the municipalities sought to increase their power of supervision and control over private associations that held water rights and canals (such as consortia that brought together all those who made use of a single canal) by attempting to acquire from them part of those rights or by imposing the control and approval of the statutes of these consortia by the communal authorities.[35]

Urban Governments, Canals, Economic Growth

The relationship between the canalization work undertaken in the twelfth and thirteenth centuries and the whole economic scenario of the time was multifaceted. Undoubtedly, the increasing demand for food resources by cities with rapidly growing populations played a decisive role in encouraging hydraulic enterprises oriented towards the exploitation of land and its cultivation. Urban governments were certainly attentive in this field, but their initiatives need to be carefully assessed and calibrated if they are not to

31 Castagnetti, 'Primi aspetti di politica annonaria'.
32 Orlando, 'Governo delle acque'.
33 Balestracci, 'La politica delle acque', p. 442; Mangolini, 'Le chiuse di Casalecchio di Reno'.
34 Campopiano, 'Gestione ordinaria'; see also the essays collected in the volume *Acque di frontiera*.
35 See for example the statutes of the Nirone (Milan, *c.* 1260): *Gli statuti delle strade e delle acque*, pp. 81–85.

be misinterpreted. On the one hand, the canalization which commenced in this phase reshaped the geography and hierarchy of agrarian transformations and made it possible to continue with the drainage and cultivation of areas marginal to the villages, even on the high plains. As stated above, this vast system of canals, precisely because of its capacity, was to constitute the real 'heart' of the irrigation network in a large part of the Po Valley, right up until the nineteenth century.[36] On the other hand, the intensive use of irrigation differed in time and intensity in the area: it began earlier and was more pronounced in western Lombardy, where in the thirteenth century the value of irrigated terrain surpassed that of arable land and the owners of the large irrigated estates were able to send substantial quantities of produce to the Milanese market. Bonvesin de la Riva, for example, estimated that the monks of Chiaravalle drew at least 3000 cartloads of hay from their irrigated meadows, which they sold in Milan.[37] In eastern Lombardy, by contrast, the exploitation of the canal network for irrigation purposes (and in particular the development of grassland) was more limited and experienced a major expansion only from the second half of the fourteenth century (particularly in the fifteenth and sixteenth centuries).[38]

Alongside the demand for foodstuffs from urban markets, it was demographic and territorial control policies which provided an important stimulus for ambitious hydraulic initiatives. This is evident in the famous case of the Veronese *campanea maior* and *palus communis*, an area whose reclamation and conversion to cropland (and grassland, central to the development of the city's wool manufacturing industry)[39] went hand in hand with the founding of new settlements (the most important of which was Villafranca), thus conferring upon this initiative a high political value in the sphere of communal control of the district.[40] A similar combination of purposes can be found in other contemporary hydraulic enterprises, such as that of Cremona, where the commune founded (or re-founded) *borghifranchi* (i.e. Ticengo and Romanengo) in a key area of the local hydrographic system; this was also of great political importance as it was the source of major conflicts with the neighbouring cities of Brescia and Bergamo over the control of the Oglio River. Here, Cremona developed its control over the existing canals, which were gradually transformed into a navigable waterway.[41]

36 Roveda, 'Il beneficio delle acque', p. 260. Menant, Campopiano, 'Agricolture irrigue'.

37 Menant and Campopiano, 'Agricolture irrigue'. For the Milanese, besides the other essays mentioned above, see Andenna, 'Dall'irrigazione dei prati', and Bertoni, 'Le campagne lombarde'.

38 Menant, *Campagnes lombardes*; Varanini, 'Per la storia agraria', pp. 90–93; on this late medieval expansion, with particular emphasis on the important role played by rural communities, see also d'Arcangelo, *Anatomia di un territorio*, pp. 85–100. See also Chittolini, 'Alle origini delle "grandi aziende"'.

39 Castagnetti, 'Primi aspetti di politica annonaria'; Varanini, 'Energia idraulica'.

40 Castagnetti, 'La pianura veronese'.

41 Menant, *Campagnes lombardes*.

If we move our attention from the countryside to urban and suburban areas, we observe that it was principally the need for power sources for mills and manufactories that inspired major canalization initiatives.[42] In contrast to the countryside, where the great pressure on water resources was chiefly determined by the conflict between agricultural needs and the use of water to power the wheels of the mills, in the city the source of major disputes was the coexistence of different activities based on diverse water uses. The problem can be understood, for example, by looking at the thirteenth-century statutes concerning the use of canals and water, which reveal the complex interplay between the interests of landowners (or grain mill owners) and proprietors of other expanding enterprises, such as textiles or leather-making, which required increasing amounts of water to power fulling mills and process raw materials.[43] The communes attempted to respond to this pressure by encouraging the zoning of economic activities, for example by locating those which were most polluting along canals or rivers expressly designated for these enterprises. In any case, urban and suburban canalization contributed to the polarization of the local manufactories: in thirteenth-century Brescia, the westward expansion of the city walls was accompanied by a series of diversions from the Garza River through the area of new growth. Over the following decades, the *domus* of the Umiliati engaged in textile production and other important manufacturing enterprises (such as shoemaking, wool processing, etc.) which sprang up along the banks of these canals.[44]

In addition to the energy supply required for the manufacturing infrastructure, the increased needs of urban markets encouraged new initiatives to connect cities with the region's fluvial network. The construction of navigable canals (to facilitate connections with specific areas of the countryside but, above all, to provide access to the main commercial routes in the Po Valley and the Adriatic) was the objective of ambitious and not always successful, but nevertheless significant communal policies.[45] In the Veneto region, Padua was perhaps the most emblematic case in terms of the dynamism and extent of modifications to the local hydrography. After an initial diversion of the Brenta River in 1142 to facilitate connections with the Venetian Lagoon, in 1209 the excavation of an artificial canal (the Piovego) from the Brenta made it possible to connect the Bacchiglione River with the Brenta and thus speed up communications with Venice.[46] Viability and commercial interests often overlapped, as is evident in the case of Mantua: here, the work carried out on the course of the Mincio River and coordinated by the engineer Alberto

42 See for example the case of Bologna (Pini, 'Porti, canali e mulini'; Rinaldi, 'La normativa') and Reggio (Fabbrici, 'Il governo delle acque', pp. 85–86).

43 Grillo, *Milano in età comunale*, pp. 215–17; Andenna, 'Dall'irrigazione dei prati', pp. 133–34. In general, see Franceschi and Taddei, *Le città italiane*, p. 96.

44 Balestrieri, 'Le acque e la loro utilizzazione'; Archetti, 'Gli Umiliati', pp. 271–73.

45 Greci, 'Le città navigabili'.

46 Orlando, 'Governo delle acque'.

Pitentino from Bergamo paved the way for the inception (from 1191) of the *nundinae*, the annual urban fairs open to neighbouring cities.[47] In Milan, the thirteenth-century enlargement of several canals, in particular the Naviglio Grande (which had originally been dug for military purposes in the years of the wars against Frederick I) should be considered in the light of the concomitant commercial agreements that the Lombard city made with Venice and other powers in the region.[48]

The waterways were also able to meet the increasing need for the transport of building materials to supply the growing number of urban construction sites. A clear example of this is the crucial role played by the Naviglio Grande from the end of the fourteenth century in bringing materials for the building of Milan Cathedral;[49] waterways however already performed this key function in previous centuries. From the twelfth century, for example, there is evidence of a *navigium* derived from the Chiese River and flowing close to the eastern walls of Brescia. It may have been a Roman or late antique construction, as suggested by the scant archaeological data available concerning a dock discovered along the course of the canal, just outside the city gate.[50] This *navigium* (later known as the Naviglio Grande, or Naviglio Bresciano) was enlarged and renewed in the mid-thirteenth century by the urban government, for transportation purposes: much of the timber extracted from the Val Sabbia was brought into the city by this route, and a flourishing extractive operation (sand and gravel) is attested along its southern bank, undoubtedly destined for the urban market.[51] The story of this canal helps us to understand how waterways of this kind must be carefully considered in their historical evolution, together with local social and economic structures. In this case, for example, despite communal investments, the use of the Naviglio as a transport route gradually declined over the following centuries, while its importance for agricultural and irrigation purposes increased: this occurred from the end of the fourteenth century onwards, as a result of investments made above all by major urban landowners who were more interested in the agrarian development of the *alta pianura* of Brescia.[52]

Technical issues were another factor that might contribute to changes in the way canals were used, either as transport routes or as agricultural infrastructure: large hydraulic structures in this area had to cope not only the more traditional maintenance requirements, but also with the hydrogeological complexity of the Po valley. This has been observed for example in the case of Parma: during the thirteenth century, the commune invested significant resources in extending a canal towards Coenzo, to connect the city with

47 Vaini, 'Il controllo delle terre e delle acque'; Gardoni, 'Uomini e acque'.

48 Mainoni, 'La fisionomia economica'.

49 Grillo, *Nascita di una cattedrale*.

50 Brogiolo, *Brescia altomedievale*, p. 55.

51 Balestrieri, 'Le acque e la loro utilizzazione', pp. 1092–93.

52 Balestrieri, 'Le acque e la loro utilizzazione'; Menant, *Campagnes lombardes*.

the Po River. Here again, the undertaking was probably responding to the transportation needs associated with the development of urban buildings: a possible link has been identified between the new canal and the start of work on the construction of the Baptistery, which required precious red marble from quarries located in the Veronese district. However, the venture had to be hastily abandoned due to challenging technical problems, particularly the silting up of the estuary as a consequence of the insufficient slope of the canal in its lower course.[53]

Techniques

The case of the Naviglio of Parma brings to light the technical implications of hydraulic transformations in the Middle Ages. Due to the lack of archaeological research carried out in the Lombard area, it is difficult to assess to what extent the social and economic transformations related to water exploitation influenced the adoption of specific hydraulic technologies, as was the case in other European regions.[54] The problem is a complex one, and traditionally scholars have tended to attribute the hydraulic development of the twelfth and thirteenth centuries to the increased number of digging initiatives rather than to improved technical knowledge.[55] In conclusion, however, I would like to highlight at least a few aspects of the issues addressed in this chapter.

The development of the hydraulic network had considerable technical, material, and management implications. There is not space here to discuss these aspects on a local scale, but it is important to remember how, in the communal period, the growth of the secondary hydraulic network (that brought water from the major arteries to the smaller derivations directed towards grasslands, mills, and other structures) encouraged greater attention to ensure the coexistence of canals and overland infrastructures. This in turn led urban governments and rural communities to draw up a series of regulations requiring, for example, the construction of bridges and overpasses (often built with stone) near canal crossings; the embankment of canals with durable materials in proximity to public roads; the establishment of the obligations of owners of canals that intersected public routes to ensure regular maintenance of embankments, roads, and bridges, etc.[56]

---

53 Greci, *Le città navigabili.*

54 In this perspective, the most important case-study is probably that of medieval Al-Andalus: see Kirchner, 'Archeologia degli spazi irrigati'; Furió, 'De la hidràulica andalusí a la feudal'.

55 See for example Menant, *Campagnes lombardes*, p. 188.

56 Some examples from thirteenth- and fourteenth-century statutes: Chiappa Mauri, *I mulini ad acqua*, pp. 86–87; Andenna, 'Dall'irrigazione dei prati', p. 135; Galetti, 'La disciplina delle acque', pp. 46–47.

The technical and material implications are even more evident if we turn our attention to the major canalization projects carried out (or at least conceived) during the communal period. The complexity of these operations concerned first and foremost the problem of their funding, as they required significant economic resources: in 1253, the commune of Brescia paid 100 *lire* only for the recruitment of the *magister* in charge of reconstructing the offshoot of the Naviglio Grande from the Chiese River: this sum did not include the cost of building materials, which the municipality promised to provide separately.[57] In the same period, in Milan, a group of investors led by the monastery of Chiaravalle invested over 300 *lire* in a hydraulic project between Porta Tosa and the Pusterla della Chiusa, near the city walls.[58] These examples clearly illustrate that this type of undertaking required significant financial resources and should be viewed in connection with the development of specific municipal government strategies to amass the financial resources (and, in some cases, the men and goods) required to complete these initiatives.[59]

Due to their complexity, these projects required specific and unusual knowledge: something more, in other words, than the know-how shared widely by rural and urban communities of the time, accumulated over the centuries of interaction between people and water that typified a wetland region such as the Po Valley. Between the twelfth and thirteenth centuries, we begin to find documentary references to engineers (*inzinerii*): these were highly-valued and therefore often itinerant figures, equipped with significant technical expertise, whose guidance was key to the coordination of the ambitious projects undertaken by urban governments.[60] The list of these engineers is fairly well known, including Alberto Pitentino, who carried out some of the most important hydraulic operations in Mantua and Bergamo at the end of the twelfth century;[61] *magister* Guintelmo and his heirs, who were a dynasty of *inzinerii* active in the construction of the new urban ditches and canals in Milan and Piacenza;[62] and donno Gnolo from Siena, a monk from St Galgano (and therefore a member of a religious community deeply interested in the hydraulic transformation of the Sienese territory) and a consultant to the Tuscan commune in its scheme to divert the Merse River in the second half of the thirteenth century.[63] The itinerant nature of the work of these experts in hydraulics should also be viewed in relation to the way communal officials moved from place to place, a phenomenon that has been widely studied in terms of its political and institutional

57 *Liber potheris*, cols 824–27.
58 Boucheron, 'Water and Power in Milan'.
59 Campopiano, 'Gestione ordinaria'.
60 Menant, *Campagnes lombardes*, pp. 189–90.
61 De Sanctis, 'Alberto Pitentino'.
62 Biscaro, 'Gli antichi "navigli"', pp. 308, 322.
63 Cortese, *L'acqua, il grano, il ferro*, p. 113.

implications, also with reference to the territorial governmental measures adopted by the various communes in the region.[64] This was also true of major hydraulic projects: it is no coincidence, for example, that some of the most important initiatives undertaken in Padua and Verona at the end of the twelfth century were promoted by Guglielmo da Osa of Milan, an itinerant *podestà* hailing from one of the areas boasting the greatest hydraulic development at the time.[65] Nevertheless, the role played by these technical experts and the circulation of hydraulic know-how in communal Italy must always be viewed in relation to the increased ability to coordinate men and resources that municipal governments, especially during the thirteenth century, were able to guarantee for such enterprises.

64 Saggioro and Varanini, *Insediamento umano*, p. 106.

65 Orlando, 'Governo delle acque', p. 260; Castagnetti, 'La pianura veronese', p. 76.

Works Cited

Primary Sources

Liber potheris communis civitatis Brixie, in *Historia patriae monumenta edita iussu Regis Caroli Alberti*, vol. 19 (Turin: Fratelli Bocca, 1899)

Gli statuti delle strade e delle acque del contado di Milano, ed. by Antonio Stella (Milan: LED, 1992)

Secondary Works

Albini, Giuliana, 'L'ospedale del Brolo di Milano e i diritti sulle acque della Muzza (sec. XIII)', in *Milano medioevale. Studi per Elisa Occhipinti*, ed. by Giuliana Albini (Milan: Pearson, 2018), pp. 3–33

Alfani, Guido, and Riccardo Rao, eds, *La gestione delle risorse collettive. Italia settentrionale, secoli XII–XVIII* (Milan: Franco Angeli, 2011)

Andenna, Giancarlo, 'Dall'irrigazione dei prati all'arte della lana, dalla terra al commercio. L'economia del borgo di Monza in età medievale attraverso i suoi statuti', in *Gli statuti medievali di Monza. Saggi critici*, ed. by Antonio Padoa Schioppa (Milan: Motta, 1993), pp. 129–49

Archetti, Gabriele, 'Gli Umiliati e i vescovi alla fine del Duecento. Il caso bresciano', in *Sulle tracce degli Umiliati*, ed. by Maria Pia Alberzoni, Annamaria Ambrosioni, and Alfredo Lucioni (Milan: Vita e Pensiero, 1997), pp. 267–314

Ardizio, Gabriele, 'La rete irrigua medievale tra Sesia e Cervo', in *I paesaggi fluviali della Sesia fra storia e archeologia. Territori, insediamenti, rappresentazioni*, ed. by Riccardo Rao (Florence: All'insegna del Giglio, 2016), pp. 125–44

Balestracci, Duccio, 'La politica delle acque urbane nell'Italia comunale', *Mélanges de l'École française de Rome. Moyen-Age*, 104.2 (1992), 431–79

Balestrieri, Enrico, 'Le acque e la loro utilizzazione', in *Storia di Brescia*, IV, *Dalla Repubblica bresciana ai giorni nostri: 1797–1963* (Brescia: Morcelliana, 1964), pp. 1085–105

Bellero, Marisa, 'I cistercensi e il paesaggio rurale. L'abbazia di S. Maria di Lucedio fra il XII e il XV secolo', *Studi Storici*, 26.2 (1985), 337–51

Bertoni, Laura, 'Le campagne lombarde nel primo Trecento. Rilettura di un caso "eccezionale"', in *La congiuntura del primo Trecento in Lombardia (1290-1360)*, ed. by Paolo Grillo and François Menant (Rome: École française de Rome, 2019), pp. 209–37

Bianca, Concetta, and Francesco Salvestrini, eds, *L'acqua nemica. Fumi, inondazioni e città storiche dall'antichità al contemporaneo* (Spoleto: Centro italiano di studi sull'alto medioevo, 2017)

Bianchi, Giovanna, and Paolo Tomei, 'Risorse e contesti insediativi nelle Colline Metallifere altomedievali: il possibile ruolo dell'allume', in *I paesaggi dell'allume. Archeologia della produzione ed economia di rete*, ed. by Luisa Dallai, Giovanna Bianchi, and Francesca Romana Stasolla (Florence: All'insegna del Giglio, 2020), pp. 155–66

Biscaro, Gerolamo, 'Gli antichi "navigli" milanesi', *Archivio Storico Lombardo*, 35 (1908), 285–326

Boucheron, Patrick, 'Water and Power in Milan, c. 1200–1500', *Urban History*, 28 (2001), 180–93

Brogiolo, Gian Pietro, *Brescia altomedievale. Urbanistica ed edilizia dal IV al IX secolo* (Mantua: Società Archeologica Padana, 1993)

Campopiano, Michele, 'Gestione ordinaria delle acque e rischi idrogeologici. L'amministrazione delle acque nella Pianura Padana tra esigenze energetiche, trasporti, irrigazione e rischi di inondazione (secoli XII–XV)', in *Gestione dell'acqua in Europa (XII–XVIII secc.). Water Management in Europe (12th–18th Centuries)* (Florence: Florence University Press, 2018), pp. 25–40

Castagnetti, Andrea, *L'organizzazione del territorio rurale nel Medioevo* (Bologna: Patron, 1982)

——, 'La pianura veronese nel medioevo. La conquista del suolo e la regolamentazione delle acque', in *Una città e il suo fiume. Verona e l'Adige*, ed. by Giorgio Borelli (Verona: Banca popolare di Verona, 1977), I, pp. 33–138

——, 'Primi aspetti di politica annonaria nell'Italia comunale. La bonifica della *palus communis Verone* (1194–1199)', *Studi medievali*, s. III, 15 (1974), 363–81

Chiappa Mauri, Luisa, 'I cistercensi e le acque in Lombardia', *Quaderni dell'abbazia*, 6 (1999), 45–53

——, *I mulini ad acqua nel milanese (secoli X–XV)* (Rome: Dante Alighieri, 1984)

Chiodi, Giovanni, 'Conflitti per l'uso delle acque nella Milano del XII secolo', in *L'acqua nei secoli altomedievali*. Atti della LV Settimana di studio del Centro italiano di studi sull'alto medioevo Spoleto 12–17 aprile 2007 (Spoleto: Centro italiano di studi sull'alto medioevo, 2008), pp. 505–82

Chittolini, Giorgio, 'Alle origini delle "grandi aziende" della bassa lombarda. L'agricoltura dell'irriguo fra XV e XVI secolo', *Quaderni storici*, 39 (1978), 828–44

Cortese, Maria Elena, *L'acqua, il grano, il ferro. Opifici idraulici medievali nel bacino Farma-Merse* (Florence: All'Insegna del Giglio, 1997)

——, *L'aristocrazia toscana. Sette secoli (VI–XII)* (Spoleto: Centro italiano di studi sull'alto medioevo, 2017)

Cortonesi, Alfio, 'Introduzione. Note sugli elementi ordinatori di alcuni paesaggi italiani (secc. XIII–XV)', in *I paesaggi agrari d'Europa (secoli XIII–XV)*. Ventiquattresimo Convegno Internazionali di Studi (Pistoia maggio 2013) (Rome: Viella, 2015), pp. 1–32

d'Arcangelo, Potito, *Anatomia di un territorio. Pizzighettone nel secondo Quattrocento* (Milan: Franco Angeli, 2012)

De Sanctis, Maria Letizia, 'Alberto Pitentino', in *Enciclopedia dell'arte medievale*, I, *Aaland-Anima* (Rome: Istituto dell'Enciclopedia Italiana, 1991), pp. 19–20

Fabbrici, Gabriele, 'Il governo delle acque negli statuti reggiani del XIII secolo', in *Acque di frontiera. Principi, comunità e governo del territorio nelle terre basse tra Enza e Reno (secoli XIII–XVIII)*, ed. by Franco Cazzola (Bologna: Clueb, 2000), pp. 79–101

Fiore, Alessio, *Il mutamento signorile. Assetti di potere e comunicazione politica nelle campagne dell'Italia centro-settentrionale (1080–1130 c.)* (Florence: Firenze University Press, 2017)

Franceschi, Franco, and Ilaria Taddei, *Le città italiane nel Medioevo, XII–XIV secolo* (Bologna: Il mulino, 2012)

Fumagalli, Vito, *Storie di Val Padana* (Bologna: Il Mulino, 1992)

Furió, Diego Antoni, 'De la hidràulica andalusí a la feudal: continuïtat i ruptura. L'Horta del Cent a l'Alzira medieval', in *L'espai de l'aigua. Xarxes i sistemes d'irrigació a la Ribera del Xúquer en la perspectiva històrica*, ed. by Diego Antoni Furió and Aureliano José Lairón Plá (Valéncia: Universitat de València, 2000), pp. 19–73

Galetti, Paola, 'La disciplina delle acque nelle normative statutarie del territorio piacentino', in *Acque di frontiera. Principi, comunità e governo del territorio nelle terre basse tra Enza e Reno (secoli XIII–XVIII)*, ed. by Franco Cazzola (Bologna: Clueb, 2000), pp. 37–51

Gardoni, Giuseppe, 'Uomini e acque nel territorio mantovano, secoli X-XIII', in *La civiltà delle acque: tra Medioevo e Quattrocento*. Atti del convegno internazionale, Mantova, 1–4 ottobre 2008, ed. by Arturo Calzona and Daniela Lamberini (Firenze: L. S. Olschki, 2010), pp. 143–76

Greci, Roberto, 'Le città navigabili. I progetti dell'età comunale', in *La civiltà delle acque: tra Medioevo e Quattrocento*. Atti del convegno internazionale, Mantova, 1–4 ottobre 2008, ed. by Arturo Calzona and Daniela Lamberini (Firenze: L. S. Olschki, 2010), pp. 177–96

Grillo, Paolo, *Milano in età comunale (1183–1276). Istituzioni, società, economia* (Spoleto: Cisam, 2001)

——, *Nascita di una cattedrale 1386–1418. La fondazione del Duomo di Milano* (Milan: Mondadori, 2017)

Kirchner, Helena, 'Archeologia degli spazi irrigati', in *L'acqua nei secoli altomedievali*. Atti della LV Settimana di studio del Centro italiano di studi sull'alto medioevo, Spoleto 12–17 aprile 2007 (Spoleto: Centro italiano di studi sull'alto medioevo, 2008), pp. 471–504

Labate, Donato, 'Archeologia delle acque a Modena: canali medievali e pianificazione urbana', *Atti e memorie della R. Deputazione di Storia Patria per le Provincie Modenesi*, s. 11, 41 (2019), 591–611

Mainoni, Patrizia, 'La fisionomia economica delle città lombarde dalla fine del Duecento alla prima metà del Trecento. Materiali per un confronto', in *Le città del Mediterraneo all'apogeo dello sviluppo medievale: aspetti economici e sociali* (Pistoia: Centro italiano di studi di storia e d'arte, 2001), pp. 141–221

Mangolini, Davide, 'Le chiuse di Casalecchio di Reno tra XIII e XV secolo: fonti storiche e ipotesi ricostruttive', *Atti e Memorie*, 68 (2018), 117–48

Matheus, Michael, Gabriella Piccinni, Giuliano Pinto, and Gian Maria Varanini, eds, *Le calamità ambientali nel tardo medioevo europeo: realtà, percezioni, reazioni* (Florence: Firenze University Press, 2010)

Menant, François, *Campagnes lombardes du Moyen Âge. L'économie et la société rurales dans la région de Bergame, de Crémone et de Brescia du Xᵉ au XIIIᵉ siècle* (Rome: École française de Rome, 1993)

Menant, François, and Campopiano, Michele, 'Agricolture irrigue: l'Italia padana', in *I paesaggi agrari d'Europa (secoli XIII–XV)*. Ventiquattresimo Convegno Internazionali di Studi (Pistoia maggio 2013) (Rome: Viella, 2015), pp. 291–332

Orlando, Ermanno, 'Governo delle acque e navigazione interna. Il Veneto nel basso medioevo', *Reti Medievali Rivista*, 12.2 (2011), 251–93

Panero, Francesco, 'Canali, fossi, rittani, pozzi sulla collina delle Langhe e del Roero nei secoli XIV e XV', in *Canali in provincia di Cuneo*, ed. by Giuseppe Carità (Cuneo: Società per gli Studi Storici Archeologici ed Artistici della Provincia di Cuneo, 1991), pp. 273–90

Pini, Antonio Ivan, 'Porti, canali e mulini a Bologna dal X al XIII secolo', in *La pianura e le acque tra Bologna e Ferrara: un problema secolare*. Atti del convegno, Cento 18–20 marzo 1983 (Cento: Centro studi Girolamo Baruffaldi, 1993), pp. 269–95

Rao, Riccardo, *I beni del comune di Vercelli. Dalla rivendicazione all'alienazione (1183–1254)* (Vercelli: Società storica vercellese, 2005)

——, *I paesaggi dell'Italia medievale* (Rome: Carocci, 2015)

Rapetti, Anna, *Campagne milanesi. Aspetti e metamorfosi di un paesaggio rurale tra X e XII secolo* (Cavallermaggiore: Gribaudo, 1994)

Rinaldi, Rossella, 'La disciplina delle acque nell'alto medioevo: problemi e letture', in *Acque di frontiera. Principi, comunità e governo del territorio nelle terre basse tra Enza e Reno (secoli XIII–XVIII)*, ed. by Franco Cazzola (Bologna: Clueb, 2000), pp. 13–35

——, 'La normativa bolognese del "200: tra la città e il suo contado"', in *Acque di frontiera. Principi, comunità e governo del territorio nelle terre basse tra Enza e Reno (secoli XIII–XVIII)*, ed. by Franco Cazzola (Bologna: Clueb, 2000), pp. 139–63

Roveda, Enrico, 'Il beneficio delle acque. Problemi di storia dell'irrigazione in Lombardia tra XV e XVIII secolo', in *Uomini, terre e acque. Studi sull'agricoltura della 'Bassa lombarda' tra XV e XVII secolo*, ed. by Enrico Roveda (Milan: Franco Angeli, 2012), pp. 260–77

Saggioro, Fabio, and Gian Maria Varanini, 'Insediamento umano, terra e acque nella pianura veronese, IX–XIV secolo: archeologia e fonti scritte', in *Acque e territorio nel Veneto medievale*, ed. by Dario Canzian and Remy Simonetti (Rome: Viella, 2012), pp. 95–114

Squatriti, Paolo, *Water and Society in Early Medieval Italy. AD 400–1000* (Cambridge: Cambridge University Press, 1998)

Vaini, Mario, 'Il controllo delle terre e delle acque nel Mantovano fra Duecento e Trecento. Vicende, istituzioni, statuti (1317)', in *Acque di frontiera. Principi, comunità e governo del territorio nelle terre basse tra Enza e Reno (secoli XIII–XVIII)*, ed. by Franco Cazzola (Bologna: Clueb, 2000), pp. 65–78

Varanini, Gian Maria, 'Energia idraulica e sviluppo urbano nella Verona comunale: l'Adige, il Fiumicello, il Fibbio (secoli XII–XIII)', in *Paesaggi urbani dell'Italia padana nei secoli VIII–XIV* (Bologna: Cappelli, 1988), pp. 331–72

——, 'Per la storia agraria della pianura bresciana nel Quattrocento. Lo stato degli studi', in *Nell'età di Pandolfo Malatesta. Signore a Bergamo, Brescia e Fano agli inizi del Quattrocento*, ed. by Giorgio Chittolini, Elisabetta Conti, and Maria Nadia Covini (Brescia: Morcelliana, 2012), pp. 83–108

Werther, Ukas, Jinty Nelson, Franz Herzig, Johannes Schmidt, Stefanie Berg, Peter Ettel, Sven Linzen, and Christoph Zielhofer, '792 or 793? Charlemagne's Canal Project: Craft, Nature and Memory', *Early Medieval Europe*, 28.3 (2020), 444–65

Wickham, Chris, *Sleepwalking into a New World: The Emergence of Italian City Communes in the Twelfth Century* (Princeton: De Gruyter, 2015)

Part II

Manufacturing

JORDI MORELLÓ BAGET

La expansión de la molinería hidráulica en Cataluña (siglos XI–XIII)

Acerca de la construcción de molinos y sus promotores

Introducción

Cualquiera que se entretenga en revisar las fuentes documentales editadas en Cataluña para la época aquí concernida, pronto se percatará de un hecho que parece estar omnipresente en toda esa documentación, y es la abundancia de referencias a molinos; en efecto, por doquier encontramos numerosas menciones a 'molendinos' en transacciones de diverso tipo;[1] da la impresión como si esos molinos — objeto frecuente de donaciones, traspasos en herencia, establecimientos, compraventas… — estuvieran ahí desde tiempo inmemorial.[2] Ahora bien, frente a la abundancia de referencias documentales — generalmente de molinos ya construidos o preexistentes —, hay comparativamente muchos menos documentos que nos informen de manera más directa al momento de su construcción. Al respecto, contamos con algunas licencias señoriales,[3] cuando no se trata de establecimientos o

1 Este trabajo se enmarca en el proyecto Petrifying Wealth: 'The Southern European Shift to Masonry as Collective Investment in Identity, c. 1050–1300', financiado por el Consejo Europeo de Investigación (ERC) en el marco del programa de investigación e innovación Horizonte 2020 de la Unión Europea (acuerdo de subvención no. 695515).

2 A veces, se hacen alusiones a un pasado más lejano o reciente; por ejemplo, en la donación realizada por Ramon Berenguer IV de la villa de Godall a favor de Guillem de Copons (1153), se incluía el molino que éste había construido junto al río Ulldecona ('quod feceris in predicta aqua'); Baiges, *Els pergamins de l'Arxiu Comtal*, IV, doc. no. 967, pp. 1570–01. En 1210, se da constancia de un lugar que tenía Bernat d'Albà cerca de Santes Creus, junto al río Gaià, 'in quo pater meus fecit molendinum'; Pardo, *Mensa episcopal de Barcelona*, doc. no. 56, pp. 87–88.

3 Algunas de esas licencias están contenidas en las cartas de población, como en la concedida por el obispo de Tortosa a los moradores de Cabassers [Priorat] (1185) o en la otorgada a los habitantes del lugar de las Beces (término de Castelldans, com. les Garrigues) en 1225; Font Rius, *Cartas de población*, doc. no. 177, pp. 245–56 y doc. no. 245, pp. 346–48. En cambio, en la carta de franquicias otorgada por el conde de Foix-vizconde de Castellbò a los habitantes de

Jordi Morelló Baget has a PhD in Medieval History from the University of Barcelona (1998).

Building and Economic Growth in Southern Europe (1050–1300), ed. by Sandro Carocci and Alessio Fiore, (Turnhout: Brepols, 2024), pp. 123–147 BREPOLS PUBLISHERS 10.1484/M.TMC-EB.5.137977

donaciones a censo instando, igualmente, a la construcción de uno o varios molinos. Las expresiones utilizadas ('ad faciendum molendinum/molendina' u otras con los verbos 'plantare', 'construere' o 'edificare') no dejan lugar a dudas sobre la intención de construirlos.

A partir de una revisión concienzuda de la documentación editada, junto con algunas referencias archivísticas y bibliográficas, he intentado elaborar un censo o inventario sobre molinos de nueva construcción.[4] Saber en qué momento se construyeron nos ha de permitir establecer una periodización dentro del amplio arco cronológico que nos sirve de referente, esto es, entre 1050 y 1300.[5]

Ya desde el siglo XI, los molinos adquirieron un valor económico sin parangón. En términos historiográficos, la proliferación de la molinería se vincula con la expansión del dominio feudal y, más concretamente, de los monopolios banales. A partir de entonces, los molinos se convirtieron en un instrumento señorial diseñado para captar nuevas fuentes de renta; añádase, igualmente, el monopolio que esos señores pasaron a ejercer sobre los recursos hídricos — el dominio jurídico sobre el agua.

A partir de cuando los molinos quedaron bajo el control de los señores, ellos mismos se encargarían de edificarlos con sus propios medios, aunque cada vez fue más habitual encomendar esa tarea a otras personas bajo ciertas condiciones. Así, por ej., es bajo el mandato del conde Ramon Berenguer IV — mediados del siglo XII — cuando se comienzan a registrar permisos de construcción de molinos, siendo los beneficiarios personas relevantes o de un cierto nivel económico. Con ello, comenzó a desvincularse la propiedad de los molinos de su explotación directa.[6]

Asimismo, la monopolización señorial de la molinería llevó a una gradual transformación o sustitución de los molinos más primitivos en instalaciones algo más complejas, y también más eficientes y productivas: aparecen, entonces, los denominados 'casals', que eran edificios más grandes conteniendo varias muelas.[7] Construir un molino se convirtió, pues, en una empresa que requería de una fuerte inversión, por no hablar también del coste que implicaría el solo mantenimiento de su maquinaria en perfecto funcionamiento.

El auge de la industria molinera, además de ser uno de los signos más visibles de la expansión económica de los siglos XII y XIII, viene a coincidir

---

Organyà (h.1233) se les facultaba para levantar casas y molinos por todas sus tierras sin tener que pedir licencia expresa.

4 Ciertamente, se han publicado numerosos inventarios de molinos de diferentes épocas o que estuvieron funcionando largos periodos de tiempo, pero la mayoría de referencias cronológicas que se dan solo sirven para establecer una *data ad quem*, que pocas veces puede ser tomada como fecha de construcción.

5 Este es el periodo establecido para todos los trabajos realizados en el marco del proyecto *Petrifying Wealth*.

6 Ortí, 'L'explotació d'una renda reial', p. 250.

7 Fernández Trabal, 'En els orígens de la indústria', p. 87.

con el fenómeno de la petrificación. Y es que también los molinos pasaron a formar parte del paisaje cotidiano del Románico.[8] Si aún quedan vestigios molineros de esa época es porque fueron levantados en piedra — a diferencia de los más primitivos, que serían de madera. A pesar de todas las transformaciones posteriores, incluidos cambios de uso y ulteriores abandonos, los hay que aún conservan parte de la estructura original fechable en los siglos centrales de la edad media. Esas construcciones suelen presentar un carácter fortificado, con anchos muros de mampostería y sillares bien labrados, de modo que no divergen mucho de otros edificios pétreos de la época, salvo por algunos elementos más específicos.

Molinería hidráulica en expansión

En las fuentes documentales tomadas en consideración, pocas veces se hace explícito que se trataba de molinos hidráulicos, sino por la proximidad de la edificación a un río, 'riera' o torrente, o por el interés en señalar el punto de provisión del agua que debía ser canalizada hasta el edificio en donde se realizaba la molienda. En Cataluña, como en otras partes de la Europa occidental, el uso del molino hidráulico ya estaba generalizado desde el siglo X. Se instalaban en cualquier lugar donde hubiera suficiente caudal de agua corriente, y ello implicaba a veces cursos de pobre caudal, de ahí que algunos molinos solo pudieran funcionar de forma estacional o intermitente. Inicialmente, fue, más que nada, en las redes fluviales secundarias donde proliferó la instalación de pequeños molinos; así se ha observado en el caso del bajo Llobregat, al sur de Barcelona.[9] Se trataba de sistemas interdependientes: dada la habitual presencia de otros molinos operando en la misma zona, cualquier nueva construcción o intervención afectando al correspondiente sistema hidráulico, debía hacerse sin causar perjuicios a otras instalaciones vecinas.[10] Asimismo, eran edificios permanentemente expuestos a las intermitentes riadas o crecidas de los ríos, por lo que debían ser reconstruidos con relativa frecuencia.[11]

Como señala Bolòs, si durante la alta edad media hubo propensión a crear hileras de pequeños molinos interconectados a lo largo de determinados cursos de agua — cada uno con una muela —, a partir de la edad media central,

---

8 Incluso en algunas zonas, como Ribagorza, se considera que se edificaron más molinos que iglesias, según apuntaba Jordi Boix en un artículo de la *Catalunya Romànica*.

9 Fernández Trabal, 'En els orígens de la indústria', p. 87. Los primeros grandes molinos alimentados con las aguas del Llobregat son los molinos reales edificados a finales del siglo XII, origen de la villa de Molins de Rei.

10 No faltan estudios incidiendo en el funcionamiento de todo el sistema hidráulico asociado a la molinería; al respecto, Batet, *L'aigua conquerida*; Kirchner, 'Hidráulica campesina'; Martí, 'Hacia una arqueología hidráulica'.

11 Más de un contrato alude a tal eventualidad; por ej., en 1171 se indica, respecto de un molino situado junto al río Segre, que, en caso de quedar destruido por inundación fluvial, debería ser reedificado; Altisent, *Diplomatari de Santa Maria de Poblet*, doc. no. 401, pp. 301–02.

proliferaron las agrupaciones de molinos con diversas muelas;[12] anteriormente ya hemos hecho referencia al 'casal' como vocablo para designar al edificio molinero.[13]

Otro aspecto tiene que ver con los usos dados a esos molinos.[14] La gran mayoría eran harineros, aunque raramente se haga explícito. No hace falta recordar la importancia que ha tenido esa molinería para el sector de la alimentación; la harina obtenida se llevaba luego al horno para la fabricación de pan; molinos y hornos conforman la industria del pan de la época. La generalización de esos molinos viene a ser un reflejo del proceso de 'cerealización' del paisaje que caracterizó al mundo rural de la Europa medieval, destinados a sustituir, aunque de manera progresiva, a los molinos manuales usados en el ámbito doméstico.[15]

Por otra parte, también comenzamos a encontrar referencias a la construcción de molinos 'drapers' (batanes), como tales asociados a la incipiente industria pañera que se fue abriendo camino en Cataluña a partir de mediados del siglo XII.[16] Estos otros artefactos molineros estaban adaptados a tundir paños mediante grandes mazos o martilletes; además del batanado, también se realizaban otras tareas, como el lavado, estirado y secado de los paños.[17] Naturalmente, esos molinos debían estar localizados, no solo cerca de cursos de agua, sino también próximos o no muy distantes de los principales centros urbanos en donde se desarrolló esa manufactura.

Ambos tipos de molinos son exponentes, pues, de la molinería hidráulica de la época;[18] y ambos suelen figurar conjuntamente en la documentación que tenemos recopilada al respecto; de hecho, parece que fue habitual instalar batanes allí donde ya había molinos harineros.[19]

Al margen de la red hídrica natural, otros molinos pasaron a construirse a lo largo de canalizaciones artificiales, como el famoso *Rec comtal* de Barcelona, que, con una longitud de unos 10 km, llevaba el agua del río Besós hasta las proximidades de la ciudad. A finales del siglo XIII, había unos 13 casals, con más de 40 muelas, además de un molino pañero.[20] Sin duda, llegó a ser una de

---

12 Bolòs, *Els orígens medievals*, p. 381.

13 'casal ubi molinum sedeat', se dice en un documento de 1152; Papell, *Diplomatari del monestir de Santes Creus*, doc. no. 52, pp. 128–29; o también 'molendinum cum domo sua vel casal' (1227); Mallorquí, *Col·lecció diplomàtica dels Cartellà*, doc. no. 80, p. 196.

14 Sobre la variedad de usos, véase Donat and Solà, 'Els molins'.

15 El molino hidráulico también fue aplicado a la molienda de las aceitunas, aunque, en estos casos, fue más habitual utilizar la fuerza animal.

16 Al respecto, Riera, 'La draperia a la Corona catalanoaragonesa'.

17 Fernández Trabal, 'Les indústries rurals', p. 386.

18 También las fraguas adoptaron los principios del molino hidráulico; Donat and Solà, 'Els molins', p. 68.

19 De hecho, devino habitual que los molinos incorporasen un aparejo para moler cereales y otro para tundir paños, según Gironella, 'La mòlta de cereals i el batanatge', I, p. 249.

20 Ello contrasta con los 16 molinos que había agrupados en cinco *casals* en la primera mitad del siglo XII; Ortí, 'L'explotació d'una renda reial', pp. 246 y 272. El mismo autor identifica

las zonas con mayor concentración molinera del ámbito catalán. Lo mismo puede hacerse extensivo a la zona situada en las inmediaciones de la ciudad de Girona, donde hay cuantificados una veintena de molinos a finales ya del siglo XI; también aquí había un *rec comtal* que desviaba el agua del Ter para la molinería, a tal punto que pasó a ser conocido como 'rec monar'. Asimismo, la zona de Lleida-Balaguer brinda numerosos ejemplos de emplazamientos molineros junto a acequias de origen andalusí. La segunda mitad del siglo XII registra un largo rosario de creación de molinos en toda el área regable del llano de Lleida.[21] Y uno de los principales promotores fue la orden templaria de Gardeny.[22] A finales del mismo siglo, hay documentados, únicamente en la comarca del Segrià, 19 molinos harineros y 3 batanes, mientras que en un cabreo de 1214 se enumeran 16 'casals' molineros conteniendo un total de al menos 25 muelas.[23] Ello representa, pues, una altísima densidad de molinos, pero quizás no tanto como en la zona transpirenaica del Rosellón, donde se han contabilizado más de una cincuentena de emplazamientos molineros para fines del siglo XIII.[24]

En términos más generales, parece que el siglo XII fue una época álgida por lo que a la construcción de molinos se refiere.[25] Más adelante veremos si podemos acotar mejor los periodos de mayor actividad constructiva. En la presente exposición queremos centrarnos, no solo en la cronología de su construcción, sino también en la identificación de sus constructores, que son dos aspectos interrelacionados.[26] Ciertamente, la palabra 'constructor' conlleva dos facetas distintas: quiénes fueron los promotores y quiénes realmente tuvieron a su cargo construirlos, lo que no tiene por qué coincidir con los constructores materiales de esos edificios. Trataré de ello al final del artículo, pero antes de nada resulta conveniente pasar revista a la infraestructura hidráulica que llevaba implícita toda instalación molinera.

---

dos momentos principales en la construcción de los molinos del *Rec Comtal*: a mediados del siglo XII (entre 1144–1153) y a mediados del XIII.

21 Sabaté, 'L'eclosió econòmica', pp. 334–35.

22 En muchas de las transacciones recogidas en el consiguiente diplomatario, se alude a la construcción, no de uno, sino de varios molinos a la vez, como en la concesión realizada en 1176 a favor de Guillem Berenguer de Riudovelles respecto a la instalación de tres molinos en distintas localizaciones de Alcanyís (Rosselló de Segrià); Sarobe, *Col·lecció diplomàtica de la Casa del Temple de Gardeny*, doc. no. 290, pp. 433–34.

23 Datos tomados del correspondiente volumen de la *Catalunya Romànica*.

24 Caucanas, *Moulins et irrigation*, p. 186.

25 Muchos molinos fueron construidos durante este siglo, según Bolòs, *Els orígens medievals*, p. 381.

26 Al decir de cierta autora, 'La cuestión de la identificación de los constructores de los molinos está estrechamente relacionada con el problema de establecer la cronología de su construcción'; Kirchner, 'Hidráulica campesina', p. 23.

Componentes de la molinería hidráulica

La construcción de un molino conllevaba poner a punto una extensa infraestructura hidráulica. Ello se refiere a elementos tanto internos como externos al edificio, tal y como suelen aparecer enumerados en la documentación de la época, comenzando por las mismas canalizaciones de agua ('recos/regos' o 'sequias', además de 'alveis', 'rigariis', 'reductibus' o 'aquaductibus'), incluidos los llamados 'capud rec' o similares ('cap rego', 'capud sequiis', 'caput aquiis' e incluso 'capud aqueductus') para referirse, en principio, al lugar donde el agua era desviada del embalse al canal.[27] Tampoco faltan menciones a las compuertas ('toledors', 'extoledors', 'estolador'...) a través de las cuales se abría y cerraba el paso del agua, regulando, pues, la cantidad de agua necesaria para llenar la balsa del molino;[28] esas balsas podían ser denominadas 'pexere', 'pexariis', 'pescatas'..., ya que se poblaban de peces para servir de sustento al molinero.[29] Otro componente imprescindible del sistema molinero era la esclusa ('resclosis'), la barrera o muro construido para subir el nivel del agua a objeto de ser desviada hacia el molino.[30] Para evitar filtraciones en las presas, se recurría a tierra compactada (gleba); así, por ej., en 1174, se indica: 'et faciatis vestrum resclosar cum petris et glebis et clausuris ibi necessariis'.[31] En algún caso, también se hace alusión al salto de agua, ya de entrada al molino, sirviendo para impulsar la rueda que había en el interior, como así aparece descrito en un documento de 1295: 'intrabat per saltum dicti molendini media aqua, vel quasi, sic quod dicta roda currebat'.[32]

Toda edificación molinera contaba con, al menos, dos dependencias. En la inferior, por donde entraba el agua a presión haciendo girar la rueda, había el cárcavo ('kakavo', 'cacavo');[33] según parece, podía designar tanto el hueco donde giraba el rodezno como el canal que iba desde la rueda hasta la pared del molino, por donde se daba salida al agua. El consiguiente movimiento creado por la fuerza hidráulica se transmitía por un eje a la muela situada en el

---

27 Según Fernández Trabal, 'En els orígens de la indústria', p. 86, sería la presa que proporcionaba el agua de toda la instalación.

28 En un molino de la Espluga de Francolí (1079), se indica que había hasta tres 'toledors'; Font Rius, *Cartas de población*, doc. no. 390.

29 También se da la equivalencia 'aqualis sive pexere'; Baraut, 'Els documents, dels anys 1191–1200', doc. no. 1.880, pp. 47–48.

30 En la riera de Merlès (cuenca alta del Llobregat), se encuentran numerosos vestigios de antiguas presas altomedievales, como revelan diversos alineamientos de agujeros excavados en las rocas, donde se colocaban las estacas para construir la barrera.

31 Rius, *Cartulario de Sant Cugat del Vallès*, doc. no. 1174, pp. 313–14. De 1233 es una indicación a cómo debía construirse cierta enclusa: 'cum petris et calse'; Ginebra, *El Manual primer*, doc. no. 2.404, p. 980. En cambio, en la construcción de otra esclusa del mismo año y zona (Vic), se indica que se hiciera con piedra seca ('sine cuneriis' ni ningún otro 'bastiment', dice el documento); Ginebra, *El Manual primer*, doc. no. 2.914, pp. 1187–88.

32 Bolòs, *Diplomatari del monestir de Serrateix*, doc. no. 228, pp. 337–39.

33 'cum kakavo et solo et superposito et cum ipsa instrumenta qui ad ipso molino pertinet' (1052); Salvadó, *El monestir benedictí de Sant Benet de Bages*, doc. no. 1122, p. 1725.

piso superior.[34] Ramón Llull expresa con meridiana claridad cómo funcionaba cada elemento del engranaje: 'En axí com lo roder se mou pel poder de l'aigua e la mola se mou per lo poder del roder'.[35]

En principio, había dos formas de accionar el mecanismo molinero: mediante rueda horizontal y eje vertical o mediante rueda vertical y eje horizontal; la primera giraba paralela al suelo, mientras la segunda lo hacía paralela a las paredes del molino. Atendiendo a las menciones documentales, se suelen establecer tres tipologías de molinos: 'todeller', 'roder' y 'cuber/cuper'.[36] Son términos derivados, cada uno, de diferentes componentes molineros: presuntamente de 'tudell' (compuerta) en el primer caso, de rueda y cubo en los otros dos. Según los diversos autores consultados, los molinos roderos, como el que ya aparece mencionado en Lleida en 1153, serían los que funcionaban con rueda vertical, mientras que los otros dos tipos debían estar equipados con ruedas horizontales (turbinas).[37] Por otra parte, se considera que la rueda horizontal era la más extendida entre los molinos harineros, mientras que la vertical fue adoptada para otros usos o aplicaciones.[38] Ahora bien, según apuntaba Fernández Trabal, la rueda vertical podía ser utilizada tanto para tundir paños como para moler harina.[39]

El tercer tipo (molino cubero) concierne aquellos que estaban provistos de un cubo o pozo por donde caía el agua con vistas a aumentar la potencia del salto. Considerado de origen andalusí, en Cataluña se difundió a partir de mediados del siglo XII.[40] Aparece referenciado, por ej., en la Espluga de Francolí (1178) como molino 'coperio'.[41] Los dos molinos de Montblanc (el Xic y el Gran) contienen, respectivamente, dos y cuatro cubos. El molino de Olius, llamado precisamente 'dels Cups', fue completamente reformado en torno a 1224; en 1258 era el propio rey, Jaime I, quien daba una licencia a un hombre de Vilamajor (Vallès oriental) para poder construir un molino 'cuper' allí donde había otro 'toeller'.[42]

---

34 'Erunt autem roda cum rodeto et cadireta operate et posite in dicto molendino in locis videlicet in quibus stare debent' (1295). La mencionada 'cadireta' parece aludir a la pieza de hierro que servía de soporte al árbol de transmisión o 'collferro'.

35 La cita en Llull, *Llibre de contemplació en Deu*, 322, 13; Planes, 'Els molins i altres indústries', p. 284.

36 Bolòs, *Els orígens medievals*, pp. 382–83.

37 Según Ortega, 'El contexto social de la molinería hidráulica', p. 89, siguiendo a Bolòs. En cambio, al decir de Ramon Planes, la denominación más corriente del molino de rueda horizontal sería la de molino rodero; Planes, 'Els molins', p. 286.

38 Además de las fargas, también los molinos papeleros pasaron a funcionar con rueda vertical; Donat and Solà, 'Els molins', p. 71.

39 Y así como todos los molinos pañeros eran de rueda vertical, no todos los molinos verticales eran pañeros; Fernández Trabal, 'En els orígens de la indústria', p. 90.

40 Planes, 'Els molins', p. 286.

41 Santacana, *El monasterio de Poblet*, doc. no. 193, p. 651.

42 Se trata del actual Molí de Dalt o de can Sunyer, en Sant Pere de Vilamajor; Aventín, *Vilamajor*, p. 124. Por esa misma época, se documentan construcciones de pequeños *casals* a

Figura 7.1. Molino dels Cups, al lado del río Cardener (Olius, com. Solsonès). Primera noticia documental: 1080 (reformado en torno a 1224). Fuente: Invarquit.

Con todo, en la documentación consultada aquí, la principal contraposición establecida parece ser entre molinos 'roders' y 'todellers', tal como ya aparece anotado en Espirà de l'Aglí (Rosellón) en 1140.[43] Al sur de los Pirineos, encontramos un par de transacciones (1163–1164) concernientes a la construcción de molinos de uno y otro tipo en Sant Quirze de Besora.[44] En 1201, se registra una donación al monasterio de las Franqueses del agua de molinos 'roders' ubicados en la *vilanova* de Balaguer, donde también se preveía la construcción de otros establecimientos molineros.[45] En 1218, el abad de Cardona encomendó construir dos o tres molinos 'tholeers' — según transcripción — donde ya había uno rodero.[46] A juzgar por esas referencias, no había incompatibilidades para poder construir molinos de uno y otro tipo en el mismo lugar, siempre que pudiera asegurarse una corriente constante de agua.

En ocasiones, también se indica el número de ruedas: de 1244 es una licencia regia a favor de varias personas: 'quod construatis quatuor rotas

lo largo del *Rec Comtal* de Barcelona, cada uno con dos molinos cuberos, uno de los cuales destinado a servir de recambio del otro; Ortí, 'L'explotació d'una renda reial', pp. 261–70.

43 'duos molendinos tudelers vel unum rotarium'; Caucanas, *Moulins et irrigation*, p. 146.

44 En este caso, aparece transcrito como 'codeier', según el regesto del siglo XVIII; Ordeig, *Diplomatari del monestir de Ripoll*, doc. no. 1.032 y 1.033, pp. 262–63.

45 Escuder, *Diplomatari de Santa Maria de les Franqueses*, doc. no. 166, pp. 254–55. En 1258, se daba permiso para construir un molino rodero en el *Rec Comtal* de Barcelona; Ortí, 'L'explotació d'una renda reial', p. 263.

46 Galera, *Diplomatari de la vila de Cardona*, doc. no. 326, pp. 393–95.

molendinorum in quatuor casalibus' del *Rec comtal* de Barcelona (esto es, una rueda en cada *casal*), además de poder realizar ampliaciones en ellos para permitir la instalación de cada una de esas ruedas. Los gastos de construcción correrían a cargo de los concesionarios, sin cuyo consentimiento no se permitiría la instalación de más ruedas o muelas ('rotas aliquas sive molas').[47]

También se indica el número de ruedas en los molinos de Alcanyís de Segrià (1282): 'in quibus sunt due rote et media' (en alusión, quizás, a una rueda de la mitad del tamaño estándar).[48] Esas ruedas podían ser bastante grandes; las del molino de Ullastret (Baix Empordà) medían 13 palmos, esto es, algo más de 2,5 m de diámetro.[49] Otras veces, lo que se indica es el número de muelas: por ej., en Alcover se enumeran varias muelas (como mínimo tres) respecto de un molino situado junto al río Francolí (1228).[50]

Un casal podía contener, pues, dos o más molinos — si seguimos el esquema 1 molino = 1 muela —; así, en 1181 se menciona 'unum parellum molendinorum in uno casallo'; y más adelante se hace mención a 'unum casal cum duos molinos'.[51] En 1291 se da constancia de un casal en Rosselló de Segrià que contenía cuatro molinos harineros.[52] Otras instalaciones tenían un número aún mayor de muelas o aparejos para moler grano.

Molinos en construcción: localizaciones

Con voluntad de ser lo más estrictos posibles, solo tenemos en cuenta aquellos documentos en los que se puede dar por sentado que la construcción se llevaría a cabo.[53] Así pues, la principal tarea ha sido discriminar qué documentos, de entre todos los que tenemos fichados, pueden ser tomados como referencia cronológica de la construcción de molinos, ya fueran de nueva planta — a veces, a partir de cambios de emplazamiento— o reedificaciones. Tenemos noventa casos recopilados que atañen a construcciones de molinos, ya se trate de permisos o de donaciones a censo (establecimientos). A partir del correspondiente inventario, el siguiente paso ha sido intentar localizar mínimamente cada uno de esos molinos sobre el mapa. Todos los molinos documentados están asociados a un curso de agua, aunque este no siempre puede ser identificado convenientemente. Por otra parte, no nos interesa tanto la localización exacta, sino su distribución global por cuencas hidrográficas. En la fig. 7.2 podemos ver cómo se distribuyen esas localizaciones.

47 Documento transcrito en Archivo Virtual Jaume I en base a la serie Cartas Reales del ACA.

48 Alturo, *Diplomatari d'Alguaire*, doc. no. 195, pp. 446–51.

49 Gironella, *Els molins empordanesos*, p. 92.

50 Pons Guri, 'Manual notarial d'Alcover', doc. no. 146, p. 196.

51 Sarobe, *Col·lecció diplomàtica de la Casa del Temple de Gardeny*, doc. no. 380–81, p. 578.

52 Alturo, *Diplomatari d'Alguaire*, doc. no. 263, pp. 561–64.

53 Algunas licencias se basan en otorgar un derecho genérico a poder edificarlos, aunque no sabemos si quienes tuvieron encomendada esa tarea la llevarían después a efecto.

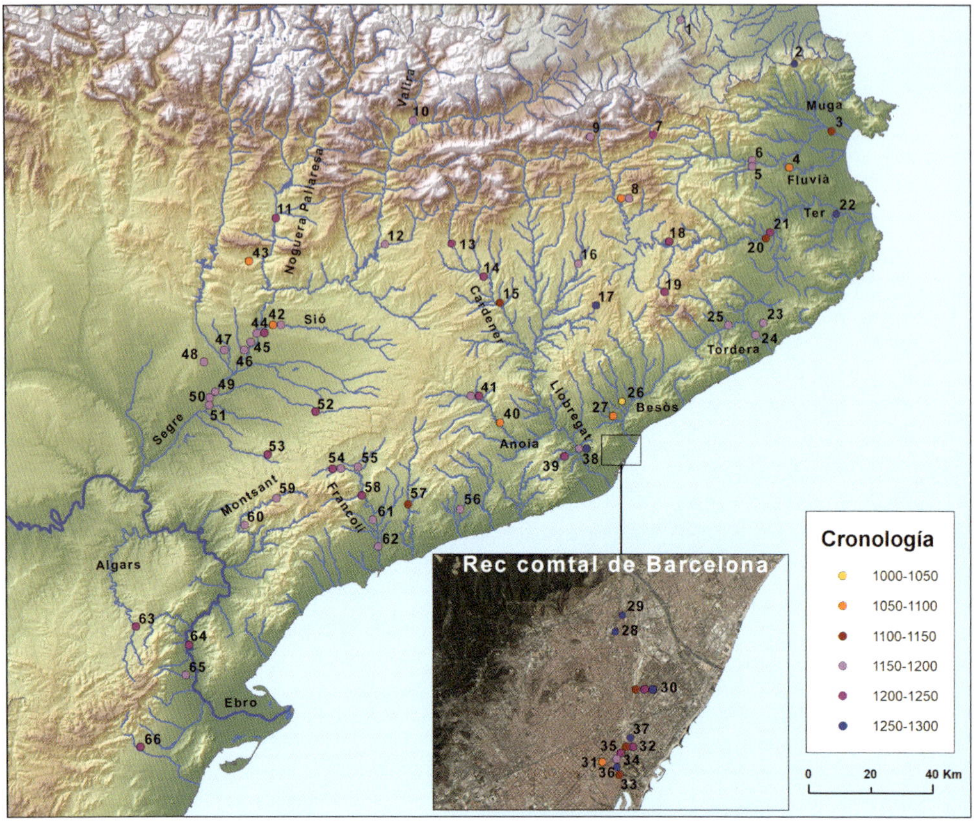

1.	Jóc	1282
2.	Requesens	1261
3.	Castelló d'Empúries	1122
4.	Parets	1065
5.	Dosquers	1169
6.	Pedrinyà	1190
7.	Segúries	1237
8.	St Quirze de Besora	1063, 1163, 1164
9.	Campelles	1190
10.	Seu d'Urgell	1189, 1196
11.	Gavet	1207
12.	Penyafiel	1199
13.	Olius	*c.* 1224
14.	Coromina de l'Almoina	1218
15.	Súria	*c.* 1137, 1142
16.	St Andreu d'Oristà	1170
17.	Moià	1258
18.	Sau	1205
19.	Viladrau	1232
20.	Salt	1141
21.	Domeny	1210
22.	Fonolleres	1286
23.	Valldemaria	1151
24.	St Esteve de Tordera	1178
25.	Ramió	1187
26.	Sta. Perpètua de Mogoda	1039
27.	Fonts de Berter	1072
28.	St Andreu	1266
29.	Bell-lloc	1286
30.	Clot	1148, 1244, 1258
31.	Merdançà	1094
32.	Molins Nous	1143, 1144, 1145, 1244
33.	Molins del Mar	1148
34.	St Pere	1153, 1244
35.	Soler	1244
36.	Malla	1253
37.	Carbonell	1264
38.	Molins de Rei	1188, 1253
39.	Cervelló	1249
40.	Piera	1067
41.	Igualada	1188, 1206
42.	Balaguer/Sió	1061, 1175
43.	Règola	1081
44.	Balaguer	1162, 1171, 1176, 1201, 1202
45.	Menàrguens	1173
46.	Farfanya	1170
47.	Corbins	1181
48.	Alcanís	1176
49.	Lleida	1152, 1174, 1182, 1190, 1194
50.	Fontanet	1191
51.	Rufea	1169
52.	Belianes	1209
53.	Besses	1225
54.	Espluga de Francolí	1150, *c.* 1153, *c.* 1161, 1178, 1205
55.	Guàrdia de Prats	1190
56.	Saifores	1152
57.	Vilardida	1130
58.	Rocacorba	1204
59.	Montsant	1164
60.	Cabassers	1185
61.	Ribarroja	1191
62.	Codony	1169
63.	Horta	1234
64.	Xerta	1222
65.	Palomera	1164
66.	Sènia	1232

Figura 7.2. La construcción de molinos en Cataluña (siglos XI–XIII). Elaborado por Enrique Capdevila Montes (IH-CSIC).

Aunque encontramos emplazamientos un poco por todas partes, es posible discernir varias zonas en donde parece existir una mayor profusión de construcciones molineras, a saber: en las cuencas del río Segre y del Francolí, además de los dos nódulos situados junto a Barcelona — en el *rec comtal* — y Girona (río Ter). Aparte, tenemos localizadas construcciones molineras junto a otros cursos fluviales (Anoia, Foix, Montsant, Tordera, Valira ...). Tal es la imagen obtenida a partir de una revisión extensa de los principales compendios documentales que tenemos consultables para la época en cuestión.

Tabla 7.1. Periodización de molinos en construcción.

Periodo	Nº de molinos	Cómputo por siglos
1000–1049	1	s.XI (8)
1050–1100	7	
1100–1149	10	s.XII (50)
1150–1199	40	
1200–1249	22	s.XIII (32)
1250–1299	10	

A la vista de los datos recogidos en la tabla 7.1, el siglo XII sería la época de mayor actividad en la construcción de molinos, pero más que nada en la segunda mitad, lo que podría prolongarse algunos años más del siglo XIII, cuando el ritmo de actividad parece disminuir. Una vez más, podría ser una cronología excesivamente condicionada por el tipo de documentación que estamos manejando. Sea como sea, no parece nada descabellado que el periodo de mayor actividad constructiva molinera se corresponda con la segunda mitad del duodécimo siglo, ya que se corresponde de lleno con una época de fuerte dinamismo y de colonización feudal por la Cataluña Nueva.

Batanes en construcción: localizaciones

Ese periodo de mayor frenesí viene a coincidir con la irrupción y consiguiente expansión de la molinería pañera. Las referencias a la construcción de esos nuevos artilugios industriales son mucho menos frecuentes. En nuestra lista, tenemos registrados una docena de molinos, aunque no de todos ellos conocemos su localización. En la figura 7.3, figuran aquellos que tenemos más o menos localizados.

Todos ellos se encuentran ubicados cerca de centros de producción textil — caso de Lleida — o próximos, si no, a rutas pañeras. La instalación de batanes en la zona del Segrià es algo bien conocido y se relaciona con el gran impulso que experimentó en esa época la industria textil en la capital del Segre.[54]

54 Bolòs, *Els orígens medievals*, p. 384 cita varios. Asimismo, Riera, 'La draperia a la Corona

Figura 7.3. La construcción de batanes en Cataluña (siglos XII–XIII). Elaborado por Enrique Capdevila Montes (IH-CSIC).

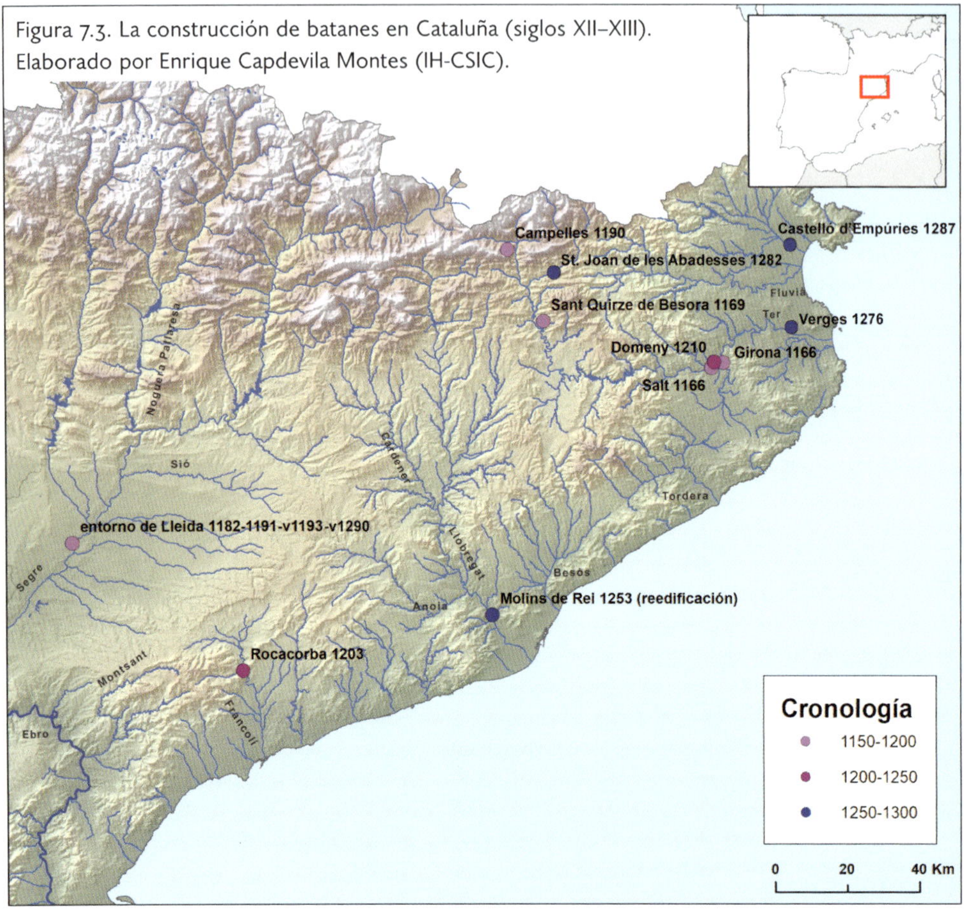

Por otra parte, no resulta extraño que se instalasen en zonas donde ya había molinos harineros funcionando. Ambos tipos de molinos suelen formar parte de concesiones conjuntas, como la donación otorgada por Guillem IV de Cervera a Pere de Tarascó de un lugar ('locum seu fundum') para construir molinos de uno y otro tipo (1191).[55]

Como es sabido, la expansión de esa nueva molinería se inició desde el norte de Cataluña: ya en 1151 se documentan molinos pañeros en Prats de Molló (Vallespir) y otros que aparecen mencionados algo más tarde en esa misma zona o ya al sur de los Pirineos, como en el caso de Banyoles. Sea como sea, aquí solo tenemos en cuenta las fechas de construcción; así, en 1166 se da constancia de dos molinos 'drapers' que se estaban construyendo, uno en

---

catalanoaragonesa' ofrece otro inventario más o menos coincidente con el anterior. En otras zonas, como en Ribagorza, los primeros molinos de este tipo se documentan ya en el siglo XIII.

55 Sarobe, *Col·lecció diplomàtica de la Casa del Temple de Gardeny*, doc. no. 579, pp. 848–49.

Salt (Girona) y otro en el Mercadal de la misma ciudad.[56] En 1169 el pavorde de Palau — adscrito al monasterio de Ripoll — estableció una heredad a favor de Pere Ermengol y su familia para la edificación de un molino 'draper' en Sant Quirze de Besora.[57] El interés del monasterio en promocionar esas instalaciones hidráulicas vuelve a ponerse de manifiesto en 1190 a propósito de otra donación realizada por uno de sus monjes — el dispensero — para la construcción de otro molino 'draper', esta vez en Sant Martí de Campelles.[58] También podemos referirnos a la donación realizada por el monasterio de Poblet a favor de Bernat de Montoliu en 1203 para que construyera molinos harineros y pañeros en Rocacorba (la Riba).[59]

A juzgar por los datos aquí reunidos, la expansión de esa industria parece concentrarse en la segunda mitad del siglo XII y principios del XIII; para ser más precisos, entre 1166 y 1210, coincidiendo con la época de mayor expansión de la molinería hidráulica.[60] Las fuentes documentales del siglo XIII aportan muchas más menciones a molinos pañeros, aunque no sabemos cuándo se construyeron, excepción hecha de los casos anotados en el mapa en cuestión.

Eventualmente, reconstruir más que construir

A veces, se trataba de molinos que estaban en mal estado o que habían quedado abandonados; por ej., en 1081, el abad de Sant Pere d'Àger encomendó a un matrimonio reedificar un molino que había recibido destruido cuando Ponç Onifred lo traspasó a la canónica.[61] Más tarde, en un establecimiento hecho a instancias de la abadesa de Sant Daniel de Girona en 1141, se alude a un molino a medio construir, de modo que se preveía completar la parte que faltaba antes de poder pasar a exigir los censos correspondientes.[62] En 1189, se señalaba un lugar junto al río Valira, cerca de la Seu d'Urgell, donde había varios molinos destruidos que debían ser puestos de nuevo en funcionamiento ('ut ibi ea reedificetis et plura de novo si poteritis edificetis').[63] En 1199, Ermessenda de Clarà, junto con su hija y nietos, encomendaba a la iglesia de Solsona reedificar dos molinos junto al río Altés, en el mismo 'casal' donde la canónica ya tenía uno.[64]

56 Donat and Solà, 'Els molins', p. 77.
57 Ordeig, *Diplomatari del monestir de Ripoll*, II, doc. no. 1063, p. 282.
58 Ordeig, *Diplomatari del monestir de Ripoll*, II, doc. no. 1181, pp. 361–62.
59 'et prefata molendina semper teneatis bene constructa et parata ad annonam et ad padnos'; Pons, *Cartulari de Poblet*, doc. no. 249, pp. 150–51.
60 De 1210 es una licencia regia para la construcción de un molino 'draper' en Domeny, junto al río Ter; Marquès, *Cartoral dit de Carlemany*, doc. no. 395; también en Alvira, *Pedro el Católico*, III, doc. no. 1000, pp. 1050–52.
61 Chesé, *Col·lecció diplomàtica de Sant Pere d'Àger*, doc. no. 120, pp. 372–73.
62 Marquès, *Col·lecció diplomàtica de Sant Daniel de Girona*, doc. no. 41, pp. 101–02.
63 Baraut, 'Els documents, dels anys 1151–1190', doc. no. 1839, pp. 341–42.
64 Bach, *Diplomatari de l'Arxiu Diocesà de Solsona*, doc. no. 604, pp. 729–30.

A propósito de esas reedificaciones, parece que ciertas intervenciones podían generar equívocos sobre si se trataba de obras realmente nuevas o bien de reconstrucciones de edificaciones preexistentes. En cualquier caso, toda nueva obra que fuera a realizarse debía contar con la previa autorización del señor o propietario del molino. Respecto de obras iniciadas sin permiso había una peculiar forma de denuncia siguiendo un determinado ritual, como el que tenemos descrito en 1295: el procurador del abad de Serrateix denunció de 'novella obra' a Bernat de Tudela y a sus dos obreros; ello se hizo lanzando tres piedras ante la presencia de la autoridad, en este caso, el *veguer* de Manresa, quien acto seguido dio orden de paralizar la obra.[65] ¿Eran obras de nueva construcción o simples reparaciones? El interpelado alegó que lo que hacían allí no era obra nueva, ya que el edificio en cuestión había sido construido por su padre cuarenta años atrás. Ciertamente, el lanzamiento de piedrecitas o guijarros para denunciar una obra nueva está recogido en las costumbres de Tortosa, concretamente, en la rúbrica titulada 'De denunciació de novella obra', donde también se advertía: 'qui edifici antic refà, no és entès que faça obra nova'; en tal caso, no era procedente llevar a cabo ninguna denuncia.[66]

Otras veces, se preveían cambios de emplazamiento. En 1094, el obispo y la canónica de Barcelona dieron licencia para poder cambiar de lugar dos molinos situados en el torrente de Merdançà (al NE de la ciudad condal), y aun levantar un tercero.[67] De 1232 es un permiso para poder elegir un nuevo emplazamiento para la construcción de un molino en la parroquia de Viladrau ('ad edificandum hoc totum de novo').[68] En 1253, Jaime I daba licencia a Berenguer Durfort para trasladar un molino (en principio uno 'draper') en Molins de Rei.[69]

Mano de obra

La construcción de un molino requería disponer de mano de obra y cuanta más mejor: en 1206 el abad de Sant Cugat del Vallès dio licencia para construir molinos en sus dominios de Igualada y para ello traspasó al concesionario las corveas u 'operas' de los hombres de la villa indicada, los cuales tendrían que acudir 'ad conplantandum et hedificandum' esos molinos.[70] Así pues, el abad hacía uso de sus prerrogativas señoriales para involucrar a parte de sus vasallos — una comunidad entera, de hecho — en los trabajos de construcción.

65 Bolòs, *Diplomatari del monestir de Santa Maria de Serrateix*, doc. no. 228, pp. 337–39.

66 Epígrafes 9.6.1./9.6.3 del citado compendio editado por Massip.

67 Además de instar a la construcción de un acueducto; Batlle, *Diplomatari de l'Arxiu Capitular*, doc. no. 1598, pp. 2476–79.

68 Ginebra, *El Manual primer*, doc. no. 1420, p. 602.

69 ACA, Canc., Pergaminos (Jaime I), no. 1348.

70 Y también 'ad aquarum destruccionem et molas adducendas'; Rius, *Cartulario de Sant Cugat*, doc. no. 1263, p. 384.

En la concesión dada por el conde Ramón Berenguer IV a favor de Bernat Folc (1160), serían los hombres de Piera quienes irían a trabajar en la construcción de varios molinos a razón de dos jornales por casa;[71] y en el establecimiento otorgado por Arnau de Cartellà, tal requerimiento se estipulaba como costumbre: 'ut nostros homines faciant operas ad illum molendinum sicut solent facere' (1178).[72] Ello no era óbice para tener que recurrir, otras veces, a la contratación de mano de obra asalariada, tanto si se trataba de obreros especializados como si no. Los señores también podían hacer uso de mano de obra servil, como así consta respecto de los batanes mandados construir por los templarios de Gardeny a finales del siglo XIII.[73] En esa misma obra, hay consignadas retribuciones a diversos operarios, al frente de los cuales había un maestro de obras (¿simple capataz?).

Plazos de construcción

Los plazos para llevar a cabo una construcción de este tipo no suelen indicarse sino en contadas ocasiones, y casi siempre se señala un año. Podemos aportar varios ejemplos al respecto: a propósito de la autorización dada por los Cervera respecto de molinos dados a construir en la Espluga de Francolí, el plazo de un año comenzaría a contar a partir del día de la conquista de Siurana (1153 o 1154);[74] en 1196, en una donación del obispo de la Seu d'Urgell, se preveía la construcción de un tercer molino en el mismo lugar en el plazo también de un año;[75] Ahora bien, en la práctica, construir un molino podía llevar más tiempo, según nos dan a entender otras anotaciones documentales; de 1286 es una licencia para construir uno junto al río Daró, afluente del Ter, en el plazo de cinco años.[76]

---

71 Baiges, *Els pergamins de l'Arxiu Comtal*, doc. no. 1067, pp. 1711–12.

72 Mallorquí, *Col·lecció diplomàtica dels Cartellà*, doc. no. 31, pp. 125–27. Retrocediendo aún más en el tiempo, encontramos otro ejemplo aportado por Fernández Trabal respecto a la obligación impuesta por los *castlans* de Castellbisbal a los pobladores de la baronía de hacer obras en los molinos (1112); Fernández Trabal, 'En els orígens de la indústria', p. 87.

73 Con trabajadores tomados, probablemente, de sus dominios de explotación directa o reservas, según Padilla, 'La construcció d'un enginy hidràulic', p. 111.

74 Altisent, *Diplomatari de Santa Maria de Poblet*, doc., no. 156, pp. 139–40.

75 Baraut, 'Els documents, dels anys 1191–1200', doc. no. 1880, pp. 47–48.

76 ADG, Pergaminos (Pia Almoina), doc. no. 3.019. Igualmente, podemos referirnos al molino del Comte (o de Palomera), situado en el barranco de la Servera (Tortosa): la construcción ya estaba acabada en 1178, pero la elección del emplazamiento se había hecho en 1164 — a tenor del correspondiente permiso regio —, a partir de cuando, supuestamente, se habrían iniciado las obras; Virgili, *Diplomatari de la catedral de Tortosa*, doc. no. 141, pp. 193–94. De todos modos, los otros dos molinos que conforman el conjunto también se fechan a finales del siglo XII.

Naturalmente, la construcción de una esclusa llevaba menos tiempo. De finales de enero de 1233 es una avenencia establecida entre dos particulares para construir una, con previsión de terminarla al cabo de cinco meses.[77]

Materiales usados

Los contratos aquí estudiados pueden contener otras disposiciones interesantes, como cuando se especifica cuál de las dos partes debía aportar las muelas: así, en el pacto suscrito por el conde Ramon Berenguer IV y Bernat Folc en 1160 — relativo a la construcción de un molino en las proximidades de Piera —, el primero le aseguraría todo lo necesario 'ad usus molendinorum', excepto las muelas, que debía aportar el segundo.[78]

Las canteras especializadas en la fabricación de muelas recibían el nombre de 'molar'. De finales del siglo XII, es una mención al 'molar' del coll del Cristià — zona de Cardona —, de donde se extraían muelas para los molinos que tenía la *Almoina* de dicha canónica.[79] En 1267, Jaime I se dirigía a los canónigos y a los hombres de Roda dándoles licencia para labrar muelas en el término del castillo de Sant Esteve del Mall.[80] Por otra parte, es de sobras conocida la cantera de Montjuïc (Barcelona) — orientada, en gran medida, a la producción de muelas —,[81] como también lo son las canteras de Peratallada (Girona), cuyo topónimo ya es bien significativo al respecto, y en las cuales aún hay trazas de la fabricación de piezas cilíndricas y, pues, de muelas. Seguramente, había muchas más repartidas por todo el territorio, de modo que no sería difícil conseguirlas gracias, también, a los circuitos comerciales creados para su distribución.

Por otra parte, la provisión de madera podía realizarse en los bosques más cercanos al lugar de la construcción: así, Arnau Moltó de l'Espluga de Francolí (v.1153) recibió permiso para poder recoger madera y leña en el término de la misma localidad, entre otras cosas, 'ad omnia molendina ipsa construenda et componenda, in casalibus et resclausis superioribus et inferioribus'.[82] En la venta suscrita en 1217 por el pavorde de Sant Joan de les Abadesses se incluía un permiso de tala en unos bosques para poder emplear la madera en las casas

77 Ginebra, *El Manual primer*, doc. no. 2404, p. 980.

78 Baiges, *Els pergamins de l'Arxiu Comtal*, doc. no. 1067, pp. 1711–12. En cambio, respecto a los molinos construidos en el *Rec Comtal* de Barcelona, era el rey quien aportaba las muelas, provenientes de sus canteras de Montjuïc; Ortí, 'L'explotació d'una renda reial', p. 256.

79 Galera, *Diplomatari de la vila de Cardona*, doc. no. 220.

80 Noticia reportada por Jordi Boix en la *Catalunya Romànica*. Asimismo, En 1233 se menciona un torrente situado en el término de Estadella — también en el antiguo condado de Ribagorça —, donde se fabricaban muelas; Marquès, 'Els pergamins del fons Monestirs diversos', doc. no. 20.

81 Aun en pleno siglo XVII, según relataba el jesuita Pere Gil, 'les moles d'ella van per tot lo mon'; Graupera, 'Usos, artífexs i comerç de la pedra', p. 248.

82 Altisent, *Diplomatari de Santa Maria de Poblet*, doc. no. 156, pp. 139–40.

y el molino del comprador.[83] Asimismo, en el pacto suscrito en 1218 entre el abad de Cardona y Bernat de Serramitjana, se preveía la repartición a medias del coste del material, ya fuera 'de petra et de ferro ac de ligno'.[84] Además de todo esto, tales edificios debían cubrirse con tejas, como así queda especificado en 1260 a propósito del molino rodero citado por Fernández Trabal.[85]

'Iure dominacionis' *vs.* 'iure plantacionis'

Tal distinción la encontramos explicitada en una donación realizada en 1175 por los condes de Urgell (Ermengol VII y Dolça e hijo) a favor de Bernat de Sió respecto a la construcción de molinos junto a los ríos Segre y Sió. El concesionario debía plantarlos y edificarlos ('quod tu hedifices et plantes ipsos molendinos de tuo de omnibus que ibi necesaria fuerint'), reservándose la mitad en concepto de 'iure plantacionis', mientras que los condes tendrían la otra mitad en concepto de 'iure dominacionis'.[86] Asimismo, el citado Bernat de Sió estaría obligado a dar 1/3 parte de los beneficios obtenidos de dichos molinos cuando 'bene plantati et hedificati fuerint', e igual proporción regiría para los gastos que surgieran a partir de entonces. Así, pues, si el propietario seguía siendo el titular del dominio directo, quien pasaba a ser titular del dominio útil tenía conferido el derecho de edificación.

En principio, eran más bien los concesionarios quienes debían hacerse cargo de los gastos de edificación.[87] Una vez edificado el molino, el constructor ya podía poner en práctica su derecho de explotación. Los beneficios solían repartirse proporcionalmente; en Cataluña, lo más habitual era 1/3 parte de la molienda a favor del propietario y 2/3 partes a favor del concesionario. También los gastos de mantenimiento podían repartirse con idénticas proporciones o ir a cargo únicamente del explotador.

Algunas concesiones adoptan ya la forma de establecimientos o donaciones a censo, mediante los cuales se estipulaba la cesión, igualmente, de un terreno o solar para poder levantar un molino a cambio de tener que pagar un derecho de entrada, que solía ser — cuando se indica — muy fluctuante, además del censo (en especie o en dinero)[88] y del diezmo que debía ser satisfecho, generalmente, a las instituciones eclesiásticas.

83 Ferrer, *Diplomatari del monestir de Sant Joan de les Abadesses*, doc. no. 222, p. 320.
84 Galera, *Diplomatari de la vila de Cardona*, doc. no. 326, pp. 393–95.
85 Fernández Trabal, 'En els orígens de la indústria', p. 91.
86 Asimismo, los donantes otorgaron a la otra parte el 'iure sucessionis'; Escuder, *Diplomatari de Santa Maria de les Franqueses*, doc. no. 31, pp. 102–03.
87 Ya se ha aludido, por otra parte, a la concesión a los habitantes del lugar de las Beces (1225), a quienes se dio permiso para edificar un molino a sus propias expensas; Font Rius, *Cartas de población*, doc. no. 245, pp. 346–48.
88 Tratándose de molinos harineros, esos censos solían ser establecidos preferentemente en especie, no así en el caso de los batanes. En los molinos dados a construir a Bonet de Fraga en 1182 en la zona del Segrià, este pagaría 14 sueldos por el molino pañero o bien 9 fanecas de

La promoción de esas instalaciones se debió, ante todo, al interés fiscal de los señores, y no por un supuesto carácter emprendedor. De hecho, a algunos de esos señores parece que les era indiferente qué tipo de molino debía construirse con tal de poder percibir una parte de los correspondientes emolumentos. Así, en 1182, el maestre templario fray Berenguer d'Avinyó, junto con los demás freires de Gardeny, hicieron donación de las aguas sobrantes del molino de Bernat de Vallseguer para la construcción de un molino 'traper' o 'blader', siendo esta una decisión dejada al arbitrio del concesionario.[89] Ello no obsta para que la misma orden decidiera emprender de manera directa la construcción de batanes a finales del siglo XIII.

Sea como sea, eran los señores, como propietarios del suelo — y de los recursos hídricos — quiénes, mediante el ejercicio del mencionado 'iure dominacionis', podían decidir de qué modo debían usarse esos recursos o qué podía construirse en esos terrenos. En ocasiones, el derecho de edificación podía ser traspasado a otros señores; así, en 1198 el conde Ermengol VIII de Urgel hizo donación de ciertos molinos a favor de la abadesa de las Franqueses; ello incluía el derecho de señorío, y asimismo el 'ius et potestatem construendi molendina'.[90]

Acto seguido, pasamos a ver qué personas o entidades figuran como otorgantes de permisos de construcción:

A/ Concedentes

Quienes aparecen actuando en la concesión de permisos de construcción de molinos son los condes-reyes, los condes de Urgel y del Ampurdán, los vizcondes de Cabrera y otros señores de entre los linajes nobles más representativos de la época (como los Cervera, los Castellvell, los Claramunt, los Cervelló…). Por otra parte, están algunos monasterios (Poblet, Ripoll, Sant Joan de les Abadesses, Casserres, Gerri, l'Estany…), siendo a veces los mismos abades o priores quienes figuran como otorgantes. La lista sigue con las órdenes militares, como los templarios de Gardeny.[91] Como ya se ha visto antes, algunos de esos señores también fueron promotores de batanes.

Desde luego, también encontramos algunos obispos, así como clérigos actuando en nombre o con el consentimiento del cabildo catedralicio.[92] Por lo que respecta al siglo XIII, podríamos destacar la serie de donaciones

---

cereal (6 de centeno y 6 de trigo) si acababa siendo 'blader'; Sarobe, *Col·lecció diplomàtica de la Casa del Temple de Gardeny*, doc. no. 416, pp. 626–27.

89 Sarobe, *Col·lecció diplomàtica de la Casa del Temple de Gardeny*, doc. no. 416, pp. 626–27.

90 Escuder, *Diplomatari de Santa Maria de les Franqueses*, doc. no. 150, p. 235.

91 Justamente, los templarios destacan por su decidida apuesta en la construcción de molinos en sus diferentes dominios, tanto en el Segrià histórico como en otras zonas del llano de Lleida; Sabaté, 'L'eclosió econòmica', p. 335.

92 Como en el caso de Pere de Nargó, prepósito de la Seu d'Urgell, cuando concedió un lugar para la construcción o reconstrucción de molinos (1189); Baraut, 'Els documents, dels anys 1151–1190', doc. no. 1839, pp. 341–42.

realizadas por los obispos de Tortosa Ponç de Torrella y Bernat d'Olivella, junto con los respectivos priores de la catedral (Guillem y Pere de Puig), respecto a molinos mandados erigir en diferentes lugares del área tortosina.[93]

No era necesario que los señores se ocuparan directamente de expedir licencias de construcción; tal cometido podía ser traspasado a sus funcionarios, como en el caso del molino mandado construir en Ribarroja — junto al río Francolí — por el bayle general de Tarragona (1191).[94] O bien eran esos mismos agentes quienes debían encargarse de la construcción, como se infiere del permiso dado por el obispo Ponç de Tortosa a su bayle, Palací de Belsa, para levantar un molino en Horta [de Sant Joan] (1234).

B/ Concesionarios y molineros

En principio, resulta imposible encasillar a los concesionarios en un único cliché.[95] Si algunas personas podían asumir individualmente el coste de levantar un molino, otras debían hacerlo asociadas, ya sea que estuvieran unidas por lazos familiares o no. Al respecto, podemos hacer referencia a la concesión realizada por los Jorba, en 1169, de unos molinos localizados en Rufea (SO de Lleida), cuyos costes de construcción parecen quedar repartidos entre varias personas — probablemente, hasta diez. Uno de los concesionarios (Torró) debía aportar 100 sueldos 'ad plantare ipsos molendinos'; otros debían invertir la misma cantidad, excepto una mujer (Guilla), que lo haría en 80 sueldos.[96] Así pues, la edificación de esos molinos debió de tener un coste total de cerca de 1.000 sueldos.

Por otra parte, no tenemos indicaciones directas de costes, excepto en el caso de los batanes mandados construir por los templarios de Gardeny a finales del siglo XIII, según las cuentas analizadas en su día por Iñaki Padilla:[97] el total arroja una suma muy elevada (más de 50 mil sueldos jaqueses). Según Riera, la construcción de molinos pañeros quedó reservada a los poderosos, ya que su alto coste estaba fuera del alcance de los pelaires.[98] Para poder acceder al dominio útil de un batan, los menestrales tenían que constituir sociedades, lo que solo aparece documentado en algunas localidades.[99]

93 En 1234, 1245, 1250 y 1259; Escolà, *Diplomatari de la catedral de Tortosa*, docs. no. 937, 1059, 1113, 1198–99, pp. 129–30, 274–75, 477–79, 566–67, 730–33.

94 Sans, *Col·lecció diplomàtica de la casa del Temple de Barberà*, doc. no. 159, pp. 244–45; también Bisson, *Fiscal Accounts of Catalonia*, doc. no. 158, pp. 284–85.

95 En relación con el *Rec comtal* de Barcelona, se observa una participación cada vez mayor de ciudadanos actuando como simples inversores, frente a otras personas que tan solo buscaban en el oficio de molinero una forma de obtener ingresos suplementarios; Ortí, 'L'explotació d'una renda reial', p. 259.

96 Altisent, *Diplomatari de Santa Maria de Poblet*, doc. no. 349–51, pp. 268–69.

97 Padilla, 'La construcció d'un enginy hidràulic', p. 108.

98 El batanero solo disponía de un derecho de usufructo sobre la máquina, el inmueble y demás equipamientos; Riera, 'La draperia a la Corona catalanoaragonesa', p. 814.

99 Por ej., en Castelló d'Empúries; Gironella, *Els molins empordanesos*, p. 113.

Quienes se hacían cargo de la construcción de un molino, también debían designar a la persona que se ocuparía luego del proceso de molienda: el molinero propiamente dicho. En el acuerdo suscrito en 1199 entre Ermessenda de Clarà y la canónica de Solsona, se hace referencia expresa al *molendinarius* que estaría a cargo de los dos molinos que debían ser reconstruidos.[100] En la donación realizada en 1204 por el abad de Poblet a favor de Bernat de Montoliu, el cenobio se comprometía a dar de comer al molinero, pero solo en el caso de que ambos molinos (uno harinero y otro pañero) estuvieran funcionando.[101] En un establecimiento suscrito en 1209, el concesionario (Bartomeu Pellicer), no solo se comprometía a levantar dos molinos, sino también a tener un molinero que se ocupase de ambos.[102] Por lo demás, hemos hallado un solo contrato que parece estar suscrito directamente con un molinero: se trata del establecimiento realizado en 1249 por Guillem de Cervelló a favor de Ferrer Moliner y su familia, en donde concesionario y molinero parecen ser una misma persona.[103]

El molinero debía tener su propio espacio para vivir, ya fuera en el propio molino o en vivienda cercana. Así, todo molino podía contar con dependencias anexas. En 1190 se habla de un 'molendinum cum domo, ortus et turriuncula' (en la torre de Vallseguer, al NE de Lleida); la correspondiente transacción de compraventa se realizó sobre la mitad de cada uno de esos elementos, incluyendo dicha torrecilla 'que est circa molendinum'.[104] También el casal molinero de Rosselló de Segrià (1291) tenía contiguas casas, así como una torre 'cum medina' [*sic*].[105] Ciertamente, todo molino acostumbraba a tener un huerto anexo para servir de abastecimiento a su inquilino; en una donación del obispo de Tortosa (1234) se preveía destinar a usos hortícolas y plantación de manzanos una parcela situada bajo el canal de riego, a la vez que se reservaba otra extensión de terreno para levantar casas y un corral.[106]

En síntesis, si hemos pasado revista a diferentes aspectos de la edificación de molinos es a partir de los datos que nos brindan la serie de contratos de establecimientos y licencias para construirlos de acuerdo con ciertos parámetros, parámetros que suelen ser similares, aunque con una casuística que resulta interesante de poner de relieve en cada caso. La expansión de la molinería hidráulica tuvo un protagonismo compartido entre los señores, en su

---

100 Bach, *Diplomatari de l'Arxiu Diocesà de Solsona*, doc. no. 604, pp. 729–30.

101 Si solo estuviese activo uno, no se le daría nada; Pons, *Cartulari de Poblet*, doc. no. 249, pp. 150–51.

102 Papell, *Diplomatari del monestir de Santes Creus*, doc. no. 485, pp. 693–94.

103 Respecto de construcciones a realizar en el mismo término de Cervelló; ACA, Canc., Pergaminos (Jaime I), no. 1157.

104 Sarobe, *Col·lecció diplomàtica de la Casa del Temple de Gardeny*, doc. no. 561, pp. 824–25. Ignoro qué uso o función tendría una pequeña torre cerca de un molino, si es que no se trataba de antiguas torres de defensa.

105 Alturo, *Diplomatari d'Alguaire*, doc. no. 263, pp. 561–64.

106 Escolà, *Diplomatari de la catedral de Tortosa*, doc. no. 937, pp. 274–75.

rol de promotores, y los distintos beneficiarios de las concesiones señoriales, actuando estos más bien como empresarios, como tales haciéndose cargo de los costes de construcción y de contratar la mano de obra. Esas obras debieron estar dirigidas, si no supervisadas, por maestros o expertos en el tipo de construcción, que las fuentes documentales consultadas aquí mantienen en el más absoluto anonimato;[107] así, pues, para la época en cuestión, no es posible saber quiénes fueron los verdaderos constructores de molinos, más allá, naturalmente, de las atribuciones que pueden ser hechas a los concesionarios o a los propios señores cuando se involucraron de forma más directa.

ABSTRACT This article addresses the construction and development of the network of hydraulic mills in Catalonia between 1050 and 1299 through a systematic analysis of the region's rich documentation, in particular the deeds by which the lords gave their permission for the construction of new mills, both for flour and for cloth. Through analysis of these texts, the article discusses topics such as the chronological development of the phenomenon, the materiality of building structures, and also the relationship between the lords (as owners of the water rights) and the concessionaires who actually built and managed the mills.

107 Con todo, a partir del siglo XIII, se tienen noticias sobre la contratación de maestros para encargarse del mantenimiento de los aparejos molineros, así como de los trabajos de construcción y conservación de sus infraestructuras; véase Gironella, *Els molins empordanesos*, p. 194.

Works Cited

Manuscripts and Archival Sources

Barcelona, Archivo de la Corona de Aragón (ACA), fondo Cancillería (Canc.)
Girona, Archivo Diocesano de Girona (ADG), Pergaminos de la Pia Almoina

Primary Sources

Altisent, Agustí, *Diplomatari de Santa Maria de Poblet. I. 960–1177* (Barcelona: Abadia de Poblet/Departament de Cultura, 1993)

Alturo, Jesús, *Diplomatari d'Alguaire i del seu monestir duple de l'orde de Sant Joan de Jerusalem (1245–1300)*, Diplomataris, 59 (Barcelona: Fundació Noguera, 2010)

Alvira, Martín, *Pedro el Católico, Rey de Aragón y Conde de Barcelona (1196–1213). Documentos, testimonios y memoria histórica*, 5 vols (Zaragoza: Inst. Fernando el Católico, 2010)

Bach, Antoni, *Diplomatari de l'Arxiu Diocesà de Solsona (1101–1200)*, 2 vols, Diplomataris, 26–27 (Barcelona: Fundació Noguera, 2002)

Baiges, Ignasi J., *Els pergamins de l'Arxiu Comtal de Barcelona, de Ramon Berenguer II a Ramon Berenguer IV*, 4 vols, Diplomataris, 48–51 (Barcelona: Fundació Noguera, 2010)

Baraut, Cebrià, 'Els documents, dels anys 1151–1190, de l'Arxiu Capitular de la Seu d'Urgell', *Urgellia*, 10 (1990–1991), 7–349

——, 'Els documents, dels anys 1191–1200, de l'Arxiu Capitular de la Seu d'Urgell', *Urgellia*, 11 (1992–1993), 7–160

Batlle, Carme, Josep Baucells, Àngel Fàbrega, Josep Hernando, and Manuel Riu, *Diplomatari de l'Arxiu Capitular de la catedral de Barcelona, segle XI*, 5 vols, Diplomataris, 37–41 (Barcelona: Fundació Noguera, 2006)

Bisson, Thomas, *Fiscal Accounts of Catalonia under the Early Count-Kings (1151–1213)* (Berkeley: University of California, 1984)

Bolòs, Jordi, *Diplomatari del monestir de Santa Maria de Serrateix (segles X–XV)*, Diplomataris, 42 (Barcelona: Fundació Noguera, 2006)

Chesé, Ramon, *Col·lecció diplomàtica de Sant Pere d'Àger fins 1192*, 2 vols, Diplomataris, 61 (Barcelona: Fundació Noguera, 2011)

Escolà, Josep Maria, Manel Pica, Montserrat Rovira, and Antoni Virgili, *Diplomatari de la catedral de Tortosa. Episcopats de Ponç de Torrella (1212–1254) i Bernat d'Olivella (1254–1272)*, vols 1–2, Diplomataris, 76–77 (Barcelona: Fundació Noguera, 2018)

Escuder, Javier, *Diplomatari de Santa Maria de les Franqueses (1075–1298)*, Diplomataris, 72 (Barcelona: Fundació Noguera, 2016)

Ferrer, Joan, *Diplomatari del monestir de Sant Joan de les Abadesses (995–1273)*, Diplomataris, 43 (Barcelona: Fundació Noguera, 2009)

Font Rius, Josep M., *Cartas de población y franquícia de Cataluña. vols 1–2* (Madrid-Barcelona: CSIC, 1969–1983)

Galera, Andreu, *Diplomatari de la vila de Cardona (966–1276)*, Diplomataris, 15 (Barcelona: Fundació Noguera, 1998)

Ginebra, Rafael, *El Manuel primer de l'Arxiu de la Cúria Fuamda de Vic (1230–1233)*, 2 vols, Acta notariorum Cataloniae, 6–7 (Barcelona: Fundació Noguera, 1998)

Mallorquí, Elvis, *Col·lecció diplomàtica dels Cartellà, cavallers de Maçanet de la Selva (1106–1301)*, Diplomataris, 67 (Barcelona: Fundació Noguera, 2015)

Marquès, Benigne, 'Els pergamins del fons "Monestirs diversos" de l'Arxiu Capitular d'Urgell (950–1582)', *Urgellia*, 18 (2011–2014), 305–99

Marquès, Josep. M., *Cartoral, dit de Carlemany, del bisbe de Girona (s. IX–XIV)*, 2 vols, Diplomataris, 1–2 (Barcelona: Fundació Noguera, 1993)

——, *Col·lecció diplomàtica de Sant Daniel de Girona (924–1300)*, Diplomataris, vol. 12 (Barcelona: Fundació Noguera, 1997)

Massip, Jesús, ed., *Costums de Tortosa*, Textos i documents, 32 (Barcelona: Fundació Noguera, 1996)

Ordeig, Ramon, *Diplomatari del monestir de Ripoll (segle XII)* (Vic: Patronat d'Estudis Osonencs, 2017)

Papell, Joan, *Diplomatari del monestir de Santa Maria de Santes Creus (975–1225)*, 2 vols, Diplomataris, 35–36 (Barcelona: Fundació Noguera, 2005)

Pardo, Maria, *Mensa episcopal de Barcelona (878–1299)*, Diplomataris, 5 (Barcelona: Fundació Noguera, 1994)

Pons, Joan, *Cartulari de Poblet* (Barcelona: Institut d'Estudis Catalans, 1938)

Pons Guri, Josep M., 'Manual notarial d'Alcover (anys 1228–1229)', *De Scriptis Notariorum* (1989), 161–294

Rius Serra, José, *Cartulario de Sant Cugat del Vallès*, 4 vols (Barcelona: CSIC, 1945–1981)

Salvadó, Joan, 'El monestir benedictí de Sant Benet de Bages. Fons documental: identificació, edició i estudi. Segles X–XI' (PhD thesis, Universitat de Lleida, 2012)

Sans Travé, Josep M., *Col·lecció diplomàtica de la casa del Temple de Barberà (945–1212)* (Barcelona: Generalitat de Catalunya/Departament de Justícia, 1997)

Santacana, Jaume, *El monasterio de Poblet (1151–1181)* (Barcelona: CSIC, 1974)

Sarobe, Ramon, *Col·lecció diplomàtica de la Casa del Temple de Gardeny (1070–1200)*, 2 vols, Diplomataris, 16–17 (Barcelona: Fundació Noguera, 1998)

Virgili, Antoni, *Diplomatari de la catedral de Tortosa (1062–1193)*, Diplomataris, 11 (Barcelona: Fundació Noguera, 1997)

Secondary Works

AADD, *Catalunya Romànica*, ed. by Antoni Pladevall, 27 vols (Barcelona: Fundació Enciclopèdia Catalana, 1984–1998)

Aventín, Mercè, *Vilamajor (872–1299). De la fi del sistema antic a la consolidació del feudalisme* (Sabadell: AUSA, 1990)

Batet, Carolina, *L'aigua conquerida. Hidraulisme feudal en terres de conquesta. Alguns exemples de la Catalunya Nova i de Mallorca* (Valencia: PUV, 2006)

Bolòs, Jordi, *Els orígens medievals del paisatge català. L'arqueologia el paisatge com a forma per a conèixer la història de Catalunya* (Abadia de Montserrat, 2004)

Caucanas, Sylvie, *Moulins et irrigation en Roussillon du IXe au XVe siècle* (Paris: CNRS, 1995)

Donat, Lídia, and Xavier Solà, 'Els molins: construccions, tipologies i usos', in *Aigua i ciutat: els recs de Banyoles, historia i futur*, ed. by Joan Nogué and Carles Puncernau (Banyoles: CECB, 2014), pp. 67–84

Fernández Trabal, Josep, 'En els orígens de la indústria. Els molins de la conca baixa del Llobregat a l'Edat Mitjana (segles XII–XVI)', *Materials del Baix Llobregat*, 6 (2000), 85–105

——, 'Les indústries rurals', in *Història agrària dels Països Catalans. 2: Edat Mitjana*, ed. by Juan M. Salrach (Barcelona: Fundació Catalana per a la Recerca, 2004), pp. 361–94

Gironella, Josep M., *Els molins empordanesos baixmedievals. Propietat, explotació i fiscalitat* (Girona: Associació d'Història Rural, 2014)

Gironella, Josep M., 'La mòlta de cereals i el batanatge de teixits al comtat d'Empúries i al vescomtat de Rocabertí (finals del segle XIII i primera meitat del XIV)', 2 vols (PhD Thesis, Universitat de Barcelona, 2013)

Graupera, Joaquim, 'Usos, artífexs i comerç de la pedra de Montjuïc de Barcelona a l'època medieval', in *Les pedreres medievals a la Corona d'Aragó*, ed. by Francesca Español and Joan Valero (Barcelona: Institut d'Estudis Catalans, 2017), pp. 237–56

INVARQUIT (*Inventari del Patrimoni Arquitectònic de Catalunya*/Direcció General del Patrimoni Cultural/Generalitat de Catalunya): http://invarquit.cultura.gencat.cat

Kirchner, Helena, 'Hidráulica campesina anterior a la generalización del dominio feudal. Casos en Cataluña', in *Hidráulica agraria y sociedad feudal. Prácticas, técnicas, espacios*, ed. by Josep Torró and Enric Guinot (Valencia: PUV, 2012), pp. 21–50

Martí, Ramon, 'Hacia una arqueologia hidráulica: la génesis del molino feudal en Cataluña', in *Arqueología medieval. En las afueras del medievalismo*, ed. by Miquel Barceló, Helena Kirchner, Josep M. Lluró, Ramon Martí, and José M. Torres (Barcelona: Crítica, 1988), pp. 165–94

Ortega, Julián M., 'El contexto social de la molineria hidráulica en el Aragón medieval (siglos XI–XIII)', in *¿Agua pasada? Regadíos en el Archivo Histórico Provincial de Zaragoza*, ed. by Julián M. Ortega and María Teresa Iranzo (Zaragoza: Gobierno de Aragón, 2008), pp. 83–97

Ortí, Pere, 'L'explotació d'una renda reial: els molins del Rec Comtal de Barcelona fins al segle XIII', in *Estudios sobre renta, fiscalidad y finanzas en la Cataluña bajomedieval*, ed. by Manuel Sánchez Martínez (Barcelona: IMF-CSIC, 1993), pp. 243–75

Padilla, José I., 'La construcció d'un enginy hidràulic. Els comptes del molí batan de Gardeny (Lleida, 1290–91)', *Ilerda*, 49.2 (1991), 105–27

Planes, Ramon, 'Els molins i altres indústries', in *L'art gòtic a Catalunya. Arquitectura. III: Dels palaus a les masies*, ed. by Antoni Pladevall (Barcelona: Enciclopèdia Catalana, 2003), pp. 284–88

Riera, Antoni, 'La draperia a la Corona catalanoaragonesa durant el segon terç del segle XIII', in *Jaume I. Commemoració del VIII centenari del naixement de Jaume I*, ed. by Maria T. Ferrer Mallol (Barcelona: Institut d'Estudis Catalans, 2013), II, pp. 763–99

Sabaté, Flocel, 'L'eclosió econòmica', in Flocel Sabaté, *Història de Lleida. 2: Alta edat mitjana* (Lleida: Pagès, 2003), pp. 316–54

MARIA ELENA CORTESE

Productive Buildings and Economic Growth

Iron-Working in Central and Northern Italy (Eleventh–Thirteenth Centuries)

A few years ago, in an essay entitled *Prima della crescita* (Before Growth), Chris Wickham noted that historians had often used mentions of merchants, craftspeople, or luxury products as evidence for establishing a chronology of economic growth in the Middle Ages; but he also underlined that before 1150 these attestations do not really tell us very much about economic structures. Indeed, only the development of the mass production — such as of fabrics, metals, and pottery — can be considered an effective proxy for understanding economic trends.[1] Medieval metal-working can certainly be studied in this perspective. The two major Italian mining and metallurgical districts — the Alps and Tuscany (including the island of Elba) — will therefore be the focus of the following pages, and they will be compared in order to identify common lines of development. However, it is necessary to briefly explain why I have chosen to deal only with the production of iron and not with that of precious metals too, which were also present in both areas.

First of all, the exploitation of precious minerals (particularly silver) must mainly be considered in relation to coinage. Even if silver was a recurrent concern for the public authorities and appears in the written sources quite often, the total volume of this raw material that was put into circulation was far lower than what was required to meet the considerable demand for iron which came from many human activities. Therefore, the production of silver reflects economic phenomena less directly than that of iron. Secondly, technological aspects are essential for interpreting the topographical location of ironworks, their management, and also the evolution of their material structure. In this regard, it should be emphasized right from the start that substantial technical innovations were introduced into iron-making in the period we are dealing with, which allowed for a real increase in productivity. This aspect, however,

1 Wickham, 'Prima della crescita'.

Maria Elena Cortese (mariaelena.cortese@unige.it)
is associate professor at the University of Genoa.

Building and Economic Growth in Southern Europe (1050–1300), ed. by Sandro Carocci and Alessio Fiore, (Turnhout: Brepols, 2024), pp. 149–168 BREPOLS PUBLISHERS 10.1484/M.TMC-EB.5.137978

is less relevant to the processing of coinage metals, whose working techniques did not undergo major changes to the same degree. But in order to understand what happened between *c.* 1050 and *c.* 1300, it is necessary to at least briefly mention the immediately preceding centuries.

Between the ninth and the tenth centuries, both in Tuscany and in northern Italy, iron production certainly took place on estates (*curtes*) owned by important churches — the only ones to have preserved written documents — which had incorporated considerable fiscal assets. Payments of rents in iron to ecclesiastical landowners are repeatedly mentioned. The analysis of these sources makes it possible to draw a distinction between the delivery of certain iron objects (*ferramenta, vomeri*, etc.) by individual tenants and that of far from negligible amounts of goods — above all raw iron (*ferrum*) — by both large or small groups of tenants who lived within *curtes* located in, or near, Alpine and pre-Alpine mining areas. In the former case we may suppose that the people involved were blacksmiths who at most could exploit modest local deposits for limited primary production; in the latter case, both the smelting and the forging took place in the context of a rather specialized activity, which would appear to have been based on the work of groups of craftsmen.[2] In the same period in Tuscany we can catch a glimpse of a rather complex system for the exploitation of Elban iron deposits, from which high-quality hematite was extracted. This activity could not have been managed only at the local level, but presupposed the existence of sea routes connecting the Tuscan archipelago's islands to southern *Tuscia*'s coast and the port of Pisa.[3] Archaeological research carried out at the end of the last century has indeed documented the processing of Elban hematite both in some sites (probably small open settlements) on the coastal strip in front of the island (Gulf of Follonica), and in urban centres (Pisa).[4] This activity thus seems to be part of a system coordinated in some way by a central power — the kings or the highest public officials in the region (the margraves of *Tuscia*) — who also exercised control over vast fiscal assets in the Maremma area.

These hypotheses seem to be strengthened by recent archaeological research carried out in the coastal hinterland of the upper Maremma and in the nearby mining district of the Colline Metallifere. In the Donoratico site, which almost certainly belonged to an important royal monastery (San Pietro a Monteverdi), the processing of Elban hematite took place at the end of the ninth/beginning of the tenth century, when the site underwent major building renovation; this initiative can be attributed to a subject with

2 Cortese, 'Beni fiscali'.

3 Concerning Pisa's maritime activity in this period, see Tangheroni and others, 'Pisa e il Mediterraneo', pp. 116–29.

4 Gulf of Follonica: Baiocco and others, *Metallurgia antica e medievale*, pp. 80, 88, 136; Cucini, 'L'insediamento altomedievale'; Cucini and Tizzoni, *Le antiche scorie*, pp. 56–58, 73. Pisa: Corretti, 'L'attività', p. 87.

a large amount of power, who was certainly also able to ensure the supply of hematite from the nearby island of Elba. All stages of the metallurgical cycle were carried out at the site, from the smelting of hematite to the forging of objects; however, the structures' remains and the amount of slag suggest the presence of small ironworks, which only functioned to meet the internal needs of the site.[5] Quite a different picture emerges from another case-study: the excavations at Vetricella, in the Pecora valley immediately behind the plain of Follonica. This site should probably be identified as the place where the central settlement of a royal *curtis* (called Valli) was located.[6] In the tenth century the main specialized production activity at Vetricella was precisely iron-working: hundreds of metal fragments have been found (many of which were probably destined for recycling), as well as slag leftover from forging, small metal bars, and ingots with traces of hammering.[7] The number of iron objects found in Vetricella is far greater than that found in numerous other excavated sites in this part of the region. As regards the productive activity on the site, as proposed by archaeologists, it is very probable that this was a management centre which coordinated the final production of iron artefacts. In other words, fragmentary objects to be recycled were brought and stored here, along with semi-finished ones (ingots, bars) which came from other places where the ore was smelted.[8] More specifically, since no remains of furnaces or slags from the first iron-working phase have been identified in Vetricella, it may be supposed that the sites with evidence of hematite reduction identified in the Gulf of Follonica were part of a more complex system, which had Vetricella at its centre.[9] Given the considerable number of artefacts, their production may have been intended to meet the needs not only of this *curtis*, but of other, more distant fiscal estates too, considering that the location of the site — at the centre of a web of canals and wetlands close to the coast — allowed easy access to the sea.

The situation in Vetricella, moreover, makes it possible in my opinion to draw a comparison with the coeval case of the royal *curtis* of Darfo, in Valcamonica (Bergamo). From a 1047 privilege granted by Emperor Henry III, we know that the inhabitants of the nearby Val di Scalve — an area in which iron deposits are plentiful and iron-working is well attested even in the following centuries — were required every year to pay the *curtis* of Darfo 'libras mille ferri' (one thousand pounds of iron), that is at least 400 kg of raw metal, in exchange for the authorization to freely trade the iron produced in the valley in a large area of the kingdom.[10] Since the privilege explicitly refers to

5 Bianchi and others, 'Archeologia di un cantiere'; Panichi, 'La produzione', p. 212.

6 Bianchi, *Archeologia dei beni*.

7 Agostini, 'The Metal Finds'.

8 Agostini, 'The Metal Finds', p. 44; Bianchi, *Archeologia dei beni*, chapter 1; Marasco and Briano, 'The Stratigraphic', p. 15.

9 See above, note 4.

10 *Heinrici III. diplomata*, ed. by Bresslau and Kehr, no. 199.

an ancient custom, it seems likely that mining and metallurgical production in the Val di Scalve dated back at least to the tenth century. The royal estate therefore appears to be a central place where iron tithes converged from the contiguous mining areas subject to imperial jurisdiction; this metal may have been destined for subsequent processing in Darfo itself, or the iron blooms may have been redistributed to other places within an economic circuit controlled by the public authorities themselves.

While during the eleventh century no significant novelties are noticeable in the written and archaeological sources, the late eleventh/early twelfth century must be identified as the real point of divergence between the productive system for precious metals and iron-working. Although both sectors were developing, in this phase they became incomparable in terms of the volume of production and amount of raw materials consumed (ore, charcoal). Secondly, the need to supply the considerable quantities of iron necessary for all the expanding sectors of the economy (agriculture, construction, craftsmanship, shipbuilding, the manufacturing of military equipment and so on) stimulated the large-scale exploitation of districts with a high concentration of good quality ore, which acquired a much greater strategic importance compared to the previous period, when even modest local deposits were used. It therefore became necessary to invest in the control of larger areas, and to carefully choose the sites for structures associated with production: the availability of vast woodlands, the abundance and quality of the mineral, access to markets and ease of transport became the determining factors about whether to enhance old metallurgical districts or to create new ones. This does not mean that iron production did not continue to satisfy local needs, since minor deposits were also exploited. For this phase, it is important to underline the coexistence of two different productive systems. This dual system is clearly visible in Tuscany, the most studied Italian region, thanks to the archaeological evidence available.

The first system involves limited smelting and forging activities under the direct control of lay and ecclesiastical landlords. Traces of Elban hematite reduction, dating back to between the eleventh and thirteenth centuries, have been identified in numerous castles both in the southern area of the region (Valli, Pero/Castellaccio, Montioni, Alma/Poggio Castello, Castel Maus, Rocca San Silvestro, Grosseto, Rocchette Pannocchieschi)[11] and in the northern one (Terrazzana, in the upper Valdinievole).[12] Iron was worked near some monastic centres, too, as is shown by the written sources for Santa Trinità di Montecalvo (Monte Amiata), by the excavation of the abbey of San Salvatore all'Amiata and by surface surveys in the Maremma area (San Quirico di Populonia, San

11 Baiocco and others, *Metallurgia antica e medievale*, pp. 85, 90, 122–23; Bruttini, 'Minatori e signorie'; Citter, ed., *Archeologia urbana*; Cucini and Tizzoni, *Le antiche scorie*, pp. 58, 75, 110–11, 123, 148, 204–05; Francovich, *Rocca S. Silvestro*, pp. 58–60, 84.

12 Quirós Castillo, *El incastellamento*, p. 63.

Pancrazio al Fango, San Bartolomeo di Sestinga).[13] The best studied case is Rocca San Silvestro: the iron-working area — located not inside a building, but sheltered by a wooden roof — included a bloomery for the reduction of the ore, a heating space for the iron blooms, and an intermediate one where the anvil was placed for beating and forging tools. The furnace was made up of a clay floor bordered on one side by a low wall to shelter the bellows from the fire. Both in Tuscany and in northern Italy, small areas for the forging and maintenance of iron tools were also frequently situated inside castles. Again, they were very simple structures, which can be classified as belonging to the bowl type, as in the case of the furnace excavated in the castle of Manzano, in Piedmont, which was located in an open space protected by a wooden shelter connected to an house.[14] However, in all these cases we should exclude any entrepreneurial role in iron production on the part of the local lords. These metallurgical activities were only linked to the phase of castle building, or they testify to a limited investment and appear to have been aimed at satisfying everyday needs in the settlements. Their topographical location also reflects the different control that local lords exercised over these limited activities, compared to their control over structures dedicated to the processing of coinage metals. The most evident case is again Rocca San Silvestro: here copper and lead ore (galena, an important source of silver) were processed inside the castle, while iron was produced in an area outside the walls.[15] A similar pattern is also repeated in the castle of Terrazzana, where the remains of a furnace for the reduction of Elban hematite were found in the immediate vicinity of the castle walls, but still outside of it.[16] In conclusion, while it is believed that from the eleventh century onward rural lords in Tuscany played a relevant role in the exploitation of coinage metals — leading both to the birth of new 'mining castles' and to the reorganizing of metallurgical settlements — there was no investment in iron-working aimed at producing a surplus for the market, as this activity was only undertaken to meet local needs.

This productive system was more or less in line with those of the previous centuries. In parallel to it, however, a new and very different form of organization was emerging in Tuscany, based on a more intense exploitation of the Elban mines. Starting from the last years of the eleventh century, the Pisan sources attest that groups of specialized artisans (*fabri*) seasonally migrated from the city toward Elba island and the Tyrrhenian coast to work the hematite extracted from the Elban mines, under the protection of the Pisan bishop (and therefore of the urban community). From this moment onward,

---

13 Cambi and Dallai, 'Archeologia di un monastero', p. 205; Cucini and Tizzoni, *Le antiche scorie*, pp. 58–59; Farinelli, 'Le risorse minerarie', pp. 43–44; Farinelli and Francovich, 'Potere e attività'.

14 On Tuscany, see Cortese, 'Il ferro a Pistoia', p. 330; Bruttini, 'Minatori e signorie', pp. 76–78; Tronti and Valenti, 'Gli spazi', pp. 225–27; on Piedmont, see Micheletto, 'Il castello di Manzano'; Micheletto, 'Archeologia dei metalli'; Negro Ponzi Mancini, ed., *S. Michele di Trino*.

15 Francovich and Wickham, 'Uno scavo archeologico'.

16 Quirós Castillo, *El incastellamento*, p. 63.

Elba and the Maremma coastal strip were affected by Pisa's expansionism; by the end of the twelfth century, they had fallen under the full control of the Pisan church and the urban commune.[17] Archaeological surveys have made it possible to identify dozens of hematite reduction sites on the island of Elba, in the Gulf of Follonica, in the Alma valley and on the promontory of Piombino, datable between the twelfth and the beginning of the fourteenth century. In these sites no traces of buildings were found, apart from short-lived structures; the furnaces were located in the open air or under wooden shelters, and probably the craftsmen themselves were housed in temporary shelters. Therefore, it does not seem as though permanent settlements linked to metallurgical activities were ever established in this scarcely populated area. The productive structures appear rather homogeneous in their main features: they were quite simple, with a limited activity over time (judging from the small size of the slag heaps), and were destroyed at the end of each smelting process to make room for new furnaces, which partially reused the remains from previous smelting cycles.[18]

The stages of production were limited to the reduction of the ore into iron blooms. Conversely, the transformation into finished products had to take place elsewhere, probably for the most part inside the city. It was thus possible to reduce the costs of transporting raw ore and charcoal, which was consumed in large quantities during the first metallurgical phase. At the same time, in Pisa — which expanded rapidly beyond its old Roman walls — iron-working no longer took place in the central area, but moved to the more peripheral one of Kinzica, beyond the Arno, where — from the twelfth century onward — a craft district had been established for the production and sale of glass and metal objects.[19] As far as the technical aspects and material structures are concerned, there is no noticeable difference between the sites related to the Pisan blacksmiths' activity and those located inside castles in the same period. However, one major difference lies in Pisa's overall organization of iron production: the city became increasingly active as a maritime centre and embarked on the wide scale exploitation of Elban deposits to satisfy the growing demand for iron, which was not only consumed within the city itself, but also traded on the Mediterranean market. In my opinion, the specific concept of 'medieval industry' can therefore be applied to this productive system, according to the meaning proposed by Philippe Braunstein and more recently reaffirmed by Chaterine Verna, namely the kind of activity 'capable

17 References to written sources and bibliography in Cortese, 'Il ferro a Pistoia', pp. 333–36, Garzella, 'Fabri e fabricae'.

18 Baiocco and others, *Metallurgia antica e medievale*; Corretti, *Metallurgia medievale*; Corretti, 'L'attività'; Cucini and Tizzoni, *Le antiche scorie*; Gelichi, 'Impianti per la lavorazione'; Martin, 'Trial Excavations'; Dallai, 'Opifici metallurgici'; Corretti, Chiarantini, Giuntoli, Benvenuti, Cambi, Firmati, Isola and Pagliantini, 'Un sito di lavorazione'.

19 Corretti, 'L'attività', p. 100; Carrera and others, 'Le ceramiche'; Garzella, 'Fabri e fabricae', pp. 46–47.

de livrer une production quantitativement importante, régulière, de qualité constante et reconnue comme telle sur le marché; une production qui dépasse les échanges locaux'.[20]

Let us now turn toward the Alps, and more specifically Lombardy. In the mining valleys, the bishops of Bergamo and Brescia had extensive lordships, as did — to a lesser extent — certain monasteries such as Santa Giulia (Brescia), Astino and Pontida (Bergamo). These churches also maintained important rights over the mines, due to the predominantly public origin of their assets.[21] However, it is very difficult to assess the role played by the rural lords in promoting iron-working in this period because, unlike in Tuscany, no archaeological research has been carried out and the written sources (with the sole exception of the aforementioned privilege bestowed by Henry III) do not mention the excavation and working of iron before the twelfth century, only referring to the 'vena argenti' (silver ore).

The lords' interest in the exploitation of iron in any case seems to have been limited, as already noted in relation to Tuscany. Considering the dossier on the Seriana Valley mines preserved by the episcopal archives of Bergamo[22] — within which only two documents concern iron — we notice that it was only at a late stage that the bishops tried to include iron in the list of their seigneurial revenues, while previously the iron deposits would appear to have been freely exploited by the valley community. In 1145, the consuls of Bergamo adjudicated between Bishop Gregory and the *vicini* of Ardesio regarding the dispute over the Monte Sicco iron ore and other mines in Ardesio valley. On the basis of the witness statements, they established that 'per plus quadraginta annis homines de Ardescie fodisse et tenuisse venas ferri in Cornelio Bagitene et Cornelio Garbiasca, et ubi invente fuissent, et carbones fecisse in comuni' (since more than forty years, the inhabitants of Ardesio had owned and mined the iron mines in Cornelio Bagitene and Cornelio Garbiasca, wherever they were located, and had in common produced charcoal), and moreover that 'ipsas venas et venam ferri in monte Sicco reperti, iure usuque homines vallis de Ardescie posse fodere et uti' (the same iron mines and the iron mine discovered in Monte Sicco could be exploited according to custom and right of the Ardesio valley inhabitants). The consuls therefore ruled that the inhabitants of the Ardesio valley could extract and work the ore without infringing upon the bishop's rights in terms of hunting and mountain grazing. Consequently they needed the bishop's permission to make charcoal for iron-working from wood collected in all

20 Braunstein, 'L'industrie'; Verna, 'Innovations et métallurgies', p. 624. See also Beck, ed., *L'innovation technique*.

21 Menant, 'Aspects', pp. 22–24.

22 'Possedimenti', ed. by Barachetti.

the forests in the valley; however, the bishop could in no way prohibit the Ardesio inhabitants from building iron furnaces.[23]

This document shows that iron production had existed for a long time in the Ardesio valley, alongside that of silver, and that the inhabitants had enjoyed the freedom to extract the ore until then. The dispute with the bishop therefore reflects the moment — in the first half of the twelfth century — when iron production had become more intense and was beginning to look like a profitable business. Only then did the bishop try to redefine relations with the rural community, by imposing his seigneurial rights on a resource over which the community had customarily exercised rights of use. But by then it was too late, as the well-established local community was capable of defending its autonomy *vis-à-vis* their lord by resorting to the support of the urban commune, which was also certainly interested in exercising control over this activity. It is also clear from this text that mining, charcoal production, and the running of furnaces were all managed by the inhabitants of the valley in a largely collective manner. Anyway, a community-based management of iron production was already visible in the aforementioned privilege granted to the inhabitants of the Val di Scalve by Henry III in 1047. Indeed the *homines habitantes in Monte Scalfi* emerge as a group capable of directly engaging with the imperial authorities to protect their commercial interests, and who were also able to ensure an extensive production of iron already in the first half of the eleventh century.[24] Other texts too show the dynamism of this community already in the first decades of the century, when the men of the Val di Scalve came into conflict with the inhabitants of the nearby village of Burno, in Valcamonica, over the exploitation of Monte Negrino, which was under the jurisdiction of the bishops of Brescia and Bergamo and of the counts of Bergamo.[25]

In 1179 the *universitas Ardesii*, which by then had its own consuls, again challenged the episcopal claims and, in return for a payment of one thousand and fifteen *lire*, obtained from Bishop Guala confirmation of a series of concessions previously granted by Oberto da Vimercate (he was a canon of the church of Bergamo, who had previously held the Ardesio *districtus* in fief) concerning matters of justice, exploitation of the woods, hunting, and the local market. The community also obtained

> potestatem utendi fluminibus et traendi aquas, levandi furnos ferri et fusinas argenti et furnellos argenti et fullos et molendinos et facere

23 'Possedimenti', ed. by Barachetti, Part II, no. V.

24 Menant, 'Pour un'histoire', p. 785: since the payment was probably 1/10 of the overall production, an annual production of between four and five tons can be assumed. See also Fiore, 'The Knots', p. 199.

25 *Codex diplomaticus civitatis et ecclesiæ Bergomatis*, ed. by Lupo, II, col. 491 (1018). See also: *I placiti del Regnum Italiae*, ed. by Manaresi, III, no. 471 (1091); *Codex diplomaticus civitatis et ecclesiæ Bergomatis*, ed. by Lupo, II, col. 775 (after 1091).

quicquid voluerint et piscandi in ipsis fluminibus atque pontes levandi et omnia predicta hedificia que iam fatta sunt sibi concessit, et etiam pontiaticum eis concessit [...] salvo omni iure et omni districto quod pertinet ad factum argenti

> (the right to use rivers and divert water, to build iron furnaces and silver workshops, fulling mills and mills, and to do everything they wanted to do, and also to fish in those rivers and to build bridges; besides he granted to them all the already existing buildings and the right to use bridges, but excluding any rights concerning the production of silver).[26]

Thus, the community's right to extract iron was implicitly confirmed (in fact, it was not mentioned at all), while it was necessary for the community to redeem its rights over water resources, woodland, and the building of production structures (metallurgical workshops, mills, and fulling mills). Moreover, from this charter it is possible to infer that there were numerous iron furnaces, as well as silver ones, and that they represented a common feature in Alpine valleys at that time. Indeed, as previously noted, to obtain large volumes of metal it was necessary to multiply the number of workshops — although, as we will see, this document seems to prove the presence in the valleys of the first technical innovation used for the processing of minerals.

In Tuscany, in this moment of economic expansion, the initiative of reorganizing the production system in a sparsely populated area had come from an urban commune. In the Alpine area, by contrast, it is clear that the local rural communities played the leading role in mining and iron processing during the central centuries of the Middle Ages. On the one hand, the likely reason for this is that for a long time iron, as a non-precious mineral, was not subject to any stringent controls by landlords. On the other hand, what probably also came into play were factors more directly related to the way in which the work was organized, since the production of much larger quantities of metal required the involvement of substantial human groups for the extraction of the metal and the initial processing stages. After all, both the documents concerning the *Scalvini* and those concerning Ardesio show that in these areas — populous ones relatively close to fast developing urban communes — it was rather difficult for the lords to control the local communities, which were already strong in the first half of the twelfth century and had had their own political institutions from at least the second half of that century.

The thirteenth century undoubtedly marked a turning point for medieval iron production, which began with the spread of some fundamental technical innovations. After a long period in which bloomery iron smelting had not enjoyed any kind of mechanization, the first change occurred with the appear-

26 'Possedimenti', ed. by Barachetti, Part II, no. VI.

ance of bloomeries equipped with water-powered hammers (often referred to by scholars as *moulins à fer*), thanks to a system that was technically not very dissimilar to that already used in fulling mills. This novelty — which made it possible to considerably reduce human work both for the hammering of the blooms and for the forging — had already appeared in several European mining districts (France, Sweden, Germany) in the first half of the twelfth century. In all likelihood, this innovation was the result of a series of small modifications and gradual improvements introduced in the production process as a whole. In Italy structures of this kind seem to be attested by the aforementioned Ardesio document (1179), in which the valley community focused on the need to have free access to the use of water for a series of craft activities, among which metallurgical ones are mentioned together with mills and fulling mills.[27]

However, the key technical innovation in iron-working was not the introduction of mechanized hammers, but the use of water power to operate the bellows. The technology involved here was more complicated and innovative: for it made it possible to obtain particularly high temperatures and, moreover, to constantly control them, thereby avoiding the kind of sudden changes that were fatal for the success of such operations. From the thirteenth century onward we therefore witness the spread of a new kind of iron bloomeries, equipped with hydraulic bellows, and a profound restructuring of the work process, which led to the achievement of higher productive levels. Indeed, more or less simultaneously throughout Europe, the written sources increasingly began to include technical terms used by notaries to refer to specialized production workshops, and which seem unmistakably connected to the use of water power.

In many European regions most bloomeries with hydraulic bellows continued to produce iron by the 'direct method', that is: the ore was transformed into spongy iron in one step and mostly also in the same furnace. But in some valleys of the Lombard Alps, the so-called 'indirect method' was also developed, whereby iron ore was first reduced to a hot liquid metal, which is called cast iron, thanks to the high temperatures reached in the furnaces (equipped with water-powered bellows). This iron had a high carbon content which had to be removed, in order to get forgeable iron, by reheating and oxidizing it; and this was achieved by blowing air into a charcoal-fired hearth using bellows.[28]

Rolf Sprandel, observing the duplication of the terms designating ironworks (*furnum* and *fucina*) in documents from this period, hypothesized that this technique appeared in the first half of the thirteenth century.[29]

27 See above, note 26.

28 General picture and bibliography in Cortese, *L'acqua, il grano, il ferro*; Verna, 'Innovations et métallurgies'.

29 Sprandel, *Das Eisengewerbe*, pp. 226–31; Sprandel, 'Die oberitalienische Eisenproduktion', pp. 315–16.

Sprandel's hypothesis was convincingly taken up by François Menant, on the basis of further attestations: in particular, a charter from Bergamo dated 1227 — which can be interpreted as evidence of the transition from rent in iron produced with the direct method to a new kind of rent in steel (*ferrum coctum*) — and the mention of steel and cast iron in the Bergamo customs tariffs (*c.* 1240).[30] Certainly, a furnace equipped with hydraulic installations located in Val di Scalve is described in a document laying out the boundaries of the communities of Schilpario, Vilmaggiore and Barzesto (1251), mentioning a 'furnum de ferro cum suis juribus et pertinentiis et clusis et acqueductibus et schirpio et utensilibus, que ipsa vicinia habet' (an iron furnace with its rights and belongings, and dams and channels, equipment and tools, belonging to the near community).[31] This change corresponded to an increasing and more selective demand for metal, both for forgeable iron bars and for steel. Some regions therefore began to specialize in production for more distant markets. In the first half of the thirteenth century production would appear to have been conspicuous, as shown by the multiplication of customs tariffs on metals — especially those on iron — in all Lombard cities, which suggests the existence of a trade network.[32] From the second half of the thirteenth century onward, the application of water power in Alpine ironworks undoubtedly also contributed to the decreasing importance of silver deposits in the Western Alps.[33] It is significant, for example, that the *teloneum ferri* (tax on the sale of ore, iron, and steel) was established by the commune of Bergamo in 1245 and became an important source of revenue, whereas previously the city government had mainly been interested in silver, as is evidenced by its disputes with the local bishop over the Ardesio mines.[34] The same change is also clear in Piedmont, in the mines of Val Chisone (in particular Perosa Argentina), where at the end of the thirteenth century the production of iron greatly exceeded that of silver.[35]

The water-powered production facilities required powerful and complex machinery, capable of simultaneously moving the bellows of the furnace, those of the refinery (in the case of an indirect process) and the hammer in the forge; and they had to be located along watercourses with an adequate capacity and a sufficient drop to spin the wheels. It was therefore in this phase that more permanent buildings appeared, which lasted a certain number of years. These were larger, built from non-perishable materials, equipped with canals and reservoirs and provided with accommodation for the workers. Furthermore, the furnace structure in the Alpine area began to develop

30 Menant, 'Pour un'histoire', pp. 784–85 and nn 7, 51, 52. This hypothesis is criticized in Arnoux, 'Moulins à fer', p. 31.

31 Finazzi, *Sulle antiche miniere*, p. 15.

32 Menant, 'Pour un'histoire', p. 785 and n. 59.

33 Belhoste, 'Mutations techniques'.

34 Mainoni, 'La politica dell'argento', p. 443.

35 Patria, 'In fodina veteri'.

considerably in height, sparking an evolution that led to the development of the 'cannecchio bresciano' and then to the blast furnace.[36] Furnaces were expensive installations which also required rights over the use of water. Moreover, these very recognizable structures in the valleys' landscape became a central element not only for production, but also for settlements and social organization. Each furnace had its own name (from the place where it stood) and in several cases metallurgical villages began to be mentioned in the documents, as did working districts in which furnaces were associated with a set of *fusine*: in Piedmont, for example, from the mid-thirteenth century onward various settlements arose in mining areas, marked by toponyms that often referred to the presence of a furnace on the site. In some cases it seems that these villages sprung up or came together precisely around this kind of productive structures.[37] They were normally owned by the local communities, which rented them out and also encouraged the building of new *fusine*, ensuring that communal woods could be exploited.

Therefore, from the end of the twelfth century onward, in settlements such as Ardesio, Bovegno, and Bormio, the working of iron stimulated the rise of an elite group of entrepreneurs — supported by the local community — who were able to negotiate their autonomy in the use of certain resources both with the old lords and with the city communes.[38] Certainly, the nearby urban communes (Bergamo, Brescia) tried to gain control over iron production and in particular to keep the final stages of the work — the most profitable — within their own walls. However, in the Alpine area, the mining valleys always remained important centres for the production of iron, steel, and also finished objects, employing hundreds of people and generating significant economic revenues. Therefore, this activity represented a very important factor that allowed local communities to maintain a degree of autonomy and made it difficult for the urban authorities and great city merchants to control them.[39]

In Tuscany too the new techniques spread in the second half of the thirteenth century in various inland areas, all rich in water and woodlands (Mount Amiata, the Merse valley, Garfagnana, Pistoiese, Casentino).[40] It was probably only in this period that larger and better organized workshops appeared and began to be run at an entrepreneurial scale, in response to the quickly developing market economy. The establishment of workshops of this kind, which had an innovative feature, led to the appearance of new technical terms, used by notaries to indicate these structures in the documents (*fabrica, fabrica aque, hedificium fabrice*).

---

36 See above, n. 28.

37 Di Gangi, *L'attività estrattiva*, pp. 351–53.

38 Menant, 'Pour un'histoire', p. 785 and n. 57; Arnoux, 'Innovation technique', pp. 217–18.

39 Menant, 'Pour un'histoire'; Menant, 'La metallurgie'.

40 Mount Amiata: Cortese, 'Opifici idraulici'; Merse valley: Cortese, *L'acqua, il grano, il ferro*, pp. 188–95; Garfagnana: Quirós Castillo, *El incastellamento*, pp. 161–63; Pistoiese: Cortese, 'Il ferro a Pistoia'; Casentino: Barlucchi, 'La lavorazione del ferro'.

Unlike in the Alpine valleys, in Tuscany water-powered ironworks processed the ore exclusively by the direct method, while the indirect method in the region dates back to the middle of the sixteenth century, when it was introduced on the initiative of Cosimo I de' Medici. In any case, the spread of the new hydraulic techniques certainly brought about a change in terms both of the location of productive districts and of the material configuration of the workshops, even though few sources explicitly mention the presence of hammers or bellows — they generally only specify that the workshops were located along rivers and streams and equipped with weirs, channels, and water reservoirs. In this phase, the furnaces were always located inside a building and no longer in the open; the buildings were characterized by a rather substantial material structure, sometimes flanked by houses for the workers and service structures, particularly charcoal deposits. To build an iron workshop powered by hydraulic energy, it was necessary to have a good level of technical knowledge and considerable accuracy in the installation of infrastructure and water wheels.

A clear example can be found in a contract drawn up in 1281 by the abbot of San Salvatore al Monte Amiata with Ranieri di Bianca, an inhabitant of Castel di Badia. This document is particularly rich in detail, and it is the first to clearly refer to the construction of an iron mill in the area. First of all, the abbot guaranteed Ranieri a ten-year concession for a fulling mill located near the castle to be converted 'ad faciendum et hedificandum fabricam aque' (into an iron workshop).[41] The concession included 'omnibus canalibus sive saiettulis et aliis edificiis necessariis ad faciendum fabricam aque' (all the channels and buildings necessary to set up the ironworks), as well as an area 'ad faciendum et edificandum unam domum pro carbonaria ad retinendum carbonem pro dicta fabrica' (to construct a building for the storing of charcoal). Secondly, the abbot granted Ranieri the woodlands of Mount Amiata, for collecting the timber for the charcoal necessary for the new *fabrica*. The clauses relating to charcoal production, moreover, suggest that this was a multi-functional workshop, in which both the reduction of the ore and the forging of finished objects was performed, because both raw ore and semi-finished iron were supplied (*venam*, *ferrum*). Finally, the contract specified that Ranieri would pay rent for four years, after which time the abbey would have the right to enter into a partnership with Ranieri and share his profits, investments, and expenses.

Another interesting document is a contract drawn up in 1296 by the commune of Seggiano, which would appear to have played a leading role in this dynamic economic period, both as the owner of iron workshops and as an economic actor supporting private investments.[42] In that year the commune

41 Siena, Archivio di Stato, Conventi, 4, 1281 luglio 16. For more details, see Cortese, 'Opifici idraulici', pp. 336–38.

42 Siena, Archivio di Stato, Diplomatico, Riformagioni, 1296 maggio 22. For more details, see

sold to a group of private entrepreneurs two parts of three water-powered workshops on the torrent Vivo, in the vicinity of the castle: a fulling mill and two iron workshops (the former seems to have been a water-powered forge, the latter were workshops for reducing the ore and forging objects). In addition, the commune granted these private entrepreneurs permission to build a new iron workshop on the Vivo, intended to be shared — again in a kind of joint venture — by the community and the entrepreneurs. Reading this document, we should note the community's concern to maintain a monopoly over production activities and to promote those controlled by the commune itself. The document also safeguarded the interests of the inhabitants of Seggiano, to whom the semi-finished products from these factories were to be sold at a set price. Great care was taken to facilitate in every way the supply of the raw materials necessary for the economic venture: the commune guaranteed the possibility of producing charcoal (and also of collecting the wood necessary for the maintenance of dams and channels) in all the woodlands within the territory of Seggiano; it also granted the entrepreneurs permission to collect all the timber necessary to build the new *fabrica*, with its dams and channels, and to build houses (*domos*: for the iron-workers?) next to the workshops. For the next five years, the entrepreneurs had the permission to buy plots of land with chestnut trees (particularly good for iron production) from private inhabitants of the district. In the whole territory of Seggiano, people were only allowed to make charcoal for these iron workshops; they could bring charcoal to the *fabricae* owned by the commune without paying any tax or toll. The management of the communal woodland, therefore, not only supported the traditional economic activities in the area, but was also promptly designed to sustain the new production activities, which were initially controlled by the commune in association with local entrepreneurs.

On the whole, a comparison between the Amiata texts and what is known about the Alpine valleys is quite revealing. In this context, too, the initiative of the local elites should be emphasized. Certainly, it is important to bear in mind that in Tuscany some Cistercian monasteries also played a leading role as promoters of iron-working; however, a careful reading of the sources shows that they became engaged in this profitable new activity later than the communities in the countryside and individual local entrepreneurs. The latter would instead appear to have taken on a leading role, seizing the opportunities offered by the increase in the demand for iron and the lowering of production costs caused by the spread of new techniques in the region.[43] A clear difference with respect to what had happened in the Alpine valleys, however, lies in the fact that the communities in the Siena territory, as time

Cortese, 'Opifici idraulici', pp. 338–41.

43 About the role played by the Cistercian monasteries of San Galgano (Merse valley) and San Salvatore al Monte Amiata, see Cortese, 'Medieval Iron-Working' and Cortese, 'Cistercian Monasteries'.

went by, completely lost control over both the production structures and the management of the woodlands, which increasingly fell under the direct or indirect control of the dominant city or of important urban of merchant and banking families.[44]

Let me now add some brief final remarks. Functional buildings for metallurgical production can provide valuable evidence when evaluating economic growth in medieval Western Europe. Indeed, a phase of intense growth usually implies a multiplication of buildings linked to economic activities, often associated with a significant material transformation of existing structures. However, as far as iron production is concerned, the two aspects must be considered separately. For a long time, as we have seen in the previous pages, medieval industry remained 'extensive' — that is, not based on the increase of individual units' productivity — yet capable of responding to the growing demand for metal essentially through the multiplication of small production structures, which continued to be more or less similar to the early medieval ones. This situation was in line with the general characteristics of the starting phase of the expansion of the European economy, already before the year 1000. In this long phase, economic growth was characterized by a gradual increase in the overall output of goods produced: we can therefore define this growth as 'extensive' or 'quantitative'. But, in this context, production increased because, along with the amount of raw materials and energy used, the number of producers also increased. Consequently, assuming that the labour productivity remained the same, the *pro capite* amount of each final product also remained roughly the same as before.[45]

When it comes to iron-working, a first phase of change and intensification is noticeable in the first half of the twelfth century in both the areas we have considered. In the Alps, we have witnessed an increase in mining and metallurgy among valley communities, as shown by the document from Ardesio (1145). This increase was accompanied by the introduction of the first technical improvement with the appearance of machinery driven by water power (so-called iron mills, equipped only with hydraulic hammers). The same intensification was recorded in Tuscany, but in this region it was the result of the stimulus provided by Pisa through the exploitation of the Elban mines. This led to a complete overhaul of the production system, based on the seasonal migration of specialized workers and on the proliferation of small ironworks in the Maremma coastal area.

Iron-working really took off, however, in the thirteenth century, when more complex and efficient production methods and equipment began to spread, which ensured a greater volume of production. Thus the energy sources used,

44 On Alpine iron-working between fourteenth and fifteenth centuries, see the contributions collected in Braunstein, ed., *La sidérurgie alpine*; on Tuscany: Barlucchi, 'Strutture produttive'; Cortese, *L'acqua, il grano, il ferro*; Cortese, 'Opifici idraulici'.

45 For a general picture see: Cortonesi and Palermo, *La prima espansione*, Chapter 2.

and the way in which they were used, became absolutely crucial. The process of reducing the ore was enhanced, on the one hand, by furnaces that proved to be more efficient in harnessing fuel energy and, on the other, by that fact that the energy of water was applied to new machinery, which made it possible to achieve the highest productivity at the lowest possible cost. It was at this time that in various parts of Europe the 'extensive' iron industry was replaced by an 'intensive' one: the productivity of single units was increased by technical improvements and innovations which, for the first time, had a major impact on the material structure of production buildings.

Works Cited

Manuscripts and Archival Sources

Siena, Archivio di Stato, Conventi, 4, 1281 luglio 16
——, Diplomatico, Riformagioni, 1296 aprile 26

Primary Sources

Codex diplomaticus civitatis et ecclesiæ Bergomatis, ed. by Mario Lupo, 2 vols (Bergamo: Typographia Vincentii Antoine, 1784–1799)

Heinrici III. diplomata, ed. by Harry Bresslau and Paul Fridolin Kehr, in Monumenta Germaniae Historica: Diplomata regum et imperatorum Germaniae, 5 (Berlin: Weidmann, 1831)

I placiti del Regnum Italiae, ed. by Cesare Manaresi, 1 (Roma: Istituto storico italiano per il Medio Evo, 1955)

'Possedimenti del vescovo di Bergamo nella valle di Ardesio: documenti dei secc. XI-XV', ed. by Gianni Barachetti, *Bergomum*, 75 (1980)

Secondary Works

Agostini, Alexander, 'The Metal Finds from the Site of Vetricella (Scarlino, Grosseto): a Revised Interpretation (8th–13th Centuries)', in *The nEU-Med Project: Vetricella, an Early Medieval Royal Property on Tuscany's Mediterranean*, ed. by Giovanna Bianchi and Richard Hodges (Florence: All'insegna del Giglio, 2020), pp. 33–50

Arnoux, Mathieux, 'Innovation technique, intervention publique et organisation du marché: aux origines du district sidérurgique de la Valteline (XIIIe-XIVe siècles)', in *La sidérurgie alpine en Italie (XIIe-XVIIe siècle)*, ed. by Philippe Braunstein (Rome: École Française de Rome, 2001), pp. 215–52

——, 'Moulins à fer et procédé indirect. Énergie hydraulique et innovation dans la sidérurgie européenne (XIIIe-XVIe s.)', in *I mulini nell'Europa medievale*, ed. by Paola Galetti and Pierre Racine (Bologna: Clueb, 2003), pp. 1–12

Baiocco, Gianni, Fausto Bucci, Luca Ferretti, Nello Geri, Rino Magagnini, and Luca Verdini, *Metallurgia antica e medievale nel golfo di Follonica* (Follonica: Comitato pro Ex Ilva, 1990)

Barlucchi, Andrea, 'La lavorazione del ferro nell'economia casentinese alla fine del Medioevo (tra Campaldino e la battaglia di Anghiari)', *Annali Aretini*, 14 (2006) 169–200

——, 'Strutture produttive industriali di proprietà comunale: fornaci, fabbriche e gualchiere nel contado della toscana interna (secoli XIII–XV)', in *Beni comuni e strutture della proprietà. Dinamiche e conflitti in area toscana fra basso medioevo ed età contemporanea*, ed. by Giuseppe V. Parigino (Florence: Associazione di studi storici Elio Conti, 2017), pp. 99–130

Beck, Patrice, ed., *L'innovation technique au Moyen Age* (Paris: Édition Errance, 1998)

Belhoste, Jean-François, 'Mutations techniques et filières marchandes dans la sidérurgie alpine entre XIIIe et XVIe siècle', in *La sidérurgie alpine en Italie (XIIe-XVIIe siècle)*, ed. by Philippe Braunstein (Rome: École Française de Rome, 2001), pp. 515–92

Bianchi, Giovanna, *Archeologia dei beni pubblici. Alle origini della crescita economica in una regione mediterranea (secc. IX–XI)* (Florence: All'Insegna del Giglio, 2022)

Bianchi, Giovanna, Giuseppe Fichera, Domenico Miriello, Nicoletta Chiarelli, and Gino Crisci, 'Archeologia di un cantiere curtense: il caso del castello di Donoratico tra IX e X secolo. Sequenze stratigrafiche e analisi archeometriche', *Archeologia dell'architettura*, 16 (2011), 34–50

Bianchi, Giovanna, and Richard Hodges, eds, *The nEU-Med Project: Vetricella, an Early Medieval Royal Property on Tuscany's Mediterranean* (Florence: All'insegna del Giglio, 2020)

Braunstein, Philippe, 'L'industrie à la fin du Moyen Âge: un objet historique nouveau?', in *La France n'est-elle pas douée pour l'industrie?*, ed. by Louis Bergeron and Patrice Bourdelais (Paris: Belin, 1998), pp. 25–40

——, ed., *La sidérurgie alpine en Italie (XIIe-XVIIe siècle)* (Rome: École Française de Rome, 2001)

Bruttini, Jacopo, 'Minatori e signorie nelle Colline Metallifere: il sistema produttivo dei metalli monetabili nel Medioevo' (unpublished doctoral dissertation, University of Siena, 2014)

Cambi, Franco, and Luisa Dallai, 'Archeologia di un monastero: gli scavi a S. Salvatore al Monte Amiata', *Archeologia Medievale*, 27 (2000), 193–210

Carrera, Francesco, Beatrice Fatighenti, and Caterina Toscani, 'Le ceramiche e le attività produttive. Recenti acquisizioni da un quartiere artigianale di Chinzica (PI)', in *Actas do X Congresso Internacional a Cerâmica Medieval no Mediterrâneo*, ed. by Maria José Gonçalves and Susana Gómez Martínez (Silves: Câmara Municipal de Silves, 2015), pp. 114–24

Citter, Carlo, ed., *Archeologia urbana a Grosseto. Origine e sviluppo di una città medievale nella 'Toscana delle città deboli'. Le ricerche 1997–2005. II: edizione degli scavi urbani 1998–2005. Dall'insediamento stabile alla città in pietra e laterizio (VII–XV secolo)* (Florence: All'Insegna del Giglio, 2007)

Corretti, Alessandro, 'L'attività metallurgica', in *Ricerche di archeologia medievale a Pisa. I. Piazza dei Cavalieri, la campagna di scavo 1993*, ed. by Silvia Bruni,

Elisabetta Abela, and Graziella Berti (Florence: All'Insegna del Giglio, 2000), pp. 83–100
——, *Metallurgia medievale all'isola d'Elba* (Florence: All'Insegna del Giglio, 1991)
Corretti, Alessandro, Laura Chiarantini, Giulia Giuntoli, Marco Benvenuti, Franco Cambi, Marco Firmati, Carlo Isola, and Laura Pagliantini, 'Un sito di lavorazione del ferro da Monte Strega (Rio nell'Elba, Livorno). Nuovi dati sulle attività dei fabri pisani all'Elba nel Medioevo', in *Atti del VI Congresso Nazionale di Archeologia Medievale* (Florence, All'Insegna del Giglio, 2012), pp. 650–55
Cortese, Maria Elena, *L'acqua, il grano, il ferro. Opifici idraulici medievali nel bacino Farma-Merse* (Florence: All'insegna del Giglio, 1997)
——, 'Beni fiscali e attività minerario-metallurgiche nell'Italia centro-settentrionale (secc. VIII-XI)', *Reti Medievali Rivista*, 24.1 (2023), 251–83
——, 'Cistercian Monasteries and Water-Powered Ironworking: Two Case-Studies in Medieval Tuscany', in *L'industrie cistercienne (XIIe–XXIe siècle)*, ed. by Arnaud Baudin and Paul Benoit (Paris: Somogy, 2019), pp. 115–26
——, 'Il ferro a Pistoia nel contesto della siderurgia medievale in Toscana: una prospettiva di lungo periodo', in *La Pistoia comunale nel contesto toscano ed europeo (secoli XIII–XIV)*, ed. by Pietro Gualtieri (Pistoia: Società Pistoiese di Storia Patria, 2008), pp. 321–48
——, 'Medieval Iron-Working on the Mount Amiata: Technology, Economy, Environments (Siena, Italy, 13th–14th Centuries')', in *Artisans, industrie — Nouvelles révolutions du Moyen Âge à nos jours*, ed. by Natacha Coquery, Liliane Hilaire-Pérez, Line Sallmann, and Catherine Verna (Lyon: ENS Editions, 2004), pp. 149–60
——, 'Opifici idraulici per la lavorazione del ferro nel comprensorio del Monte Amiata (secc. XIII–XIV)', in *I mulini nell'Europa medievale*, ed. by Paola Galetti and Pierre Racine (Bologna: Clueb, 2003), pp. 329–50
Cortonesi, Alfio, and Luciano Palermo, *La prima espansione economica europea. Secoli XI–XV* (Rome: Carocci, 2019)
Cucini, Costanza, 'L'insediamento altomedievale del podere Aione (Follonica – GR)', *Archeologia medievale*, 16 (1989), 499–512
Cucini, Costanza, and Marco Tizzoni, *Le antiche scorie del golfo di Follonica (Toscana). Una proposta di tipologia* (Milan: Edizioni Et, 1992)
Dallai, Luisa, 'Opifici metallurgici sul promontorio di Piombino. Primi dati topografici', in *II congresso nazionale di archeologia medievale*, ed. by Gian Pietro Brogiolo (Florence: All'Insegna del Giglio, 2000), pp. 186–201
Di Gangi, Giorgio, *L'attività mineraria e metallurgica nelle Alpi occidentali italiane nel Medioevo* (Oxford: BAR, 2001)
Farinelli, Roberto, 'Le risorse minerarie amiatine e il loro sfruttamento', in *Carta archeologica della provincia di Siena, II, Il Monte Amiata*, ed. by Franco Cambi (Siena: Periccioli, 1996), pp. 39–55
Farinelli, Roberto, and Riccardo Francovich, 'Potere e attività minerarie nella Toscana altomedievale', in *La storia dell'Alto Medioevo italiano (VI–X secolo)*

alla luce dell'archeologia, ed. by Riccardo Francovich and Ghislaine Noyé (Florence: All'Insegna del Giglio, 1994), pp. 443–63

Fiore, Alessio, 'The Knots and the Nets: Fisc, Rural Estates and Cities in the Written Sources (Northern Italy, c. 800–1000)', in *The nEU-Med Project: Vetricella, an Early Medieval Royal Property on Tuscany's Mediterranean*, ed. by Giovanna Bianchi and Richard Hodges (Florence: All'insegna del Giglio, 2020), pp. 197–206

Finazzi, Giovanni Maria, *Sulle antiche miniere di Bergamo* (Milan: Società per la pubblicazione degli annali universali delle scienze e dell'industria, 1860)

Francovich, Riccardo, *Rocca S. Silvestro* (Rome: Leonardo-De Luca, 1991)

Francovich, Riccardo, and Chris Wickham, 'Uno scavo archeologico ed il problema dello sviluppo della signoria territoriale: Rocca S. Silvestro ed i rapporti di produzione minerari', *Archeologia Medievale*, 21 (1994), 7–30

Garzella, Gabriella, 'Fabri e fabricae *a Pisa: una presenza nel cuore della città medioevale*', in *Ricerche di archeologia medievale a Pisa. I. Piazza dei Cavalieri, la campagna di scavo 1993*, ed. by Silvia Bruni, Elisabetta Abela, and Graziella Berti (Florence: All'Insegna del Giglio, 2000), pp. 37–49

Gelichi, Sauro, 'Impianti per la lavorazione del ferro sul promontorio di Piombino. Contributo archeologico alla conoscenza di attività proto-industriali sulla costa tirrenica', *Ricerche Storiche*, 14.1 (1984), 37–47

Mainoni, Patrizia, 'La politica dell'argento e del ferro nella Lombardia medievale', in *La sidérurgie alpine en Italie (XIIe-XVIIe siècle)*, ed. by Philippe Braunstein (Rome: École Française de Rome, 2001), pp. 418–54

Marasco, Lorenzo, and Arianna Briano, 'The Stratigraphic Sequence at the Site of Vetricella (Scarlino, Grosseto): Preliminary Results from the Study of an Early Medieval Assemblage', in *The nEU-Med Project: Vetricella, an Early Medieval Royal Property on Tuscany's Mediterranean*, ed. by Giovanna Bianchi and Richard Hodges (Florence: All'insegna del Giglio, 2020), pp. 9–22

Martin, Sally, 'Trial Excavations on Monte Serra, Elba: a Medieval Workshop', *Archeologia Medievale*, 21 (1994), 233–50

Menant, François, 'Aspects de l'économie et de la société dans les vallées lombardes aux derniers siècles du moyen âge', in *La sidérurgie alpine en Italie (XIIe-XVIIe siècle)*, ed. by Philippe Braunstein (Rome: École Française de Rome, 2001), pp. 3–30

——, 'La métallurgie lombarde au Moyen Age', in *Hommes et travail du métal dans les villes médiévales*, ed. by Paul Benoit and Denis Cailleaux (Paris: Association pour l'édition et la diffusion des études historiques, 1988), pp. 127–62

——, 'Pour une histoire médiévale de l'entreprise minière en Lombardie', *Annales. Economies, Sociétés, Civilisations*, 42.4 (1987), 779–96

Micheletto, Egle, 'Archeologia dei metalli in Piemonte dall'età tardoromana al medioevo. Appunti per una schedatura preliminare', in *Miniere, fucine e metallurgia nel Piemonte medievale e moderno*, ed. by Rinaldo Comba (Cuneo: Società per gli Studi Storici di Cuneo, 1999), pp. 1–25

——, 'Il castello di Manzano. Note su uno studio in corso nel territorio di Cherasco', *Alba Pompeia*, 11 (1990), 65–79

Negro Ponzi Mancini, Maria Maddalena, ed., *S. Michele di Trino (VC). Dal villaggio romano al castello medievale* (Florence: All'insegna del Giglio, 1999)

Panichi, Francesca, 'La produzione medievale del ferro nella Toscana meridionale' (unpublished doctoral dissertation, University of Siena, 2008)

Patria, Luca, 'In fodina veteri: prospezioni minerarie e pratiche metallurgiche nelle Alpi Cozie (secoli XII–XIV)', in *Miniere, fucine e metallurgia nel Piemonte medievale e moderno*, ed. by Rinaldo Comba (Cuneo: Società per gli Studi Storici di Cuneo, 1999), pp. 27–64

Quirós Castillo, Juan Antonio, *El incastellamento en el territorio de la ciudad de Luca (Toscana). Poder y territorio entre la Alta Edad Media y el siglo XII* (Oxford: Oxford University Press, 1999)

Sprandel, Rolf, *Das Eisengewerbe in Mittelalter* (Stuttgard: Hiersemann, 1968)

——, 'Die oberitalienische Eisenproduktion im Mittelalter', *Rivista trimestrale di storia sociale ed economica*, 52.3 (1965), 289–329

Tangheroni, Marco, Catia Renzi Rizzo, and Graziella Berti, 'Pisa e il Mediterraneo nei secoli VII–XIII: l'apporto congiunto delle fonti scritte e di quelle archeologiche', in *Il mare, la terra, il ferro. Ricerche su Pisa medievale (secoli VII–XIII)*, ed. by Marco Tangheroni, Catia Renzi Rizzo, and Graziella Berti (Pisa: Pacini, 2004), pp. 109–42

Tronti, Carlo, and Marco Valenti, 'Gli spazi del settore B', in *Poggio Imperiale a Poggibonsi: dal villaggio di capanne al castello di pietra*, ed. by Marco Valenti (Firenze: All'Insegna del Giglio, 1996), pp. 225–31

Verna, Catherine, 'Innovations et métallurgies en Méditerranée occidentale (XIIIe-XVe siècles)', *Anuario de Estudios Medievales*, 41.2 (2011), 623–44

Wickham, Chris, 'Prima della crescita: quale società?', in *La crescita economica dell'Occidente medievale. Un tema storico non ancora esaurito*, ed. by Franco Franceschi (Pistoia: Centro Italiano di Studi di Storia e d'Arte, 2017), pp. 93–106

ALESSIO FIORE

Building for the Market

Residential Properties in Medieval Italy (c. 1070–1250)

In the present contribution I will investigate the construction and management of urban residential buildings by focusing on the more strictly 'economic' implications of these dynamics.[1] I will instead leave aside the kind of identity-defining and social aspects which the *Petrifying Wealth* project has generally investigated. Thus, while the object of my enquiry will be the same as that of many studies undertaken within the framework of this project, the point of view from which I will examine it will be a radically different one. The area to which I will direct my attention is central-northern Italy, while, from a chronological perspective, I will focus on the period between the late eleventh century and the early decades of the thirteenth century. I have chosen to have such a broad time span because of the very nature of the documentation that pertains to urban houses: this evidence is for the most part rather limited as far as the period under investigation is concerned; moreover, it has almost invariably reached us through ecclesiastical archives, and this has certain consequences in terms of these documents' representativeness. A wide range of case studies makes it possible to limit (albeit not to completely eliminate) the distorted perspective of the documentary evidence. I have therefore analysed published documents pertaining to different cities in central-northern Italy, including Pisa, Florence, Genoa, Savona, Milan, Novara, Vercelli, and Bologna, while drawing upon Étienne Hubert's important studies on the topic in relation to Rome.[2] Within this framework, the case that emerges most clearly from

1 The publication of this research was financed by the European Research Council (ERC) under the European Union's Horizon 2020 research and innovation programme (grant agreement 695515), project *Petrifying Wealth: The Southern European Shift to Masonry as Collective Investment in Identity, c. 1050–1300*.

2 Hubert, *Espace urbain*; *Le carte della canonica della cattedrale di Firenze*, ed. by Piattoli; *Codice diplomatico Padovano*, ed. by Gloria; *Le carte del monastero di S. Stefano di Bologna*, ed. by Rinaldi; *Gli atti privati milanesi*, ed. by Santoro and others; *Carte dell'archivio capitolare di Pisa*, ed. by Falaschi; *Le carte del monastero di S. Maria in Firenze*, ed. by Schiaparelli; *Il regesto*

Alessio Fiore (alessio.fiore@unito.it) obtained his PhD at the University of Pisa, and is currently professor of Medieval History at the University of Turin.

Building and Economic Growth in Southern Europe (1050–1300), ed. by Sandro Carocci and Alessio Fiore, (Turnhout: Brepols, 2024), pp. 169–186 BREPOLS PUBLISHERS 10.1484/M.TMC-EB.5.137979

the available documentary evidence is probably Genoa owing to the notary registers that, from as early as the mid-twelfth century, give us a picture of economic real estate transactions that is far richer and more focused than the one we get from other urban centres. We have a considerable number of leases, sales, property exchanges, and inheritance divisions, involving a far more varied range of social and economic actors than is usually the case. But we also find genuine building contracts between commissioning parties and the *magistri* who directed the building sites. Furthermore, the fact that the Genoese evidence has chiefly reached us via notary registers removes that ecclesiastical filter that in the other cases constitutes the most serious problem as far as the representativeness of the available sources goes. This peculiar richness (from a quantitative as much as qualitative perspective) obviously presents a great research opportunity, but it also raises the question of how representative Genoa is of more general processes that were typical of central-northern Italy as a whole. In this regard, a preliminary point I wish to make is that the dynamics that emerge in Genoa in relation to properties with either a residential function or a mixed one (i.e. buildings used as both dwellings and workplaces) do not strike me as extraordinary compared to the rest of central-northern Italy. As far as I have been able to determine by comparing the plentiful and detailed data from Genoa with the more or less scattered evidence from other coeval cities (particularly as regards properties owned by laymen), what we have is a relatively homogeneous scenario: the chronologies are not all that different and the processes at play are also quite similar, notwithstanding the inevitable local divergences — likewise as regards the chronology of the processes, which varies slightly depending on the context.[3] In my view, Genoa's economic peculiarities when compared to the Italian context in the same period lie elsewhere: for example, in the importance and mobility of commercial capital, rather than in the management of the real estate stock. In this contribution I will therefore employ the Genoese data (also) as a guide to the more general context of central-northern Italy, while taking into account the fact that no two urban centres are ever alike, and hence that the Genoa case is bound to differ in certain respects from those of Rome or Florence.

Obviously, in relation to the period under investigation, the more strictly economic aspect that I will often be focusing on cannot be completely detached from other forms of social relations such as personal loyalty, kinship ties, or the connection between parishioners and their churches. We are dealing

---

del capitolo di Lucca, ed. by Guidi and Calleri; *Le carte del capitolo della cattedrale di Verona*, ed. by Lanza; and *Le carte dell'archivio capitolare di S. Maria di Novara*, ed. by Gabotto.

3 However, it should be emphasized that Genoa belongs to that group of more dynamic Italian cities (which also includes, for example, Genoa and Milan, but also Florence), where the most advanced (and profit-driven) management methods in the management of real estate assets are visible a few decades earlier than in economically less lively contexts (such as Volterra and Pistoia, but also Rome).

with a context in which economic relations (or rather, those relations that contemporary scholars interpret as economic) are encapsulated within a broader and more complex system of relations: they do not constitute a completely autonomous sphere.[4] However, it is possible to identify specific areas in which the actions and choices of some (or many) of the actors involved appear to be determined by strictly 'economic' calculations and concerns; and it is precisely to these contexts that I will turn my attention in the following pages. I have chosen to focus on cities because property dynamics are different there compared to those in the countryside, where in most cases houses and fields form an integrated property, which makes it almost impossible to develop an enquiry into residential buildings alone. Judging from the available sources, *borghi* (towns) of 2000–3000 inhabitants instead present dynamics that are largely comparable to those we will be seeing at work in urban centres, although the overall evidence for our period is too sparse to allow us to develop a general analysis.[5]

Before embarking on the actual investigation, which — as anticipated — will concern residential (and mixed) property in Italian urban centres, I will try to explain why it is worth discussing this specific category.

The first obvious, yet crucial, observation to be made is that urbanism is a fundamental component of the process of economic growth that took place between the late eleventh and the late thirteenth centuries.[6] At this stage cities were not just centres for the demand and consumption of goods, as in the previous period, but also places in which goods were manufactured. One of the major differences compared to the Carolingian economic model — albeit not the only one — concerns precisely the different role played by cities within the system of production and trade. At least from the eleventh century onwards, cities became trading hubs, as well as significant manufacturing centres, and one of the goods manufactured, everywhere, was of course houses. As we shall later see in greater detail, within this new economic context residential buildings, even non-luxury ones, became the object of numerous transactions: they were not just valuable assets but represented a form of speculative investment — designed to increase the value of the capital invested within a few years — and a means of ensuring steady revenue (particularly through renting). Houses were thus built in order to be let or even sold, once their value had gone up.

In this framework, a profound change in the residential urban fabric occurred through the gradual transition from perishable materials to stone and (especially) brick, which became the real star of urban development in

4 On these topics, the classic reference point is Polany, *The Great Transformation*.

5 Some examples of sales of houses placed in little towns of Liguria and Corsica, see *Petrus Rufi (Genova 1213–1214)*, ed. by Boem and Calleri, doc. 150 (1213), pp. 136–37 (on Bonifacio); doc. 238 (1213), pp. 212–13 (on Portovenere); doc. 278 (1213), p. 245 (on Rapallo).

6 For a detailed discussion on the urban development in Italy, see Hubert, 'La construction de la ville'

that age. Apart from this, the construction of residential buildings provided an enduring and long-term stimulus for the urban economy. Although the best-documented and most widely investigated construction projects are major ones involving cathedrals, basilicas, or city walls, we should not forget that the continuous process of building and rebuilding residential properties played an important role in the urban economy as a whole: like a beat in the background, it set the rhythm for this growth process. It created employment and fuelled new manufacturing activities: kilns for tiles and bricks, stone quarries, and also joineries.[7] There was more to it than just the expansion of the building fabric; it was a process of reconstructing the city in new and more developed forms — especially in an upward direction — that continued throughout the period under investigation. The constant fires and episodes of destruction also played their part, contributing to the overall renewal of the urban fabric.

We should not take the occurrence of this process for granted: the large 'urban' manufacturing sites of the Carolingian age, namely *emporia*, consisted of exclusively wooden residential and productive buildings which were far simpler and more functional.[8] The new demand for durable building materials initially led to the reuse of bricks and building blocks from Roman ruins. Then, from the first half of the twelfth century onwards, at least in the earliest cases (illustrated for instance by the recent investigations in Pisa, particularly the Kinzica district), increasingly widespread use was made of new bricks.[9] Starting in the mid-twelfth century we find more and more mentions of the presence of kilns and clay quarries in the cities' environs, as well as of craftspeople producing bricks and tiles. But we also find citizens in forests located dozens of kilometres away from their home cities, acting as intermediaries in the purchase of large pieces of high-quality timber (ash or oak wood) to be used as beams or floor slabs for buildings' upper storeys. This is the case with those citizens of Ferrara who around 1140 were operating in the fluvial forests near Ostiglia, some fifty kilometres away from their city (the timber purchased would then be transported to Ferrara on the river).[10] The switch to durable materials did not occur overnight. Particularly in newly built areas, where the owners of a property would grant a plot of land for the construction of a house according to a tight time schedule, as late as the mid-thirteenth century wooden buildings continued to be predominant at an initial stage (which varies in duration depending on the area). This was the case, for example, in various suburbs of Pavia — including Borgoratto, which had quite a few wooden houses as late as the 1270s — and in the Giudecca

7 Significant reflections on this issue, based on the case of Bruges, can be found in Sosson, *Pour une approche économique*.

8 On the *emporia*, see Lebeq, 'The New *wiks*'.

9 Baldassarri, 'Another Brick'.

10 Fiore, 'Ostiglia around 1100'

area of Venice.[11] Nevertheless, these were only provisional solutions: within a few years, wood would be replaced by other, more durable building materials. In areas with a long history of urban development by the early decades of the thirteenth century, wooden buildings had become rather uncommon, to the point of being singled out in the written sources. For instance, shortly after 1200 a house belonging to the prominent Squarciafico family, located not far from the Genoa cathedral, is referred to as *domus lignaminis* in a document, suggesting that it stood out in a context in which brick and stone had become utterly predominant.[12]

This change of materials is associated with a transformation in the shape and size of houses, as well as in the use of their spaces. In the late twelfth century, mentions of home workshops become increasingly frequent in the sources. These are mixed buildings in which residential spaces (usually on the upper floors) are combined with a space (usually on the ground floor) reserved for craftsmanship, storage, and/or trade. It therefore becomes increasingly common to find a household's living and work spaces being combined within the same building: a solution that seems hardly surprising, given the growing weight of manufacturing activities in urban contexts.[13] As far as the construction of wooden houses is concerned, it has been suggested that most labour was provided by the future dwellers themselves, who were probably grouped together with their future neighbours in teams led by professional joiners. Things were obviously quite different in the case of brick (and stone) houses, which required more specific and professional skills. Among the twelfth-century notary deeds from Genoa, we find a few pertaining to the building (or rebuilding) of brick dwellings, with *magistri* in charge of all aspects of the work, from the supplying of building material to builders' wages, for a total sum of around 20 lire (in this case we are probably dealing with a rather large *domus*, on several floors).[14] In the case of luxurious buildings, prices shoot up: in 1191 *magister* Ottobono, who was in charge of the construction of a luxury *domus* in Genoa (with capitals, a balcony, and ashlar masonry), asked for no less than 45 lire, not including the marble, (unhewn) columns and capitals, timber, and iron, which the commissioning party was expected to furnish.[15] To get a better idea of the materials' price, we might consider the fact that around 1140 the oak logs for the Ferrara property market probably cost well over two *solidi* each (on the urban market), given that the right to fell a tree alone cost one *solidus* — owed to the wood's owner — to which we must then add all the expenses for transportation (50 km via river) as

11 On Pavia, see Andreolli, 'Pavia nei documenti'.

12 Guglielmotti, *Agnacio seu parentella*, p. 99.

13 Degrassi, *L'economia artigiana*; on Liguria see the overview offered by Mannoni, 'Case di città e case di campagna', pp. 239–49.

14 *Oberto Scriba de mercato (1186)*, ed. by Chiaudano, doc. 234 (a. 1186), p. 87.

15 *Guglielmo Cassinense*, ed. by Hall-Cole and others, II, n. 1415 (1191), pp. 119–20.

well as the woodcutters and carpenters' labour.[16] The difference in prices is an element that already emerges quite clearly upon an initial survey of the sources. Even if we limit our analysis to a relatively short-time period and to one or two cities, this difference does not grow significantly smaller, so it merits discussion. The price range for residential buildings in Genoa and Savona in the two decades at the turn of the 1200s, a period for which several dozen appraisals are available, is from 4–5 lire for inexpensive houses to around 200. The average price is between 20 and 50 lire (if we rule out dwellings with a tower and a *statio* — storeroom — which could fetch even higher prices). This wide range is explained not only by price differences between different urban areas, but also by the varying quality of the buildings themselves (as luxury features could significantly increase their value) and obviously their size. Thus, in 1192 a Genoese *domus* without any distinguishing features was sold for 142 lire, whereas a dozen years later, in 1201, an apparently similar one changed owner for only 40 lire.[17] If we then turn to the upper end of the market, namely aristocratic mansions with a courtyard and tower, we often come across appraisals close to 1000 lire. These might seem like extremely high prices, but they find confirmation in coeval sources from Florence.[18] In those years a building complex of this kind was essentially worth as much as a medium-size castle, including its jurisdictional rights over the surrounding countryside. Just to give another example, an inexpensive dwelling cost only a little more than a young Saracen female slave on the Genoese market, namely 4–5 lire.[19]

The construction of residential buildings (or mixed ones, namely dwellings with areas reserved for trade or craftsmanship) fuelled a range of highly specialized economic activities, ranging from the supplying and processing of building materials to the salaries of those labourers specializing in construction work (stonecutters, sculptors, joiners, decorators, etc.). When viewed from this perspective, building work acted as one of the driving forces for urban (and suburban) economic development, according to dynamics that become more visible and noticeable in relation to the modern and contemporary ages.[20] The construction of (residential or mixed) buildings in urban or suburban areas reflects other, even more direct economic dynamics which have to do

16 Fiore, 'Ostiglia around 1100'.

17 *Guglielmo Cassinsense*, ed. by Hall-Cole and others, II, doc. 1530 (a. 1192), pp. 165–66; *Giovanni di Guiberto*, ed. by Hall-Cole and others, I, n. 260 (a. 1201), pp. 131–32.

18 As far as particularly valuable properties are concerned, a house with a tower is sold in the early thirteenth century for 416 lire: *Petrus Rufi (Genova 1213–1214)*, doc. 511 (a. 1214), ed. by Boem and Calleri, pp. 439–40; while half of a house with a tower, the same year, changes hands for 550 lire (with a total valuation of the property thus exceeding 1000 lire); see *Petrus Rufi (Genova 1213–1214)*, ed. by Boem and Calleri, doc. 456 (a. 1214), pp. 396–97. On the dataset about Firenze, see Faini, *Firenze*, p. 63.

19 In the same years slave-girls are sold in Genoa for 3–6 lire (see *Guglielmo Cassinense*, ed. by Hall, II, n. 1278 (a. 1191), p. 66; and n. 1410 (a. 1191), p. 118.

20 For an at least partly similar perspective, see Sosson, *Pour une approche economique*.

with building work as an investment to produce wealth. In this regard, the two questions we must seek to answer are: how was wealth extracted from these buildings? What social actors were involved in this process?

A first way to make money from the buildings was to purchase or build a house as an investment, which is to say in order to increase the capital invested through the upward revaluation of the property over time. A house was not just an asset, but could constitute a speculative investment — clearly, within certain limits. Certainly, it was not the most dynamic form of investment (as is clear in a lively commercial context such as late twelfth- or early thirteenth-century Genoa). Nevertheless, it was a kind of investment that could ensure an increase in capital. Furthermore, building development would lead to rising property prices in already urbanized areas as a city expanded. Purchasing or building a house meant investing one's capital in something the value of which tended to increase, at least in the period between the early twelfth and the late thirteenth century. We find that the price of houses in urban areas underwent a marked and steady increase in this period, an increase far greater than the inflation rate, which was especially high in the last decades of the twelfth century. In Rome, for instance, a one-storey house near the Coliseum, which was the object of a transaction between laymen in 1152, was sold by the people who had inherited it some twenty years later at a price roughly 30 per cent higher — this, it should be noted, was in a context that was not particularly dynamic from an economic perspective.[21] Not only that, but this increase is greater than that which cropland experienced, as Enrico Faini has highlighted in relation to Florence through the systematic analysis of a wealth of documentary evidence; but the same trend emerges from the (less plentiful) data pertaining to other cities, such as Verona and Novara.[22] The ownership and building of (residential and mixed) buildings in the urban or suburban space, however, does not concern only the attempt to increase the value of one's capital, but also the possibility of extracting revenue through rents. Houses would of course be granted by members of the elite as a means of establishing — or consolidating — patronage bonds with socially inferior individuals. In certain cases, such as in Padua or Verona, the documents suggest that these were relations explicitly based on vassalage.[23] The aim was to build a series of houses around a prominent family's dwelling, often with one or more towers, and place these houses under the control of allies or clients who would be mobilized during the frequent military clashes between the members of the urban elite's main factions. This model is clearly visible in numerous

---

21 Hubert, *Espace urbain*, p. 331.

22 Faini, *Firenze*, pp. 76–100. Diverso ovviamente il discorso per le aree periurbane interessate dall'aumento della produzione orticola destinata al crescente mercato urbano e appetibili come aree edificabili in vista dell'espansione del tessuto urbano. On Verona and Novara I used the sources edited in *Le carte del capitolo della cattedrale di Verona*, ed. Lanza; and *Le carte dell'archivio capitolare di S. Maria di Novara*, ed. by Gabotto, II.

23 See for example Varanini, 'Torri e casetorri'.

cities, from Padua and Verona to Florence, Rome, and Genoa. In this case buildings had an instrumental value as a means of accessing social relations and displaying a kinship group's power by extending its control over as vast an urban area as possible. These dynamics have been well known since Heers' studies on Genoa, and even recently they have been the object of important new studies, such as Sandro Carocci and Nicoletta Giannini's one on Rome.[24] But house ownership in an urban context was not governed by this logic alone: it also reflects more strictly economic dynamics. Granting someone a house (or a plot of land on which to build a house) was often — indeed, increasingly often — an operation that chiefly served an economic purpose.

Before dealing with houses, however, it is worth focusing on the land on which these buildings were built, and which are the focus of countless transactions attested in the available sources.

In an initial phase, up until the mid-twelfth century at least, ownership of a plot of land was often (yet not always) separate from ownership of the buildings erected on it, as is especially evident in Genoa, Bologna, Pisa, and Rome.[25] The owner of the plot would remain as such: he would only grant someone the right to construct a small building on it by assigning the plot as a long-term concession (the contracts involved are generally twenty-nine-year leases or *emphyteutic* ones valid for three generations). These concessions are defined as contracts *ad domum aedificandum* or *pro faciendo edificio*. Especially in the earliest period, we find clauses specifying the right to purchase the building at a special price, but these mostly disappear at a later date. The advantage for the landowner was that all building expenses would fall on the concessionaire. The owner only had to provide the building land, at no cost. In a context of the built surface's growth such as that just described, large, compact plots of previously cultivated suburban land would be parcelled out, and each parcel would be granted to a different concessionaire so as to reap economic profit from them. Judging from the documentary evidence, the biggest landowners were urban churches (for example, we have a fine series of texts pertaining to Santo Stefano in Bologna and San Michele in Borgo in Pisa). However, the documents from Liguria show that the lay urban aristocracy became increasingly involved in such operations, and it is conceivable that elsewhere, too, laypeople played a more prominent role than what the ecclesiastical evidence suggests.[26]

Regardless of the landowners' identity, the real problem lies in the fact that the fees paid for these concessions are generally very small. Historians have tended to see these recognition fees as a relative failure on the part of

---

24 Carocci and Giannini, 'Portici, palazzi, torri e fortezze'.

25 Per un'introduzione a questo problema vedi Hubert, 'Urbanisation', e più in generale tutti i saggi raccolti in *Le sol et l'immeuble*.

26 On S. Michele in Borgo, in Pisa, see Garzella, 'La proprietà frazionata'; on the abbey of S. Stefano, in Bologna, see Rinaldi, 'Forme di gestione'; Bocchi, 'Lo sviluppo urbanistico'.

ecclesiastical institutions to make the most of their rights as landowners, particularly in the long run. In addition to these very small fees (often just 1 *denarius* around 1100, or 5–6 *denarii* in the second half of the twelfth century), institutions would only receive an entry fee upon each sale of the building. This usually amounted to 12–15 *denarii* per *lira*, i.e. to 5–6 per cent of the total sum paid by the buyer: a significant sum, particularly in a context of high property turnover, which greatly increased the opportunities for landowners to receive an entrance fee. Moreover, the fact that this was a percentage, rather than a fixed sum, made it possible to stay abreast of inflation. A church that held rights over some lands would further profit from its new tenants' inclusion in its parish (which entailed the payment of alms and especially burial fees). The creation of spiritual bonds based on residence had strictly economic repercussions as well, as has been highlighted for instance in relation to San Michele in Borgo in Pisa.[27]

It seems reasonable to infer that something is still missing from this picture, however. First of all, emphyteutic leaseholders were probably required to pay an entry fee when the concession was first granted: presumably, this fee was so small that it has not been recorded for archival reasons except in some cases, significantly pertaining to laypeople — such as Ildebrando, who was active in Bologna in the second half of the twelfth century. Furthermore, alongside the entry fee it is possible that at least certain institutions held customary rights that entailed payments in kind (or services) by the leaseholders, according to mechanisms that are occasionally visible in the countryside during the same period.[28] Some interesting evidence in this respect is provided by the documents from the church of Sant'Ilario in Venice. Here, alongside a dense and homogeneous series of very small recognition fees in exchange for rights over plots of land, we unexpectedly find, for the year 1197, mention of an annual fee of no less than 12,000 *coppi* (tiles) owed by a pair of leaseholding craftsmen (who were evidently desirable tenants, as they could provide their services to the local monastery).[29] In the (much larger) registers from the hospital of Sant'Andrea in Vercelli, dating from the early fourteenth century, we find references to labour services, the provision of foodstuffs by butchers, of hemp ropes by ropemakers, of shoes by shoemakers, and so on, which suggests a far more complex system of levies than the one we can infer from lease contracts alone.[30] In other words, the nature of the documentary evidence might conceal a degree of economic exploitation on the landowners' part much greater than what would seem to have weighed upon the leaseholders at first sight.

---

27 Garzella, 'La proprietà frazionata'.

28 On these mechanisms in rural frameworks, see Tabarrini, 'Le operae e i giorni'.

29 Niero, 'Edilizia minore', p. 152.

30 Olivieri, 'Il volto nascosto'; for the relationship between S. Andrea and Vercelli craftsmen in the previous period, see Degrandi, *Artigiani nel Vercellese*.

If we move from land rents to the renting of houses (or of a housing block along with its land, as became increasingly common), we find ourselves dealing with a different situation. Up until the mid-twelfth century, long-term leases were predominant, often in the form of twenty-nine-year *libelli* or emphyteutic leases, such as those binding the tenants of the dwellings to the Lateran basilica. In this case, in the last third of the century, the rent ranged from one *denarius* to a dozen, although most contracts were closer to the bottom of this range.[31] As this last example clearly illustrates, in this case as well the contracts were based on small fees, which were probably combined — just as in the case of the renting of land, or indeed more so — with forms of customary taxation that are generally not mentioned in the written records. Less often we find much higher fees, which seem to me consistent with this model: for example, already by the late eleventh century the leaseholders of a house (and its grounds) belonging to the monastery of San Stefano in Padua were paying the considerable sum of 24 *denarii*, in addition to a focaccia and a pork shoulder.[32] From the mid-twelfth century onwards, these forms of long-term leases were progressively replaced by shorter contracts, with a duration of only a few years and with far higher rents than in previous years. Contracts of this sort obviously enabled the owners to reap a fair profit and to keep up with inflation, which in the second half of the twelfth century began to make itself felt. The figures vary considerably and obviously depend on a wide range of factors. Indeed, it is very difficult to understand what the standard percentage of a property's value was in order to calculate an annual rent, or even if there was one at all. Be that as it may, while land fees in the second half of the twelfth century amounted to a few *denarii* (5, 6, 7, and rarely over 10), rent amounted to several *solidi* (4, 5, or even 9 or 10): in the first decade of the thirteenth century, in some rare but not exceptional cases, it could be as high as 5 ½ lire.[33] To take a couple of Genoese examples, in 1192 a twenty-nine-year lease *pro faciendo edificio* granted by the hospital of Rivarolo to a cobbler came with an annual fee of 15 *denarii*, whereas in 1203 a smith paid a nobleman 5 *solidi* as rent for his house.[34] This development, however, would not appear to have occurred everywhere at the same time. In Genoa and other urban centres such as Pisa, Florence, and Milan, it occurred earlier than in other contexts, such as Rome and Pistoia, which were a few decades behind in this respect. It is therefore conceivable that more dynamic circumstances from a

31 Lauer, 'Un inventaire inédit'.

32 *Codice diplomatico padovano*, ed. by Gloria, I, doc. 300 (a. 1089), pp. 323–24.

33 *Guglielmo Cassinense*, ed. by Hall-Close and others, II, doc. 1845 (a. 1192), p. 284 (12 *solidi* per year for half of a house) *Lanfranco*, ed. by Krueger and Reynolds, I, n. 650 (a. 1210), p. 290; *Giovanni di Guiberto*, ed. by Hall-Cole and others, II, doc. 1457 (a. 1206), p. 155 (2 lire per year for three years); *Giovanni di Guiberto*, ed. by Hall-Cole and others, I, doc. 545 (a. 1203), p. 253 (26 *solidi* per year).

34 *Guglielmo Cassinense*, ed. by Hall-Close and others, II, doc. 1557, *Giovanni di Guiberto*, ed. by Hall-Cole and others, I, doc. 54 (a. 1200), pp. 25–26 (between two laypeople, 4 *solidi* per year).

commercial and manufacturing perspective were the first to experience these transformations in the management of property, which — significantly — went in the direction of increased economic exploitation. By contrast, in urban centres with a less dynamic and more peripheral economy, such as Rome, it took longer for these innovations to take hold from at least the second half of the twelfth century, as these centres remained tied to traditional management systems for a more prolonged period.

A further indicator of the transformations that occurred is to be found in changes to the material structure of leased buildings. Their owners sought to keep up with market trends by investing in the kind of buildings that were most sought after by renters. In Genoa around 1200, we find increasing mentions of the renting of 'mixed' buildings, which is to say of houses including manufacturing, retail, and/or storage spaces.[35] These were generally home workshops, with a ground floor that could be used as a workplace and an upper floor intended as a dwelling. Besides, these were versatile spaces that could be adapted to suit different professional needs: just outside one of the gates of Genoa, a home workshop was let first to an innkeeper, and then to a butcher; in another contract, an owner who has let his house to a smith commits himself to providing a millstone at his own expense.

In the sources we also find a few, yet significant, cases of tenants subletting a house. They would exploit existing long-term contracts to reap a profit from rising rent prices through shorter subleases. Owners sought to oppose such practices by explicitly forbidding it in contract clauses, which crop up in the evidence now and again. These are all indicators of the property market's increasingly dynamic and complex nature. We also witness the appearance of tenants who can afford to pay a high price for annual rent, even as much as 4–6 lire around the year 1200.[36] Clearly, these were individuals who needed a 'luxury' building for reasons connected to their social image, but who at the same time could not (or did not wish) to invest their capital in a big purchase. Significantly, up until 1210 or thereabouts, almost all cases of this kind that I have been able to identify occur in Genoa or its environs: a very dynamic context in which money could reap quite a profit if invested in commercial enterprises, meaning that people with more modest capital often preferred to pour it into more dynamic activities in the hope of increasing it. This was certainly the case with an individual engaged in overseas trade in 1203, who paid an annual rent of 26 *solidi*.[37]

We then find even shorter leases, day- or week-long ones, reserved for merchants: while for obvious reasons we find no information about this form of management in sources from our period, the literary sources describe it as profitable business from as early as the end of the eleventh century — the

35 Bezzina, *Artigiani genovesi*.
36 *Lanfranco*, ed. by Krueger and Reynolds, I, n. 650 (a. 1210), p. 290.
37 *Giovanni di Guiberto*, ed. by Hall-Cole and others, I, n. 545 (a. 1203), p. 253.

poem known as *Versus Eporediensis*, for example, speaks of the existence of a large number of such structures in Pavia in that period.[38] Already in the twelfth century, however, we find more and more references to activities of this kind, and we have clear mentions concerning Lodi, Milan, Como, Susa, and — again — Pavia, just to provide a partial list.[39] As far as we can tell, these renting opportunities were especially common in centres located along the main road axes (such as Susa and Como) or in major trading hubs (such as Milan or Pavia). As far as this early stage is concerned, however, the *hospicia* category (a broad term used in the sources) seems to include not so much large-size, specialized structures as much smaller buildings, with one or two rooms set aside for paying guests.[40]

The parcelling of land and building concessions naturally led to an increase in the number of small property owners, which are clearly visible in the documentary evidence. But alongside them we also find large ecclesiastical or lay landowners who could own as many as several dozen houses (and/or plots of land). Santo Stefano in Bologna had at least eighty plots of land, while several Roman churches had over a hundred: in the late twelfth century, Santa Maria in Campo Marzio owned no fewer than 154 houses, while a few decades later the Lateran basilica had roughly 220, at least three-fourths of which were leased.[41] What is interesting, however, is that laypeople as well increasingly invested in property, and it is here that the data pertaining to Genoa prove crucial for trying to assess the weight of this (generally elusive) presence. If we look at the data for rents from Genoese notary registers during the twelfth century and the first half of the thirteenth, we find that most owners of houses for let are laypeople, and that a considerable percentage within this group (although under 50 per cent) is represented by large landowners. In the earlier notary registers, which were compiled between the late twelfth century and the beginning of the thirteenth, we find references to several prominent Genoese families as owners of properties that would be let to members of the lower classes in exchange for an annual rent. The interesting thing is that this practice would not appear to be specifically based on patronage ties, but rather to reflect a logic (at least partly) centred on profit. More generally it may be argued that the data from Genoa, however partial they may be, stem from a much broader and far less distorted set of documents than the data for other cities. Besides, despite the heavy ecclesiastical filter, numerous lay owners emerge from the documentary evidence pertaining to cities such

38 *Versus eporediensis*, ed. by Dümmler, pp. 245–53, the poem speaks (with obvious rhetorical amplification) of 100 rooms for rent in Pavia. The first documentary mention, again concerning Pavia, of *hospicia* managed by private individuals and intended to house and feed foreigners is instead from the last years of the twelfth century, and thus at least a century later; see Soriga, 'Il memoriale dei consoli', pp. 114–15.

39 For a detailed reference to socurces, see Mainoni, 'Un'economia cittadina', pp. 325–27.

40 Crotti, 'Le strutture di accoglienza'

41 Hubert, *Espace urbain*, pp. 311–12.

as Milan, Bologna, Padua, Lucca, Florence, and Pisa from as early as the eleventh century.[42]

The widespread presence of laypeople, and especially of members of the elite, among large property owners can therefore be taken for granted (differences between individual cities notwithstanding). What is more complex is the question of the size of individual families' property patrimonies, and of the part that urban houses may have played within them. An interesting, if somewhat murky, picture emerges in relation to the houses owned by the Tossico kinship group, which was a rather prominent one in Genoa in the second half of the twelfth century, although it was not particularly rich. When in 1197 four brothers split the (mobile and immobile) properties they had just inherited from their recently-deceased father, buildings (including half a tower with half of the large warehouse annexed to it) accounted for over half of the overall patrimony. Some of these properties were luxury ones (appraised at over 200 lire); they were located in the city centre and used by the four brothers as their private dwellings. Then there was a block of *domos* located in the suburbs just to the west of the city centre, Pré, which was appraised at 400 lire (in that period the price of a non-luxury house in Genoa ranged between 15 and 30 lire, so the block in question presumably comprised around twenty residential units).[43] These houses were certainly let to members of the lower classes. In a cartulary by Guglielmo da Sori, who in the years 1200–1201 drafted many deeds for the powerful Embriaci family, we find that the latter not only engaged in maritime trade, money-lending, and the purchase of extra-urban property, but also bought a rather ordinary house (for 29 lire), clearly as a form of investment.[44] Notary cartularies also show other prominent families investing significant capital not in houses that had already been built, but in the purchase of farmland from private individuals or religious institutions in the suburbs just outside the city centre, areas likely to undergo urban development. Thus, in 1161 the Rataldos invested no less than 106 lire in a large plot of land near the hospital of Santo Stefano, near the walls, clearly with the intention of parcelling it up.[45] Transactions of this

42 By way of example, see: *Gli atti privati milanesi*, ed. by Santoro and others, I, doc. 60 (a. 1013), pp. 139–40; doc. 134 (a. 1025), pp. 305–06; *Le carte del monastero di S. Stefano di Bologna*, ed. by Rinaldi and Villani, I, doc. 41 (a. 1071), pp. 72–73; *Codice diplomatico Padovano*, ed. by Gloria, I, doc. 204 (a. 1069), p. 233; *Carte dell'archivio capitolare di Pisa*, ed. by Falaschi, I, doc. 23 (a. 1001), pp. 72–73; doc. 44 (1017), pp. 125–26; doc. 53 (a. 1067), pp. 141–43; *Le carte del monastero di S. Maria in Firenze*, ed. by Schiaparelli, I, doc. 26 (a. 1019), pp. 67–68; doc. 147 (a. 1099), pp. 340–42; *Il regesto del capitolo di Lucca*, ed. by Guidi and Calleri, I, doc. 102 (a. 1021), p. 37.

43 Filangieri, *Famiglie e gruppi*, p. 174, n. 752.

44 *Guglielmo da Sori*, ed. by Oreste and others, I, doc. 185 (a. 1200), pp. 151–52.

45 *Codice diplomatico del monastero di S. Stefano*, ed. by Calleri, I, doc. 137 (a. 1161), pp. 230–31; see Filangieri, *Famiglie e gruppi*, p. 177. The purchase of a well on an adjacent piece of land, conceivably to supply water to the new housing complex, must be understood in this light; see *Codice diplomatico del monastero di S. Stefano*, ed. by Calleri, I, doc. 144 (a. 1167), p. 240.

sort could lead to the construction of a significant number of buildings to be let within a relatively short time. In the mid-thirteenth century, again in Genoa, the Ventos leased at least two houses, seven home workshops, and four stores; the Dorias, a dozen houses and home workshops.[46] Obviously these are small figures compared to the property patrimony of the religious institutions previously discussed, but it must be noted that, at least as far as the most prominent families are concerned, the picture we have is very limited. Furthermore, as regards the comparison between the urban elite's patrimonies and those of religious institutions, it is conceivable that the former invested far greater sums in more dynamic and lucrative activities compared to land and real estate investment (such as trade and money-lending). An excellent example in this respect is the aforementioned one of the Tossico family, half of whose patrimony in 1195 consisted of liquid assets.[47]

To conclude, it seems useful to return to the chronological element in order to try to ascertain what a discussion of the economic dynamics revolving around urban residential buildings can tell us about the overall economic trends in central-northern Italy in the period under investigation.

First of all, sources from the last decades of the eleventh century and the early twelfth clearly point to an expansion of the urban fabric, providing a picture of increasingly frequent home purchases and concessions of land plots for the construction of dwellings. It is only from the second half of the twelfth century (slightly earlier in economically more advanced centres like Milan, Genoa, or Pisa), however, that a genuine urban 'property market' emerged, governed by an increasingly market-like logic and way of operating — although this was not entirely predominant. We find economic operators (laypeople and churches) investing in the purchase of residential and mixed buildings, or of plots of land to be developed, and in the construction of housing stock to be rented. Property was no longer seen as a merely defensive form of investment, designed to safeguard one's capital; rather, it was seen as an investment that could bring in some profit based on the reappraisal of the value of the capital invested, and which could also ensure regular revenues for an owner through shorter and more onerous rents compared to the past. Cities were the linchpin for this restructuring of the economic system, and it is in urban contexts that the market logic became increasingly important and pervasive. The management of residential property offers an effective vantage point to examine this economic vitality. Significantly, the turning point as far as property management is concerned coincides — at least in more advanced centres, such as Genoa — precisely with the second half of the twelfth century. In the period in which growth become more intense — at

46 Bezzina, *Artigiani*, p. 180 (it should be pointed out that these are very partial data, reconstructed from the analysis of surviving notarial registers and not overall photographs of family assets).

47 Filangieri, *Famiglie e gruppi*, p. 174 n. 752.

any rate, according to the most recent reconstructions — and the first signs emerge of what was to become the great acceleration of the thirteenth century, urban actors' way of envisaging (and managing) housing stock also changed.[48] This development would appear to have occurred at the same time as certain transformations affecting the material structure of buildings, particularly the spread of multi-storey home workshops, which become increasingly visible in the documentary evidence — but also in the archaeological record (for instance, in the excavations in the Kinzica district of Pisa) — and in the spread of newly produced bricks for the construction of buildings.[49] In other words, the material aspect of houses changed to suit a new and more dynamic social and manufacturing context, but what also changed — in parallel with this — was the way in which housing stock was managed, as owners increasingly sought to reap a profit from their properties, first in those cities at the forefront of the growth process, and shortly afterwards elsewhere as well.

A logic of profit, a capacity to develop new strategies to extract profit from buildings, and a desire to invest capital to make the most of a noticeable economic upswing: these emerge as closely interconnected processes that become increasingly evident from the second half of the twelfth century. They reveal a new attitude and a new awareness on the part of social actors that we can regard as both indicators and essential components of a general economic take-off.

48 On the chronologies of economic growth, see Wickham, 'Prima della crescita'.

49 Baldassarri, 'Another Brick'.

Works Cited

Primary Sources

Gli atti privati milanesi e comaschi del sec. 11, ed. by Caterina Santoro, Carlo Manaresi, and Giovanni Vittani, 4 vols (Milan: Hoepli, 1953–1969)

Carte dell'archivio capitolare di Pisa, ed. by Emma Falaschi, I (Rome: Storia e letteratura, 1971)

Le carte dell'archivio capitolare di S. Maria di Novara, ed. by Ferdinando Gabotto, II (Pinerolo: Società storica subalpina, 1915)

Le carte della canonica della cattedrale di Firenze, ed. by Renato Piattoli, I (Rome: ISIME, 1938)

Le carte del capitolo della cattedrale di Verona, ed. Emanuele Lanza, 2 vols (Rome: Viella, 1998–2006)

Le carte del monastero di S. Maria in Firenze (Badia), ed. by Luigi Schiaparelli, I (Rome: ISIME, 1990)

Le carte del monastero di S. Stefano di Bologna e di S. Bartolomeo di Musiano, ed. by Rossella Rinaldi and Carla Villani, I, 1001–1125 (Cesena: Badia di S. Maria del Monte, 1984)

Il cartolare del notaio Stefano di Corrado di Lavagna, Chiavari-Lavagna (1288), ed. by Marta Calleri (Genoa: Società Ligure di Storia Patria, 2012)

Il cartolare di 'Uberto', I. Atti del notaio Giovanni, Savona (1213–1214), ed. by Antonella Rovere and Marco Castiglia (Genoa: Società Ligure di Storia Patria, 2013)

Il cartolare di 'Uberto', II. Atti del notaio Guglielmo, Savona (1214–1215), ed. by Marco Castiglia (Genoa: Società Ligure di Storia Patria, 2009)

Il cartulario del notaio Martino: Savona (1203–1206), ed. by Dino Puncuh (Genoa: Società Ligure di Storia Patria, 1974)

Codice diplomatico padovano, ed. by Andrea Gloria, 2 vols (Venice: Deputazione di storia patria per le Venezie, 1877)

Codice diplomatico del monastero di Santo Stefano, ed. by Marta Calleri, I, (965–1200) (Genoa: Società Ligure di Storia Patria, 2009)

Guglielmo Cassinese (1190–1192), ed. by M. W. Hall-Cole, R. G. Reinert, H. C. Krueger and R. L. Reynolds, I (Genoa: Società Ligure di Storia Patria, 1938)

Giovanni di Guiberto (1200–1211), ed. by M. W. Hall-Cole, R. G. Reinert, H. C. Krueger and R. L. Reynolds, I (Genoa: Società Ligure di Storia Patria, 1939)

Giovanni di Guiberto (1200–1211), ed. by M. W. Hall-Cole, R. G. Reinert, H. C. Krueger and R. L. Reynolds, II (Genoa: Società Ligure di Storia Patria, 1940)

Guglielmo da Sori. Genova-Sori e dintorni (1191, 1195, 1200–1202), ed. by Giuseppe Oreste, Dino Puncuh, and Valentina Ruzzin (Genoa: Società Ligure di Storia Patria, 2015)

Lanfranco (1202–1226), ed. by H. C. Krueger and R. L. Reynolds, I (Genoa: Società Ligure di Storia Patria, 1951)

Lanfranco (1202–1226), ed. by H. C. Krueger and R. L. Reynolds, II (Genoa: Società Ligure di Storia Patria, 1951)

Lanfranco (1202–1226), ed. by H. C. Krueger and R. L. Reynolds, II.1 (Genoa: Società Ligure di Storia Patria, 1953)

Lauer, Philippe, 'Un inventaire inédit des revenus fonciers de la basilique du Latran au XIIe siècle', *Melanges de l'école francaise de Rome*, 42 (1925), 117–24

Oberto Scriba de Mercato (1186), ed. by Mario Chiaudano (Genoa: Società Ligure di Storia Patria, 1940)

Oberto Scriba de Mercato (1190), ed. by Mario Chiaudano and Raimondo Morozzo della Rocca (Genoa: Società Ligure di Storia Patria, 1938)

Petrus Rufi (Genova 1213–1214), ed. by Chiara Boem and Marta Calleri (Genoa: Società Ligure di Storia Patria, 2021)

Il regesto del capitolo di Lucca, ed. by Pietro Guidi and Oreste Calleri, I (Rome: Loescher, 1910)

Versus eporediensis, in Dümmler, Emst, 'Gedichte aus Ivrea', in *Zeitschrift für deutsches Altertum*, 14 (1869), 245–65, edition at pp. 245–53

Secondary Works

Andreolli, Maria Pia, 'Pavia nei documenti: l'area occidentale. Immagini della città e della 'Campagna' nel secolo XIII', *Annali di storia pavese*, 27 (1999), 113–30

Baldassarri Monica, 'Another Brick in the Wall: edilizia residenziale e uso dei Laterizi nell'area di Palazzo Franchetti e in Chinzica (XII–XV secolo)', in *Le case di Pisa: edilizia privata tra Età romana e Medioevo*, ed. by Federico Cantini (Florence: All'insegna del Giglio, 2020), pp. 133–40

Bezzina, Nicole, *Artigiani a Genova nei secoli XII–XIII* (Florence: Firenze University Press, 2015)

Crotti, Renata, 'Le strutture di accoglienza in città: pubblico e privato a confronto. Prime indagini', *Annali di storia pavese*, 27 (1999), 131–44

Bocchi, Francesca, 'Lo sviluppo urbanistico', in *Bologna nel Medioevo*, ed. by Ovidio Capitani (Bologna: Bononia University Press, 2007), pp. 187–308

Carocci, Sandro, and Nicoletta Giannini, 'Portici, palazzi, torri e fortezze. Edilizia e famiglie aristocratiche a Roma (XII–XIV secolo)', *Studia Historica. Historia Medieval*, 39.1 (2021), 7–44

Degrandi, Andrea, *Artigiani nel vercellese nei secoli XII e XIII* (Pisa: GISEM-Edizioni ETS, 1996)

Degrassi, Donata, *L'economia artigiana nell'Italia medievale* (Rome: Carocci, 1996)

Faini, Enrico, *Firenze nell'Età Romanica (1000-1211) L'espansione urbana, lo sviluppo istituzionale, il rapporto con il territorio* (Florence: Olschki, 2010)

Filangieri, Luca, 'Famiglie e gruppi dirigenti a Genova. (secoli XII-metà XIII)' (PhD Thesis, University of Florence, 2010)

Fiore, Alessio, 'Ostiglia around 1100: A Window on the Transformation of Local Power in the Countryside', in *Krise und Aufbruch*, ed. by Étienne Doublier (Rome: DHI, forthcoming)

Garzella, Gabriella. 'La proprietà frazionata nella gestione immobiliare di un ente monastico pisano (secoli XII–XIII)', in *Le sol et l'immeuble. Les formes dissociées de propriété immobilière dans les villes de France et d'Italie (XIIe-XIXe siècle)*, ed. by Oliver Faron and Étienne Hubert (Rome: École Française de Rome, 1995), pp. 169–84

Guglielmotti, Paola, *'Agnacio seu parentella'. La genesi dell'albergo Squarciafico a Genova (1297)* (Genoa: Società Ligure di Storia Patria, 2017)

Hubert, Étienne, *Espace urbain et habitat à Rome du Xe siècle à la fin du XIIIe siècle* (Rome: École Française de Rome, 1990)

——, 'La construction de la ville. Sur l'urbanisation dans l'Italie medievale', *Annales. Histoire, Sciences Sociales*, 59.1 (2004), 109–39

——, 'Urbanisation, propriété et emphytéose au Moyen Âge: remarques introductives', in *Le sol et l'immeuble. Les formes dissociées de propriété immobilière dans les villes de France et d'Italie (XIIe-XIXe siècle)*, ed. by Oliver Faron and Étienne Hubert (Rome: École Française de Rome, 1995), pp. 1–8

Lebeq, Stephan, 'The New *wiks* or *emporia* and the Development of a Maritime Economy in the Northern Seas (7th–9th Centuries)', in *From One Sea to Another: Trading Places in the European and Mediterranean Early Middle Ages*, ed. by Sauro Gelichi and Richard Hodges (Brepols: Turnhout, 2012), pp. 11–24

Mainoni, Patrizia, 'Un'economia cittadina nel XII secolo: Vercelli', in *Vercelli nel secolo XII. Atti del quarto Congresso storico vercellese* (Vercelli: Società storica vercellese, 2005), pp. 311–52

Mannoni, Tiziano, 'Case di città e case di campagna', *Atti della società ligure di storia patria*, n.s., 44.2 (2004), 227–60

Niero, Marina, 'Edilizia minore a Venezia tra XIII e XIV secolo' (PhD thesis, Università di Venezia, 2015)

Olivieri, Antonio, 'Il volto nascosto dell'economia ospedaliera. L'ospedale di Sant'Andrea di Vercelli nei secoli XIV e XV', *Reti Medievali Rivista*, 17.1 (2016), 189–217

Polany, Karl, *The Great Transformation: The Political and Economic Origins of Our Time* (New York: Farrar & Rinehard, 1944)

Rinaldi, Rossella, 'Forme di gestione immobiliare a Bologna nei secoli centrali del Medioevo tra normativa e prassi', in *Le sol et l'immeuble. Les formes dissociées de propriété immobilière dans les villes de France et d'Italie (XIIe-XIXe siècle)*, ed. by Oliver Faron and Étienne Hubert (Rome: École Française de Rome, 1995), pp. 169–84

Soriga, Renato, 'Il memoriale dei consoli del comune di Pavia', *Bollettino della società pavese di storia patria*, 13 (1913), 114–15

Sosson, Jean-Pierre, *Pour une approche économique et sociale du bâtiment: l'exemple des travaux publics à Bruges aux xive et xve siècles* (Brussels: Bulletin de la Commission Royale des Monuments et des Sites, 1972)

Tabarrini, Lorenzo, 'Le *operae* e i giorni: un elenco di censi e servizi dell'abbazia di S. Michele di Passignano (ultimo quarto del secolo XII) tra paleografia e storia', *Quaderni storici*, 152.2 (2016), 383–411

Varanini, Gian Maria, 'Torri e casetorri a Verona in età comunale: assetto urbano e classe dirigente', in *Paesaggi urbani dell'Italia padana nei secoli VIII–XIV* (GEM: Bologna, 1988), pp. 173–249

Chris Wickham, 'Prima della crescita: quale società?', in *La crescita economica dell'Occidente medievale. Un tema storico non ancora esaurito*, ed. by Franco Franceschi (Pistoia: Viella, 2017), pp. 93–109

Part III

Connecting

PAOLO TOMEI

Petrified Nodes

Bridges and Economic Growth (Tuscany, 1050–1200)

What exactly were the dynamics behind the leap forward that underpinned the European economic take-off in the latter part of the twelfth and thirteenth centuries? What trajectory did they follow, and what was the driving force behind them? The answer to these questions may lie in an interpretation of the transformation of the landscape and the pattern of settlement, both of which underwent a process of petrification over the same period. To reach a better understanding of these phenomena and way they are interrelated, I have taken the work of Chris Wickham as a starting point.[1] Addressing the theme of growth, this British scholar has recently focused on the study of distribution networks. Wickham's thesis can be summed up by the juxtaposition of 'donkey' and 'boat', with the emphasis on the first element. The creation of a system of interconnections would have made possible the development of regional economies, a prerequisite for the subsequent opening up to international commerce. This system is also at the centre of the model proposed by Richard Britnell some thirty years ago: the 'commercialization thesis'.[2] Its development started with the study of bridges and hospitals, which were often built in their immediate vicinity. Britnell focused, specifically, on the case of Rochester.[3] Bridges really were at the centre of the connective tissue linking cities, small towns, and medium-sized settlements, and the countryside.

There is a long-running debate among Italian medievalists on how best to categorize the various nodes in the settlement network. This discussion, and in particular Maria Ginatempo's synthesis articles over the last decade, have led me to believe that a strong argument can profitably interact with

* This paper was conceived during a research grant funded by the PRIN 2017 *Fiscal Estate in Medieval Italy: Continuity and Change (9th–12th centuries)*.

1 Wickham, 'Prima della crescita'; Wickham, *The Donkey and the Boat*.

2 Britnell and Campbell, eds, *A Commercialising Economy*; Britnell, *The Commercialisation of English Society*.

3 Britnell, 'Rochester Bridge'.

Paolo Tomei (paolo.tomei@cfs.unipi.it) is research fellow in Medieval History at the University of Pisa. His main research interests are the material and symbolic structures of power in Italy between the sixth and thirteenth centuries.

Building and Economic Growth in Southern Europe (1050–1300), ed. by Sandro Carocci and Alessio Fiore, (Turnhout: Brepols, 2024), pp. 189–214 BREPOLS PUBLISHERS 10.1484/M.TMC-EB.5.137980

Figure 10.1. 'Cittadine borghigiane' and major communication routes. **Green:** 'cittadine borghigiane' with populations of over 3000 inhabitants in the early fourteenth century as estimated by Maria Ginatempo; **Blue:** the oldest 'petrified nodes'. Fucecchio is in both categories.

Wickham's thesis. It is worth noting the distribution in the Italian peninsula of what Cinzio Violante termed the 'cittadine borghigiane', a possible precondition and certainly a result of demographic and economic growth (Figure 10.1). There are no small towns at all on the Tyrrhenian coast between Pisa and Civitavecchia, or on the Adriatic coast between Venice and Rimini. Many settlements of this type are however to be found concentrated along the main 'road area', the Via Francigena, in an arc stretching from Colle Val d'Elsa to Rivoli, precisely on the various routes along which the oldest and most important bridges were built.[4]

Despite their obvious relevance, little progress on the historiography of bridges has been made over recent years. The work of Thomas Szabó is still the main frame of reference: in the 1980s, Szabó re-proposed Johan

4 Ginatempo, 'Vivere a modo di città'; Ginatempo, 'La popolazione dei centri minori'; Ginatempo, 'Piccole patrie'.

Plesner's concept of 'road revolution', but used a completely new approach, putting in place the key features of a great narrative.[5] Following on from Britnell's thesis and Nicholas Brooks' articles of the early 1990s,[6] a revival of a sort took place at the beginning of this century with David Harrison and Alan Cooper's essentially complementary monographs on English bridges.[7] The former outlines the process of petrification, which began in the twelfth century and by the middle of the thirteenth had already established the system of infrastructure that still characterized the English landscape as late as the mid-eighteenth century. The latter is less interested in the economic aspect of bridge building than its relationship with the history of power, in particular of royal ideology.

Generally speaking, a certain narrowness of perception tends to prevail in studies on the subject. In complete contrast to the approach suggested by Wickham, bridges and other infrastructure put in place to facilitate the movement of people and goods have often been treated as incidental to the political and economic fabric in which they were embedded, and used mainly by outsiders, be they pilgrims or merchants.

The aim of this paper is to verify Szabó's model, to compare it with the direction of Wickham's research, and to draw some lines of synthesis from a regional study. My research centres on the territory focused on by both these scholars and which, together with Lombardy, was at the forefront of the late medieval economic take-off. I shall concentrate on central-northern Tuscany prior to the thirteenth century, paying particular attention to the two major river systems: the Arno, which flows through both Florence and Pisa, and the Serchio, whose course at that time ran through the plains of Lucca and Pisa, and was divided into the *Auser* and the *Auserculus*.[8] The region boasts a documentary base of excellent consistency and continuity from the early Middle Ages, and has been the subject of a wealth of archaeological studies, particularly the volumes edited by Juan Antonio Quirós Castillo and Federico Cantini.[9] This is only a first and, for reasons of space, limited exploration of a line of research that offers great potential. A future comparison might include

5 Szabó, *Comuni e politica stradale*; Szabó, 'I ponti tra antichità e medioevo'.

6 Brooks, 'Rochester Bridge'; Brooks, 'Medieval Bridges'.

7 Harrison, *The Bridges of Medieval England*; Cooper, *Bridges, Law and Power*.

8 The study of these two river systems in the Middle Ages has been revitalized thanks to new methodologies of archaeological research. See Gattiglia, *MAPPA*; Salvini and others, 'Ricostruzione del paleoalveo del fiume Serchio'. No systematic survey exists of bridges over the Arno. For the Serchio, the starting point is still *Inventario*, ed. by Bongi, I, pp. 310–16.

9 Quirós Castillo, ed., *L'ospedale di Tea*; Cantini, ed., *Costruire lo sviluppo*. For an overview of published and unpublished sources, see Ghignoli, 'Le edizioni per la storia delle città toscane'. On economic growth in Tuscany, see Petralia, 'Le navi e i cavalli'; Poloni, *Lucca nel Duecento*; Faini, *Firenze nell'età romanica*; Tabarrini, 'When Did Clerics Start Investing?'; Cortese, 'I destini di un gruppo dominante'; Collavini, 'La crescita pieno medievale in Toscana'; Collavini, 'Tra campagne e centri minori'; Paganelli, 'Montieri, l'argento e altre risorse strategiche'.

the other area identified by Ginatempo as the most densely populated in the medieval settlement network, namely the heart of the Po basin between the rivers Adda and Oglio.

Premises

Before introducing and discussing Szabó's great narrative, I shall address some preliminary questions that touch on the problematic cores of materiality and representation.

What petrification?

Written and/or archaeological sources do not always allow us to ascertain which materials were used in the construction of a bridge. I have focused my attention on these structures, which I call 'petrified nodes', in whose construction one can infer at least a partial use of stone because of the monumentality and complexity of the investment involved. Bridges are characterized by the construction of a hospital and *domus* in their immediate vicinity, with a church or monastery, and sometimes fortifications, in the surrounding space.

The first example I shall consider is the *ponte Bonifilii* which spanned the river Arno at Fucecchio (built before 1002).[10] As we move into the twelfth century, the frequency of the references to 'petrified nodes' became gradually tighter: they increase in their absolute number and investments were also repeated in the same node. In addition to the Fucecchio Bridge over the Arno, which from 1138 was associated with the church of S. Maria, and was rebuilt three times before the thirteenth century (between 1122 and 1134, between 1154 and 1159, and around 1178),[11] the following bridges were built over the Serchio, going up this river: Rosaiolo Bridge near the castle of the same name (before 1168);[12] Marquis's Bridge or S. Pietro Bridge (before 1064) along with the eponymous hospital and church, where there was already a *nave Eriprandi*;[13] S. Quirico Bridge near the church of the same name (before 1147),

10 Lucca, Archivio Storico Diocesano, Diplomatico Arcivescovile, † R 23.

11 Lucca, Archivio di Stato, Diplomatico, Altopascio, 01–1135, 22–04–1138, 11–11–1156, 20–01–1173; Grégoire, 'Temi tipologici della Vita di sant'Allucio'; Lucca, Archivio Storico Diocesano, Diplomatico, †† F 83. For the history of the bridge, see Spicciani, 'La realtà storica di sant'Allucio'; Malvolti and Morelli, 'L'ospedale di S. Jacopo di Altopascio'; Wickham, *Legge, pratiche e conflitti*, pp. 169–73.

12 Ceccarelli Lemut, *Medioevo pisano*, pp. 376, 491–95; *Regesto del Capitolo di Lucca*, ed. by Guidi and Parenti, no. 1501.

13 *Regesto del Capitolo di Lucca*, ed. by Guidi and Parenti, no. 308. See Wickham, *Legge, pratiche e conflitti*, pp. 138–42. In the analysis of the rich dossier on the church and *domus* of the bridge, *ponte Marchionis* cannot be distinguished from *ponte Sancti Petri*, as assumed by Belli Barsali, 'La topografia di Lucca', p. 521. By contrast, the *ponte petrino* which was the subject of a dispute (1157) studied by Savigni, *Episcopato e società cittadina*, pp. 89–90, and Wickham, *Legge, pratiche e conflitti*, pp. 68–69, should be considered a different structure. It stood in the

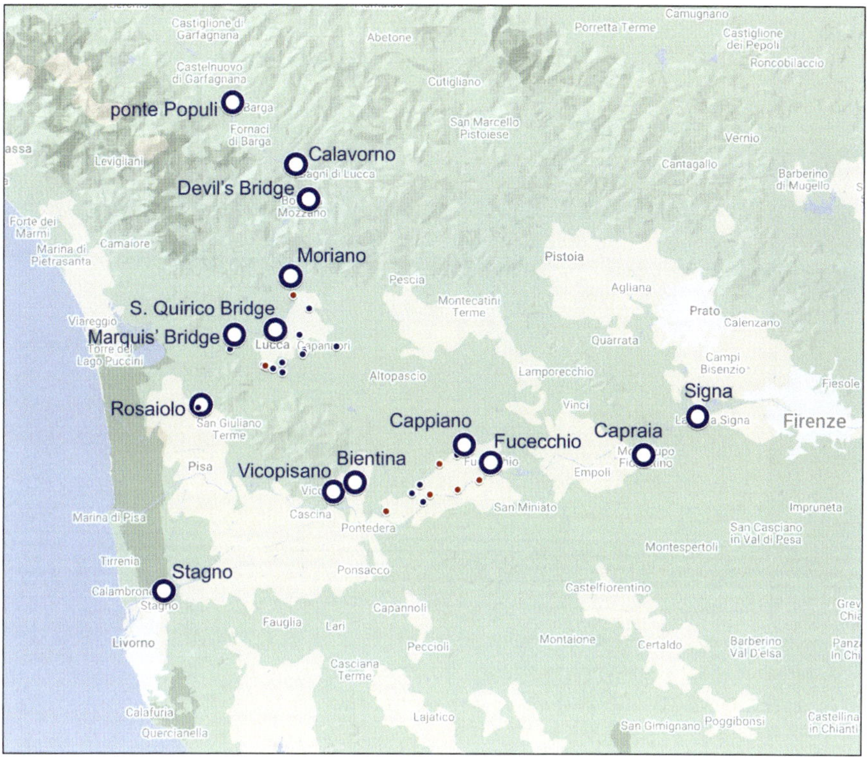

Figure 10.2. River crossings and docking points.
Blue: the 'petrified nodes' with major bridges indicated; **Red:** the 'mobile nodes'.

at the vicinity of which, but on the opposite bank, the rectory of S. Frediano built the church of S. Leonardo (1187);[14] Moriano Bridge (before 1113) along with the hospital and church of S. Ansano;[15] Calavorno Bridge (before 1122) together with the hospital of S. Leonardo;[16] *ponte Populi* near Fiattone, together with the hospital and church of S. Jacopo (1176).[17]

In my review I have also included both 'movable nodes', that is, docking and crossing points involving boats and pontoons; and 'fossil nodes', those

eastern suburb in front of the church of S. Maria Forisportam. See Lucca, Archivio di Stato, Diplomatico, S. Maria Forisportam, 28–02–1141, 08–05–1157, 18–08–1164, 05–02–1182.

14 *Regesto del Capitolo di Lucca*, ed. by Guidi and Parenti, no. 1019; Lucca, Archivio di Stato, Diplomatico, Archivio di Stato, 30–12–1187. See Wickham, *Legge, pratiche e conflitti*, pp. 132–35.

15 Lucca, Archivio Storico Diocesano, Diplomatico Arcivescovile, †† O 55, AC 67, †† P 32. See Savigni, *Episcopato e società cittadina*, pp. 101–02; Wickham, *Comunità e clientele*, pp. 62, 107–08.

16 Lucca, Archivio Storico Diocesano, Diplomatico Arcivescovile, †† R 95; Lucca, Archivio di Stato, Diplomatico, Miscellanee, 19–02–1187. See Tomei, *Milites elegantes*, pp. 122–24, 196.

17 *Papsturkunden in Italien*, ed. by Kehr, III, no. 15; *Acta Pontificum Romanorum Inedita*, ed. by von Pflugk-Harttung, III, no. 256. See Tomei, *Milites elegantes*, pp. 122, 126.

bridges only attested as relicts by toponymy. Incidentally, it is worth noting that, unlike Rome and other areas of central Italy, the region under review can boast no monumental Roman structures capable of continuity — such as the Augustus Bridge at Narni.[18] A close and multifaceted relationship persists between the three categories of node. The plain of Lucca is a good example of this. Here, on the branches of the *Auser* and the *Auserculus*, three fossil nodes are identifiable: from the north, clockwise around the city, we find *Ponteferrato*, Pontetetto, and *Pontearsiccio*. Near the first two locations, to the east and south of Lucca, there were respectively *ponte Petri*, *ponte Uberti*, and *ponte Preite Amichi*; *nave Hoti*, *ponte Homici Biti*, and *ponte Lei Buçi*.

If we add together the three types of node, the result is a grand total of forty river crossings and docking points in this area alone (Figure 10.2).

Petrification stimulates the production of written documentation

Even before the eleventh century, and prior to the widespread use of stone, bridges were already landmarks. Following the petrification of the landscape they become gathering places, where the interests of key political figures converged and social tensions were released. The construction of a petrified node was usually documented early on, and it left traces: bridges were places where charters were drawn up, and they also received 'cycles of donations'.[19] With regard to other petrified structures that were the object of conspicuous and repeated investments during the transition from the eleventh to the twelfth century, bodies called *operae* or *domus* were formed, whose duty it was to manage a structure's growing resources and maintenance, converting it into a legal entity.[20] The first to undergo this process was the Marquis's Bridge (before 1106).[21]

Most importantly, a petrified node could be both a cause and object of conflict. A large number of the court cases and dispute resolutions in twelfth-century Tuscany analysed by Wickham related to bridges.[22] Again, there was an increase in these cases as the century progressed. Eight disputes concern the Marquis's Bridge (1140, 1145, 1150, two in 1166, 1172, 1191, and 1199).[23] Three disputes involve the Moriano Bridge (1179, two in 1192).[24] The first *libellus querimoniae* preserved in Lucca, dated around 1210, refers to two previous

18 D'Angelo, *Narni e i suoi santi*.
19 For this concept, see Wickham, *The Mountains and the City*.
20 Ronzani, 'Dall'edificatio ecclesiae all'Opera di S. Maria'.
21 *Regesto del Capitolo di Lucca*, ed. by Guidi and Parenti, no. 661, no. 770, no. 775, no. 792, no. 810, no. 828, no. 887, and no. 890.
22 Wickham, *Legge, pratiche e conflitti*, exact references in previous footnotes.
23 *Regesto del Capitolo di Lucca*, ed. by Guidi and Parenti, no. 944, no. 1000, no. 1056, no. 1057, no. 1250, no. 1254, no. 1297, and no. 1816; Lucca, Archivio di Stato, Diplomatico, S. Frediano, 23-08-1191.
24 Lucca, Archivio Storico Diocesano, Diplomatico Arcivescovile, A 47, † B 28, †† P 26.

disputes relating to the S. Quirico Bridge.[25] Central to the reconstruction of the history of the Fucecchio Bridge is the dispute of 1173 which was heard before the imperial court of San Miniato.[26]

This growing presence of bridges in documents is linked to their increasingly stable territorial entrenchment

As Quirós Castillo has shown, the twelfth century marked an onomastic turning point.[27] Underlying this is an evolution which I call a process of de-personalization. Prior to this period, less enduring structures had taken their names from individuals who had distinguished themselves as builders, financiers, benefactors, or simple managers; later on, however, toponymy specifications became more frequent. The petrified node at Fucecchio is a paradigmatic case: the first time it was destroyed, in around 1106, references to the genitive *Bonifilii* disappeared and it became known as Fucecchio Bridge or Arno Bridge par excellence. The other docking and crossing points identified in the heart of the Valdarno before the twelfth century were also characterized by anthroponyms: *pontone Cicculi* (945) and *porto Acti* (1053).[28]

Notwithstanding the fragmentary nature of the records, this phenomenon was even more commonplace in the plain of Lucca on the branches of the *Auser* and the *Auserculus*, which formed a sort of belt around the city. Here the following are attested from the north in a clockwise direction: *nave Iohanni* (984); *ponte Winiberti* (981); *ponte Berteradi* (984); *ponte Petri* (1074); *ponte Uberti* (1074); *ponte Preite Amichi* (1132); *ponte Deruli* (979); *ponte de Formica* where there was once a *guado* — ford — *de Formica* (1117); *nave Hoti* (820); *ponte Homici Biti* (1014); *ponte Lei Buçi* (1071); and *nave Eriprandi* (910).[29] In the twelfth century, these increasingly petrified nodes referred no longer to people, but to places.[30] I interpret this phenomenon as a reflection of the process of the territorialization of power, which in Tuscany accelerated sharply with the decline of the March, a regional political framework with a public matrix, and the onset of the 'seigneurial transformation'.[31]

---

25 Guidi, 'Per la formazione delle circoscrizioni parrocchiali'.

26 Lucca, Archivio di Stato, Diplomatico, Altopascio, 20–01–1173.

27 Quirós Castillo, ed., *L'ospedale di Tea*, p. 50.

28 Lucca, Archivio Storico Diocesano, Diplomatico Arcivescovile, †† I 91, †† K 21.

29 *Chartae Latinae Antiquiores*, ed. by Magistrale and others, LXXIV, no. 48; Lucca, Archivio Storico Diocesano, Diplomatico Arcivescovile, † B 39, † I 4, † O 51, †† B 100, †† A 67, * O 4; *Regesto del Capitolo di Lucca*, ed. by Guidi and Parenti, no. 380, no. 403, no. 751, and no. 836; Lucca, Archivio di Stato, Diplomatico, S. Maria Forisportam, 14–04–1076, S. Giovanni, 25–05-1132.

30 Two examples: Lappeto Bridge (1165) and Verciano Bridge (1177). See *Regesto del Capitolo di Lucca*, ed. by Guidi and Parenti, no. 1238, no. 1375, and no. 1376.

31 Wickham, 'La signoria rurale in Toscana'; Tomei, *Milites elegantes*.

Times and Forms

In Szabó's view, the transition to the twelfth century represents a veritable 'road revolution'.[32] After this date, bridges became petrified bodies, juridically organized with the *operae*. A new network of roads was created simultaneously with the development of urbanization and the creation of a new system of small and medium-sized settlements. This is the decisive step in the great circular narrative outlined by the Hungarian-German scholar. It moves from the sacred to the public sphere (put simply, from *pontifex* to state) in a double cycle. Once the first sequence of the Roman age was over, the early Middle Ages entered a period of prolonged decline that would lead, after the final attempt to revive the Carolingian empire, to the disintegration of the ancient public structures. The construction and maintenance of bridges would have become the responsibility chiefly of the bishops who would have done their best not to squander this inheritance, against a backdrop characterized by disorder and localization.

The reversal of this decline was brought about by the expansion of the communal world, which restored civilization and brought with it security, as well as being a consequence of urban growth. This was the backdrop to a growing interest in, and awareness and appreciation of communication routes, which were vital to the economic and political development of cities. Szabó attributed the recovery of Roman law, and the inclusion among the *regalia* first of roads in Roncaglia, then of bridges in Constance, to an almost exclusively communal will. He described a process of diffusion that advanced from the urban centre to the periphery. During the twelfth century, cities shaped the territory over which they ineluctably established their dominion by carrying out interventions in settlement and infrastructure network. Tolls therefore became a source of revenue and concern. A significant series of agreements and pledges were made, initially within the urban direct sphere of influence; and from the middle of the century, with foreign territorial powers on a reciprocal basis.

The obsolescence of this narrative with respect to the new historiographic paradigms on the early and high Middle Ages is evident. In particular, regarding the matter in hand, it clashes with the modern interpretation of the structuring of seigneurial and communal powers on the territory and the imperial presence at the time of the Staufers, especially between the Diet of Roncaglia (1154, 1158) and the death of Henry VI (1197).[33] Nevertheless, even if de-contextualized from Szabó's interpretative key, I feel that a number of elements of his narrative still hold firm: the change of course at the transition between the eleventh and twelfth centuries, which Szabó describes using a

32 Szabó, *Comuni e politica stradale*; Szabó, 'I ponti tra antichità e medioevo'.

33 Carocci, 'Signoria rurale, prelievo signorile e società contadina'; Wickham, *Sleepwalking*; Fiore, 'L'impero come signore'; Fiore, 'La dimensione locale del potere imperiale'; Collavini, '*Iugum eius nobis videbitur suave*'; Provero, 'Tra Germania e Italia'.

mutationist lexicon that has recently undergone a successful resemantization;[34] and the change of pace in the middle of the twelfth century, during the reign of Frederick Barbarossa, which Szabó perceives through the analysis of political relations. On the economic and material side, it is indeed in this last historical period that Wickham, one of the most significant contributors to the renewal of interpretative frameworks, has situated the changes that preceded the growth and expansion experienced by Milan after 1150, and by northern Tuscany half a century or a century later. In this he is supported by the archaeological data systematized by Alessandra Molinari and Federico Cantini.[35]

Having established these key points, I shall now propose a possible way of reading, and providing a rhythm to, the process of petrification of bridges.

First Phase, Before the Middle of the Twelfth Century, divided into Two Stages

Initially, before the outbreak of the civil wars between Henry IV and Gregory VII, petrified nodes were created in the restricted belt around cities or in 'accumulation areas', namely those crossed by main roads, where a cluster of movable nodes was already in place, and where large fiscal *curtes* existed and small towns often sprang up. Investment was the deciding factor behind the selection of a privileged point of passage, and also acted as a driving force for the further development of the surrounding economic and settlement fabric.

The earliest initiatives were promoted by public authorities, namely the Cadolingi Counts at Fucecchio, and the Marquises near Lucca, where the main route linking the Po valley to Rome crossed the Arno and Serchio rivers respectively. Evidence of the centrality and dynamism of the rural area through which the Arno and its tributary *Arme* (today known as Usciana) flowed (Figure 10.3), is provided by the string of *burgi*, the first to appear in the documentation and attested in the same decades in which the Fucecchio Bridge was built: along the same route we find *Burgo Sancti Martini* (1018), *Burgonovo* (985), and *Burgo Sancti Genesii* (991).[36] As a result of petrification, *ponte Bonifilii* established itself as the heart of this hub, replacing a movable node, *pontone Cicculi* (945), situated near the *curtis* of the Queen at *Catiana*.[37] For many years Fucecchio was the sole bridge over the Arno between Pisa and Florence.

---

34 Wickham, 'The Feudal Revolution'; Fiore, *Il mutamento signorile*.

35 Molinari ed., 'Mondi rurali'; Cantini, 'Ritmi e forme della grande espansione economica'.

36 Lucca, Archivio Storico Diocesano, Diplomatico Arcivescovile, †† P 23, * E 90, * Q 22, AE 71. Located along the Via Francigena, they correspond to Borgo in the Cerbaie forest, Fucecchio, and San Genesio in the plain below San Miniato. See Malvolti, *La comunità di Fucecchio*, pp. 60–61, 74, 90, 100; Tomei, *Locus est famosus*; Tomei, *Milites elegantes*, pp. 105–09.

37 Lucca, Archivio Storico Diocesano, Diplomatico Arcivescovile, †† L 91. It was located further downstream, in the area of Castelfranco. See Pescaglini Monti, *Toscana medievale*, pp. 343–44; Tomei, *Milites elegantes*, pp. 42, 60, 94–95, 98.

There is a clear continuity between boats and docking, and petrified structures. The Fucecchio Bridge was built near *Burgonovo* at the landing and crossing point of *Vadocigni* (985). A port is documented here from 1024.[38] Marquis's Bridge was built near *nave Eriprandi* and the port at *Luto Asini* (910, 914);[39] and Moriano Bridge near *Navelongora* and the port at *Quercia Georgii* (1115, 1116).[40] However, the dynamic does not always proceed in the same direction. This was the case at Fucecchio, where a boat crossing was re-established when the bridge was temporarily destroyed (1114).[41]

With the 'seigneurial transformation' petrified nodes began to multiply, within or as junctions of the new territorial spheres of power. The construction of bridges represented a decisive moment in the structuring phase of the seigneurial districts. At Moriano (before 1113), the initiative was contemporary with the appearance of the episcopal *palatium* (1111) and the oath sworn by the 280 men of the local seigneurial *curtis* to the bishop of Lucca (1121).[42] At Calavorno (before 1122), the bridge was built following the creation of distinct *domus* within the marquisal aristocratic entourage and their common establishment as a power network in the upper and middle Serchio valley, following in the footsteps of Countess Matilda. The bridge preserved and petrified the link between these *domus*.[43]

As mentioned earlier, we can observe two profound transformations which are common to bridges and other political and social structures. In the decades straddling the eleventh and twelfth centuries, on the one hand, the territorialization process underwent a significant acceleration.[44]

38 Lucca, Archivio Storico Diocesano, Diplomatico Arcivescovile, †† P 23, † Q 93.

39 Lucca, Archivio Storico Diocesano, Diplomatico Arcivescovile, † B 39, * E 85.

40 Lucca, Archivio Storico Diocesano, Diplomatico Arcivescovile, †† A 20, † F 25.

41 Lucca, Archivio Storico Diocesano, Diplomatico Arcivescovile, AF 11.

42 Lucca, Archivio Storico Diocesano, Diplomatico Arcivescovile, † B 56, † L 91. See Wickham, *Comunità e clientele*, pp. 93–144.

43 Tomei, *Milites elegantes*, pp. 383–93.

44 Lauwers and Ripart, *Représentation et gestion de l'espace*; Mazel, *L'évêque et le territoire*;

Figure 10.3. Confluence of the Arno and the *Arme*: tenth to eleventh centuries. **Blue:** the 'petrified nodes'; **Red:** the 'movable nodes'; **Grey:** the *burgi*; **Gold:** the *curtis* of the Queen.

On the other, there was a juridical-institutional redefinition with the setting up of *domus*, from both an abstract and a concrete point of view. To use an expression coined by Claude Lévi-Strauss, and cited by Mario Nobili, this period saw the establishment of a 'société à maisons'.[45]

Bührer-Thierry and others, eds, *Genèse des espaces politiques*.

45 Nobili, *Gli Obertenghi e altri saggi*, pp. 288–89.

Second Half of the Twelfth Century: 'Dialectical Convergence'

As the twelfth century progressed, tolls became a permanent feature of the lexicon of power: this becomes evident if we glance at the index of noteworthy items in any edition of charters. The movement of people and goods not only became an important source of income. It also took centre-stage in the political arena, emerging as a subject of confrontation and conflict between the political forces dealing with the renewed imperial presence.

After being conducted on a more modest scale for thirty years, power struggles became more of a regional phenomena in Tuscany in the 1140s. The disputes revolved around new levies on the transit of goods and people introduced after the deaths of Matilda (1115) and the last of the Cadolingi counts (1113). The main area of conflict were the territories traversed by the major communication routes: the Middle Valdarno and Versilia. The Empire, with the Staufer dynasty at its head, put itself forward as a peacemaker, claiming the Matildic and Cadolingian inheritance and seeking to take control of the complex political mosaic, thereby providing legitimacy and recognition to princes, landlords, and communities. Furthermore, the Empire became one of the forces which was active both in local and regional affairs: with the reactivation of the Cadolingian *curiae* of Pescia and Fucecchio and the installation of a direct representative in San Miniato, the Empire now occupied the very heart of Tuscany, where the river Arno meets the Via Francigena.[46]

Petrified nodes became a feature of the landscape of power and were habitually mentioned in documentary sources. Investments and disputes increased in number and frequency (Figure 10.4). In addition to the examples cited above, mention should be made of the urban bridges built in Florence after the extraordinary flooding of the Arno in 1177 and in Pisa in 1182, which caused tensions within the dynamic political life of the city communes.[47] It is also worth mentioning the initiatives promoted in 1154 in the area of Porto Pisano by the archbishop of Pisa, who entrusted the rector of the hospital and the bridge of S. Leonardo on the Ugione with the foundation and endowment of an eponymous hospital and bridge, on the tombolo that closed off the Stagno lagoon. The second bridge required immediate restoration following the destruction caused by the floods of 1167, as recounted by the chronicler Bernardo Maragone.[48]

---

46 Ronzani, 'I conti Guidi, i conti Alberti e Pistoia'; Ronzani, 'L'affermazione dei comuni cittadini'; Cortese, 'Poteri locali e processi di ricomposizione politico-territoriale'; Cortese, 'L'Impero e la Toscana'; Cotza, *Prove di memoria*.

47 On the reconstruction of the *ponte vecchio* in Florence, see Faini, *Firenze nell'età romanica*, pp. 193–95. On the building of the *ponte novo* in Pisa, see Ronzani, 'I giurisperiti e il comune di Pisa'; Ronzani, 'La casa di Gontolino'.

48 On the hospital and bridge at Stagno, see Ciccone and Polizzi, *Liburna e Planum Portus*; Ceccarelli Lemut, *Medioevo pisano*, pp. 370–71, 391–432.

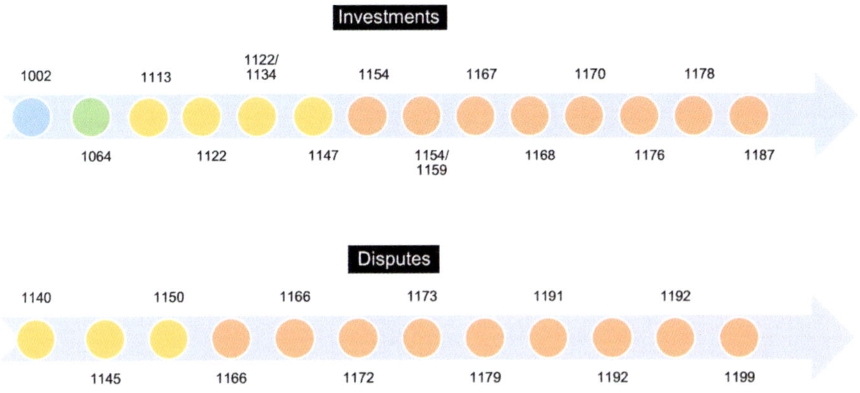

Figure 10.4. Investments and disputes over bridges: temporal rhythm. Each change of colour in the diagrams marks the passage of a half-century.

The construction of stone bridges and hospitals did not occur as a result of the political and economic conquest of the countryside and its shaping by the city communes. There was in fact simultaneous activity in several key areas, occurring at different speeds and with varying intensity. A close analogy can be established with the phenomenon of the 'terre nuove', the new towns that sprang up along the main communication routes through both seigneurial and communal initiatives, as shown by Maria Elena Cortese and Paolo Pirillo in the case of Tuscany.[49] A wave of development cannot be traced within a diffusionist model, from the city to the countryside. There was also movement in the opposite direction.[50]

The dialectical convergence between the various forces operating in the area was an impulse that drove the processes of reconstruction. There was a subsequent development of interconnecting networks. In this second phase, we begin to see the establishment of long-distance links between a number of hospitals and bridges. A key example of this is S. Jacopo at Altopascio.[51] Founded at the beginning of the civil wars between Henry IV and Gregory VII, this hospital, together with two others — S. Stefano at Rosaia and S. Ercolano at Campugliano — was entrusted with the management of the Fucecchio Bridge at the time of its first reconstruction, between 1122 and 1134, by the will of the assembly tasked with dividing up the region's Cadolingian inheritance. Thanks to imperial protection and support, in the Swabian period

49 Cortese, 'Castra e terre nuove'; Pirillo, *Creare comunità*.

50 For instance, consider the agreement made by the consuls of the urban confraternity of S. Simeone of Lucca in 1188, who entrusted the church to the rector of S. Jacopo of *ponte Populi*, in Garfagnana, in return for the construction of a new rectory and concern for its officiating. See Lucca, Archivio di Stato, Diplomatico, S. Ponziano, 19–09–1188.

51 Schneider, *Toskanische Studien*; Spicciani, *L'ospedale lucchese di Altopascio*.

Altopascio succeeded in gaining full control of the bridge and asserting a kind of monopoly over hospital structures in the Middle Valdarno, the area where the influence of Swabian officials held sway. Further towards the coast, another example of long-distance control can be found in the hospital and church of S. Leonardo at Stagno. In addition to the link with the bridge over the Ugione established at the time of its foundation, S. Leonardo received the newly-founded hospital of S. Leonardo on the Linaglia (1155) near Cecina, as a gift from the Gherardeschi counts.[52] An intense flow of donations followed, reaching as far afield as Corsica and Sardinia in the 1170s.

A study of donation charters brings to light the widening of the range of solidarity networks. In the last quarter of the twelfth century, these included multiple petrified nodes. In Lucca for example, the network set up by Morettino and Sassolino's provisions *pro anima* included the Fucecchio Bridge, the Marquis's Bridge, and S. Quirico Bridge (1178, 1185).[53]

Thirteenth Century: 'Integrated Complexity'

After the major arteries had been established, what we might metaphorically call a capillary circulatory system came into operation. It was in the thirteenth century that a network was established linking all the nodes, both in the heart of the region and in the valleys further away from the major road areas. In this third phase we can speak of integrated complexity.

In the Arno-*Arme* system — a privileged observatory due to its central position (Figure 10.5) — a series of pairs of bridges and ports was fully formed on the routes that passed through the Cerbaie forest at Cappiano, Rosaiolo, Montefalcone, Pozzo, Santa Maria a Monte, and Montecalvoli. In the decades preceding the foundation of the Lucchese new towns of Castelfranco and Santa Croce (1252), the following bridges are attested for the first time: Cappiano Bridge; Rosaiolo Bridge (1241) and Pozzo Bridge (1225), associated with fishponds held by Altopascio; the bridge at *Porto Acti* (1221) — after its collapse here a boat transported Altopascio's sheep; and the bridge at Santa Maria a Monte (1202), constructed on the initiative of the bishop of Lucca. If we widen our gaze to observe the entire course of the Arno, we perceive that the Fucecchio Bridge's bi-secular hegemony had come to an end. After the appearance of the Vicopisano Bridge (1170) and the Bientina Bridge (1179), coinciding with the refoundation of the settlements by the archbishop of Pisa, the Capraia Bridge (1204) and the Signa Bridge (1245) were added. The construction of the latter was a momentous event: here finally we witness the petrification of a movable node which, at least from the middle of the tenth century, had been of primary importance for

52 Ceccarelli Lemut, *Medioevo pisano*, pp. 193–95.

53 Lucca, Archivio di Stato, Diplomatico, S. Maria Forisportam, 20-10-1178, S. Giovanni, 14-01-1185.

Figure 10.5. Confluence of the Arno and the *Arme*: twelfth to thirteenth centuries. **Blue:** the 'petrified nodes'; **Red:** the 'movable nodes'; **Gold:** the new towns.

communication and transit between Florence and the sea.[54] Furthermore, this period saw a flurry of bridge building in the cities of Florence and Pisa.[55]

Petrified nodes are widely distributed across the region and, between the end of the twelfth and the beginning of the thirteenth century, are accompanied in the sources by elements suggesting demographic and economic expansion, even at some distance from the major arteries. Along the middle and upper course of the river Serchio, for example, the documentary data corresponds with the archaeological research coordinated by Quirós Castillo and Giulio Ciampoltrini.[56] The sources mention *burgi* at the head of Moriano Bridge

---

54 Pirillo, 'Il fiume come investimento'; Malvolti, 'Il ponte di Cappiano'; Pescaglini Monti, *Toscana medievale*, pp. 328–32, 578–79. Ceccarelli Lemut, *Medioevo pisano*, pp. 484–89; Salvestrini, 'Navigazione, trasporti e fluitazione del legname'.

55 In Florence, *ponte novo* (1218), *ponte Rubaconte* (1237), and *ponte Santa Trinita* (1252), see Salvestrini, *Libera città su fiume regale*, pp. 21–34. In Pisa, *ponte della Spina* (1262), and lastly *ponte a Mare*, see Garzella, *Pisa com'era*, p. 248.

56 Quirós Castillo, ed., *L'ospedale di Tea*; Ciampoltrini, ed., *Medioevo in Garfagnana*.

(1192), one of the few concentrated settlements in the plain of Lucca, as well as that of Marquis's Bridge (1195).[57] This period saw the start of a cycle of donations to the Maddalena Bridge or Devil's Bridge together with the hermitage of S. Francesco (before 1247). These were agreed by the *burgum* of Mozzano and by *fora* located along the river Lima and at its confluence with the Serchio, the connection point between the routes that descended from Garfagnana and the Pistoia mountains.[58]

The process of bridge building was a lengthy one, which gained momentum throughout the twelfth century; during the first half of the thirteenth century the connective network with bridges at its heart was in essence not so very different from the one we see today. This infrastructure attained a more complete degree of integration and complexity at the same time as the 'commercial revolution' broke out through an abrupt and rapid take-off.[59] A study of the interrelationship between this latter process and the dynamics reconstructed so far would however require a degree of focus and extended reflection beyond my field of expertise, and does not fall within the limitations of this paper.

Actors and Experiences

Bridges are structures that belong to the 'central zone' of society, that is, the public and sacred sphere. They therefore offer a privileged vantage point from which to observe those members of society who wish to distinguish themselves in the political community — in life as well as in death — by contributing to the common good with a huge expenditure of resources.[60] This applies above all to public officials, the highest-ranking of these in Tuscany being the Marquis-Duke, even in the phase of decline of the marquisal institutions following the death of Matilda. The only mention of *ponte de Lignaria* (866), ancestor of Rosaiolo Bridge, describes it as bordering on royal land.[61] The link with the *publicum* of S. Pietro Bridge is confirmed by its toponymy and by the land boundaries: it is called Marquis's Bridge; nearby there is a locality called *Teupascio*, meaning 'royal water', along with other evidence of royal lands, of the imperial abbeys of S. Ponziano and S. Giustina, and of S. Michele di Quiesa, founded by the daughter of Marquis Hugh (1025).[62] At Moriano Bridge

57 Lucca, Archivio Storico Diocesano, Diplomatico Arcivescovile, †† P 26. See Wickham, *Comunità e clientele*, p. 62. Lucca, Archivio di Stato, Diplomatico, S. Giustina, 19–03–1195.

58 Lucca, Archivio di Stato, Diplomatico, S. Agostino, 07–12–1247, 13–09–1251, 04–09–1252, 07–07–1255. See Savigni, 'Fenomeni migratori e vie dei commerci', p. 68.

59 Poloni, *Lucca nel Duecento*; Poloni, 'Italian Communal Cities'.

60 This also applies to the walls, see Menzinger, 'Mura e identità civica', and in general with the urban decor, see Internullo, '*Decus urbis*'.

61 *Chartae Latinae Antiquiores*, ed. by Gattagrisi and others, LXXXII, no. 18.

62 *Regesto del Capitolo di Lucca*, ed. by Guidi and Parenti, no. 308, no. 320, no. 342, no. 460, and no. 1198; Lucca, Archivio di Stato di Lucca, Diplomatico, S. Ponziano, 16–04-1042, 17–09-1071, 01–01-1079, 25–08-1081, 22–03-1185.

there was *terra de marcha* (1113).[63] The land on which the *domus* of S. Quirico Bridge was built was donated by Marquis Conrad between 1120 and 1129.[64]

From the last quarter of the twelfth century onwards, emperors and popes took a leading role. They interacted with all those individuals and groups who were keen to invest in the building of petrified nodes. As mentioned earlier, imperial support was crucial for S. Jacopo of Altopascio. For its part, the papacy played a decisive role in the creation of S. Jacopo of *ponte Populi* (1176) and S. Leonardo at S. Quirico Bridge (1187), as well as in the allocation of S. Pietro at Marquis's Bridge (1186) to the rectory of the mother church of S. Martino. From the 1180s onwards, the papacy also conceded a series of privileges to Stagno Bridge: in order to encourage the flow of donations for its reconstruction and maintenance, they granted thirty days of indulgence to the faithful of the kingdom of Sicily, of Tuscany, and Genoa, with the later including Corsica and Sardinia.[65]

A whole range of figures who were actively engaged in political competition, monocratic authorities and communities, in both urban and rural settings, addressed those political forces with universalistic claims. There was also room for personal initiatives. The most emblematic case is that of Allucio, who earned an aura of sanctity by moving in the former Cadolingian power space as a promoter of hospitals and bridges. His profile can be reconstructed by cross-referencing information from the dispute over the Fucecchio Bridge in 1173 and from the *Vita Allucii*, a hagiographic text dedicated to him.[66]

An examination of the documentary evidence regarding bridges permits us to trace the institutional definition process of 'collective bodies' with a horizontal matrix, in both the city and the countryside. Of particular note is the gradual creation of urban communal structures, whose representatives were instrumental in resolving disputes and imposing penalties.[67] Initially it is judicial officials, *consules causarum* and *consules de placito*, who are in evidence at Marquis's Bridge near Lucca; after the middle of the twelfth century, they are replaced by the more fully formed consular institutions and a generic and abstract *potestas*; finally, in 1190, we witness the presence of one of the first Podestà of Lucca, Pagano Ronzini.[68] The same charters also show how limits

---

63 Lucca, Archivio Storico Diocesano, Diplomatico Arcivescovile, †† P 32.

64 Wickham, *Legge, pratiche e conflitti*, p. 133.

65 *Papsturkunden in Italien*, ed. by Kehr, III, no. 15; *Acta Pontificum Romanorum Inedita*, ed. by von Pflugk-Harttung, III, no. 256; Lucca, Archivio di Stato, Diplomatico, Archivio di Stato, 30 12 1187; *Regesto del Capitolo di Lucca*, ed. by Guidi and Parenti, no. 1539. See *Italia Pontificia*, ed. by Kehr, III, pp. 375–76, 454, 465–66.

66 Spicciani, 'La realtà storica di sant'Allucio'.

67 It is also worth noting that at the same time as Stagno expanded its reach into the Mediterranean, the urban authorities in Pisa regulated activities at sea more clearly, defining the concept of piracy. See Cotza, 'Pace di Corso e gli altri mercanti'.

68 *Regesto del Capitolo di Lucca*, ed. by Guidi and Parenti, no. 944, no. 1000, no. 1056, no. 1057, no. 1250, no. 1296, and no. 1297; Lucca, Archivio di Stato, Diplomatico, S. Ponziano, 24–07-1144, Archivio dei Notari, 11–08-1190.

were placed on the actions of these authorities, which calls into question the traditional image of an early and uncontested urban predominance over the countryside. At Moriano Bridge in 1183, the coercive power in charters was attributed to the bishop of Lucca, the consuls of Moriano, and the generic *potestas* that exercised here the *districtio*.[69] At the Fucecchio Bridge, the consuls of Lucca appeared only for the reconstruction between 1154 and 1159; subsequently imperial activity in Valdarno clearly prevailed.[70]

Furthermore, bridges were connective and unifying elements that facilitated institutional experiments and efforts to achieve political and territorial reconstruction. They were, in fact, a matter of common interest, and required continuous and substantial investment, rendering them a constant work-in-progress; hence their plural, associative dimension. The charters relating to Marquis's Bridge give us a glimpse of a lively succession of characters.[71] There was a high turnover of rectors for the *opera pontis*, a body which took on a separate identity from the church of S. Pietro at the end of the twelfth century. There is, then, a patron of the bridge: Bernardo, son of the late Bulgarino, who was active between 1140 and 1157 and sought distinction in the ranks of the urban *militia*.[72] From 1172 onwards, we find the first bridge consuls who established a symbiotic relationship, so to speak, with the consuls of the millers of the city gates of S. Donato and S. Frediano. Thus, in parallel with the emergence of the bridge community and the proximity of its church, the parish of S. Pietro, we witness the creation of the first non-merchant trade association in Lucca, a very early kind of corporation, as Alma Poloni has observed.[73] After the bridge was granted to S. Martino in 1186, the parish priests in charge of the neighbouring baptismal churches were also involved in its management.

In addition, petrified nodes were crucial for the recovery and reconstitution of the Cadolingian and Matildic inheritance, both of which were major issues at the heart of the political debate in twelfth-century Tuscany. At the time of the first reconstruction of the Fucecchio Bridge, entrusted in joint management to the hospitals of Altopascio, Rosaia, and Campugliano, an agreement was made with Saint Allucio by the leading local figures: Countess Imillia Guidi, on behalf of the abbey of S. Salvatore; Countess Cecilia, remarried to Tancredi Nontigiova Alberti; the bishop of Lucca; and the *boni homines* of Fucecchio, that is the leaders of the local community. It was around the bridges of the middle and upper Serchio valley that members of a 'macro-consorteria' in the

---

69 *Regesto del Capitolo di Lucca*, ed. by Guidi and Parenti, no. 1492.

70 Lucca, Archivio di Stato, Diplomatico, Altopascio, 11–11–1156, 20–01–1173; Lucca, Archivio Storico Diocesano, Diplomatico Arcivescovile, †† F 83.

71 *Regesto del Capitolo di Lucca*, ed. by Guidi and Parenti, no. 770, no. 887, no. 944, no. 1000, no. 1056, no. 1057, no. 1162, no. 1185, no. 1254, no. 1296, no. 1532, no. 1656, no. 1726, and no. 1816.

72 On the patron Bernardo, see also *Regesto del Capitolo di Lucca*, ed. by Guidi and Parenti, no. 955.

73 Poloni, 'Strutturazione del mondo corporativo'. This evidence reveals the fundamental link between timber supply and rafting, mill activity, and other river infrastructure. On this, see Paganelli, 'I boschi, le navi, i mulini'.

province of Garfagnana converged: this was a political-territorial structure comprised of aristocratic households and castle communities which were already connected by virtue of belonging to Matilda's *domus*.

Bodies that were on the ascendant sought to distinguish themselves by investing in this kind of infrastructure. S. Jacopo of Altopascio and S. Frediano of Lucca are the two ecclesiastical institutions at Lucca registered with the highest amounts in the *estimo* of 1260, 6700 and 5300 *librae* respectively.[74] Thanks to the patronage of universalistic powers, between the twelfth and thirteenth centuries Altopascio and S. Frediano acquired a lot of possessions and dependencies from a wide area that extended far beyond the borders of Tuscany. They succeeded in fighting off rival powers to secure a place in the network of petrified nodes, thus contributing to both its increased complexity and integration.[75]

We should not be misled by the name: petrified nodes are all about dynamism. These were points in which the ferments that animated society manifested and accumulated, spaces of encounter and confrontation, and of circulation for the flow of people and resources. The objects of contention were, in a nutshell, the land gained or lost due to the presence of the river, on its banks or on the islands; structures built near the bridge pillars and on the road that might hinder free movement and result in the imposition of tolls; and the ecclesiastical framework of the new settlements that emerged and prospered at the immediate vicinity of bridges. Another recurring source of dispute were the activities of the rectors of those bodies in charge of the bridges' custody and management, in the land market and in credit.

The following instances provide an indication of the order of magnitude. At the Marquis's Bridge, initiatives followed one another in close succession: an investment of 9 *librae* and 8 *solidi* led, in 1192, to a new institutional set-up with a clearer distinction between the church of S. Pietro and the *opera pontis*; 12 *librae* from the millers' consuls helped finance the rebuilding of the hospital in 1195.[76] At the Moriano Bridge, the toll *de lignamine et bestiis* was used to recover a credit of 65 *librae* owed by the bishop to the Commune of Moriano in 1192.[77] The 1173 dispute over Fucecchio Bridge gives the following figures: the annual income from the bridge, after deducting expenses, would have been 50 *librae*; according to witnesses, there would have been a sum varying between 5 and 100 *librae* kept in the safe of its *domus*. In around 1156 Altopascio, advancing 60 *librae* for reconstruction costs, sought to secure absolute control of the bridge, and in 1175 obtained the waiver of rights over the bridge from the hospital of Campugliano for the sum of 56 *librae*.[78]

---

74 *Rationes Decimarum Italiae*, ed. by Guidi and Giusti, I, no. 4996.

75 The history of S. Frediano in this phase and its relationship with S. Giovanni in Laterano are yet to be properly investigated. An overview of its dependencies in *Inventario*, ed. by Bongi, I, pp. 12–13.

76 *Regesto del Capitolo di Lucca*, ed. by Guidi and Parenti, no. 1656, and no. 1726.

77 Lucca, Archivio Storico Diocesano, Diplomatico Arcivescovile, † B 28.

78 Lucca, Archivio di Stato, Diplomatico, Altopascio, 26-05-1158, 20-01-1173, 19-04-1175.

One final note on the qualitative side: it was common practice to combine bridges with other functional structures, with a view to boosting the economy.[79] Landing and crossing points, whether movable or petrified, were generally located at the confluence of watercourses in the major rivers (the Cerchia for the Marquis's Bridge, the Molerna for Moriano Bridge) or on bends, often marked by the toponym *Flexo*, where fishponds and cataracts were located — as was the case on the Serchio at what is now Montuolo (1025, 1140).[80] Associated with these nodes, even at some distance, is documentary evidence of mills and fullers — see the endowment charter of S. Jacopo of *ponte Populi* (1176).[81] The same applies to kilns, both before the period of growth, when brick was used sporadically, and between the twelfth and thirteenth centuries, when it was reintroduced and widely used in building initiatives. There was a specialized brick production centre near Marquis's Bridge in the second half of the tenth century where *manentes* made up the workforce. The toponyms *Teulaia* and *Figline* also refer to this. A brick kiln reappeared here at the end of the fourteenth century, but there is no clear evidence of continuity.[82] Lastly, a *furnace Iohanni* is mentioned in the oath to Altopascio sworn by around sixty men from Fucecchio, relating to the bridge and toll over the Arno (1180).[83]

* * *

It is time to bring together the threads of my discourse and draw some provisional conclusions. I have followed the time span already delimited by studies on the specific theme of bridges and, more generally, of petrification in relation to economic growth, seeking to provide new content, and to mark out and structure in stages the historical process that led to the creation of a complex system of interconnections on a regional scale. I have attempted to gain an insight into these initiatives, to put them in context, and to give a voice to their protagonists. What has emerged is a polyphonic ensemble that fragments and breaks down what has traditionally been considered a single voice: the proliferation of stone bridges as a reflection of communal order and prosperity. Rather, what emerges is the multiplicity of actors who interacted, clashed, and made connections, on a local level in a convergence of initiatives from above and below, characterized by intense institutional experimentalism. Bridges are a feature of twelfth-century competition, an indicator and generator of dynamism with a complex matrix, in which the political and economic dimensions are closely entwined. They constitute essential elements in the transformation of the landscapes of power, in which it was possible to locally intercept, feed, and connect the flow of wealth.

---

79 Pirillo, 'Il fiume come investimento'.

80 Lucca, Archivio di Stato, Diplomatico, S. Ponziano, 26–09–1025, 27–05–1140.

81 *Acta Pontificum Romanorum Inedita*, ed. by von Pflugk-Harttung, III, no. 256.

82 Tomei, 'Sulle tracce dei manentes altomedievali', pp. 6, 8; Savigni, 'Fenomeni migratori e vie dei commerci', p. 71.

83 Lucca, Archivio di Stato, Diplomatico, Altopascio, 27–05–1180.

Works Cited

Archival Sources

Lucca, Archivio Storico Diocesano, Diplomatico Arcivescovile
Lucca, Archivio di Stato, Diplomatico

Primary Sources

Acta Pontificum Romanorum Inedita, ed. by von Julius von Pflugk-Harttung, III (Stuttgart: Kohlhammer, 1886)

Chartae Latinae Antiquiores, ed. by Francesco Magistrale, Clelia Gattagrisi, and Paolo Fioretti, LXXIV (Dietikon: Urs Graf, 2004)

Chartae Latinae Antiquiores, ed. by Clelia Gattagrisi, Pasquale Cordasco, and Corinna Drago, LXXXII (Dietikon: Urs Graf, 2013)

Inventario del Regio Archivio di Stato di Lucca, ed. by Salvatore Bongi, I (Lucca: Giusti, 1872)

Italia Pontificia, ed. by Paul F. Kehr, III (Berlin: Weidmann, 1908)

Papsturkunden in Italien, ed. by Paul F. Kehr, III (Vatican City: Biblioteca Apostolica Vaticana, 1977)

Rationes Decimarum Italiae nei secoli XIII e XIV. Tuscia, ed. by Pietro Guidi and Martino Giusti, I (Vatican City: Biblioteca Apostolica Vaticana, 1932)

Regesto del Capitolo di Lucca, ed. by Pietro Guidi and Oreste Parenti (Rome: Loescher, 1910–1939)

Secondary Works

Belli Barsali, Isa, 'La topografia di Lucca nei secoli VIII–XI', in *Lucca e la Tuscia nell'alto medioevo*, Congressi del Centro Italiano di Studi sull'Alto Medioevo, 5 (Spoleto: Centro Italiano di Studi sull'Alto Medioevo, 1973), pp. 461–554

Britnell, Richard H., *The Commercialisation of English Society, 1000–1500* (Manchester: Manchester University Press, 1996)

——, 'Rochester Bridge, 1381–1530', in *Traffic and Politics: The Construction and Management of Rochester Bridge, AD 43–1993*, ed. by Nigel Yates and James M. Gibson (Woodbridge: Boydell, 1994), pp. 41–106

Britnell, Richard H., and Bruce M. S. Campbell, eds, *A Commercialising Economy: England 1086 to c. 1300* (Manchester: Manchester University Press, 1995)

Brooks, Nicholas P., 'Medieval Bridges: A Window onto Changing Concepts of State Power', *The Haskins Society Journal*, 7 (1995), 11–30

——, 'Rochester Bridge, AD 43–1381', in *Traffic and Politics: The Construction and Management of Rochester Bridge, AD 43–1993*, ed. by Nigel Yates and James M. Gibson (Woodbridge: Boydell, 1994), pp. 1–40

Bührer-Thierry, Geneviève, Steffen Patzold, and Jens Schneider, eds, *Genèse des espaces politiques IXe–XIIe siècle: autour de la question spatiale dans les royaumes francs et post-carolingiens*, Collection Haut Moyen Âge, 28 (Turnhout: Brepols, 2018)

Cantini, Federico, ed., *'Costruire lo sviluppo': la crescita di città e campagna tra espansione urbana e nuove fondazioni (XII–prima metà XIII secolo)* (Florence: All'Insegna del Giglio, 2019)

——, 'Ritmi e forme della grande espansione economica dei secoli XI–XIII nei contesti ceramici della Toscana settentrionale', *Archeologia medievale*, 37 (2010), 113–27

Carocci, Sandro, 'Signoria rurale, prelievo signorile e società contadina (secoli XI–XIII): la ricerca italiana', in *Pour une anthropologie du prélèvement seigneurial dans les campagnes médiévales (XIe–XIVe siècles): réalités et représentations paysannes*, ed. by Monique Bourin and Pascual Martínez Sopena (Paris: Publications de la Sorbonne, 2004), pp. 63–82

Ceccarelli Lemut, Maria Luisa, *Medioevo pisano. Chiesa, famiglie, territorio* (Pisa: Pacini, 2005)

Ciampoltrini, Giulio, ed., *Medioevo in Garfagnana. Contributi archeologici* (digital reprint, 2018) <https://archive.org/details/MedioevoInGarfagnana.ContributiArcheologici> [accessed 25 August 2024]

Ciccone, Gaetano, and Salvatore Polizzi, *Liburna e Planum Portus: ricerche sul territorio livornese nel medioevo fino all'inizio del XIV secolo* (Livorno: Ugo Bastogi, 1984)

Collavini, Simone M., 'La crescita pieno medievale in Toscana tra campagna e città. Prime riflessioni a partire da un seminario', in *'Costruire lo sviluppo': la crescita di città e campagna tra espansione urbana e nuove fondazioni (XII–prima metà XIII secolo)*, ed. by Federico Cantini, (Florence: All'Insegna del Giglio, 2019), pp. 147–52

——, '*Iugum eius nobis videbitur suave*. Una lettura politica della prima versione (1195/97) della *Summa Trium Librorum* di Rolando da Lucca', *Studi medievali*, 55 (2014), 495–519

——, 'Tra campagne e centri minori: forme della mobilità sociale nella Toscana rurale del XII secolo', in *La mobilità sociale nel Medioevo italiano. 4: Cambiamento economico e dinamiche sociali: secoli XI–XIII*, ed. by Simone Maria Collavini and Giuseppe Petralia, I libri di Viella, 255 (Rome: Viella, 2019), pp. 1–26

Cooper, Alan R., *Bridges, Law and Power in Medieval England: 700–1400* (Woodbridge: Boydell, 2006)

Cortese, Maria E., '*Castra* e terre nuove. Strategie signorili e cittadine per la fondazione di nuovi insediamenti in Toscana (metà XII–fine XIII sec.)', in *Le terre nuove*, ed. by David Friedman and Paolo Pirillo (Florence: Olschki, 2004), pp. 283–318

——, 'I destini di un gruppo dominante nell'età della crescita: la media aristocrazia del territorio fiorentino (1150–1250 ca.)', in *La mobilità sociale nel Medioevo italiano. 4: Cambiamento economico e dinamiche sociali: secoli XI–XIII*, ed. by Simone Maria Collavini and Giuseppe Petralia (Rome: Viella, 2019), pp. 27–64

——, 'L'Impero e la Toscana durante il regno di Federico Barbarossa', *Reti Medievali Rivista*, 18 (2017), 49–88

——, 'Poteri locali e processi di ricomposizione politico-territoriale in Toscana (1100–1200 ca.)', in *Poteri centrali e autonomie nella Toscana medievale e moderna*, ed. by Giuliano Pinto and Lorenzo Tanzini (Florence: Olschki, 2012), pp. 59–81

Cotza, Alberto, 'Pace di Corso e gli altri mercanti. Pirateria, società e istituzioni a Pisa nella seconda metà del XII secolo', *Società e storia*, 176 (2022), 215–39

——, *Prove di memoria: origini e sviluppi della storiografia nella Toscana medievale (1080–1250 ca.)* (Rome: Carocci, 2021)

D'Angelo, Edoardo, *Narni e i suoi santi: storia, liturgia, epigrafia, agiografia* (Spoleto: Centro Italiano di Studi sull'Alto Medioevo, 2013)

Faini, Enrico, *Firenze nell'età romanica (1000–1211): l'espansione urbana, lo sviluppo istituzionale, il rapporto con il territorio* (Florence: Olschki, 2010)

Fiore, Alessio, 'La dimensione locale del potere imperiale: assetti istituzionali e linguaggi politici nel regno d'Italia (1177–1197)', *Rivista storica italiana*, 122 (2010), 1088–120

——, 'L'impero come signore: istituzioni e pratiche di potere nell'Italia del XII secolo', *Storica*, 30 (2004), 31–60

——, *Il mutamento signorile. Assetti di potere e comunicazione politica nelle campagne dell'Italia centro-settentrionale (1080–1130 c.)* (Florence: Firenze University Press, 2017)

Garzella, Gabriella, *Pisa com'era. Topografia e insediamento dall'impianto tardoantico alla città murata del secolo XII* (Naples: Liguori, 1990)

Gattiglia, Gabriele, *MAPPA. Pisa medievale: archeologia, analisi spaziali e modelli predittivi* (Rome: Nuova Cultura, 2013)

Ghignoli, Antonella, 'Le edizioni per la storia delle città toscane dalla metà degli anni Sessanta a oggi: un bilancio per le carte e le fonti diplomatiche', in *Per la storia delle città toscane. Bilancio e prospettive delle edizioni di fonti dalla metà degli anni Sessanta a oggi*, ed. by Anna Maria Pult Quaglia and Aurora Savelli (Florence: Consiglio Regionale della Toscana, 2013), pp. 15–28

Ginatempo, Maria, 'Piccole patrie: le peculiarità dell'urbanesimo minore nell'Italia centrosettentrionale del Basso Medioevo', in *La ciudad de los campesinos: villas nuevas, pequeñas villas, villas mercado*, Semana de Estudios Medievales, 46 (Pamplona: Gobierno de Navarra, 2020), pp. 91–118

——, 'La popolazione dei centri minori dell'Italia centrosettentrionale nei secoli XIII–XV. Uno sguardo d'insieme', in *I centri minori italiani nel tardo Medioevo: cambiamento sociale, crescita economica, processi di ristrutturazione (secoli XIII–XVI)*, ed. by Federico Lattanzio and Gian Maria Varanini (Florence: Firenze University Press, 2018), pp. 31–80

——, 'Vivere a modo di città: i centri minori italiani nel Basso Medioevo: autonomie, privilegio, fiscalità', in *Città e campagne del Basso Medioevo: studi sulla società italiana offerti dagli allievi a Giuliano Pinto* (Florence: Olschki, 2014), pp. 1–30

Grégoire, Réginald, 'Temi tipologici della Vita di sant'Allucio († 1134)', in *Un santo laico dell'età postgregoriana: Allucio da Pescia (1070 c.a–1134). Religione e società nei territori di Lucca e della Valdinievole*, ed. by Cinzio Violante (Rome: Jouvence, 1991), pp. 15–54

Guidi, Laura Maria, 'Per la formazione delle circoscrizioni parrocchiali a Lucca: la *ecclesia sancti Leonardi pontis S. Quirici*', in *Pisa e la Toscana occidentale nel medioevo. A Cinzio Violante nei suoi 70 anni*, ed. by Gabriella Rossetti (Pisa: ETS, 1991), II, pp. 181–202

Harrison, David F., *The Bridges of Medieval England: Transport and Society 400–800* (Oxford: Oxford University Press, 2006)

Internullo, Dario, '*Decus urbis*. Un'altra prospettiva sui *Mirabilia* di Roma e le origini del decoro urbano (secoli XII–XV)', *Quaderni storici*, 55 (2020), 159–83

Lauwers, Michel, and Laurent Ripart, *Représentation et gestion de l'espace dans l'Occident médiéval (V^{e}–XIIIe siècle)*, in *Rome et l'état moderne européen*, ed. by Jean-Philippe Genet (Rome: École Française de Rome, 2007), pp. 115–71

Malvolti, Alberto, *La comunità di Fucecchio nel Medioevo* (Vicopisano: Tipografia Monteserra, 2014)

——, 'Il ponte di Cappiano e il Padule di Fucecchio dal Medioevo all'età lorenese', in *Il ponte mediceo di Cappiano: storia e restauro*, ed. by Giorgio Galletti and Alberto Malvolti (Fucecchio: Edizioni dell'Erba, 1989), pp. 7–64

Malvolti, Alberto, and Paolo Morelli, 'L'ospedale di S. Jacopo di Altopascio e il Valdarno inferiore nel Medioevo: dipendenze e proprietà, funzioni', in *Altopascio, un grande centro ospitaliero nell'Europa medievale* (Altopascio: Comune di Altopascio, 1992), pp. 73–110

Mazel, Florian, *L'évêque et le territoire: l'invention médiévale de l'espace* (Paris: Seuil, 2016)

Menzinger, Sara, 'Mura e identità civica in Italia e in Francia meridionale (secc. XII–XIV)', in *Cittadinanze medievali. Dinamiche di appartenenza a un corpo comunitario*, ed. by Sara Menzinger (Rome: Viella, 2017), pp. 65–111

Molinari, Alessandra, ed., 'Mondi rurali: insediamenti, struttura, economia. Secoli X–XIII', *Archeologia Medievale*, 37 (2010), 11–284

Nobili, Mario, *Gli Obertenghi e altri saggi* (Spoleto: Centro Italiano di Studi sull'Alto Medioevo, 2006)

Paganelli, Jacopo, 'I boschi, le navi, i mulini. Alcune riflessioni sul ruolo del legname nella crescita del XII secolo (a partire dalle fonti toscane)', *Ricerche storiche*, 53 (2023), 59–78

——, 'Montieri, l'argento e altre risorse strategiche nella Tuscia del XII secolo. Alcune riflessioni a partire da un dossier inedito', *Mélanges de l'École française de Rome – Moyen Âge*, 134 (2022), 67–91

Pescaglini Monti, Rosanna, *Toscana medievale: pievi, signori, castelli, monasteri (secoli X–XIV)* (Pisa: Pacini, 2012)

Petralia, Giuseppe, 'Le navi e i cavalli: per una rilettura del Mediterraneo pienomedievale', *Quaderni storici*, 35 (2000) 201–22

Pirillo, Paolo, *Creare comunità: Firenze e i centri di nuova fondazione della Toscana medievale* (Rome: Viella, 2007)

——, 'Il fiume come investimento: i mulini e i porti sull'Arno della Badia a Settimo (secc. XIII–XIV)', *Rivista di storia dell'agricoltura*, 29 (1989), 18–44

Poloni, Alma, 'Italian Communal Cities and the Thirteenth-Century Commercial Revolution: Economic Change, Social Mobility, and Cultural Models', in *Social Mobility in Medieval Italy (1100–1500)*, ed. by Sandro Carocci and Isabella Lazzarini (Rome: Viella, 2018), pp. 353–72

——, *Lucca nel Duecento: uno studio sul cambiamento sociale* (Pisa: Pisa University Press, 2009)

——, 'Strutturazione del mondo corporativo e affermazione del Popolo a Lucca nel Duecento', *Archivio storico italiano*, 165 (2007) 449–86

Provero, Luigi, 'Tra Germania e Italia: luoghi regi sotto Federico I Barbarossa (1152–1190)', in *Los espacios del rey: poder y territorio en las monarquías hispánicas (siglos XII–XIV)*, ed. by Fernando Arias Guillén and Pascual Martínez Sopena (Bilbao: Universidad del País Basco, 2018), pp. 207–25

Ronzani, Mauro, 'L'affermazione dei Comuni cittadini fra Impero e Papato: Pisa e Lucca da Enrico IV al Barbarossa (1081–1162)', in *Poteri centrali e autonomie nella Toscana medievale e moderna*, ed. by Giuliano Pinto and Lorenzo Tanzini (Florence: Olschki, 2012), pp. 1–57

——, 'La casa di Gontolino. Origine, sviluppo genealogico e attività pubblica della famiglia dei Sismondi fino ai primi decenni del Duecento', *Bollettino storico pisano*, 75 (2005), 503–22

——, 'I conti Guidi, i conti Alberti e Pistoia dall'inizio del secolo XII al 1177', *Bullettino Storico Pistoiese*, 112 (2010), 91–108

——, 'Dall'*edificatio ecclesiae* all'Opera di S. Maria: nascita e primi sviluppi di un'istituzione nella Pisa dei secoli XI e XII', in *Opera. Carattere e ruolo delle fabbriche cittadine fino all'inizio dell'età moderna*, ed. by Margaret Haines and Lucio Riccetti (Florence: Olschki, 1996), pp. 1–70

——, 'I giurisperiti e il comune di Pisa nell'età delle sperimentazioni istituzionali', in *Legislazione e prassi istituzionale a Pisa (secoli XI–XIII): una tradizione normativa esemplare*, ed. by Gabriella Rossetti (Naples: Liguori, 2001), pp. 91–130

Quirós Castillo, Juan Antonio, ed., *L'ospedale di Tea e l'archeologia delle strade della Valle del Serchio* (Florence: All'Insegna del Giglio, 2000)

Salvini, Riccardo, Enrico Guastaldi, Nadia Coscini and Nicola Del Seppia, 'Ricostruzione del paleoalveo del fiume Serchio (Lucca) tramite rilievi Lidar, foto aeree ed immagini Quick Bird', *Il Quaternario*, 19 (2006), 299–310

Salvestrini, Francesco, *Libera città su fiume regale: Firenze e l'Arno dall'antichità al Quattrocento* (Florence: Nardini, 2005)

——, 'Navigazione, trasporti e fluitazione del legname sulle acque interne della Toscana fra Medioevo e prima Età moderna', *Bollettino Storico Pisano*, 78 (2009), 1–42

Savigni, Raffaele, *Episcopato e società cittadina a Lucca da Anselmo II († 1086) a Roberto († 1225)*, Studi e testi Accademia Lucchese di Scienze Lettere ed Arti, 43 (Lucca: San Marco Litotipo, 1996)

——, 'Fenomeni migratori e vie dei commerci in Garfagnana nei secoli XII–XIV', in *Viabilità, traffici, commercio, mercati e fiere in Garfagnana dall'antichità all'unità d'Italia*, ed. by Giordano Bertuzzi (Modena: Aedes Muratoriana, 2006), pp. 59–103

Schneider, Fedor, *Toskanische Studien. Urkunden zur Rechtsgeschichte von 1000 bis 1268* (Aalen: Scientia, 1974)

Spicciani, Amleto, *L'ospedale lucchese di Altopascio: storia economica e finanziaria nei secoli XI–XII*, Quaderni della Biblioteca Capitolare di Pescia, 14 (Pisa: ETS, 2006)

——, 'La realtà storica di sant'Allucio e la storicità della *vita Allucii*', in *Un santo laico dell'età postgregoriana: Allucio da Pescia (1070 c.a–1134). Religione e società nei territori di Lucca e della Valdinievole*, ed. by Cinzio Violante (Rome: Jouvence, 1991), pp. 331–57

Szabó, Thomas, *Comuni e politica stradale in Toscana e in Italia nel medioevo*, Biblioteca di storia urbana medievale, 6 (Bologna: CLUEB, 1992)

——, 'I ponti tra antichità e medioevo. La ridefinizione di una struttura organizzativa', in *Ponti, navalestri e guadi: la via Francigena e il problema dell'attraversamento dei corsi d'acqua nel Medioevo*, ed. by Renato Stopani (Florence: Centro Studi Romei, 1998), pp. 17–28

Tabarrini, Lorenzo, 'When Did Clerics Start Investing? Abbot Uberto and the Economics of the Monastery of S. Michele di Passignano (c. 1190–c. 1210)', *Annali della Scuola Normale Superiore di Pisa Classe di Lettere e Filosofia*, 10 (2018), 399–434

Tomei, Paolo, *Locus est famosus. Come nacque San Miniato al Tedesco (secoli VIII–XII)* (Pisa: ETS, 2018)

——, *Milites elegantes. Le strutture aristocratiche nel territorio lucchese (800–1000 c.)* (Florence: Firenze University Press, 2019)

——, 'Sulle tracce dei *manentes* altomedievali', *Reti Medievali Rivista*, 22 (2021), 173–96

Wickham, Chris J., *Comunità e clientele nella Toscana del XII secolo. Le origini del comune rurale nella Piana di Lucca* (Rome: Viella, 1995)

——, *The Donkey and the Boat: Rethinking Mediterranean Economy, 950–1180* (Oxford: Oxford University Press, 2023)

——, 'The Feudal Revolution and the Origins of Italian City Communes', *Transactions of the Royal Historical Society*, 24 (2014), 29–55

——, *Legge, pratiche e conflitti. Tribunali e risoluzione delle dispute nella Toscana del XII secolo* (Rome: Viella, 2000)

——, *The Mountains and the City: The Tuscan Appennines in the Early Middle Ages* (Oxford: Oxford University Press, 1988)

——, 'Prima della crescita: quale società?', in *La crescita economica dell'Occidente medievale: un tema storico non ancora esaurito*, Centro Italiano di Studi di Storia e Arte Pistoia, 25 (Rome: Viella, 2017) pp. 93–106

——, 'La signoria rurale in Toscana', in *Strutture e trasformazioni della signoria rurale nei secoli X–XIII*, ed. by Gerhard Dilcher and Cinzio Violante (Bologna: Il Mulino, 1996), pp. 343–409

——, *Sleepwalking into a New World: The Emergence of Italian City Communes in the Twelfth Century* (Princeton: Princeton University Press, 2015)

PINUCCIA F. SIMBULA

Porti, cantieri e arsenali

Una premessa

In un saggio dedicato alla portualità nell'alto medioevo Sauro Gelichi nel 2008, a proposito della semplificazione delle infrastrutture economiche seguita alla fine dell'età antica, invitava a spostare l'attenzione dalla ricerca dei segni materiali di continuità/discontinuità alle sfumature di questa transizione, alla variabilità che discende dalla frammentazione del sistema di comunicazione e di scambi.[1] Tale suggestione può essere estesa ai secoli centrali del medioevo per individuare le dinamiche e i tempi della costituzione delle reti di infrastrutture di cui i porti rappresentano gli annodi marittimi. Il tema è indissolubilmente legato alla crescita economica dell'Occidente medievale, oggetto di un risalente quanto attuale dibattito storiografico, ripreso in un importante volume curato da Franco Franceschi nel quale, alla luce delle ricerche recenti, sono discussi in prospettiva teorica e metodologica i risultati di puntuali analisi descrittive e i tentativi di misurare la crescita con un approccio empirico.[2]

Sintetizzando schematicamente l'ampio ventaglio di posizioni, la periodizzazione dello sviluppo può essere ricondotta a due tesi di fondo: una, con Michael McCormick, individua i segni della ripresa in età carolingia, negli empori e nella circolazione monetaria e commerciale a lunga distanza tra Occidente, Oriente bizantino e islamico riattivata dagli intermediari dei centri campani e adriatici e dal decisivo rafforzamento delle relazioni dell'area padana che con i Franchi apre il Mediterraneo all'Europa continentale; l'altra, con Chris Wickham, sposta i primi indizi dell'avvio al X–XI secolo e la crescita tra la seconda metà del XII e il XIII secolo.[3] Nella serrata critica alla carenza di elaborazione di modelli affidabili in grado di spiegare i meccanismi dello sviluppo, Wickham ha insistito sulla debolezza delle letture basate sulle attestazioni più o meno precoci dello slancio urbano, sulla presenza di mercanti

1 Gelichi, 'Infrastrutture marittime', pp. 283–86.

2 Franceschi, *La crescita economica.*

3 Petralia, 'Tra storia e archeologia'; Petralia, 'Le "navi" e i "cavalli"'; McCormick, *Origins of the European Economy*; Wickham, *Framing the Early Middle Ages.*

Pinuccia F. Simbula (simbula@uniss.it) is Associate Professor of Medieval History at the University of Sassari. Her interests deal with the economic and social history in the Mediterranean area between the 11th and 15th centuries.

Building and Economic Growth in Southern Europe (1050–1300), ed. by Sandro Carocci and Alessio Fiore, (Turnhout: Brepols, 2024), pp. 215–242 BREPOLS PUBLISHERS 10.1484/M.TMC-EB.5.137981

e di attività commerciali e artigianali, di per sé non sufficienti a chiarire il funzionamento delle strutture economiche e i meccanismi della crescita.[4]

I dati sulla circolazione delle maioliche d'importazione e delle anfore da trasporto con sempre maggiore chiarezza restituiscono l'articolazione degli scambi, i livelli dei consumi e le intersezioni tra aree di produzione e mercati che convergono nel disegnare una pluralità di sistemi locali e regionali che con diversa intensità si vanno gradualmente integrando.[5] Nel Mediterraneo Occidentale, per Roma e il Lazio, la Campania e la Sicilia gli indicatori materiali confermano flussi economici mai del tutto venuti meno, mentre nell'Alto Tirreno i segnali della riattivazione delle rotte si pongono tra la fine del X–primi dell'XI secolo, con la presenza di produzioni di provenienza mediterranea islamica (Sicilia, Tunisia) e bizantina. Fenomeno ancora marginale, acquista consistenza con il progressivo dilatarsi degli orizzonti delle relazioni, tra XI e XII secolo, come documentano i ritrovamenti di vasellame proveniente dalla Penisola iberica, dalla Campania e dalla Puglia oltre che dal Mediterraneo orientale, presenti nei diversi contesti tirrenici in quantità variabile.[6]

La successione temporale e la provenienza dei ritrovamenti costituiscono un attendibile indicatore per delineare i ritmi degli scambi e i tempi della ripresa economica dell'Occidente, sul mare imperniata sui porti. Punta avanzata di un sistema di infrastrutture, i poli portuali aggregano con varia densità le complesse relazioni tra territorio, mare e mercati, in rapporto alle quali devono essere analizzati. Tuttavia, osservare le trasformazioni in atto dall'angolazione strettamente portuale attraverso le caratteristiche delle attrezzature è poco agevole per più ragioni. Sviluppo degli impianti portuali e crescita economica sono strettamente associati, ma collegare l'importanza economica di uno scalo tra l'XI-XII secolo alle installazioni presenti sul fronte portuale è fuorviante. Sul piano delle evidenze materiali nei secoli centrali, con poche eccezioni, con l'occasionalità delle indagini archeologiche la configurazione dei porti nell'Occidente sconta la fragilità delle strutture. Il pescaggio delle imbarcazioni fino alla rivoluzione nautica e commerciale, i cui effetti si avvertono tra XIII e XIV secolo, richiedeva dotazioni minime: situati nelle anse riparate del litorale, preferibilmente all'interno di specchi lagunari o alla foce dei corsi d'acqua, con poche eccezioni, i porti disponevano tuttalpiù di qualche pontile o banchina di legno per garantire le operazioni di carico e scarico al naviglio del tempo.[7]

L'aspetto è lontano dall'immagine evocata dal termine porto che richiama specchi d'acqua protetti da moli, con banchine, fari e torri. Le strutture

4 Wickham, 'Prima della crescita'.

5 Molinari, 'Le anfore medievali'; Petralia, 'Tra storia e archeologia', p. 17.

6 Arcifa and others, 'Archeologia della Sicilia islamica'; Baldassarri, 'Strutture portuali'; Baldassarri, 'Approdi, rotte e distribuzione'; Benente, 'La ceramica d'importazione'; Cantini, 'Ritmi e forme'; Gelichi and Molinari, 'Introduzione'; Molinari, 'Riflessioni sulle economie'; Meo, 'L'ordinario e l'eccezione'; Wickham, 'Prima della crescita', p. 102.

7 Luciano, *Porti e approdi*; Luciano, 'The Wooden Medieval Ports'; Beltrame, *Archeologia*, pp. 263–67.

dell'Occidente nei secoli centrali sono elementari e talvolta lo sono ancora nel tardo medioevo, l'età in cui i porti assumono maggiore complessità anche sotto il profilo architettonico.[8] Basti richiamare i caricatori stagionali siciliani, privi di qualunque attrezzatura eppure nodali per l'esportazione dei cereali incanalati in direzione dei centri mediterranei, o un grande scalo come Barcellona, una spiaggia relativamente coperta dai venti incuneata nell'ansa creata dai cordoni sabbiosi delle Tasques, a metà del XV secolo priva di moli, come la stessa Venezia nella sua peculiare forma di città-porto.[9] A questa varietà di scali nel suo insieme fa riferimento la definizione giuridica elaborata nella seconda metà del XIII secolo. Se nel VII secolo le *Etymologiae* di Isidoro di Siviglia ricalcano senza variazioni la formula di Ulpiano ('un porto è un luogo chiuso dentro il quale le merci sono importate e esportate'), nelle Siete Partidas (1265) di Alfonso X di Castiglia si incontra una precisazione del termine porto, ritenuto 'palabra dudosa'.[10] Pur rimanendo nel perimetro tracciato da Ulpiano, il testo precisa che 'sono porti anche tutti i luoghi dove la nave può svernare all'ancora; ma gli altri, dove può stare alla fonda senza potersi difendere da grandi tempeste, sono detti spiaggia o pelago'.[11] A prescindere dalla consistenza delle attrezzature, nel novero entrano a buon diritto tutti i luoghi attrezzati dove avviene il transito delle merci, nei quali le autorità dispongono di funzionari per la riscossione dei diritti doganali e d'uso, indipendentemente dalla delimitazione di un recinto portuale e si includono i ripari dove la nave può sostare per trovare rifugio.[12]

I contorni concreti della giurisdizione e lo stesso intrico della riscossione delle imposizioni sul transito delle merci tra XI e XII secolo sono poco lineari. Gli apparati preposti dalle autorità all'amministrazione dei porti con l'essenzialità hanno ambiti di competenza non privi di interferenze. Fra tutti, i grovigli con i diritti ecclesiastici e signorili, destinati a trascinarsi a lungo.[13]

8 Balard, 'Conclusion', pp. 279–80; Balard, 'Città portuali', pp. 11–20; Tranchant, 'Les ports maritimes' pp. 27–28.

9 Bresc, 'Le caricatore méditerranéen'; Soberón, 'Caixes i pontons'; Riera i Mora and others, 'Evolució del front marítim', pp. 89–112.

10 Piergiovanni, 'Dottrina e prassi', pp. 171–92; Balard and Picard, *La Méditerranée au Moyen Âge*, p. 96.

11 Alfonso X, *Las Siete Partidas*, Septima Partida, Titulo 33, ley 8.

12 Gautier Dalché, 'Qu'est-ce qu'un port?', pp. 233–39.

13 Il tema, come altri che andrebbero approfonditi con analisi specifiche, esula da queste pagine. Alcune indicazioni in: Castagneto and Trevisan, 'Politica marittima', pp. 40–42 per Piombino; Bordone, 'Le origini del comune', pp. 242–43; Guglielmotti, *Ricerche sull'organizzazione*, pp. 41–42; Vallerani, 'La riscrittura dei diritti', pp. 154–56; Sulla *decima maris* riscossa a Genova dall'arcivescovo: Krueger, *Navi e proprietà navale*, pp. 6–7; Mainoni, 'Sperimentazioni fiscali', pp. 740–43; Polonio, 'Gli spazi economici'. I conti di Barcellona nel 1127 rivendicano il potere di riscossione del diritto di ancoraggio per le navi che fanno sosta tra Nizza e Salou, oltre Tarragona: Bonnassie, 'Le littoral', p. 269 e più ampiamente pp. 251–71; Bastardes, *Usatges*, cap. 57–58-59, pp. 92–95. Concessioni di franchigie o alcuni diritti a singoli o alla cattedrale di Barcellona nel XII secolo in De Capmany i de Montpalau, *Memorias Históricas*, II, docc. 1, 3, 4. Catafau, 'La Catalogne et la mer', pp. 101–14.

Privilegiando i porti maggiori, meglio studiati e documentati, senza per questo sottovalutare le molte differenze e il ruolo fondamentale dei porti regionali e locali lasciati sullo sfondo, con generalizzazioni che appiattiscono i singoli contesti, si possono individuare alcuni elementi di fondo che caratterizzano la portualità nei secoli antecedenti il XIII secolo e le coordinate cronologiche delle tappe che nell'Occidente latino ne scandiscono l'evoluzione.

Porti tra selezioni, fondazioni e ri-fondazioni

Un primo punto riguarda la localizzazione dei porti e i fattori che tra i secoli centrali e il tardo medioevo concorrono a determinare i mutevoli assetti.[14] La topografia rimanda insistentemente alla dislocazione degli approdi nei contesti fluvio-lagunari, la cui importanza per i porti antichi è stata ben messa in risalto da Pascal Arnaud, mentre per il Medioevo è sottostimata.[15] Nei secoli di transizione e fino al primo Duecento, in linea con l'eredità del passato, la portualità mediterranea tende a ricalcare o privilegiare questi ambienti. Gli approdi della laguna veneta fondati nell'alto medioevo o i tanti porti ancorati alle foci dei corsi d'acqua nei litorali sabbiosi dell'Adriatico, del Tirreno o delle coste iberiche sono alcuni tra i tanti esempi.[16] Scali con queste caratteristiche si confrontavano inevitabilmente con il problema ricorrente dell'accentuata esposizione a processi di interramento per l'apporto terrigeno dei corsi d'acqua e la progradazione dei litorali. In antico, così come nel tardo medioevo, quando la rilevanza economica o militare rendeva economicamente proficuo l'intervento, l'evoluzione dei fondali e l'isolamento dal mare erano superati con escavazioni, prolungamenti delle banchine e dei moli o drastiche rifondazioni degli scali per mantenere vitali le funzioni economiche dell'area.[17] Guardando al passato si può ricordare il dragaggio effettuato fra la fine del IV ed il III secolo a. C. nel porto di Napoli per rifunzionalizzare l'insenatura, i molti porti di Roma sorti a breve distanza di tempo o gli interventi sugli scali di Costantinopoli.[18] Al radicale mutamento seguito alla 'fine della complessità' del mondo antico, rappresentato sul piano

---

Sulla giurisdizione dei porti in Catalogna e le competenze degli ufficiali regi: Ferrer i Mallol, 'Jurisdició i control', pp. 113–14.

14 Schmiedt, 'I porti italiani', saggio, che pur datato, costituisce ancora un imprescindibile punto di riferimento.

15 Chioffi and others, *Documentando città portuali*, in particolare i saggi Mayer, 'Algunos aspectos', e Ibba, 'Porti'; Arnaud, 'Entre mer et rivière'; Arnaud, 'Les Infrastructures'; Marriner, and Morgange, 'Geoscience of Ancient Mediterranean Harbours'.

16 Augenti, *Città e porti*; Gelichi, 'L'archeologia'; Gelichi and Negrelli, *Adriatico*; Pirani, 'Città, insediamenti', pp. 162–66; Mayer, 'Algunos aspectos'; Ibba, 'Porti'; Simbula, 'I porti nello sviluppo'.

17 Morhange and others, 'Perché studiare'; Slim and others, *Le littoral de la Tunisie*, pp. 43–45.

18 Carsana and others, 'Evoluzione del paesaggio costiero'; Giraudi and others, 'Portus (Fiumicino-Roma)'; Preiser-Kapeller, 'Heptaskalon and Other'.

materiale dalla diminuzione della circolazione dei beni di consumo e dalla contrazione qualitativa e quantitativa dei traffici marittimi, nell'Occidente cristiano si accompagna la minore necessità delle infrastrutture portuali e di investimenti per il loro funzionamento, all'origine almeno in parte della decadenza di molti impianti di età classica.[19]

La continuità d'uso di un sito non necessariamente implica la stretta sovrapposizione topografica con gli impianti preesistenti. Gli eventi idrogeologici che caratterizzano la costante mobilità degli impianti del *Portus Pisanus* esemplificano le pressioni imposte dall'innalzamento dei fondali fin dall'età antica. Per contrastare le conseguenze dell'impaludamento del *Sinus Pisanus* periodicamente si resero necessarie modifiche. Il nuovo complesso di torri, moli, banchine, bitte per l'ancoraggio ed edifici, avviato intorno alla metà del XII secolo (1156), fu collocato in posizione avanzata, a meridione rispetto alle precedenti strutture, adattate ai mutamenti ambientali, fino allo spostamento trecentesco degli impianti in mare aperto nel XIV secolo nelle acque antistanti Livorno.[20]

Approdi abbandonati talvolta conoscono un rilancio a distanza di secoli, in Occidente e non solo. Il porto di Cagliari, rifondato dai Pisani nel primo Duecento riporta l'approdo sul sito di età romana, entrato in decadenza nell'alto medioevo con lo spopolamento della città e l'esodo degli abitanti ai margini della vicina laguna.[21] Nei territori dell'impero islamico, Alessandria, Rosetta, Damietta, Tinnis o Tripoli sono tra i porti antichi rimasti in funzione sui quali gli Arabi impostano l'avvio dell'espansione marittima; altri lungo la costa dell'Ifriqiya, meno rispondenti alle strategie militari e commerciali, inizialmente lasciati al loro destino, sono rifondati nei secoli successivi, come Bugia (Béjaïa, in Algeria), Sousse (Hadrumetum) o Mahdia (al-Mahdiyya, in Tunisia).[22] Quest'ultimo, riattivato su iniziativa dei Fatimiti al principio del X secolo, contava su un bacino artificiale preesistente, risalente al periodo punico, un *cothon* scavato nell'arenaria appositamente riattato, a cui si accedeva da una struttura architettonicamente complessa, fatta di canali di comunicazione con il mare, di un arsenale e di un sistema difensivo murario.[23] Sul versante iberico, Almeria insisteva su un precedente sito romano entrato in crisi nella tarda antichità e rilanciato nel IX secolo come sede dei principali arsenali califfali.[24]

---

19 Gelichi, 'Infrastrutture marittime', pp. 283–85.

20 Baldassarri, 'Approdi, rotte'; Baldassarri, 'Strutture portuali'; Ceccarelli Lemut, 'Il sistema portuale'; Vaccari, 'Infrastrutture'.

21 Cadinu, 'Porti e strutture portuali', pp. 57–58; Simbula, 'I porti nello sviluppo', pp. 275–77; 281–83.

22 Valérian, 'Le pouvoir', pp. 77–79; Valérian, *Bougie*, pp. 247–330; Valérian, *Ports et réseaux*, pp. 53–87.

23 Slim and others, *Le littoral de la Tunisie*, pp. 43–45.

24 Torres Balbás, 'Atarazanas', pp. 178–79; Martínez Nicolás, 'Un caso de destrucción'; Picard, *La mer et les musulmans*, p. 137.

Nella Penisola italiana intorno all'XI secolo il paesaggio portuale presentava un'irregolare maglia di fortificazioni e arsenali che si dissolveva superata la linea del Mezzogiorno. La densità era concentrata sul versante tirrenico, nei centri campani, lungo la sfrangiata fascia di frontiera tra Islam, Oriente e Occidente saldata dalle navi dei *middleman* della Costiera, che avevano mantenuto ininterrotta la relazione con il mare.[25]

Nel Mediterraneo settentrionale i segnali dei cambiamenti si avvertono nel XII secolo, con le sistemazioni del fronte portuale avviate a Pisa e a Genova. Gli interventi nelle due città sono inscindibili dalla contemporanea monumentalizzazione della trama urbana e dall'ideologia sottesa al desiderio di legittimazione del proprio ruolo politico, si tratti del riconoscimento del papato o dell'impero.[26] Le stesse imprese sul mare dall'XI secolo, tra spedizioni antislamiche e partecipazione alla crociata, si inseriscono all'interno di questo quadro. Se Genova si modella nella Ripa, per Pisa, lontana dal mare, l'imponenza architettonica dell'avamporto enfatizza il programma urbanistico avviato dentro le mura. Tappa della costruzione degli spazi di preminenza politica ed economica, in entrambe il potenziamento delle infrastrutture avviene in corrispondenza con la riorganizzazione degli spazi destinati alle attività commerciali e produttive e con rafforzamento del controllo delle vie di accesso ai mercati, di mare e di terra.[27] La rilevanza delle evidenze, la relativa abbondanza di fonti e studi e la cronologia alta, rendono i porti di Genova e Pisa paradigmatici su grande scala della molteplicità di dinamiche che entrano in gioco nella conformazione delle infrastrutture in cui il porto e le attività che vi si imperniano sono poste a cardine dell'economia.

Per la città ligure le indagini archeologiche consentono di stabilire l'assenza di interventi precedenti l'inizio del XII secolo, quando nell'arco di un cinquantennio, di pari passo alla realizzazione della cinta muraria, si precisano le direttrici dello sviluppo urbanistico. L'orientamento della trama insediativa abbandona l'assialità romana ed è ribaltato sulla *Ripa Maris* lungo la quale la città si andrà distendendo e farà convergere i servizi con una redistribuzione delle attività funzionali al porto e al commercio. I consoli con il lodo del 1133 indirizzano la riqualificazione degli edifici sulla *Ripa*: fissano dimensioni e caratteri costruttivi del porticato voltato addossato agli

---

25 Feniello, 'Mercati, mercanti'. Sul ruolo dei centri monastici direttamente impegnati nelle attività di scambio: Del Treppo, 'La marina napoletana', p. 38; Marazzi and Frisetti, 'Porti "monastici" in Campania'; Petralia, 'Per una visione d'insieme'.

26 Petralia, 'Le "navi" e i "cavalli"', pp. 208–10; Bordone, 'Le origini del comune', pp. 254–56; Musarra, 'Genova e il mare'.

27 Guglielmotti, *Ricerche sull'organizzazione*, pp. 41–56; Balard, 'Vendere nel dominio'; Mannoni, 'Quando il mare'; Mannoni, 'Rapporti tra i porti e la rete stradale'; Grossi Bianchi and Poleggi, *Una città portuale*, pp. 51–66. Per Pisa, oltre al saggio di Paolo Tomei in questo stesso volume, cfr. Petralia, 'Pisa e la Sicilia', pp. 217–21; Garzella, 'Porti e approdi'; Salvatori, 'Pisa e le città del Midi'; Castagneto and Trevisan, 'Politica marittima e istituzioni'; Figliuolo, 'Le relazioni tra Pisa e Amalfi'; Salvatori, 'Lo spazio economico'; Ouerfelli, 'Les premiers contacts'.

edifici esistenti; intervengono sui materiali, sulle misure e sulle forme delle coperture da impostare su *columpne* di pietra. La struttura, libera da ostacoli e protetta da paramuri, basamenti compatti di pietra sotto la quota stradale, è calibrata per l'alaggio delle piccole imbarcazioni e il ricovero delle merci nei fondi degli edifici e rimanda alla prevalenza di un traffico di cabotaggio. Nell'ansa interna del Mandraccio, il porticciolo antico, è impiantato un primo troncone di molo in pietra fondato su palificate con calate scandite da pontili di legno, coronato nel 1173 dall'edificazione della chiesa di San Marco. Nel 1163 è avviato l'esproprio dei terreni tra il fossato Buccebovis e la chiesa del Santo Sepolcro, destinati dal Comune alla realizzazione dei nuovi scali, segno dell'insufficienza di quelli in funzione e della vitalità della cantieristica.[28]

L'azione dei consoli va oltre l'ambito urbano e sviluppa politiche che investono i centri costieri e i nodi di accesso alle vie di transito padane. La città, come nota la Guglielmotti, dal terzo decennio del XII secolo accompagna il consolidamento delle istituzioni comunali con una determinata politica di inquadramento degli insediamenti del territorio a Levante e a Ponente e nell'area retrostante verso l'Oltregiogo: 'l'effetto complessivo è un sostanziale arretramento dalla costa dei diversi poteri signorili'.[29] Nel 1113 è edificato il *castrum* di Portovenere, estremo limite a Oriente di uno spazio in costruzione, caposaldo che segna lo sbarramento all'espansione pisana. Significativo è che nella distrettuazione ecclesiastica con la creazione nel 1133 dell'arcidiocesi di Genova, Innocenzo II assegni, oltre alle diocesi in Corsica, i monasteri di Bobbio, Brugnato e nell'isola del Tino di San Venerio, in prossimità di Portovenere, le cui chiese saranno integrate nel 1162. Chiavari, passaggio verso l'area padana, nell'ultimo quarto del secolo è oggetto di interventi di fortificazione e politiche di incentivazione insediativa.[30]

Negli stessi anni il Comune di Pisa è impegnato a intensificare il proprio ruolo nel Tirreno, sancito nel 1162 dal riconoscimento da parte di Federico I di una forma di protettorato sugli scali costieri da Civitavecchia a Portovenere, dal potere di vietare la fondazione di nuovi porti e di concedere l'autorizzazione a esercitarvi il commercio. Il diploma, sul piano concreto privo di efficacia, delinea la traiettoria della città per rinsaldare la propria preminenza nell'area tirrenica. Nel 1154 con l'espansione demografica prende avvio l'edificazione della nuova cinta muraria e in sequenza è varato l'allestimento delle installazioni per il traffico fluviale e l'adeguamento della rete di collegamento tra avamporto e città. Gli interventi sulle strutture lungo il fiume iniziano intorno al 1160 con

---

28 Grossi Bianchi and Poleggi, *Una città portuale*, pp. 51–66; Grossi Bianchi, 'La costruzione', pp. 284–85; Grossi Bianchi, 'Gli approdi delle consorterie', pp. 302–03 e le tabelle (p. 306) con lista terre espropriate per gli scali comunali e per la nuova strada nel 1163; Cabona, 'Navi e porto', p. 44; Cagnana, 'Pietre per il vescovo', pp. 43–44. Sul significato di 'mandraccio' e sulla diffusione del termine in Occidente cfr. Ritter, 'Naval Bases', pp. 201–02.

29 Guglielmotti, *Ricerche sull'organizzazione del territorio*, pp. 43–47 (la citazione è a p. 45).

30 Guglielmotti, *Ricerche sull'organizzazione del territorio*, pp. 43–53; Basso, 'Politiche signorili', pp. 114–17.

la creazione di un edificio, forse un magazzino per le merci e una *darsana*, uno spazio delimitato riservato alla costruzione delle navi del Comune, oltre alla *domus Decatie*, vicino a San Vito, sede della dogana del porto.[31] Sul fronte marittimo il complesso prende corpo tra il XII e il XIII secolo. Al faro eretto nelle secche della Meloria nel 1156, segue la realizzazione di due torri nel porto, completate tra il 1162 e il 1164 e la sistemazione dell'area del Magnale. Nel 1165 si completano altri edifici 'per utilità dei marinari' ed è tesa la catena nell'accesso al porto, delimitato dalla palizzata lignea e dai moli. Dotato di acqua dolce per rifornire le navi, nel 1177 dispone di un fondaco e di una chiesa. Negli stessi anni è progettato e non realizzato un canale navigabile, il *carisium* che doveva facilitare i collegamenti con la città.[32] I casi di Genova e Pisa non esauriscono il panorama e nella loro specificità mostrano la stretta relazione tra lo sviluppo di uno scalo e le serrate iniziative che modellano la rete di servizi, le infrastrutture urbane e le connessioni senza le quali il porto sarebbe privo di sostegno.

Il XIII secolo segna un salto di qualità negli assetti e nell'articolazione dei complessi portuali. Nella stagione delle fondazioni (e rifondazioni) duecentesche la maglia portuale si ispessisce sulla spinta di esigenze tecniche, commerciali e egemoniche. La competitività tra le nascenti potenze occidentali per il controllo di mercati e risorse si riflette nella conflittualità innescata dalle politiche espansionistiche. Si possono ricordare le direttive federiciane sui porti del Mezzogiorno, l'edificazione di Aigues-Mortes intorno al 1240, affidata da Luigi IX alla perizia di costruttori genovesi o la creazione delle basi di Alghero e Castelgenovese volute dai Doria in Sardegna nell'ultimo quarto del secolo.[33] La crescita dei consumi con l'intensificazione dei ritmi dei viaggi e del volume delle merci favorisce l'incremento della stazza media delle imbarcazioni, soprattutto delle navi destinate al trasporto a lunga distanza di grandi carichi con un impatto diretto sulla configurazione dei porti. Gli impianti sono ripensati e attrezzati, spesso dislocati in posizione avanzata rispetto alle precedenti installazioni con la creazione di frangiflutti o colmate che portano in acque più profonde la linea di attracco. Moli o dighe per ampliare la capacità degli specchi portuali diventano elementi ricorrenti, come gli accessi sorvegliati da torri e chiusi da catene che, pur non rappresentando una novità assoluta o una sistematica presenza, accentuano il carattere difensivo dei porti, in certi casi quasi castrense.

L'adeguamento alle esigenze duecentesche a Venezia si ripercuote invece nelle misure contenimento delle dimensioni del naviglio per garantire la circolazione nei canali della laguna, affiancate dalla messa a punto delle galee da mercato, nel Trecento distintive della flotta della Repubblica, militare e commerciale a un tempo. In Catalogna lo scalo di Barcellona — la spiaggia, come è chiamata nella documentazione — mantiene la sua competitività con

31 Garzella, 'Pisa: la forma urbana', pp. 151–54.

32 Ceccarelli, 'Il sistema portuale', pp. 121–22.

33 Basso, *Strutture insediative*, pp. 74–76; Simbula, 'I porti nello sviluppo', pp. 287–91.

il potenziamento dei servizi per il trattamento delle merci, il coordinamento degli approdi minori e nel serrato confronto con i *barquers* cittadini che disimpegnano le operazioni per le navi in rada che solo nel pieno XV secolo potranno disporre di un ormeggio interno. In entrambe le città, più che le opere strettamente portuali sono le infrastrutture disseminate nel tessuto urbano e gli arsenali a fissarne la dimensione economica e militare.[34]

Attorno ai poli principali si raccordano con diversa densità approdi minori su cui si intrecciano rotte di cabotaggio e connessioni regionali e interregionali.[35] La trama tra XI e XIII secolo si va componendo e scomponendo nella fluida geografia degli assetti politici ed economici in via di definizione: la conquista da parte dei Normanni della Sicilia islamica, in piena crisi politica e gli attacchi ai regni degli Ziridi dell'Ifriqiya, le iniziative delle flotte di Pisa e Genova, l'avanzata dei regni cristiani nella Penisola iberica e l'avvio le crociate nell'arco di un secolo moltiplicano gli attori sul mare. Porti un tempo secondari sono avvantaggiati dalla posizione negli assi di comunicazione in relazione al mutare degli assetti politici, insediativi e produttivi.

Nelle isole è immediato cogliere gli assestamenti e i rimescolamenti delle gerarchie. In Sicilia, il passaggio dalla dominazione bizantina a quella araba segna il declino dei porti sulla costa orientale, come Siracusa, a favore degli approdi che guardano al Nord Africa e di quelli tirrenici, con l'affermazione di Palermo e di centri come Trapani e Mazara; scali, questi ultimi, ridimensionati nell'XI secolo, con la conquista normanna quando Messina, in concorrenza con Palermo, nel sistema del regno sarà il porto privilegiato.[36] Scelte politiche, iniziative economiche e mercantili incidono sul ruolo dei porti nel territorio e nei complessivi equilibri mediterranei.

Cantieri e arsenali tra commercio e guerra

Tra gli aspetti centrali, soprattutto nella fase iniziale in cui la presenza dell'Occidente sul mare si accentua, vi è quello delle navi e delle strutture sulle quali poggia la cantieristica. L'alto numero di imbarcazioni ricordate nelle fonti presuppone un elevato potenziale costruttivo e la presenza diffusa di maestranze con competenze altamente tecniche. Nell'XI secolo le imprese veneziane di Pietro II Orseolo in Adriatico e la mobilitazione in soccorso dell'impero, le spedizioni militari di Pisa e di Genova nelle Baleari, in Sardegna, in Sicilia e in Nord Africa o gli attacchi dei Normanni contro le terre dell'Impero bizantino, contavano tutte sulla disponibilità di ingenti flotte. Le cifre, trattandosi di testi cronachistici, annali e opere celebrative, pur prese con le dovute cautele, sono spia della notevole capacità armatoriale.

34 Anche attraverso una serie di scali minori coordinati dalla capitale del Principato.

35 Per la Toscana: Ceccarelli, 'I porti minori', pp. 49–67.

36 Balard and Picard, *La Méditerranée*, pp. 96–98; Bresc, 'Conclusions'; Corrao, 'Arsenali'; Martin, 'Les Normands d'Italie', p. 465; Martin and Noyé, 'Les façades maritimes'.

Ibn-el-Athīr, attribuisce 400 unità alle forze congiunte pisano-genovesi integrate da un contingente amalfitano che nel 1087 attaccò Bona. Nello stesso anno a Mahdia sono ricordate 300 navi e nel 1092 le imbarcazioni delle due città intervenute nel blocco di Tortosa ben 400. Nel 1113 per le forze congiunte della spedizione nelle Baleari, tra quelli giunti da Pisa, Genova, Catalogna, Provenza e Linguadoca, sono stati calcolati circa 500 scafi. Di Pisa si ricordano anche 120 navi messe a disposizione per la prima crociata.[37] E per Venezia Martino da Canal, riferendosi al 1171, segnala 100 galee realizzate in 100 giorni.[38]

Accantonando i numeri e le strategie all'origine dell'impegno dei centri tirrenici e dei progetti normanni, tra i vuoti vi è che poco sappiamo dei cantieri che supportano le iniziative marittime. Nelle fonti appare evidente che le flotte erano destinate al trasporto, al trasferimento di uomini in armi, cavalcature e macchine belliche da riversare a terra per le operazioni militari. Il *Liber Maiorichinus* tra le imbarcazioni della spedizione guidata da Pisa nel 1113 ricorda un composito campionario di 'gatti, drumones, garabi celeresque galee, barce, currabii, lintres grandesque sagine et plures alie variantes nomina naves', una tipizzazione navi da guerra/navi commerciali molto sfumata, frutto dell'evidente complementarietà degli usi e della modalità di raccolta delle flotte, composte da molte imbarcazioni di privati cittadini e integrate dalle unità commissionate per l'occasione.[39]

Nel XII secolo, prima della comparsa degli arsenali, si individuano spazi riservati dalle autorità alla costruzione le cui modalità di gestione non sono precise. A Genova si interviene nell'aumento degli scali intono alla metà del XII secolo;[40] a Pisa, l'area destinata è quella di San Vito dove nel primo Duecento sorgeranno gli arsenali comunali;[41] a Barcellona si accenna alle strutture nel tratto vicino alla Porta del Regomir sotto l'autorità dei conti di Barcellona e a Venezia un cantiere pubblico è in funzione prima della creazione degli arsenali duecenteschi.[42]

Struttura di diretta emanazione pubblica, almeno come complesso di edifici collegati alla navigazione, la tradizione dell'arsenale non era venuta meno nel

37 Renzi Rizzo, 'Lo spazio economico di Pisa'; Salvatori, 'Lo spazio economico', pp. 17, 27, 35–40; Musarra, 'Genova e il mare', pp. 124–47.

38 Tucci, 'Navi e navigazioni', p. 275 e, più in generale, sulla capacità veneziana tra XI e XII secolo, Tucci, 'L'impresa marittima', pp. 627–31.

39 Pisano, *Liber Maiorichinus*, pp. 192–99. Le spedizioni dell'XI–XII secolo conservavano l'aspetto di un esercito feudale in marcia: Tucci, 'L'impresa marittima', pp. 4–7; Petralia, 'Le "navi" e i "cavalli"', pp. 207–08; Musarra, 'La guerra', pp. 95–98.

40 Balletto, 'I lavoratori', pp. 110–11. A Savona, centro cantieristico di primaria importanza dal XII secolo, gli statuti trecenteschi prevedevano l'assegnazione degli scali in prossimità del porto ai maestri d'ascia che ne facevano richiesta, seguendo una rotazione annuale.

41 Garzella, 'Pisa: la forma urbana', pp. 152–54.

42 Estrada-Rius, *La Drassana reial*, pp. 18–19; Crouzet-Pavan, 'L'Arsenal de Venise', pp. 129–31; Tucci, 'L'impresa marittima', pp. 21–22.

Mezzogiorno bizantino e nelle riarticolazioni longobarde.[43] Sulla costa ionica la presenza era poco diffusa e anche i materiali utilizzati rimandano a una certa precarietà: l'arsenale in piedi a Brindisi in età normanna era in legno e di dimensioni ridotte, tanto che Federico II nel 1239, nelle misure di rilancio dei porti del regno, ne dispose il rifacimento in muratura, prevedendo un ampliamento tale da consentire il ricovero di venti galee.[44] Anche in Sicilia gli impianti erano pochi e solo in età normanna all'arsenale di Palermo si aggiunse quello di Messina.[45] Complessi chiusi, come Amalfi, erano invece fabbricati in pietra e disponevano di ampie navate destinate alla custodia di materiali e al ricovero delle galee.[46]

Rispetto al modello di arsenale che si diffonderà nel Mediterraneo settentrionale quello islamico aveva uno spettro di funzioni più ampio. Gli studi di Picard hanno sottolineato come ancor prima che uno spazio cantieristico l'arsenale era un'istituzione di diretta emanazione pubblica che rappresentava l'autorità del sovrano sul mare in tutti i suoi aspetti: flotta, equipaggi, attività militari e commercio marittimo. La valenza ne faceva un luogo emblematico del potere, centrale anche sotto il profilo economico-fiscale. Al suo interno, raccoglieva i funzionari califfali, gli uffici commerciali e doganali, botteghe artigianali e aree cantieristiche.[47]

L'arsenale entra nell'orizzonte dell'Occidente latino nel XIII secolo come 'fabbrica delle galee', di pari passo con lo sviluppo di iniziative espansionistiche militari. Venezia e Pisa, con alle spalle iniziative di intervento diretto nella cantieristica, all'inizio del Duecento sono le prime a dotarsi di arsenali, destinati alla realizzazione e al mantenimento delle unità da guerra, seguite dalla Corona catalano-aragonese e dalla Castiglia. La comparsa e il rafforzamento di queste strutture è ritmata dall'emergere nel Mediterraneo del Duecento di ambizioni talassocratiche tra le potenze dell'Occidente militarmente impegnate nella

---

43 Per Amalfi si rimanda ai saggi di Gargano, 'Arsenali e scaria' e alla relativa bibliografia; per Napoli, cfr. Del Treppo, 'La marina napoletana', pp. 40–42; Feniello, 'Alle origini di Napoli', p. 569; Alaggio, 'L'evoluzione urbana di Brindisi', pp. 112–13; Alaggio, 'Finis Europae', in part. pp. 86–87; De Vitis, Silvia, 'Taranto', pp. 22–24; Leone, 'Porto dela cita', pp. 44–45; Martin and Noyé, 'Les façades maritimes', pp. 507–08. Qualche indicazione per il Salento nella tarda età normanno - angioina anche in Auriemma, 'Nuovi dati'.

44 Mignone, *La riforma portuale di Federico II*.

45 Corrao, 'Arsenali'.

46 Gargano, 'Arsenali e scaria'; Gargano, 'Un esempio di ricerca'. Sul piano tecnico, pur senza particolari innovazioni, le esperienze costruttive del Mezzogiorno intorno al Mille confermano conoscenze mutuate dalla tradizione classica riprese dalle maestranze che nel XII secolo intervengono nei centri dell'Alto Tirreno e in quelle seguite ancora fino al tardo medioevo. Il molo di Otranto, realizzato tra il 1150 e il 1280, la sostituzione dei pontili di legno con opere in muratura tra il XIV e il XV secolo, e nel XV secolo, i lavori del molo di Barcellona sono eseguiti secondo le tecniche romane: Auriemma, 'Nuovi dati'; Soberón, 'Caixes i pontons'.

47 Picard, 'Les arsenaux', pp. 694–99. Nei porti islamici del Mediterraneo occidentale una nuova fase di interventi sugli arsenali si rileva nel XII secolo: Amores Carredano, *Las atarazanas almohades*; Navarro Paredes, 'Las atarazanas andalusíes'.

difesa di spazi economici e politici, fatti di conquiste territoriali e controllo di *enclaves*.[48] A conferma dell'interesse tardo per gli arsenali e della centralità mantenuta dai cantieri fino al Duecento, sul versante iberico si può osservare che nel XII secolo la nascente Corona d'Aragona, pur acquisendo diversi impianti islamici, per un lungo periodo non li impiegò e tantomeno pianificò rifacimenti o adeguamenti. Nelle coste meridionali della Catalogna Nuova i conti di Barcellona nel 1148 entrarono in possesso della *drassana* di Tortosa situata sull'Ebro. Il complesso, fondato intorno al 945 dal califfo Abd al-Rahman III, aveva il perimetro difeso da una cinta muraria fortificata con diciassette torri.[49] L'interramento ne aveva compromesso il funzionamento e a breve distanza dalla conquista, nel 1149 Ramon Berenguer IV ne donava una parte alla comunità ebraica della città per edificarvi sessanta case.[50] Opere furono intraprese alla fine del secolo successivo per riattare alcune parti dell'arsenale che riprese le attività in modo intermittente dai primi del Trecento.[51] Analogamente a Maiorca l'arsenale cristiano sorgerà nella seconda metà del Duecento, all'interno della pianificazione delle opere portuali e degli interventi urbanistici, in posizione opposta rispetto a quello islamico.[52] A Barcellona i grandi arsenali sui quali la Corona modellerà la facciata marittima e il ruolo di potenza mediterranea vedranno la luce nell'ultimo quarto del Duecento, negli anni del Vespro e dello scontro con gli Angioini quando emergerà l'esigenza di una flotta navale per i collegamenti e la difesa dei regni marittimi.[53]

L'arsenale non ovunque ha lo stesso peso. Gli estremi possono essere rappresentati dalla forma accentrata veneziana, nel Trecento un'industria navale di stato, e da quella di Genova, dove, per dirla con Balard, le costruzioni navali sono un affare privato.[54] Potenza navale senza flotta, dotata di arsenali alla fine del Duecento (1285), la città ligure è scarsamente interessata a monopolizzare il settore, preferendo armamenti estemporanei e soprattutto il ricorso all'iniziativa privata.[55]

L'avvento dell'arsenale crea una specializzazione, per quanto non rigida, tra costruttori del naviglio commerciale e militare: nella stessa Venezia, dove l'intervento pubblico della flotta è centrale, nel Duecento, quando le attività costruttive della Repubblica si andavano concentrando nell'*arsena communis*, all'occorrenza galee erano commissionate ai maestri negli squeri della laguna per conto del Comune.[56]

48 Sulle strategie e la rete di insediamenti portuali genovesi cfr. Basso, *Strutture insediative*.

49 Guidi Sánchez, 'Barcelona y la red marítima', pp. 169–78; Guidi Sánchez, *Els ports i la navegació*.

50 Carreras Candi, *Les dreçanes*, p. 7.

51 Estrada-Rius, 'Les Drassanes', pp. 30–32.

52 A Maiorca saranno edificati anche arsenali municipali che conviveranno con quelli regi: Cateura Bennàsser, 'Urbanizacion y finanzas', pp. 161–72.

53 Estrada-Rius, 'Les Drassanes'; Estrada-Rius, *La Drassana reial*.

54 Balard, 'Les arsenaux', pp. 59–57; Dotson, 'Shipbuilding'.

55 Tucci, 'L'Impresa marittima'; Basso, 'Tra crociata e commercio'.

56 Sul funzionamento dell'arsenale veneziano: Tucci, 'L'impresa marittima'; Crouzet-Pavan,

Navi e maestranze

Le domande sul funzionamento dei cantieri, l'organizzazione del lavoro, l'approvvigionamento dei materiali e il profilo delle maestranze sono insolute e in buona parte destinate a rimanere tali. Le abilità tecniche dei costruttori tirrenici nel XII secolo godevano di grande fama tra i contemporanei. L'*Historia Compostelana*, a proposito delle difese apprestate dalla Galizia in seguito agli attacchi di squadre normanne e musulmane, racconta delle richieste inviate a Pisa, Genova e Arles dal vescovo Diego Gelmírez, per richiamare esperti costruttori di navi da guerra ('Arelatum, Guenuam et Pisam nuntios suos miserat, qui ad se peritissimos navium artifices illinc venire facerent'). Nel 1115 a Iria Flavia sotto la guida del genovese Ogerio 'peritissimum navium artifex', furono varate due galee e nel 1122 'quoniam in partibus Gallaeciae homines nauticae artis periti non habebantur' il cantiere era affidato a 'cuiusdam juveni nomine Fuxoni Pisana Civitate oriundo, probo et nauticae artis peritissimo'.[57] La notizia, con il patrimonio di conoscenze tecniche relativamente diffuse, accenna alla mobilità delle maestranze originarie dei centri con una certa tradizione. Caratterizzati da una grande flessibilità, maestri d'ascia e calafati eseguono commesse private e pubbliche, disposti a lavorare anche in località distanti: negli archivi liguri si rintracciano genovesi in Sicilia, ad Ancona, in Provenza, chiamati a prestare temporaneamente la loro opera.[58] La mobilità è tra le clausole dei contratti di apprendistato del XIII secolo, che vincolano chi intraprende il mestiere a seguire i maestri negli spostamenti vicini e lontani.[59]

Quali fossero i canali attraverso i quali si tramandavano i saperi di un'arte in cui la perizia richiesta era elevatissima non è chiaro. Le imbarcazioni per la pesca e il cabotaggio potevano avere un unico committente ed essere realizzate da un unico artigiano, mentre quelle di maggiore dimensione e complessità richiedevano competenze tecniche per la progettazione e squadre di maestri d'ascia, carpentieri, calafati e altri lavoranti. Il cosiddetto *conto navale pisano*, noto per essere il più antico documento interamente scritto in volgare che si sia tramandato, è un frammento di spese sostenute per la riparazione o la costruzione di una galea o più imbarcazioni tra la fine dell'XI e i primi del XII secolo, pochi anni dopo la prima crociata (1095–1099) e quasi contemporaneamente all'impresa alle Baleari (1113–1115). La sequenza di voci con la razionale gestione del cantiere, degli acquisti e lo stoccaggio dei materiali acquistati in corso d'opera, denota la presenza di maestranze qualificate e un tessuto di artigiani coinvolti nelle forniture di legname, ferro, velature e parti speciali come i timoni, acquistati già pronti. Lo spaccato descrive un settore

---

'L'Arsenal de Venise'; Doumerc, 'Flottes publiques'; Dotson, 'Shipbuilding'.

57 Falque Rey, *Historia Compostelana*, lib. I, cap. LXXV; lib. I, cap. CII; Lib. I, cap. CIII; Lib. II, cap. XXI; Lib. II, cap. LXXV; Lib. III, cap. XXV; Burgoa, 'La Armada gallega', pp. 75–114.

58 Sulla mobilità delle maestranze liguri: Balletto, 'I lavoratori', pp. 123–29.

59 Balletto, 'I lavoratori', pp. 124–25.

collaudato e una suddivisione dei compiti definita, come meglio confermano i più tardi protocolli liguri del XII–XIII secolo.[60]

I maestri d'ascia, nel contesto genovese studiato da Laura Balletto, costituivano piccole imprese solitamente a carattere familiare, integrate all'occorrenza da altro personale. All'interno degli schemi contrattuali erano previste la tipologia dell'opera, il prezzo e la data di consegna e una serie di elementi concordati di volta in volta. I committenti ingaggiavano maestri d'ascia per imbarcazioni finite o solo per lo scafo, rivolgendosi separatamente ad altri artigiani per il calafataggio, la velatura e le parti necessarie.[61] La fornitura del materiale poteva essere a carico del committente (circostanza ricorrente) o dell'esecutore e incideva nella determinazione del compenso, regolarmente stabilito a monte e versato per stati di avanzamento dei lavori. Variabili che rendono impossibile calcolare gli introiti e i salari dei lavoratori.[62]

L'approvvigionamento del legname, dei materiali e di quanto necessario per la realizzazione della *machina navis* tra il XII e il principio del XIII secolo coinvolgeva numerosi artigiani e botteghe, con una ricaduta sull'indotto difficile da quantificare. Componenti semilavorate come tavolame per l'opera viva e la tolda, antenne, alberi o parti finite come scalmi, timoni, remi, oltre a vele, ancore, chiodi e altri elementi metallici, confluivano nei cantieri per la rifinitura e la messa in opera.[63] L'attenzione per la selezione delle essenze adeguate alle diverse parti dell'imbarcazione è ben presente e il legname è merce richiesta. I boschi retrostanti e le importazioni dai centri della costa o via mare dalla Corsica alimentavano la richiesta e dalla stessa Liguria dai primi del Duecento carichi di tavolame di faggio, platano e quercia e remi finiti prendevano la via della Provenza.[64] Sullo sfondo dell'intensificazione dello sfruttamento boschivo locale, Savona alla fine del XII secolo si impegna in politiche di controllo delle risorse, acquistando tra l'altro nel 1191 la foresta appartenuta ai del Carretto per le necessità pubbliche.[65]

L'ossatura dell'industria navale poggia innanzitutto sulle infrastrutture umane, le maestranze specializzate in grado di progettare e realizzare le svariate tipologie di imbarcazioni, indipendentemente da strutture fisse. Gli impianti stabili più facilmente sono presenti in area urbana o nei centri rivieraschi maggiori dove magazzini per lo stivaggio, botteghe e fornitori contribuivano a un sistema in grado di assicurare anche la continua manutenzione degli scafi in porto.[66] Gran parte dei cantieri aveva carattere temporaneo, che non incideva

60 Mastruzzo, 'Il conto navale', pp. 191–95; Baldelli, 'La carta pisana'; Antoni, 'The Pisan Paper', pp. 105–07.

61 Balletto, 'I lavoratori', pp. 116–18; 129–39.

62 Balletto, 'I lavoratori', pp. 123–29; 142–50.

63 Balletto, 'I lavoratori', pp. 129–38; cfr. Ciciliot, 'Les chantiers navals', pp. 259–71.

64 Balletto, 'I lavoratori', pp. 130–31; Noberasco and Scovazzi, *Storia di Savona*, pp. 243–44.

65 Ai cantieri di Savona all'occorrenza si rivolgeva la stessa Genova: Noberasco and Scovazzi, *Storia di Savona*, pp. 243–44.

66 Balletto, 'I lavoratori', pp. 108–11; 113–15; 132–34.

sulla capacità delle maestranze disponibili di soddisfare le richieste. I siti allestiti all'occorrenza avevano caratteristiche ricorrenti: erano individuati in prossimità dei centri abitati, spesso borghi di pescatori, riparati e ben collegati ai canali di rifornimento dei materiali. Dotati tuttalpiù di qualche capanno precario per riporre quanto utile per i lavori, i cantieri con la conclusione dell'opera scomparivano senza lasciare traccia.[67]

La costruzione di una imbarcazione comportava un investimento cospicuo. Le rilevazioni di Eugene Hugh Byrne e di Hilmar C. Krueger sui costi della *navis* nella seconda metà del XII secolo oscillano tra un minimo di 90–100 lire e un massimo di 1920 e 2480 lire di moneta genovese, mentre nella prima metà del secolo successivo i valori si attestano intorno alle 400–2250 lire. Per le galee i dati sono esigui, cinque valori compresi tra 126 e le 264 lire, nettamente più bassi rispetto ai velieri e eccessivamente pochi per trarne valutazioni attendibili sulla struttura della flotta del XII secolo.[68] La prassi diffusa era la compartecipazione tra più investitori con una divisione della proprietà in *loca*, quote ideali dello spazio della nave. Lo stesso committente o la società costituita per finanziare l'opera alcune volte ricorrevano alla vendita anticipata dei *loca* per disporre di liquidità per le spese.[69]

Nell'evoluzione duecentesca, riconducibile agli effetti della rivoluzione nautica si avverte una differenziazione tra imprese di costruttori. A fianco alla cantieristica 'familiare', che occupa il segmento del naviglio minore, nella seconda metà del secolo si affacciano imprenditori con maggiore intraprendenza e capacità economica che traendo opportunità dalla crescente richiesta, a fianco alle commesse tradizionali, a proprio rischio costruiscono e immettono sul mercato imbarcazioni come 'oggetto finito', pronte per la vendita.[70]

L'origine del capitale per il finanziamento delle navi nel XII secolo è una questione piuttosto in ombra, sulla quale meritano di essere riprese le considerazioni del Krueger basate sui cartolari notarili genovesi. Lo spoglio, per gli anni compresi tra il 1154 e il 1200, ha restituito 400 proprietari di imbarcazioni di cui lo studioso americano ha ricostruito il profilo. La disomogeneità e la consistenza del campione su cui si basano le deduzioni inducono alla prudenza e lasciando le aleatorie percentuali numeriche pare invece utile sottolineare l'evoluzione delle tendenze indicate da quelle cifre. Per il decennio tra il 1155 e il 1164 i 65 nomi dei proprietari di navi appartengono a molti protagonisti della vita pubblica cittadina, marginalmente coinvolti nei traffici mercantili, 'anzi, i modesti investimenti commerciali dell'intero gruppo dei proprietari di nave, in contrasto con l'elevata posizione politica e familiare di tanti di loro, suggerisce che nel decennio di Giovanni Scriba (1155 al 1164), la percentuale

67 Sulle specializzazioni dei centri cantieristici liguri: Balard, 'Les arsenaux', pp. 60–61, 64–66.

68 Byrne, *Genoese Shipping*, pp. 22–24; Krueger, *Navi e proprietà navale*, pp. 155–56, 164–65. Tito Antoni ipotizza il costo di una galea ai primi del secolo intorno alle 50 lire: Antoni, 'The Pisan Paper', p. 106.

69 Chiaudano, 'I "Loca navis" nei documenti', pp. 411–16; Krueger, *Navi e proprietà navale*, pp. 13–14.

70 L'esempio ligure più antico è del 1274: Balletto, 'I lavoratori', pp. 142–43.

maggiore del capitale per la costruzione e l'armamento delle navi provenisse da fonti non commerciali'. In sostanza, molti esponenti delle élites cittadine di stirpe viscontile, pur mantenendo l'interesse nelle rendite fondiarie, a metà secolo indirizzano i propri capitali nei crescenti e redditizi investimenti nelle navi e nelle attività commerciali.[71]

A fine secolo i profili comuni dei proprietari di quote di imbarcazione si identificano soprattutto con i mercanti. A pieno titolo, queste figure posseggono navi e partecipano direttamente ai traffici in tutti i settori del Mediterraneo, compreso l'Oriente, in misura decisamente superiore rispetto agli omologhi dei decenni precedenti. La terra mantiene la sua importanza ma gli investimenti si estendono a immobili in città o nei centri vicini dove la consapevolezza delle 'crescenti necessità economiche e sociali' rende altamente proficuo l'acquisto di 'luoghi di lavoro e di commercio', con una diversificazione degli introiti.[72]

Contrariamente a quanto sostenuto da Eduard Heyck a proposito della forza e della ricchezza dei proprietari di navi del XII secolo basata esclusivamente sul commercio, Krueger mette in risalto il ruolo della rendita e della ricchezza fondiaria di cui inizialmente si servirono i genovesi per i capitali da investire nella proprietà di imbarcazioni.[73] Il tema richiama quello sollevato a suo tempo da José Enrique Ruiz Domènec, a proposito dell'origine del capitale investito negli affari mercantili nella Barcellona degli stessi anni. Più che una contrapposizione tra ceto mercantile e aristocrazia, ancor meno attinente al contesto ligure, affiora l'importanza delle risorse della terra destinate a sostenere un settore economico in espansione e la rilevanza dalle attività marittime che vedono tra gli attori esponenti di primo piano della società cittadina.[74] Processi e dinamiche non lineari, che riportano l'attenzione sulla struttura economica e sociale da approfondire nei singoli contesti.

Qualche considerazione conclusiva

Tirando le fila del discorso, in primo luogo risulta evidente che misurare un porto restringendo il campo alle opere presenti sul fronte marittimo limita la comprensione delle dinamiche, dei modi e dei tempi della riorganizzazione della maglia di approdi. Le infrastrutture portuali si definiscono e sviluppano nel sistema economico di cui sono parte, in serrata interazione con le possibilità di innesto ai mercati, per vie di terra e di mare.[75] Superare lo 'spazio' porto ed entrare nella trama urbana, nelle politiche di inquadramento del territorio

71 Byrne, *Genoese Shipping*; Krueger, *Navi e proprietà navale*, pp. 53–55; Balletto, 'I lavoratori', pp. 103–53. Alcune considerazioni sulla base patrimoniale dei proprietari di navi per Pisa in Wickham, *Sonnambuli*, pp. 105–19.

72 Balletto, 'I lavoratori', pp. 135–36.

73 Heyck, *Genua und seine Marine*; Krueger, *Navi e proprietà navale*, pp. 35–54.

74 Ruiz Domènec, *Ricard Guillem*; Bonnassie, 'Le littoral catalan', pp. 267–71; Petralia, 'Le "navi" e i "cavalli"', p. 214.

75 Mannoni, 'Quando il mare', pp. 89–92.

e delle sue risorse, consente di osservare nel loro insieme le strutture delle attività commerciali e artigianali legate alla distribuzione dei beni, ai trasporti, alla cantieristica e ai servizi per la nave.

Gli indicatori delineano tra XI e XII secolo una rete di approdi in via di definizione. I poli che emergono con una sufficiente caratterizzazione sono favoriti dalla capacità di controllare gli assi di comunicazione e sfruttare le capacità di intessere relazioni tra territori e mercati. L'essenzialità degli impianti dei secoli centrali è dettata dalle modeste esigenze della navigazione e dalla consistenza dei traffici del tempo. La precocità delle installazioni di Pisa e Genova, i casi qui presi in esame, è in stretta relazione con i programmi urbanistici che rimodellano le due città, nella fase in cui sono impegnate nella costruzione di una propria dimensione politica, inscindibile dagli intenti propagandistici che passano per il ruolo militare svolto sul mare. Il che non significa sottovalutare o ridimensionare lo slancio economico alla base di quegli investimenti, quanto piuttosto sottolineare la rilevanza del retroterra su cui si sostengono e la molteplicità dei fattori che entrano in gioco.

Su un piano generale, che indubbiamente appiattisce la cronologia sfumata dei singoli contesti, lo scarto si avverte nel Duecento, l'età in cui i porti sono oggetto di profondi ripensamenti. Ristrutturazioni, ampliamenti e nuove fondazioni accompagnano lo sviluppo di infrastrutture dettato dalle esigenze tecniche della navigazione e del commercio. Le architetture non sono solo materiali: all'interno di congiunture mobili alle arterie maggiori si saldano le connessioni locali e regionali. Le intersezioni, tra iniziativa mercantile e azione politica, orientano gli spazi economici e sono esse stesse parte dell'infrastruttura su cui poggia la rete dei traffici. Vale la pena richiamare le considerazioni di Marco Tangheroni a proposito delle caratteristiche del commercio mediterraneo. Nella sua proposta si individuano tre fasi: una prima, tra l'XI e parte del XII secolo, nella quale gli scambi — e gli alti profitti che ne derivano — sono caratterizzati dall'intermediazione in prevalenza di merci di lusso, in cui non si può ancora parlare di un'economia di mercato; una seconda, tra il XII–XIII secolo, nella quale si moltiplicano le iniziative e il numero dei mercanti attivi nelle piazze mediterranee e, soprattutto, si accresce il volume e la varietà delle merci che entrano nei circuiti con operazioni a carattere speculativo e non monopolistico, come accadrà per alcuni settori produttivi nel tardo medioevo, in quella che Tangheroni individua come terza fase.[76]

Un ulteriore passaggio cruciale tra XII e XIII secolo si ravvisa nella graduale istituzionalizzazione dei rapporti commerciali con accordi internazionali e nello sviluppo delle basi di un diritto marittimo comune.[77] All'interno di coordinate cronologiche aperte, dove i singoli contesti sono suscettibili di molti approfondimenti, la scansione dell'organizzazione del commercio si allinea ai tempi delle trasformazioni delle infrastrutture portuali, fin qui genericamente e sommariamente trattate.

76 Tangheroni, 'I diversi sistemi economici', pp. 53–55.
77 Tangheroni, 'I diversi sistemi economici', p. 55.

ABSTRACT While focusing on ports, shipyards, and arsenals, the essay examines the evolution of facilities in the Latin West between the eleventh and thirteenth centuries. These considerations highlight the economic, technical, and material elements that mark the steps in building infrastructure related to navigation and maritime activities. Within a blurred chronology, the gap with the central centuries of the Middle Ages becomes significantly perceptible during the thirteenth century. The port network from this age underwent an intense phase of foundations, re-foundations, and adaptations of facilities extending into the late Middle Age, creating a system of connections and hierarchies modelled on the economic and political transformations of the West.

Works Cited

Primary Sources

Alfonso X, *Las siete partidas del Rey Don Alfonso el Sabio, cotejadas con varios códices antiguos por la Real Academia de la Historia. Tomo tercero. Partida Quarta, Quinta, Sexta y Séptima* (Madrid: Imprenta Real, 1807)

Pisano, Enrico, *Liber Maiorichinus de gestis Pisanorum illustribus*, introduction and critical edition by Giuseppe Scalia; comments by Alberto Bartola; translation by Marco Guardo (Florence: Sismel-Edizioni del Galluzzo, 2017)

Usatges de Barcelona. El codi a mitjan segle XII, ed. by Joan Bastardes (Barcelona: Fundació Noguera, 1984)

Secondary Works

Alaggio, Rosanna, 'L'evoluzione urbana di Brindisi in età normanno-sveva', in *Città di mare del Mediterraneo medievale. Tipologie* (Amalfi: Centro Studi di Storia Amalfitana, 2005), pp. 111–39

——, '*Finis est Europae contra meridiem*. Immagini da una frontiera dell'occidente medievale', *I Quaderni Del m.æ.S. — Journal of Mediæ Ætatis Sodalicium*, 11.1 (2008), 85–118

Amores Carredano, Fernando, 'Las atarazanas almohades de Isbiliya (Sevilla)', *Archivo Hispalense*, 101.306–08 (2018), 37–63

Antoni, Tito, 'The Pisan Paper of Philadelphia. Naval Account of the First Decades of the XII Century', *The Accounting Historians Journal*, 44.1 (June 2017), 105–07

Arcifa, Lucia, Alessandra Bagnera, and Annliese Nef, 'Archeologia della Sicilia islamica: nuove proposte di riflessione', in *Villa 4, Histoire et archéologie de l'occident musulman (VIIIe-XVe siècle): Al-Andalus, Maghreb, Sicile*, ed. by Philippe Sénac (Toulouse: Presses Universitaires du Midi, 2012), pp. 241–74

Arnaud, Pascal, 'Entre mer et rivière: les ports fluvio-maritimes de Méditerranée ancienne: modéles et solutions', in *Les ports dans l'espace méditerranéen antique: Narbonne et les systèmes portuaires fluvio-lagunaires*, Actes du colloque international tenu à Montpellier du 22 au 24 mai 2014, ed. by Corinne Sanchez and Marie-Pierre Jézégou (Montpellier-Lattes: Éditions de l'Association de la Revue archéologique de Narbonnaise, 2016), pp. 1–17

——, 'Les Infrastructures Portuaires Antiques', in *The Sea in History — The Ancient World*, ed. by Christian Buchet, Pascal Arnaud, and Philip de Souza (Woodbridge: Boydell, 2016), pp. 224–42

Augenti, Andrea, *Città e porti dall'Antichità al Medioevo* (Rome: Carocci, 2010)

Auriemma, Rita, 'Nuovi dati dalla costa adriatica e ionica del Salento', *Historia Antiqua*, 21 (2012), 543–46

Balard, Michel, 'Les arsenaux génois au Moyen Age', in Michel Balard, *Gênes et la mer. Genova e il mare* (Genoa: Società Ligure di Storia Patria, 2017), I, pp. 59–67

——, 'Città portuali del Medioevo', in Michel Balard, *Gênes et la mer/Genova e il mare* (Genoa: Società Ligure di Storia Patria, 2017), I, pp. 11–20

——, 'Conclusion', in *Ports maritimes et ports fluviaux au Moyen Age, XXXVe Congrès de la SHMES, La Rochelle, 2004* (Paris: Editions de la Sorbonne, 2005), pp. 277–81

——, 'Vendere nel dominio e fuori; botteghe di città e colonie mercantili', in *Storia della cultura ligure*, ed. by Dino Puncuh (Genoa: Società Ligure di Storia Patria, 2004), I, pp. 99–116

Balard, Michel, and Christophe Picard, *La Méditerranée au Moyen Âge. Les hommes et la mer* (Paris: Hachette, 2014)

Baldassarri, Monica, 'Approdi, rotte e distribuzione delle ceramiche in area altotirrenica (VIII–XIII secolo): riflessioni in margine ai recenti studi', in *Navi, relitti e porti: il commercio marittimo della ceramica medievale e post-medievale, Atti XLV Convegno Internazionale della Ceramica, Savona 2012* (Albenga: Tipolitografia Bacchetta, 2013), pp. 17–34

——, 'Strutture portuali e comunicazioni marittime nella Toscana medievale alla luce della fonte archeologica (VIII-inizi XIII sec. d.C.)', in *I sistemi portuali della Toscana mediterranea*, ed. by Giuseppe Petralia (Pisa: Pacini, 2010), pp. 81–116

Baldelli, Ignazio, 'La carta pisana di Filadelfia. Conto navale in volgare pisano dei primi decenni del sec. XII', *Studi di filologia italiana*, 31 (1973), 5–33

Balletto, Laura, 'I lavoratori nei cantieri navali (Liguria XII–XV secolo)', in *Artigiani e salariati: il mondo del lavoro nell'Italia dei secoli XII–XV*, Atti del Decimo Convegno di Studi tenuto a Pistoia nei giorni 9–13 ottobre 1981 (Bologna: Centro Italiano di Studi di Storia e d'Arte Pistoia, 1984), pp. 103–53

Basso, Enrico, 'Politiche signorili e comunali: villaggi scomparsi nella Liguria bassomedievale', in *Assetti territoriali e villaggi abbandonati (secoli XII–XIV)*, ed. by Francesco Panero and Giuliano Pinto (Cherasco: CISIM, 2012), pp. 109–34

——, *Strutture insediative ed espansione commerciale: la rete portuale genovese nel bacino del Mediterraneo* (Cherasco: CISIM, 2011)

——, 'Tra crociata e commercio: le relazioni diplomatiche fra Genova e i regni iberici nei secoli XII-XIII', *Medievalismo*, 19 (2009), 11–56

Beltrame, Carlo, *Archeologia marittima del Mediterraneo. Navi, merci e porti dall'antichità all'età moderna* (Rome: Carocci, 2012)

Benente, Fabrizio, 'La ceramica d'importazione dal Mediterraneo tra X e XIV secolo. Aggiornamenti e dati di sintesi per la Liguria', in *Pensare/classificare. Studi e ricerche sulla ceramica medievale per Graziella Berti*, ed. by Sauro Gelichi and Monica Baldassarri (Florence: All'Insegna del Giglio, 2010), pp. 53–70

Bonnassie, Pierre, 'Le littoral catalan durant le haut Moyen Âge', in *Zones côtières littorales dans le monde méditerranéen au Moyen Âge. Défense, peuplement, mise en valeur*, ed. by Jean-Marie Martin (Rome: École Française de Rome, 2001), pp. 251–71

Bordone, Renato, 'Le origini del comune di Genova', in *Comuni e memoria storica. Alle origini del Comune di Genova*, Atti del Convegno di Studi. Genova, 24–26 settembre 2001 (Genoa: Società Ligure di Storia Patria, 2002), pp. 237–59

Bresc, Henri, 'Le caricatore méditerranéen, fragment d'un espace maritime éclaté (XIe-XVe siècles)', in *Les ports et la navigation en Méditerranée au Moyen Âge*, Actes du colloque de Lattes, 12, 13, 14 novembre 2004, Musée Archéologique Henri Prades, ed. by Ghislaine Fabre, Daniel Le Blévec, and Denis Menjot (Paris: Le Manuscrit, 2009), pp. 149–60

——, 'Conclusions', in *Villes portuaires de Méditerranée occidentale au Moyen Age, îles et continents, XIIe-XVe siècles*, ed. by Jean-Andre Cancellieri and Vannina Marchi van Cauwelaert (Palermo: Associazione Mediterranea, 2015), pp. 283–96

Burgoa, Juan J., 'La Armada gallega de Diego Gelmírez', *Nalgures*, 8 (2012), 75–114

Byrne, Eugene H., *Genoese Shipping in the Twelfth and Thirteenth Centuries* (Cambridge, MA: The Medieval Academy of America, 1930)

Cabona, Danilo, 'Navi e porto. L'evoluzione del porto di Genova nel Medioevo tramite i contributi dell'archeologia e della storia', in *Genova porta d'Europa. La logistica delle merci tra il porto di Genova e l'Europa nei secoli XII–XXI*, ed. by Danilo Cabona and Giovanna Massaro (Florence: All'Insegna del Giglio, 2003), pp. 43–48

Cadinu, Marco, 'Strutture portuali, architetture e forme urbane medievali tra XI e XIV secolo. Lo spazio tirrenico toscano, la Sardegna, le isole', *Infraestructures portuàries d'època medieval i moderna a la Mediterrània occidental, Rodis*, 2 (2020), 57–88

Cagnana, Aurora, 'Pietre per il vescovo, per il signore per le comunità. Tecniche murarie e assetti sociali fra X e XV secolo nella Repubblica di Genova', in *Il Paesaggio pietrificato. La storia sociale dell'Europa attraverso l'archeologia del costruito*. Atti del convegno (Arezzo, 7–8 febbraio 2020), ed. by Fabio Giovannini and Alessandra Molinari (Florence: All'insegna del Giglio, 2021), pp. 37–51

Cantini, Federico, 'Ritmi e forme della grande espansione economica dei secoli XI–XIII nei contesti ceramici della Toscana settentrionale', *Archeologia Medievale*, 37 (2010), 113–27

De Capmany i de Montpalau, Antonio, *Memorias Históricas sobre la Marina, Comercio y Artes de la antigua ciudad de Barcelona*, riedizione ed. by Emili Giralt y Raventós, and Carmen Battle y Gallart (Barcelona: Cambra Oficial de Comerç i Navegació de Barcelona, 1961–1963)

Carreras Candi, Francesc, *Les dreçanes barcelonines sos inventaris y restauració* (Barcelona: Tàber, 1928)

Carsana, Vittoria, Stefania Febbraro, Daniela Giampaola, Carmella Guastaferro, Giolanda Irollo, and Maria Rosaria Ruello, 'Evoluzione del paesaggio costiero tra Parthenope e Neapolis', *Méditerranée*, 112 (2009), 14–22

Castagneto, Pierluigi, and Rossella Trevisan, 'Politica marittima e istituzioni portuali a Pisa nella seconda metà del XII secolo. Relazioni con l'Oriente, la Sardegna, il Midi e la Lunigiana', *Memorie della Accademia lunigianese di scienze Giovanni Capellini. Scienze storiche e morali*, 88 (2019), 65–121

Catafau, Aymat, 'La Catalogne et la mer aux Xe-XIIe siécles: l'autre frontiére', *Les Cahiers de Saint-Michel de Cuxa*, 48 (2017), 101–14

Cateura Bennàsser, Pau, 'Urbanizacion y finanzas de una ciudad portuaria: Palma de Mallorca en la edad media (siglos XIII–XV)', in *Villes portuaires de Méditerranée occidentale au Moyen Âge*, ed. by Jean-André Cancellieri and Vannina Marchi van Cauwelaert (Palermo: Associazione Mediterranea, 2015), pp. 159–83

Ceccarelli Lemut, Maria Luisa, 'I porti minori della Toscana', in *La repubblica di Noli e l'importanza dei porti minori del Mediterraneo nel Medioevo*, ed. by Mauro Darchi and Francesca Bandini, Quaderni dell'Istituto di storia della cultura materiale, 3 (Florence: All'Insegna del Giglio, 2004), pp. 49–67

——, 'Il sistema portuale pisano e le sue infrastrutture: riflessioni su una problematica aperta', in *Un filo rosso. Studi antichi e nuove ricerche sulle orme di Gabriella Rossetti in occasione dei suoi settanta anni*, ed. by Gabriella Garzella and Enrica Salvatori (Pisa: ETS, 2007), pp. 115–26

Chiaudano, Mario, 'I "Loca navis" nei documenti genovesi dei secoli XII e XIII', in *Studi di storia e diritto in onore di Enrico Besta per il XL anno del suo insegnamento* (Milan: Giuffrè, 1939), IV, pp. 411–16

Ciciliot, Furio, 'Les chantiers navals en Ligurie du Moyen Âge à l'époque moderne (XIIe – XVIe siècles)', *Cahiers de la Méditerranée*, 84 (2012), 259–71

Corrao, Pietro, 'Arsenali, costruzioni navali e attrezzature portuali in Sicilia (sec. XI–XV)', in *Arsenali e città nell'Occidente europeo*, ed. by Ennio Concina (Florence: NIS, 1987), pp. 33–50

Crouzet-Pavan, Elisabeth, 'L'Arsenal de Venise', in *The Sea in History: The Medieval World — La mer dans l'histoire*, ed. by Christian Buchet and Michel Balard (Woodbridge: Boydell, 2017), pp. 128–37

Del Treppo, Mario, 'La marina napoletana nel Medioevo: porti, navi, equipaggi', in *La fabbrica delle navi. Storia della cantieristica nel Mezzogiorno d'Italia*, ed. by Arturo Fratta (Naples: Electa 1990), pp. 31–46

De Vitis, Silvia, 'Taranto dall'età romana agli angioini', in *Taras e i doni del mare*, ed. by Eva Degl'Innocenti, Danilo Leone, Maria Turchiano, and Giuliano Volpe (Bari: Edipuglia 2022), pp. 21–24

Dotson, John E., 'Shipbuilding in the Medieval Adriatic', in *The Sea in History: 2. The Medieval World*, ed. by Christian Buchet and Michel Balard (Woodbridge: Boydell, 2017), pp. 115–27

Doumerc, Bernard, 'Flottes publiques, flottes privées à Venise (XIIe–XVe siècles)', in *The Sea in History: The Medieval World — La mer dans l'histoire*, ed. by Christian Buchet and Michel Balard (Woodbridge: Boydell, 2017), pp. 138–47

Estrada-Rius, Albert, *La Drassana reial de Barcelona, Barcelona. Organització institucional i construcció naval a la Corona d'Aragó* (Barcelona: Museu Marítim de Barcelona, 2004)

——, 'Les Drassanes Reials de Barcelona a la baixa edat mitjana: notes d'estudi', *Drassana: revista del Museu Marítim*, 11 (2003), 36–49

Falque Rey, Emma, *Historia Compostelana* (Madrid: Akal, 1994)

Feniello, Amedeo, 'Alle origini di Napoli capitale. Il porto, la terra, il denaro', *Mélanges de l'École française de Rome — Moyen Âge*, 124.2 (2012), 567–84

——, 'Mercati, mercanti, diritto mercantile in uno spazio di confine: il Mezzogiorno italiano (IX–XII secolo)', in *La crescita economica dell'Occidente medievale. Un tema storico non ancora esaurito*, ed. by Franco Franceschi (Rome: Viella, 2017), pp. 161–74

Ferrer i Mallol, Maria Teresa, 'Jurisdició i control de la navegació a la Ribera i mar de Barcelona', *Anales de la Universidad de Alicante. Historia medieval*, 12 (1999), 113–33

Figliuolo, Bruno, 'Le relazioni tra Pisa e Amalfi in Età Medioevale', in *Interscambi socio-culturali ed economici fra le città marinare d'Italia e l'Occidente dagli osservatori mediterranei*, Atti del Convegno Internazionale di Studi, Amalfi, 14–16 maggio 2011, ed. by Bruno Figliuolo and Pinuccia F. Simbula (Amalfi: Centro di Cultura e Storia amalfitana, 2014), pp. 445–67

Franceschi, Franco, 'Introduzione', in *La crescita economica dell'Occidente medievale. Un tema storico non ancora esaurito*, ed. by Franco Franceschi (Rome: Viella, 2017), pp. 1–24

Gargano, Giuseppe, 'Arsenali e scaria di Amalfi nel contesto del Meridione medievale', in *Ricoveri per navi militari nei porti del Mediterraneo antico e medievale*, ed. by David J. Blackman and Maria Costanza Lentini (Bari: Edipuglia, 2010) pp. 133–40

——, 'Un esempio di ricerca storica ed archeologica: l'analisi dell'area 'maritima' di Amalfi', *Rassegna del Centro di Cultura e Storia Amalfitana*, N.S., 7 (1997), 137–80

Garzella, Gabriella, 'Pisa: la forma urbana e gli impianti portuali sul fiume', in *Pisa e il Mediterraneo. Uomini, merci, idee dagli Etruschi ai Medici*, Catalogo della mostra (Pisa, 13 settembre – 9 dicembre 2003), ed. by Marco Tangheroni (Milan: Skira, 2003), pp. 151–56

——, 'Porti e approdi nelle acque interne della Toscana medievale', in *I sistemi portuali della Toscana mediterranea. Infrastrutture, scambi, economie dall'antichità ad oggi*, ed. by Giuseppe Petralia (Pisa: Pacini, 2011), pp. 133–46

Gautier Dalché, Patrick, 'Qu'est-ce qu'un port? Les données des portulans', in *Les ports et la navigation en Méditerranée au Moyen Age*, Actes du colloque de Lattès 12–14 novembre 2004, ed. by Ghislaine Fabre, Daniel Le Blévec, and Denis Menjot (Montpellier: Le Manuscrit, 2009), pp. 233–39

Gelichi, Sauro, 'L'archeologia nella laguna veneziana e la nascita di una nuova città', *Reti Medievali Rivista*, 11, 2 (2010), 137–67

——, 'Infrastrutture marittime nell'Alto Medioevo: una prospettiva archeologica', in *L'acqua nei secoli altomedievali* (Spoleto: Centro Italiano di studi sull'alto medioevo, 2008), pp. 283–314

Gelichi, Sauro, and Claudio Negrelli, *Adriatico altomedievale (VI–XI secolo). Scambi, porti, produzioni* (Venice: Edizioni Ca' Foscari, 2017)

Gelichi, Sauro, and Alessandra Molinari, 'Introduzione', in *I contenitori da trasporto altomedievali e medievali (VIII–XII secolo) nel Mediterraneo. Centri produttori, contenuti, reti di scambio*, ed. by Sauro Gelichi and Alessandra Molinari, *Archeologia medievale*, 45 (2018), 9–10

Giraudi, Carlo, Cristiana Tata, Giovanni Ricci, and Lidia Paroli, 'Portus (Fiumicino-Roma): il colmamento sedimentario dei bacini del porto di Claudio e Traiano nell'ambito dell'evoluzione ambientale tardo-antica e medievale del delta del Tevere', *Archeologia medievale*, 33 (2006), 1–12

Grossi Bianchi, Luciano, 'La costruzione del fronte monumentale marittimo genovese nel mediterraneo medievale', in *Città di mare del mediterraneo medievale: tipologie* (Amalfi: Centro di cultura e storia amalfitana, 2005), pp. 283–96

——, 'Gli approdi delle consorterie e il porto del Comune di Genova', in *Le città portuali del Mediterraneo*, ed. by Ennio Poleggi (Genoa: Sagep, 1989), pp. 299–307

Grossi Bianchi, Luciano, and Ennio Poleggi, *Una città portuale del medioevo. Genova nei secoli X–XVI* (Genoa: Sagep, 1987)

Guglielmotti, Paola, *Ricerche sull'organizzazione del territorio nella Liguria medievale* (Florence: Florence University Press, 2005)

Guidi Sánchez, José Javier, 'Barcelona y la red marítima de la Catalunya Nova en la Edad Media. Una aproximación a sus puertos, el comercio y la defensa del litoral mediterráneo entre los siglos XI-XIV', *Barcelona quaderns d'història*, 21 (2014), 169–84

——, *Els ports i la navegació de la Catalunya Nova (Tarragona-Delte de l'Ebre) a l'edat mitjana: la xarxa portuària, les rutes i els sistemes de navegació entre Al-Àndalus i la Corona Catalano-Aragonesa (segles X–XIV)* (Barcelona: Museu Marítim de Barcelona, 2016)

Heyck, Eduard, *Genua und seine Marine in Zeitalter der Kreuzzüge* (Innsbruck: Verlag der Wagner'schen Universäts-Buchhandlung, 1886)

Ibba, Antonio, 'Porti (e non approdi) in Sardinia', in *Documentando città portuali*, Atti del convegno internazionale, Capri 9–11 maggio 2019 ed. by

Laura Chioffi, Mika Kajava, and Simo Örmä (Rome: Institutum Romanum Finlandiae, 2021), pp. 205–09

Kreuger, Hilmar C., *Navi e proprietà navale a Genova (seconda metà del XII secolo)* (Genoa: Società Ligure di Storia Patria, 1985)

Leone, Danilo, 'Porto dela cita optimo. Le infrastrutture portuali a Taranto dall'antichità all'età moderna', in *Taras e i doni del mare*, ed. by Eva Degl'Innocenti, Danilo Leone, Maria Turchiano, and Giuliano Volpe (Bari: Edipuglia, 2022), pp. 41–46

Luciano, Alessandro, *Porti e approdi fluviali in Italia peninsulare: Dall'età romana all'anno mille* (Oxford: Holywell Press, 2019)

——, 'The Wooden Medieval Ports', in *Proceedings of the 18th Symposium on Mediterranean Archaeology*, Wroclaw – Poland, 24–26 April 2014, ed. by Blazej Stanislawski and Hakan Öniz (Oxford: Archaeopress, 2016), pp. 17–26

Mainoni, Patrizia, 'Sperimentazioni fiscali e amministrative', in *Sperimentazioni fiscali e amministrative nell'Italia del nord (secoli XII – inizio XIII)*, Atti della XVI Settimana internazionale di Studi medievali sul tema Pensiero e sperimentazioni istituzionali nella Societas Christiana (1046–1250), Centro di Cultura Passo della Mendola, Trento, 26–31 agosto 2004, ed. by Giancarlo Andenna (Milan: Vita e Pensiero, 2007), pp. 705–59

Mannoni, Tiziano, 'Quando il mare diventa una grande via di comunicazione', *Storia della cultura ligure*, ed. by Dino Puncuh, *Atti della Società Ligure di Storia Patria, nuova serie*, 44.2 (2004), 69–98

——, 'Rapporti tra i porti e la rete stradale in Liguria dall'età romana al medioevo', in *Rotte e porti del Mediterraneo dopo la caduta dell'Impero romano di Occidente*, ed. by Lorenza De Maria and Rita Turchetti (Soveria Mannelli: Rubettino, 2004), pp. 275–90

Marazzi, Federico, and Alessia Frisetti, 'Porti "monastici" in Campania fra VIII e X secolo', *Hortus artium medievalium*, 22 (2016), 227–37

Marriner, Nick, and Christophe Morgange, 'Geoscience of Ancient Mediterranean Harbours', *Earth-Science Reviews*, 80 (2007), 137–94

Martin, Jean-Marie, 'Les Normands d'Italie et la mer (XIe–XIIe siècle)', in *The Sea in History: The Medieval World — La mer dans l'histoire*, ed. by Christian Buchet and Michel Balard (Woodbridge: Boydell, 2017), pp. 245–54

Martin, Jean-Marie, and Ghislaine Noyé, 'Les façades maritimes de l'Italie du Sud: défense et mise en valeur (IVe–XIII siècle)', in *Zones côtières littorales dans le monde méditerranéen au Moyen Âge; défense, peuplement, mise en valeur*, ed. by Jean-Marie Martin (Rome: École Française de Rome, 2001), pp. 467–512

Martínez Nicolás, Maria del Mar, 'Un caso de destrucción del patrimonio histórico-artístico: las Atarazanas de Almería', *Cuadernos De Arte De La Universidad De Granada*, 22 (1991), 75–85

Mastruzzo, Antonino, 'Il conto navale nel panorama grafico della Pisa altomedievale', in *Pisa e il Mediterraneo. Uomini, merci, idee dagli Etruschi ai Medici*, Catalogo della mostra (Pisa, 13 settembre–9 dicembre 2003), ed. by Marco Tangheroni (Milan: Skira, 2003), pp. 191–95

Mayer y Olivé, Marc, 'Algunos aspectos de los puertos de la costa de la Hispania citerior (conventus Tarraconensis y Carthaginiensis)', in *Documentando città portuali*, Atti del convegno internazionale, Capri 9–11 maggio 2019 ed. by Laura Chioffi, Mika Kajava, and Simo Örmä (Rome: Institutum Romanum Finlandiae, 2021), pp. 229–48

McCormick, Michael, *Origins of the European Economy: Communications and Commerce AD 300–900* (Cambridge: Cambridge University Press, 2001)

Meo, Antonino, 'L'ordinario e l'eccezione. Per un aggiornamento cronologico dell'introduzione dei bacini islamici a Pisa', in *XIth Congress AIECM3 on Medieval and Modern Period Mediterranean Ceramics Proceedings*, (19–24 October, EKIM 2015, Antalya), ed. by Filiz Yenişehirlioğlu (Ankara: Vekam, 2018), pp. 59–73

Mignone, Alfonso, *La riforma portuale di Federico II* (Molfetta: La Nuova Mezzina, 2017)

Molinari, Alessandra, 'Le anfore medievali come proxy per la storia degli scambi mediterranei tra VIII e XIII secolo?', *Archeologia medievale*, 45 (2018), 293–306

——, 'Riflessioni sulle economie dei secoli X e XI: Palermo e Roma a confronto', in *Italy and Early Medieval Europe: Papers for Chris Wickham*, ed. by Ross Balzaretti, Julia Barrow, and Patricia Skinner (Oxford: Oxford University Press, 2018), pp. 155–70

Morhange, Christophe, Maria Giovanna Canzanella-Quintaluce, David Kaniewski, Nick Marriner, Marinella Pasquinucci, Elda, Russo Ermolli, and Matteo Vacchi, 'Perché studiare l'ambiente dei porti antichi?', in *Documentando città portuali*, ed. by Laura Chioffi, Mika Kajava, and Simo Örmä (Rome: Institutum Romanum Finlandiae, 2021), pp. 27–39

Musarra, Antonio, 'Genova e il mare nell'Alto Medioevo', *Bullettino dell'Istituto Storico Italiano per il Medio Evo*, 119 (2017), 109–48

——, 'La guerra sul mare', in *Guerre ed eserciti nel Medioevo*, ed. by Paolo Grillo and Aldo A. Settia (Bologna: il Mulino, 2018), pp. 279–307

Navarro Paredes, Claudio, 'Las atarazanas andalusíes. Funciones y características dentro de la red portuaria de al-Ándalus', *DAMA*, 4 (2019), 87–106

Noberasco, Filippo, and Italo Scovazzi, *Storia di Savona*, I (Savona: Tipografia Italiana, 1926)

Ouerfelli, Mohamed, 'Les premiers contacts diplomatiques entre l'Ifrīqiya et la commune de Pise au XIIe siècle', in *De la guerre à la paix en Méditerranée médiévale: acteurs, propagande, défense et diplomatie*, ed. by Elisabeth Malamut and Mohamed Ouerfelli (Aix-en-Provence: Presses universitaires de Provence, 2021), pp. 207–23

Petralia, Giuseppe, 'Le "navi" e i "cavalli": per una rilettura del Mediterraneo pieno medioevale', *Quaderni Storici*, 35, 103.1 (2000), 201–22

——, 'Per una visione d'insieme: stagioni e congiunture amalfitane e campane nella storia del Mediterraneo medievale', in *Interscambi socio-culturali ed economici fra le città marinare d'Italia e l'Occidente dagli osservatori mediterranei*, Atti del Convegno Internazionale di Studi, Amalfi, 14–16 maggio 2011, ed. by Bruno Figliuolo and Pinuccia F. Simbula (Amalfi: Centro di Cultura e Storia amalfitana, 2014), pp. 529–39

——, 'Pisa e la Sicilia', in *Pisa e il Mediterraneo: uomini, merci, idee dagli Etruschi ai Medici*, ed. by Marco Tangheroni (Milan: Mailand, 2003), pp. 217–22

——, 'Tra storia e archeologia: Mediterraneo altomedioevale e spazi regionali "italiani" (intorno al secolo VIII)', *Studi storici*, 56.1 (2015), 5–28

Picard, Christophe, 'Les arsenaux musulmans de la Méditerranée et de l'océan Atlantique (VIIIe-XVe siècle)', in *Chemins d'outre-mer, Études d'histoire sur la Méditerranée médiévale offertes à Michel Balard*, ed. by Damien Coulon, Catherine Otten-Froux, Paule Pagès, and Dominique Valérian (Paris: Éditions de la Sorbonne, 2004), pp. 691–710

——, *La mer et les musulmans d'Occident au Moyen Âge: VIIIe-XIIIe siècle* (Paris: Presses universitaires de France, 1997)

Piergiovanni, Vito, 'Dottrina e prassi nella formazione del diritto portuale: il modello genovese' in *Norme, scienza e pratica giuridica tra Genova e l'Occidente medievale e moderno, Atti della Società Ligure di Storia Patria*, n.s., 52.1–2 (2012), 171–92

Pirani, Francesco, 'Città, insediamenti costieri e strutture portuali nel medio Adriatico', in *Attività economiche e sviluppi insediativi nell'Italia dei secoli XI–XV*, ed. by Enrico Lusso (Cherasco: CISIM, 2014), pp. 163–64

Polonio, Valeria, 'Gli spazi economici della Chiesa genovese', in *Gli spazi economici della chiesa nell'occidente mediterraneo (secoli XII-metà XIV)*, Pistoia, 16–19 maggio 1997 (Pistoia: Centro Italiano di Studi di Storia e d'Arte, 1999), pp. 231–57

Preiser-Kapeller, Johannes, 'Heptaskalon and Other Selected Moorings on the Golden Horn', in *The Byzantine Harbours of Constantinople*, ed. by Falko Daim and Ewald Kislinger (Heidelberg: Propylaeum, 2022), pp. 140–50

Renzi Rizzo, Catia, 'Lo spazio economico di Pisa: la provvista multiforme e incontrollata del secolo X', *Bullettino dell'Istituto storico italiano per il medio evo*, 115 (2013), 97–118

Riera i Mora, Santiago, Ramón Julià Brugués, and Carme Miró i Alaix, 'Evolució del front marítim de la zona portuària de Barcelona de la tardoantiguitat a l'edat moderna', *Rodis*, 2 (2019), 89–112

Ritter, Max, 'Naval bases, Arsenals, Aplekya: Logistics and Commands of the Byzantine Navy (7th–12th C.)', in *Seasides of Byzantium Harbours and Anchorages of a Mediterranean Empire*, ed. by Johannes Preiser-Kapeller, Taxiarchis G. Kolias, and Falko Daim (Mainz: Romisch-Germanisches Zentralmuseum, 2021), pp. 201–02

Ruiz Domènec, José Enrique, *Ricard Guillem. Un sogno per Barcellona* (Naples: Edizioni Athena, 1999)

Salvatori, Enrica, 'Pisa e le città del Midi tra XI e XII secolo', in *Pisa e il Mediterraneo. Uomini, merci, idee dagli Etruschi ai Medici*, Catalogo della mostra (Pisa, 13 settembre–9 dicembre 2003) ed. by Marco Tangheroni (Milan: Skira, 2003), pp. 257–61

——, 'Lo spazio economico di Pisa nel Mediterraneo: dall'XI alla metà del XII secolo', *Bullettino dell'Istituto storico italiano per il medioevo*, 115 (2013), 119–52

Schmiedt, Giulio, 'I *porti* italiani nell'*alto medioevo*', in *La navigazione mediterranea nell'alto medioevo, XXV Settimana di studio del CISAM, Spoleto 1977* (Spoleto: CISAM, 1978), pp. 129–258
Simbula, Pinuccia F., 'I porti nello sviluppo economico della Sardegna medievale', in *Attività economiche e sviluppi insediativi nell'Italia dei secoli XI–XV*, ed. by Enrico Lusso (Cherasco: CISIM, 2014), pp. 269–305
Slim, Hédi, Pol Trousset, Roland Paskoff, and Ameur Oueslati, *Le littoral de la Tunisie. Etude géoarchéologique et historique* (Paris: CNRS Éditions, 2004)
Soberón, Mikel, 'Caixes i pontons. Els aspectes tècnics en la construcció del primer port medieval de Barcelona, 1439–1455', *Barcelona quaderns d'història*, 21 (2014), 125–38
Tangheroni, Marco, 'I diversi sistemi economici: rapporti e interazioni. Considerazioni generali e analisi del caso sardo', in *Le Italie del tardo Medioevo*, ed. by Sergio Gensini (Pisa: Pacini, 1990), pp. 291–320
Torres Balbás, Leopoldo, '*Atarazanas hispano musulmanas*', *Al-Andalus*, 11 (1946), 175–209
Tranchant Mathias, 'Les ports maritimes en France au Moyen Âge', in *Ports maritimes et ports fluviaux au Moyen Age*, XXXVe Congrès de la SHMES, La Rochelle, 2004 (Paris: Éditions de la Sorbonne, 2005), pp. 21–31
Tucci, Ugo, 'L'impresa marittima: uomini e mezzi', in *Storia di Venezia. Dalle origini alla caduta della Serenissima*, II, *L'età del comune*, ed. by Giorgio Cracco and Gherardo Ortalli (Rome: Istituto dell'Enciclopedia Italiana, 1995), pp. 627–70
——, 'Navi e navigazioni all'epoca delle crociate', in *Genova, Venezia, il Levante nei secoli XII–XIV*, ed. by Gherardo Ortalli and Dino Puncuh, Atti del Convegno Internazionale di Studi, Genova – Venezia, 10–14 marzo 2000, Atti della Società Ligure di Storia Patria. Nuova serie, 41.1 (Genoa: Società Ligure di Storia Patria, 2001), pp. 273–94
Vaccari, Olimpia, 'Infrastrutture e regolamenti del porto di Livorno dal Medioevo alla prima età moderna', in *I porti della penisola italiana*, ed. by Gabriella Garzella and Olimpia Vaccari (Pisa: Pacini 2011), pp. 183–208
Valérian, Dominique, *Bougie, port maghrébin, 1067–1510* (Rome: École française de Rome, 2006), pp. 247–330
——, *Ports et réseaux d'échanges dans le Maghreb medieval* (Madrid: Casa de Velázquez, 2019)
——, 'Le pouvoir et les espaces portuaires dans le Maghreb médiéval', in *Espaces d'échanges en Méditerranée. Antiquité et Moyen Âge*, ed. by François Clément, John Tolan and Jérôme Wilgaux (Rennes: Presses universitaires de Rennes, 2006), pp. 77–88
Vallerani, Massimo, 'La riscrittura dei diritti nel secolo XII: astrazione e finzione nelle sentenze consolari', in *Zwischen Pragmatik und Performanz. Dimensionen mittelalterlicher Schriftkultur*, ed. by Christoph Dartmann, Thomas Scharff, and Christoph Friederich Weber (Turnhout: Brepols, 2011), pp. 133–64

Villain-Gandossi, Christiane, 'La révolution nautique médiévale (XIIIe-XVe siècles)', in *The Sea in History: The Medieval World — La mer dans l'histoire*, ed. by Christian Buchet and Michel Balard (Woodbridge: Boydell, 2017), pp. 70–89

Wickham, Chris, *Framing the Early Middle Ages: Europe and the Mediterranean, 400–800* (Oxford: Oxford University Press, 2005)

——, 'Prima della crescita: quale società?', in *La crescita economica dell'Occidente medievale. Un tema storico non ancora esaurito*, ed. by Franco Franceschi (Rome: Viella, 2017), pp. 93–106

——, *Sonnambuli verso un nuovo mondo. L'affermazione dei comuni italiani nel XII secolo* (Rome: Viella 2017)

SANDRO CAROCCI

Conclusions

In the context of the ERC project *Petrifying Wealth. The Southern European Shift to Masonry as Collective Investment in Identity, c. 1050–1300*, this book stands at the margins.[1] The collective research project was primarily social, political, and cultural in nature. By contrast this volume focuses on the economic aspect of building with masonry via an analysis of buildings and other structures whose purpose was to facilitate production and trading activities; more generally it explores the link between construction and the economy. Since it examines types of buildings that have received less attention elsewhere in the project, it is probing rather than systematic in nature.

The book nevertheless arrives at some interesting results, which are worth summarizing at the very outset. The articles contained in this volume examine the centuries of preparation for and the flowering of the medieval economic growth from a novel perspective, taking as their focus buildings that were used for production and trade. Every article published here lends support to the increasingly widespread interpretation that brings the date of this economic growth in southern Europe forward to the second half or even the final decades of the twelfth century. This is true of both the level of production and technology, particularly as regards the enlargement of markets and the supply of goods. At the same time, it is precisely the history of building that reminds us how this great change was made possible by the participation of a wide range of protagonists who played an active part in the growth of production and the expansion of demand to new social groups. The difference with the previous situation becomes all the more clear if one thinks of the significant role played by emperors, kings, and their officials in the economic exploitation of public goods up until the middle of eleventh century, and more generally if one considers the elitist and episodic nature

1 The publication of this research was financed by the European Research Council (ERC) under the European Union's Horizon 2020 research and innovation programme (grant agreement 695515), project *Petrifying Wealth: The Southern European Shift to Masonry as Collective Investment in Identity, c. 1050–1300*.

Sandro Carocci (carocci@lettere.uniroma2.it) is Professor of Medieval History at the University of Roma Tor Vergata.

Building and Economic Growth in Southern Europe (1050–1300), ed. by Sandro Carocci and Alessio Fiore, (Turnhout: Brepols, 2024), pp. 243–258 BREPOLS PUBLISHERS 10.1484/M.TMC-EB.5.137982

of the earliest major building initiatives, which were restricted to a modest number of ecclesiastical projects, or to sites under the control of public officials.

If this is the overall interpretation to be drawn from the volume as a whole, it is necessary to dwell on a number of aspects of the research, and to consider how it was conducted. I shall therefore organize my reflections around two points: firstly, I shall briefly attempt to clarify and, in some respects, to shed new light on the role played by economics in a research project that does after all include the term 'wealth' in its title, at the same time questioning the actual connection between petrification and productive changes; secondly, I shall reflect, much more broadly, on the key players involved in the investment in functional buildings and in structures linked to specific production or exchange processes, and on the chronology of these investments.

Petrification and Wealth

Titles can sometimes be misleading. *Petrifying Wealth* is not an economic history project, and the subtitle, which qualifies the phenomenon as *Collective Investment in Identity*, makes it clear that economics, or *Wealth*, is not the central theme. The process under investigation was far more complex than a simple economic phenomenon. The economy most certainly had its part to play, and I shall shortly return to this point, but the project's principal focus was on the material and technical aspects of building in stone; its ideological and religious significance; the role played by individual, family, and group social identities; the symbols and ostentation involved; and the significance of political-military affirmation. Petrification was more a social and cultural transformation process than an economic phenomenon. However, this process was also intricately linked with the economy, because it manifested itself at the material level and required a huge amount of resources. Gradually at first, and then at an ever-accelerating pace, a building frenzy took place; some of the resulting constructions were of finer quality than others, but all these buildings were more complex and costly than their predecessors.[2] This was building for the future, and the structures were designed to last. In cities in Italy and elsewhere, soil levels ceased to rise, and the past was no longer buried.[3] A process through which lifestyles changed was set in motion, paving the way for living practices and landscapes which would survive for many centuries, indeed right up until recent times.

It would be wrong to assert that economic dynamics were the catalyst and principal driver behind the petrification process. In most cases, the emergence of durable construction does not appear to be related to the

2 Analyses of the technical and construction changes of the phenomenon are collected in Giovannini and Molinari, eds, *Il paesaggio pietrificato*.

3 Molinari, 'La "pietrificazione" del costruito', p. 277, which elaborates on a suggestion by Carandini, 'L'ultima civiltà sepolta'.

rise in incomes as a result of economic growth. A good illustration of this phenomenon is the Italian private tower, the building that more than any other today symbolizes eleventh–thirteenth century urban construction, and whose existence is largely confined to the Italian peninsula, being virtually unknown in the Iberian peninsula and highly unusual in the French Midi.[4] At first glance, it would be tempting to attribute the proliferation of this type of tower to an economic take-off that occurred in Italian cities earlier than in other regions. The appearance of these towers at an earlier date in Genoa, Pisa, Gaeta, and other port cities would also seem to confirm this reading. Such an assumption would however be erroneous. By the end of the eleventh century, private towers had sprung up in a whole host of locations, including cities where an economic take-off was still only a distant prospect, and even in small towns with far fewer economic resources and different economic trends. In fact, the reasons behind the spread of this type of building were related to politics and identity, rather than the economy. The towers were first and foremost the product of the new political context that arose in the last decades of the eleventh century due to the collapse of public, supra-city power structures; this led to the emergence of forms of urban self-government that relied on fierce and often violent competition between noble families. In this new reality, the tower established itself as an indispensable means for all relatively important city families to assert themselves symbolically, politically, and militarily. The economic resources at the disposal of such families might remain unchanged, but they were now directed towards building activity and tower construction to a much greater extent than in the past. In those cases such as the large port cities where we can infer an actual increase in available funds, we must bear in mind that, while economic growth certainly stimulated the creation of new buildings, it was not the principal factor behind this construction activity.

Things changed in part during the twelfth century, when the effects of an expanding economic dynamic became more evident. The epoch-making watershed represented by the proliferation of buildings of all kinds would not have gained momentum or been consolidated over time without a growing economy to provide new resources. The importance of this is evident in the petrification process, especially if we consider the mass phenomenon it eventually became, and the success it achieved in the secular world. The reason why towers and other buildings linked to the aristocracy multiplied at such an extraordinary rate during the twelfth and thirteenth centuries was because the city as a whole, along with the nobility, had access to new resources. But once again, these building choices were primarily determined by elements of a broadly cultural and social character, rather than any of an economic nature. Even when the economy was booming, the link with the petrification process was neither obvious nor direct. Outside Italy, far fewer

4 In what follows, I refer to Carocci, 'Nobility, Conflicts, and Buildings'.

towers and fortified palaces were built, even in cities that had begun to experience robust economic growth. The case of Islamic Sicily, which could boast both wealth and a highly complex economy but where large-scale lime mortar-bound constructions were absent, is a good example of how lasting construction was determined by the forms of ostentation and the ways of expressing identity chosen by those involved, and not by the mechanical reflection of any economic vitality.[5]

There was however a specific economic facet to the petrification of wealth. This took the form of structures whose purpose was to improve production and trade, and it is precisely this aspect which is dealt with by this volume. More generally, petrification is a powerful indicator of the processes of growth and increased spending capacity of institutions, households, and collectives; it also greatly influenced the economy both directly and indirectly. The construction of urban property endowed families with something that up until that point had been less significant in terms of value and as a source of income. This unprecedented utilization of architecture had a disproportionate effect on the entire economy of the construction sector, ultimately leading to its expansion and transformation into something new. Skilled craftsmen who, due to the scarcity of complex building initiatives had hitherto been obliged to move from city to city, or between large rural building projects, now no longer needed to travel around; more importantly, they grew in number and became ever more specialized. Limestone was extracted from newly-opened quarries, and brickmaking resumed. The need for a constant supply of building materials resulted in the emergence of new trades and transport infrastructure. This increase in building activity and in the number of specialized workers brought down unit costs, generalizing and making accessible to many the complex production cycles that were indispensable to durable construction, and that were previously reserved for ecclesiastical and public buildings. Subsequently the processes of the commercialization and monetization of the economy further stimulated the construction sector. In many respects, construction is an area in which cultural change — that is, the new meanings that the various social actors attributed to construction and which, more than anything else, led to the massive increase in building demand — galvanized and in some respects determined economic change.[6]

---

5 Molinari, 'La "pietrificazione" del costruito', p. 280.

6 A guide to these changes, and to the earlier bibliography that dealt with them, can be found in the publications that appeared within the *Petrifying Wealth* project itself, and especially: Giovannini and Molinari, eds, *Il paesaggio pietrificato*; *La petrificación de la riqueza*; Maira Vidal and Rodríguez, eds, *El coste de la construcción*; *Construir para perdurar*.

Workers and Lords

The aspect of petrification on which this book provides the greatest wealth of information is the wide range of participants who in one way or another were instrumental in the promotion of building projects aimed at creating useful structures for economic activity. In the following pages, I shall attempt to offer a brief overview of these, while also paying heed to the chronologies of their initiatives.

The first point to be emphasized concerns the complex nature of identifying the investments in building for production made by those principally responsible for production itself, i.e. the workers. The absence of evidence for investments in building for production on the part of this particular group in either written and material sources comes in many respects as no surprise, precisely because the labour force made very little contribution to building for the economy, financially or otherwise. Their participation would appear to have been out of the question for both urban and rural wage earners, whose spending power was either very modest or non-existent; the same was apparently true for artisans. From the end of the twelfth century onwards, a change appears to have taken place, indicated by the increased number of references to mixed buildings containing both residential and working spaces (Fiore). However, it is difficult to establish exactly who was behind this change, and to determine the nature of its productive results. The data illustrated in this book concerns *case-bottega* (house-workshops) with ecclesiastical and aristocratic landowners. Even if other *case-bottega* resulted from direct investments by the artisans themselves, the question remains as to the actual productive effects of these properties. It seems inappropriate to characterize them as investments for production: any craftsman who, after a great deal of effort, succeeded in building himself a house-workshop must have been motivated not by the desire to increase labour productivity, but rather by the benefits associated with an investment in housing, such as saving rent, improving their quality of life, acquiring a store of value and a possible source of income through partial rental.

A similar ambivalence exists regarding the building investments undertaken by peasants who were either owners or very long-term tenants of the land they cultivated. Especially after the middle of the twelfth century and even more so in the thirteenth century, peasants' homes began to be constructed with durable materials, although this chronology has yet to be properly ascertained in many regions.[7] As was the case with the *casali* of the Roman Campagna, the *cassine* and *poderi* of Lombardy and Tuscany, and the Catalan *mas*, these were often buildings that the peasants made use of but had not built with their own hands (Farías Zurita, Tabarrini). Moreover, even where the dwellings

7 Research on the archaeology of architecture struggles to arrive at concordant dates: see e.g. Zoni, *Edilizia residenziale*, and Cagnana, 'Recensione'.

had been built by the peasants themselves, it is difficult to determine, as with the artisans' house-workshops, to what extent we can consider these buildings as investments intended for production. Certainly they contained stables, warehouses, storerooms, and other spaces related to agricultural work; after all, a productive investment was also the very possibility of less cramped, safer and perhaps healthier housing. There is however no doubt that, while the contribution of peasant landowners or tenants to economic growth was fundamental, it followed other trajectories, being expressed in minute investments and only exceptionally in building. Peasant investments were made first and foremost through the clearing of new tracts of land, the purchase of better tools and livestock, the planting of crops for the market, and numerous minor agrarian improvements (planting of trees and vines, terracing, or small water drainage systems).

Mills are one of the few instances of peasant investment in production buildings, although the example of Catalonia shows that new constructions were promoted by the lords, and that only on rare occasions did the subjects of the lords chose to build the new facilities come from the peasant world (Morelló Baget). In fact, in the era examined in this volume, the most significant examples in the rural world of direct and massive investments in building for production are those undertaken by communities. This can be seen to some extent in the participation of rural communities in the canalization works embarked on by sovereigns and lords in the kingdom of Aragon, and by urban communes and lords in the Po Valley. Their role was, however, of a subordinate nature, as major canalization initiatives required technical knowledge and investment which would have been beyond the reach of rural communities (Pagnoni, Torró). Conversely, in the case of iron metallurgy in the Alpine area, it was precisely rural communities who took the lead in what constituted a revolution in both technology and productivity. These communities promoted the resumption of mining activities on a larger scale between the eleventh and twelfth century; again, from the late twelfth century onwards, the increase in production generated by the introduction of bloomeries equipped with water-powered hammers can be attributed to the communities' initiative. The same is true of the fundamental technological and production innovations in the thirteenth century linked to 'the spread of a new kind of iron bloomeries equipped with hydraulic bellows, which led to the achievement of higher productive levels' (Cortese).

If we shift our attention from the peasants to the rural aristocracies, we naturally find many more instances of investment in structures destined for economic activity than in those situations where labourers were the chief participants. Rural lords figure among the promoters of many productive initiatives: the canalization work undertaken in northern Italy and the kingdom of Aragon (Pagnoni, Torró); the process of restructuring and diffusion of the *mas*, the farms of Old Catalonia (Farías Zurita); the construction of the bridges of Tuscany at an early stage, prior to the middle of the twelfth century, when bridges were one of the manifestations of the new seigniorial powers

(Tomei); the proliferation of mills (Morelló Baget); the processing of coinable metals (Cortese); and episodically on many other occasions.

These examples should not however obscure the fundamental fact that the lords, in the fullest sense of the term, i.e. with territorial and jurisdictional powers, were not as engaged in the creation of structures for production and trade as one might expect of figures of such economic and political standing. Where metallurgical activities were concerned, the lords in Italy participated only in the processing of coinable metals, remaining completely uninvolved in the much larger and more important aspects of iron-working (Cortese); in Catalonia, they stimulated the multiplication of flour mills and fulling mills without contributing to the expenses, and their interest was of a fiscal rather than an entrepreneurial nature (Morelló Baget); and in central-northern Italy they were completely absent from the construction of *casali, poderi, cassine,* and other agrarian enterprises oriented towards speculative, market-related agriculture (Tabarrini). In the period under consideration, it is rare to find entrepreneurial lords like those who between the fourteenth and sixteenth centuries invested directly in proto-industry; examples of these were the lords of Valencia who, in the early fourteenth century, brought skilled craftsmen from Andalusia and built glass mills to produce highly prized glazed ceramics;[8] or the later feudal lords-entrepreneurs of the kingdom of Naples, who invested their income in the construction of fulling and paper mills, tanneries, and cloth factories.[9] The seigniorial lack of interest in the promotion of artisan activities was in reality part of a more general attitude of substantial alienation from involvement in production, even in a sector as fundamental as agriculture: with very few exceptions, the territorial lords in southern Europe appropriated the products of the land, but had very little to do with the production processes.[10]

Despite these limitations, we must be careful not to underestimate the economic importance of the new type of lordship that became widespread after the mid-eleventh century, and the very extent of the investments in construction carried out by these noblemen. Their investment in buildings was significant, but this was directed specifically towards castles, which strictly speaking are not buildings that were used for production. The lords greatly increased the number of castles and, most importantly, transformed their material appearance.[11] Masonry replaced palisades and earthworks, and there was considerable growth in the size and complexity of the structures. Mighty walls were created to enclose the summit area, and there was extensive construction of palaces, towers, cisterns, and churches. Building a castle

8 Furió and Almenar Fernández, 'Land, Ceramics and Seigniorial Rents'.

9 Cirillo, *Il vello d'oro*.

10 On this aspect of the lordships of southern Europe, I refer to Carocci, *Lordships of Southern Italy*, pp. 476–89.

11 The bibliography on medieval castles is immense. A good recent overview, however, is Augenti and Galetti, eds, *L'incastellamento: storia e archeologia*.

was clearly not a productive initiative; its purpose was instead political and military, with connotations of ostentation, legitimation, and emulation. The historiography however emphasizes the great economic importance of castles and castle-villages in a number of ways. Some interpretations view castles as a means of directing and consolidating demographic and agrarian growth, and of appropriating its benefits.[12] Others regard castles and particularly castle-villages as an important aspect of the expansion of small-scale and inter-regional exchange networks, all the more so in the mid- and late twelfth century, when the increase in the size and population of some castle-villages transformed them into proto-urban centres. These acted as social, commercial, and productive referents for the surrounding areas, and as hubs of an increasingly articulated network of economic relations, which made them an essential element of that 'integrated complexity' observed by Tomei when speaking of the spread of bridges.[13] More generally, a recently updated interpretation portrays territorial lordship as a major agent of European economic life. The rise of seigniorial powers would have led to an increase in pressure on peasants, and this was to be the main cause of the upsurge in agricultural production that formed the basis of the great period of medieval growth.[14] Although not constructed for production purposes, there can be no doubt that, as a fundamental aspect of these new lordships, building a castle had major economic repercussions.

Lay and Ecclesiastical Landowners

In the case of productive building promoted by city landowners, the survey looks exclusively at north-central Italy, an area where urban landowners appear to have been the most active investors in buildings designed for production and trade. For these investors, the already mentioned probing as opposed to the systematic character of the survey of building for the economy within the overall organization of the *Petrifying Wealth* project is particularly evident.

The list of different productive structures is extensive. It includes several that I have already mentioned, such as the farm buildings established from the late twelfth century onwards in the countryside around Milan, Rome, and several other cities; urban artisan workshops of various kinds, for which no specific report has yet been produced, but for which excellent evidence has been produced through recent archaeological research;[15] and last but not least,

12 This line of interpretation ranges from Toubert, *Les structures du Latium*, to the recent Feller, 'Abruzzes'.

13 e.g. the recent work by Collavini, 'La crescita pieno medievale'.

14 Duby, *Guerriers et paysans*; and more recently Wickham, *The Donkey and the Boat*.

15 From this point of view, the city which has undergone the most thorough investigation is Pisa, where a vast area ('Ex Laboratori Gentili') was also excavated; here, from the end of the twelfth century, workshops were set up for the production of glass, iron, and copper alloy artefacts; by the mid-thirteenth century these had reached a degree of specialization and

shipbuilding. Shipbuilding activity, in truth, testifies to the instability of the connections that in certain cases existed between building and production activities. Prior to the emergence of public dockyards in the thirteenth century, the albeit fundamental shipbuilding industry, promoted independently by private individuals and institutions, relied on human rather than material infrastructure. Shipbuilding was dependent on the availability of a highly skilled workforce, while permanent construction facilities were few and far between; most construction sites were equipped only with small temporary wooden structures, destined to disappear without trace once the work was completed (Simbula).

In all these cases, the origin of the capital invested in construction and the minds that appear to guide that investment all suggest economic dynamism. From the end of the twelfth century, the capital used to build the farm holdings in the countryside around Rome and Milan often had its origins in finance and commerce. Even the decision to build a new type of farm with closer ties to the markets bears witness to the fact that entrepreneurial and speculative minds were becoming involved in agriculture in a way that had not been the case in previous centuries (Tabarrini).

It is pointless to seek to identify the nature of the capital invested by city landowners in what was undoubtedly the largest construction investment by citizens: urban housing. Indeed, this investment was on such a large scale and so socially widespread that it is impossible to identify which type of capital was prevalent. Income from work, land, and seigniorial rents, profits from trade and finance, and benefits drawn from war and political activity all contributed to construction. Residential buildings have not been a primary focus of this study because clearly their purpose was not to directly promote production and trade activities. They were however undoubtedly the most valuable artefacts to be built in cities, both individually and as part of a whole, and should be taken into account because 'the continuous process of building and rebuilding residential properties played an important role in the urban economy as a whole: like a beat in the background, it set the rhythm for the growth process' (Fiore). The rise of property prices above inflation and the cost of agricultural land meant that houses represented a profitable investment which increased the value of capital. Moreover, as was the case with peri-urban farms, after the middle and especially at the end of the twelfth century we witness the advance of more dynamic economic attitudes, made manifest by profit-seeking modes of management. On the other hand, it should be emphasized that the economic value of this investment in residential buildings was accompanied by a much more pronounced social and political significance than was the case for other building investments made by individual families. Houses could certainly protect and increase capital and provide good incomes,

massification 'almost to an industrial level' of production itself (Carrera, 'Le lavorazioni dei metalli', p. 62, and more generally Cantini and Rizzitelli, eds, *Una città operosa*).

but for the city nobility — the social group that invested most in urban real estate — these structures were primarily a means of asserting kinship within the urban fabric and political life.[16]

All the essays collected in this volume demonstrate that the investment in productive structures undertaken by ecclesiastical landowners of all kinds, be they bishops, churches, monasteries, or religious orders, appears to have been less significant than that of lay landowners. There are, however, both exceptions and chronological differences. The exceptions concern specific religious orders. From the first decades of the twelfth century, the Cistercians engaged in the creation and management of granges and vast areas for cultivation (Tabarrini); in the mid-thirteenth century, the Aragonese Templars promoted and coordinated canalization projects (Torró). But they are, as I said, exceptions in an overall context of limited ecclesiastical activity.

Chronology is however key. In the first part of the period examined in this volume, the role of ecclesiastical investments was apparently less marginal. Areas where there is evidence of ecclesiastical intervention, albeit on a modest scale, include a number of canalization works at the end of the eleventh century (Pagnoni), the construction of bridges in Tuscany in the twelfth century (Tomei), the building of a number of *cassine* and *casali* in the countryside around Milan and Rome beginning in the final decades of the twelfth century (Tabarrini), and the coeval realization of several conspicuous patrimonies of houses for rent (Fiore). Then there is the vast sphere of the participation of bishops, and to a lesser extent monasteries and churches, in the new investment in castle and castle-villages that began in the late eleventh century and continued into the twelfth century with initiatives that were sometimes of great importance. Even in the case of castles and castle-villages, however, there are instances of a complete absence of ecclesiastical interest in building investment. Churches and monasteries even went so far as to place the burden of petrifaction directly on the shoulders of their subordinates: one such case is to be found at the beginning of the twelfth century at Poiano and Marzana, where the canons of Verona delegated the transition to masonry to the rural communities in exchange for reductions in the seignorial burden.[17] From the late twelfth century onwards, however, the clergy appears to have played a much-reduced role in investing in productive structures. In the second half of the twelfth century, churches and monasteries engaged only indirectly in canalization projects, conferring benefits on the local communities on which the initiative fell; in Tuscany, no new bridges were built under episcopal auspices after 1202; the creation of *cassine*, *casali*, and also *poderi* by ecclesiastical institutions continued to be attested in the thirteenth century, but these constituted only a fraction of the overall number of initiatives.

16 On the subject, most recently Carocci, 'Nobility, Conflicts, and Buildings'.

17 Settia, *Castelli medievali*, pp. 102–12.

A study of buildings functional to production and trade thus clearly establishes a fundamental characteristic of the late twelfth- and thirteenth-century economic take-off: albeit with regional differences, this economic boom was a largely secular phenomenon. There were many lay figures of all descriptions involved, but far fewer were from ecclesiastical institutions. In economic life as a whole, bishops, monasteries, and churches were destined to play a far less significant role than they had done in the preceding centuries: those of the early Middle Ages, sometimes described as an era of 'Temple Society';[18] the Carolingian and post-Carolingian period; and again the whole of the eleventh century and part of the following.

Institutions of Government

Last but not least, one of the key players in building for production to appear in the chapters contained in this volume are the institutions of government. These were the aforementioned territorial lords, the cities, and of course the large-scale political entities: the empire, kingdoms, and principalities.

By and large, the role of the latter appears to have been relatively limited until the late twelfth century; its influence however grew significantly in the thirteenth century and expanded further in the following centuries. In this volume, this dynamic is illustrated by the canalization of Aragon (Torró), and by the example of ports and dockyards: as far as these were concerned it was only in the late thirteenth century that western Christendom succeeded in matching the achievements of the Islamic world (Simbula). At the conference which marked the starting point for this book, attention was also paid to investment in roads and bridges.[19] The whole picture seems to suggest a prevalence of expenditure on structures associated with trade but in reality we know that rulers sometimes also invested in the organization of production. The most striking cases are perhaps the *masserie*, *aratie*, and *marestalle* created by Frederick II in southern Italy: these were arable and livestock farms whose purpose was to produce food and other goods for the court, public institutions, and the market; and at which the sovereign also promoted formidable building initiatives, in the shape of warehouses, production facilities, houses, and prestigious residences.[20]

However, it is best to avoid narratives based on a linear chronological evolution, marked by the transition from weak to strong sovereigns. The *masserie* of Frederick II themselves underwent a sharp decline in grandeur as early as the second half of the thirteenth century. In this volume, the impossi-

18 Wood, *The Christian Economy in the Early Medieval West*.

19 In a contribution by Almudena Blasco Vallés (see Blasco Vallés, 'Wealth in Stone').

20 On the southern *masserie* in the thirteenth century and related studies, see Violante, 'La conduzione delle terre demaniali'; for the analysis of a specific case, Favia, *Ordona XII*, pp. 161–85, provides guidance on recent archaeological research on the subject.

bility of an evolutionary reading is well illustrated by the curious case of the disappearance of granaries from the central-northern Italian countryside in the twelfth century, as expounded by G. Bianchi on the basis of the results of a collective research project in which she played a prominent role.[21] The story of the granaries reveals profound changes when compared to the previous situation, and a marked decline in public investment in production structures. Between 960 and the first decades of the eleventh century, the proliferation of granaries was linked to the tremendous investment made by the emperors of the Ottonian dynasty and public officials within the estates of the imperial treasury. Large-scale investments were made in the fiscal estates of the Italic kingdom linked to the exploitation of specific resources, such as iron and salt; the first castles were built and the natural and anthropic landscape was transformed. As a consequence, a marked process of economic growth was set in motion on the extensive properties of the imperial treasury, although the low level of trade and relations with the outside world seems to have limited its general effects. After the middle of the eleventh century, a combination of the collapse of public structures, the privatization of fiscal estates, and the genesis of territorial lordship put an end to the economic prominence of these estates and the productive investments of which they were the object.[22] In this new context, granaries, which had been one of the material and symbolic markers of the public programme of the economic revival of public goods, were replaced by other storage systems.

Lastly we turn to the communes, the form of urban self-government that developed in Italy in the twelfth century. It is evident that, in many cities, investment in functional buildings and structures linked to specific production or exchange processes reached substantial levels. However, this phenomenon is only briefly touched on by the contributions in this volume. Of the cases examined, the earliest and most striking examples are the harbour front works undertaken in Genoa and Pisa in the fourth and fifth decades of the twelfth century respectively. This is the earliest evidence available to us of initiatives that in the thirteenth century would spread to every port, in response to the new infrastructural requirements that resulted from the increase in traffic and the size of ships, and which were often accompanied by the building of a dockyard (Simbula). Pagnoni illustrates the ambitious projects carried out by communes in northern Italy with the aim of developing a network of canals that was functional for transport and the supply of hydraulic energy to mills and factories, and therefore crucial for the development of urban economies. By contrast, there has been no opportunity to provide examples of urbanization initiatives promoted by the communes, especially from the middle of the thirteenth century, for political, health, and aesthetic reasons, but also in order to better adapt the urban space to production and trade: the

21 Bianchi, *Archeologia dei beni pubblici*.

22 Collavini, 'Mutazione signorile e beni fiscali'.

paving of streets and the establishment of a sewer network; the creation of squares and market areas; or the construction of aqueducts and fountains.[23] In the countryside, city governments were active not only in the construction of canals, but also in the improvement of communication routes. The main contribution of the communes to building investment in the countryside aimed at increasing production and trade seems, however, to have been institutional: by providing fiscal, judicial, and military protection for citizens' possessions, the commune represented a favourable legal and administrative framework for investments carried out independently by urban landowners.[24]

When a grand narrative looms large in studies, caution must be exercised, as we are at risk of being conditioned by entrenched cultural paradigms. In this case, the grand narrative is that of the Italian city and its driving role in the economic growth and commercial and financial supremacy of the Peninsula. Two notes of caution must therefore be sounded. On the one hand, the partial nature of the survey carried out runs the risk of over-stating the importance of Italian cities because comparative data with other European cities is not provided, with the exception of ports and shipbuilding (Simbula). On the other hand, it should be noted that even the essays collected here have downplayed the role of the city in a number of areas. One example of this is the clear absence of urban influence in the quantitative and technological growth of the iron mining industry in the north (Cortese). This observation is however also valid with regard to the formation of the dense network of overland routes which were so vital for economic growth, and which are attributed to 'a convergence of initiatives from above and below'; a wide range of participants lay behind this undertaking, and it can therefore no longer be read as 'a reflection of communal order and prosperity' (Tomei). The same institutional protection that the city government offered to investments in the territory must be considered within a negative political context of great fragmentation and inter-city conflict, which increased transaction costs and limited the geographical scope of investments.[25] This ultimately confirms the doubts and cautions raised by more recent research on the dynamism and economic centrality of cities: I do not refer to the thirteenth century, but instead to the phases leading up to the cities' take-off, phases that ended in the mid-twelfth century in the cases of the earliest development, such as Milan and some port cities, and a generation or two later in other cities.

* * *

To conclude: the essays published in this volume remind us of the need to proceed with caution in areas open to debate such as the nature and rhythms of the economic growth in southern Europe. However, they also provide

23 For an overview, see Bocchi, *Per antiche strade*.
24 This is the interpretation of Cammarosano, 'Città e campagna', p. 329.
25 Wickham, 'I cambiamenti economici'.

numerous stimuli to help us better understand a process of massification of a type of consumption that took a hitherto insignificant phenomenon like masonry construction to such levels that it became a radically new and fundamentally important production and product sector. In this context, investments in material structures for production and trade became widespread. We can observe the wide range of participants in this phenomenon in different ways and chronologies, and perceive how, even from this angle, for much of the twelfth century the city does not seem to have taken on the leading role attributed to it in the past. We also see the non-chronologically linear nature of certain evolutions but, at the same time, we note the clear gap in economic dynamism that separates the earliest phase, prior to the mid- and especially more often the late twelfth century, from the subsequent period. We observe a decline in the activism of ecclesiastical institutions and an increase in that of the secular world. Finally, we have confirmation of the lordship's impulse to place itself outside and downstream of the production process, while stimulating it in depth by its mere existence.

Works Cited

Secondary Sources

Augenti, Andrea, and Paola Galetti, eds, *L'incastellamento: storia e archeologia. A 40 anni da Les structures di Pierre Toubert* (Spoleto: CISAM, 2018)

Bianchi, Giovanna, *Archeologia dei beni pubblici. Alle origini della crescita economica in una regione mediterranea (secc. IX–XI)* (Florence: All'Insegna del Giglio, 2022)

Blasco Vallés, Almudena, 'Wealth in Stone: Building Activity of the Viscounts of Béarn on the Pilgrimage Roads of the Atlantic Pyrenees (ca. 1063–ca. 1130)', *Journal of Medieval Iberian Studies*, 15.1 (2023), 24–49. DOI: 10.1080/17546559.2023.2168721

Bocchi, Francesca, *Per antiche strade. Caratteri e aspetti delle città medievali* (Rome: Viella, 2013)

Cagnana, Aurora, 'Recensione' of Federico Zoni, *Edilizia residenziale medievale dell'Appennino reggiano (secoli XI–XIV). Maestranze, committenti e ambienti tecnici* (Florence: All'Insegna del Giglio, 2019), *Archeologia dell'Architettura*, 25 (2020), 281–82

Cammarosano, Paolo, 'Città e campagna: rapporti politici ed economici', in *Società e istituzioni dell'Italia comunale: L'esempio di Perugia. Secoli XII–XIV* (Perugia: Deputazione di Storia Patria per l'Umbria, 1988), pp. 303–49

Cantini, Federico, and Claudia Rizzitelli, eds, *Una città operosa. Archeologia della produzione a Pisa tra Età romana e Medioevo* (Florence: All'Insegna del Giglio, 2018)

Carandini, Andrea, 'L'ultima civiltà sepolta o del massimo oggetto desueto, secondo un archeologo', in *Storia di Roma*, III. 2. *L'età tardoantica. I luoghi e le culture* (Turin: Einaudi, 1993), pp. 11–38

Carocci, Sandro, *Lordships of Southern Italy: Rural Societies, Aristocratic Powers and Monarchy in the Twelfth and Thirteenth Centuries* (Rome: Viella, 2018)

——, 'Nobility, Conflicts, and Buildings in Italian Cities (c. 1050–1300)', in *Petrified Conflicts: Buildings as Cause, Object and Mirror of Confrontation (Southern Europe, 1000–1300)*, ed. by Sandro Carocci and Federico Del Tredici (Turnhout: Brepols, forthcoming)

Carrera, Francesco Marco Paolo, 'Le lavorazioni dei metalli delle botteghe artigianali degli Ex Laboratori Gentili', in *Una città operosa. Archeologia della produzione a Pisa tra Età romana e Medioevo*, ed. by Federico Cantini and Claudia Rizzitelli (Florence: All'Insegna del Giglio, 2018), pp. 55–64

Cirillo, Giuseppe, *Il vello d'oro. Modelli mediterranei di società pastorali: il Mezzogiorno d'Italia (secc. XVI–XIX)* (Manduria: Lacaita, 2003)

Collavini, Simone M., 'La crescita pieno medievale in Toscana tra campagna e città. Prime riflessioni a partire da un seminario', in *'Costruire lo sviluppo'. La crescita di città e campagna tra espansione urbana e nuove fondazioni (XII-prima metà XIII secolo)*, ed. by Federico Cantini (Florence: All'Insegna del Giglio, 2019), pp. 151–56

——, 'Mutazione signorile e beni fiscali', in *La gestione del patrimonio fiscale tra IX e XII secolo. Uno specchio delle trasformazioni economiche medievali?*, ed. by Lorenzo Tabarrini (forthcoming)

Construir para perdurar. Riqueza petrificada e identidad social. Siglos xi–xiv (XLVII Semana Internacional de Estudios Medievales. Estella-Lizarra. 20/23 de julio de 2021) (Estella-Lizarra: Gobierno de Navarra/Nafarroako Gobernua, 2022)

Duby, Georges, *Guerriers et paysans. VIIe-XIIe siècle. Premier essor de l'économie européenne* (Paris: Gallimard, 1973)

Favia, Pasquale, *Ordona XII. Un casale nel Tavoliere medievale* (Bari: Edipuglia, 2018)

Feller, Laurent, 'Abruzzes adriatiques. L'apport de la documentation écrite', in *L'incastellamento: storia e archeologia. A 40 anni da Les structures di Pierre Toubert*, ed. by Andrea Augenti and Paola Galetti (Spoleto: CISAM, 2018), pp. 405–12

Furió, Antoni, and Luis Almenar Fernández, 'Land, Ceramics and Seigniorial Rents in the Late Middle Ages: The Manor of Manises in the Kingdom of Valencia, c. 1400–1575', *Historia agraria*, 90 (2023), 39–69

Giovannini, Fabio, and Alessandra Molinari, eds, *Il paesaggio pietrificato. La storia sociale dell'Europa tra X e XII secolo attraverso l'archeologia del costruito. Atti del Convegno (Arezzo, 7–8 febbraio 2020)*, special issue of *Archeologia dell'Architettura*, 26 (2021)

Maira Vidal, Rocío, and Ana Rodríguez, eds, *El coste de la construcción medieval. Materiales, recursos y sistemas constructivos para la petrificación del paisaje entre los siglos XI y XIII* (Madrid: CSIC, 2021)

Molinari, Alessandra, 'La "pietrificazione" del costruito nell'Europa meridionale del pieno medioevo. Considerazioni comparative dalla prospettiva archeologica', *Archeologia dell'Architettura*, 26 (2021), 275–87

La petrificación de la riqueza: construcción e identidad en la Península ibérica e Italia, siglos XI–XIII, special issue of, *Studia historica. Historia medieval*, 39.1 (2021), 3–240

Settia, Aldo A., *Castelli medievali* (Bologna: Il Mulino, 2017)

Toubert, Pierre, *Les structures du Latium Médiéval. Le Latium méridional et la Sabine du IXe à la fin du XIIe siècle* (Rome: École française de Rome, 1973)

Violante, Francesco, 'La conduzione delle terre demaniali', in *Eclisse di un regno. L'ultima età sveva*, Atti delle diciannovesime giornate normanno-sveve, Bari, 12–15 ottobre 2010, ed. by Pasquale Cordasco (Bari: Adda, 2012), pp. 163–96

Wickham, Chris, 'I cambiamenti economici in Italia centrosettentrionale tra 1050 e 1150 e le loro conseguenze politiche; e viceversa', in *Periodizzare il medioevo. Una discussione su continuità e cambiamento nell'Italia dei secoli XI e XII* (forthcoming)

——, *The Donkey and the Boat: Reinterpreting the Mediterranean Economy, 950–1180* (Oxford: Oxford University Press, 2023)

Wood, Ian, *The Christian Economy in the Early Medieval West: Towards a Temple Society* (Santa Barbara: Punctum books, 2022)

Zoni, Federico, *Edilizia residenziale medievale dell'Appennino reggiano (secoli XI–XIV). Maestranze, committenti e ambienti tecnici* (Florence: All'Insegna del Giglio, 2019)

Index